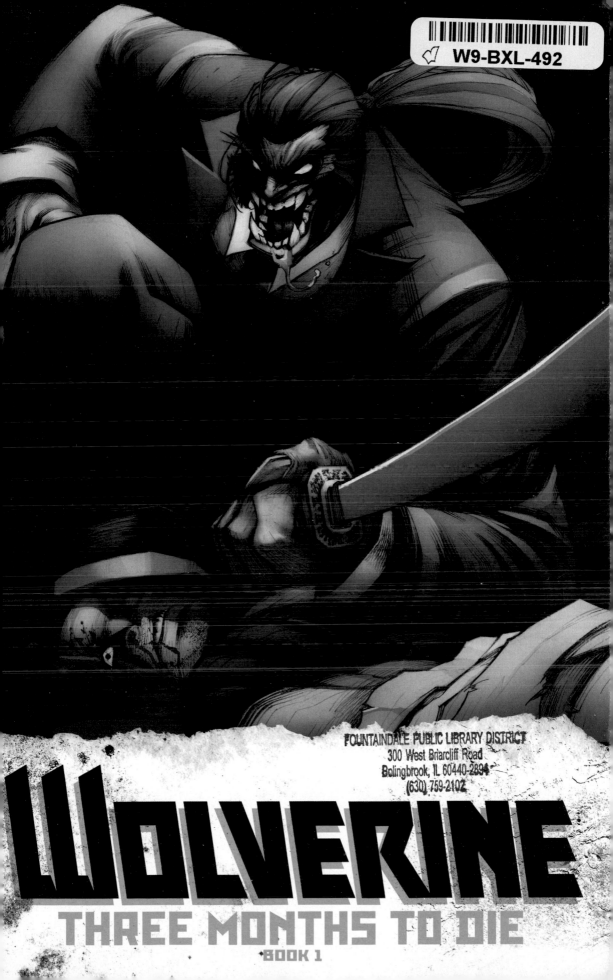

WOLVERINE

THREE MONTHS TO DIE

◆BOOK 1

COLLECTION EDITOR: **JENNIFER GRÜNWALD**
ASSISTANT EDITOR: **SARAH BRUNSTAD**
ASSOCIATE MANAGING EDITOR: **ALEX STARBUCK**
EDITOR, SPECIAL PROJECTS: **MARK D. BEAZLEY**
SENIOR EDITOR, SPECIAL PROJECTS: **JEFF YOUNGQUIST**
SVP PRINT, SALES & MARKETING: **DAVID GABRIEL**
BOOK DESIGNER: **RODOLFO MURAGUCHI**

EDITOR IN CHIEF: **AXEL ALONSO**
CHIEF CREATIVE OFFICER: **JOE QUESADA**
PUBLISHER: **DAN BUCKLEY**
EXECUTIVE PRODUCER: **ALAN FINE**

WOLVERINE: THREE MONTHS TO DIE BOOK 1. Contains material originally published in magazine form as WOLVERINE #1-7. First printing 2014. ISBN# 978-0-7851-5419-8. Published by MARVEL WORLDWIDE, INC., a subsidiary of MARVEL ENTERTAINMENT, LLC. OFFICE OF PUBLICATION: 135 West 50th Street, New York, NY 10020. Copyright © 2014 Marvel Characters, Inc. All rights reserved. All characters featured in this issue and the distinctive names and likenesses thereof, and all related indicia are trademarks of Marvel Characters, Inc. No similarity between any of the names, characters, persons, and/or institutions in this magazine with those of any living or dead person or institution is intended, and any such similarity which may exist is purely coincidental. **Printed in Canada.** ALAN FINE, EVP - Office of the President, Marvel Worldwide, Inc. and EVP & CMO Marvel Characters B.V.: DAN BUCKLEY, Publisher & President - Print, Animation & Digital Divisions; JOE QUESADA, Chief Creative Officer; TOM BREVOORT, SVP of Publishing; DAVID BOGART, SVP of Operations & Procurement, Publishing; C.B. CEBULSKI, SVP of Creator & Content Development; DAVID GABRIEL, SVP Print, Sales & Marketing; JIM O'KEEFE, VP of Operations & Logistics; DAN CARR, Executive Director of Publishing Technology; SUSAN CRESPI, Editorial Operations Manager; ALEX MORALES, Publishing Operations Manager; STAN LEE, Chairman Emeritus. For information regarding advertising in Marvel Comics or on Marvel.com, please contact Niza Disla, Director of Marvel Partnerships, at ndisla@marvel.com. For Marvel subscription inquiries, please call 800-217-9158. **Manufactured between 5/30/2014 and 7/7/2014 by SOLISCO PRINTERS, SCOTT, QC, CANADA.**

10 9 8 7 6 5 4 3 2 1

WOLVERINE
THREE MONTHS TO DIE
BOOK 1

WRITER:
PAUL CORNELL

PENCILERS, #1-4:
RYAN STEGMAN
WITH **DAVID BALDEON** (#4)

INKERS, #1-4:
MARK MORALES WITH **RYAN STEGMAN** (#3-4),
JOHN LIVESAY (#3) & **SCOTT HANNA** (#4)

ARTIST, #5-7:
GERARDO SANDOVAL

COLORIST:
DAVID CURIEL

LETTERER:
VC'S CORY PETIT

COVER ART: **RYAN STEGMAN** & **EDGAR DELGADO**

ASSISTANT EDITORS: **FRANKIE JOHNSON** & **XANDER JAROWEY**

EDITORS: **TOM BRENNAN, JEANINE SCHAEFER** & **MIKE MARTS**

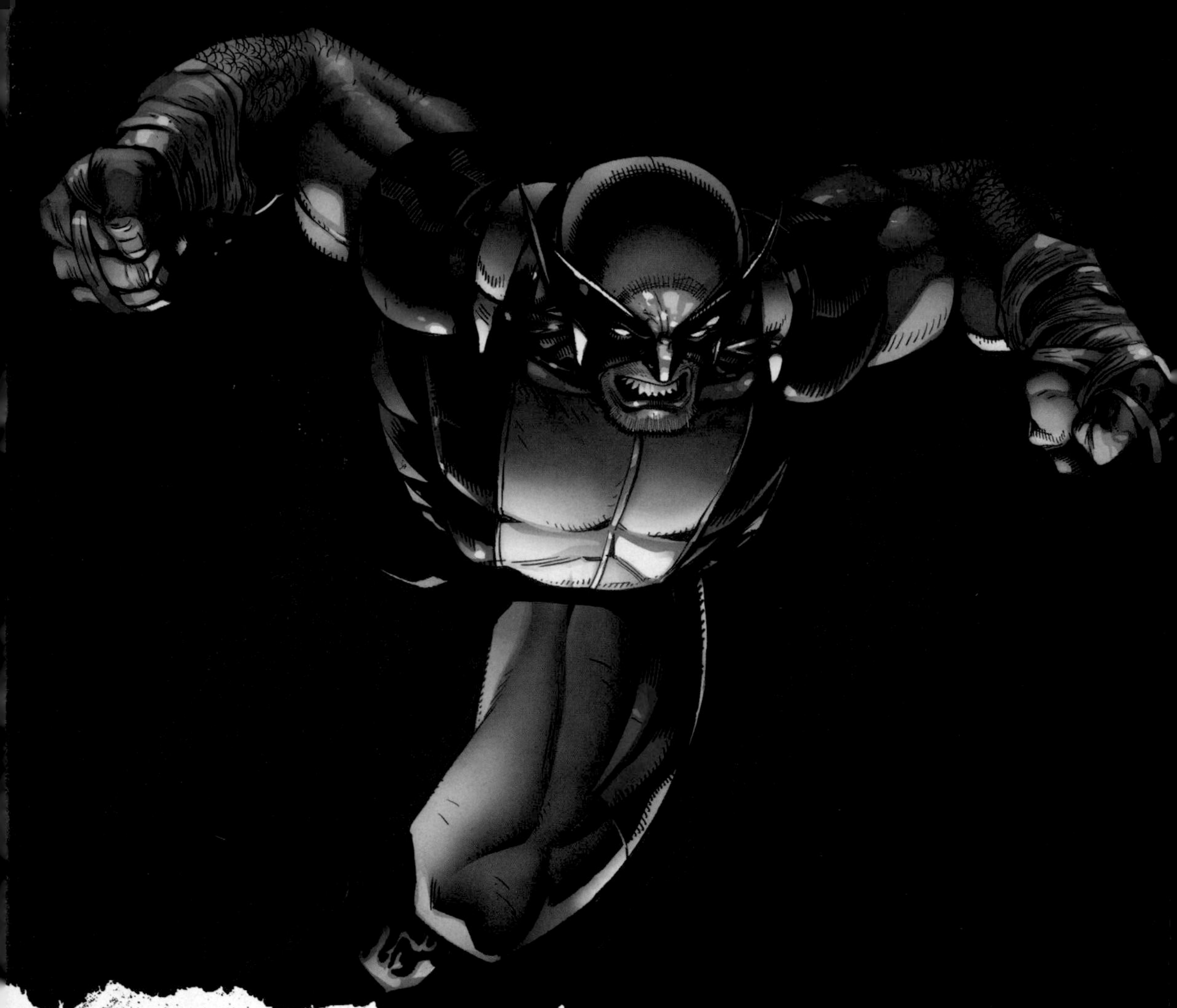

LOGAN, the man called Wolverine, has been many things in his life — a child of privilege, a wild man of the woods, a soldier, a killer, a hero and a teacher — but for all the roads he has traveled, Logan has always striven to do right.

Recently, a virus stripped him of his superhuman healing factor, rendering him mortal and killable. With a world full of enemies, Logan had to relearn how to defend himself, and in the process found himself on the losing end of a battle with his lifelong enemy, Sabretooth.

Beaten, bloodied and scarred, Logan returned to his old life as leader of the Jean Grey School, an academy for superhuman children, with a cryptic message:

"THE WOLVERINE IS DEAD."
LONG LIVE THE...

WOLVERINE

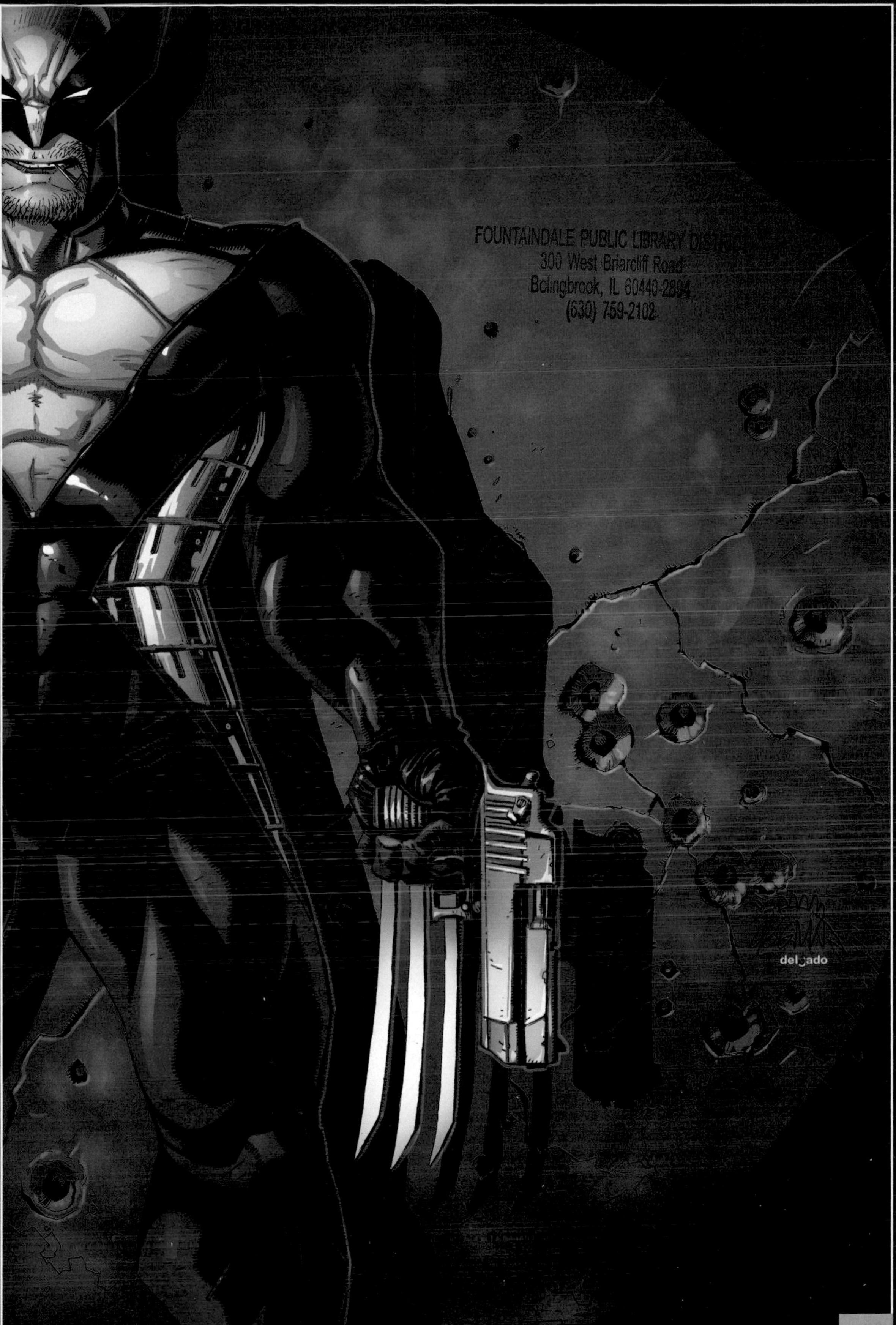
delgado

#1

ROGUE LOGAN PART 1

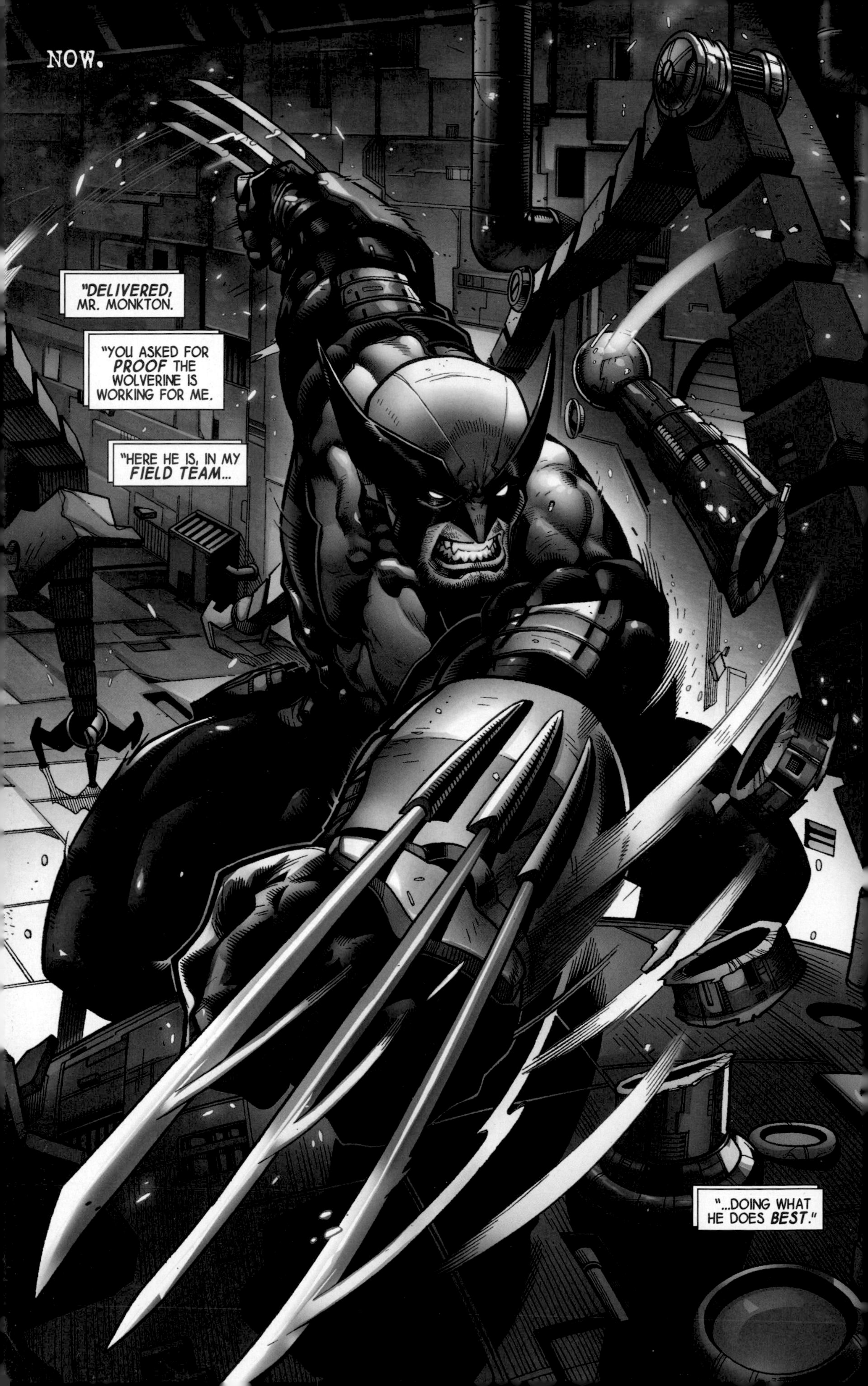
NOW.
"DELIVERED, MR. MONKTON.
"YOU ASKED FOR PROOF THE WOLVERINE IS WORKING FOR ME.
"HERE HE IS, IN MY FIELD TEAM...
"...DOING WHAT HE DOES BEST."

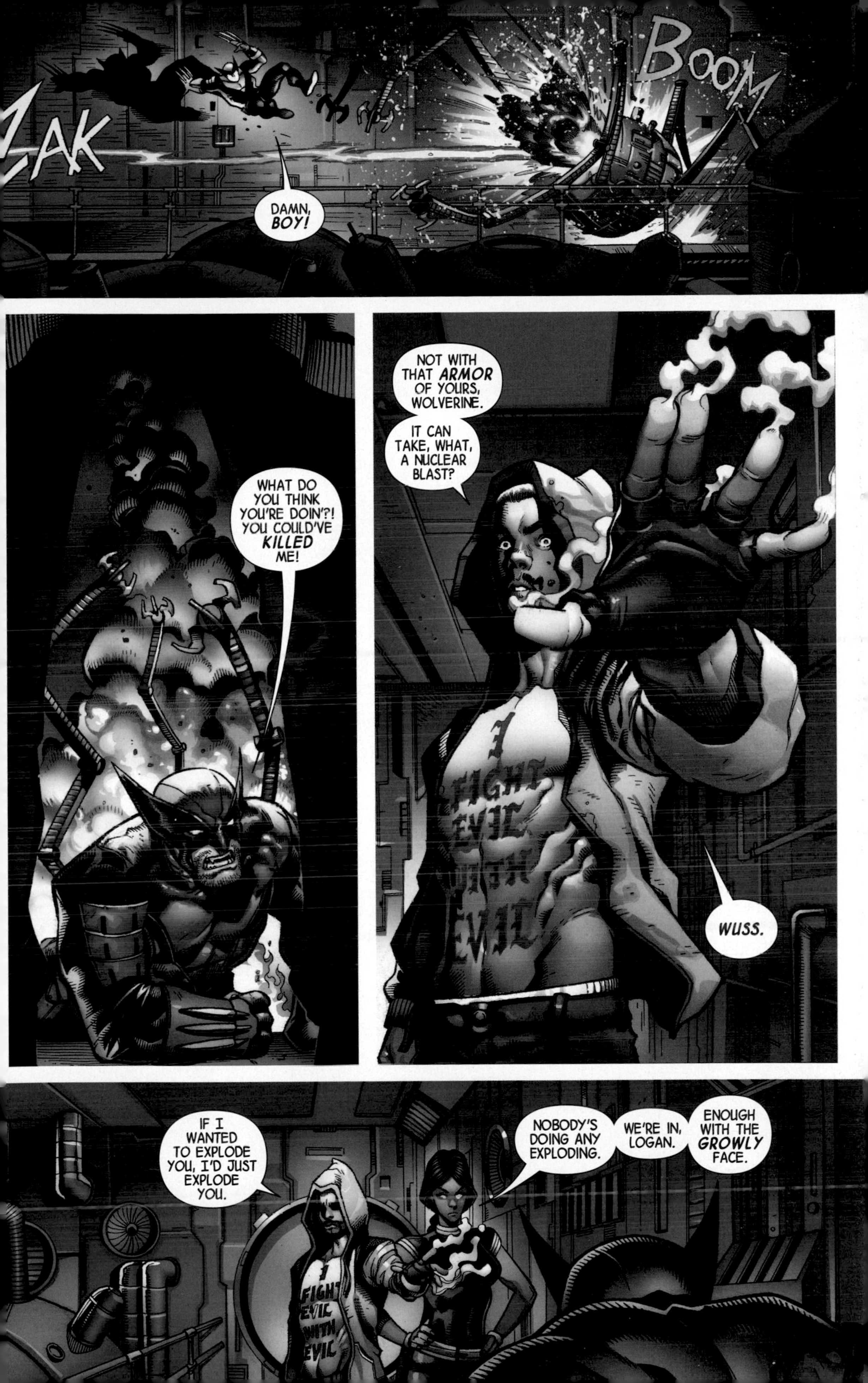
ZAK
BOOM
DAMN, BOY!
WHAT DO YOU THINK YOU'RE DOIN'?! YOU COULD'VE KILLED ME!
NOT WITH THAT ARMOR OF YOURS, WOLVERINE.
IT CAN TAKE, WHAT, A NUCLEAR BLAST?
I FIGHT EVIL WITH EVIL
WUSS.
IF I WANTED TO EXPLODE YOU, I'D JUST EXPLODE YOU.
NOBODY'S DOING ANY EXPLODING.
WE'RE IN, LOGAN.
ENOUGH WITH THE GROWLY FACE.

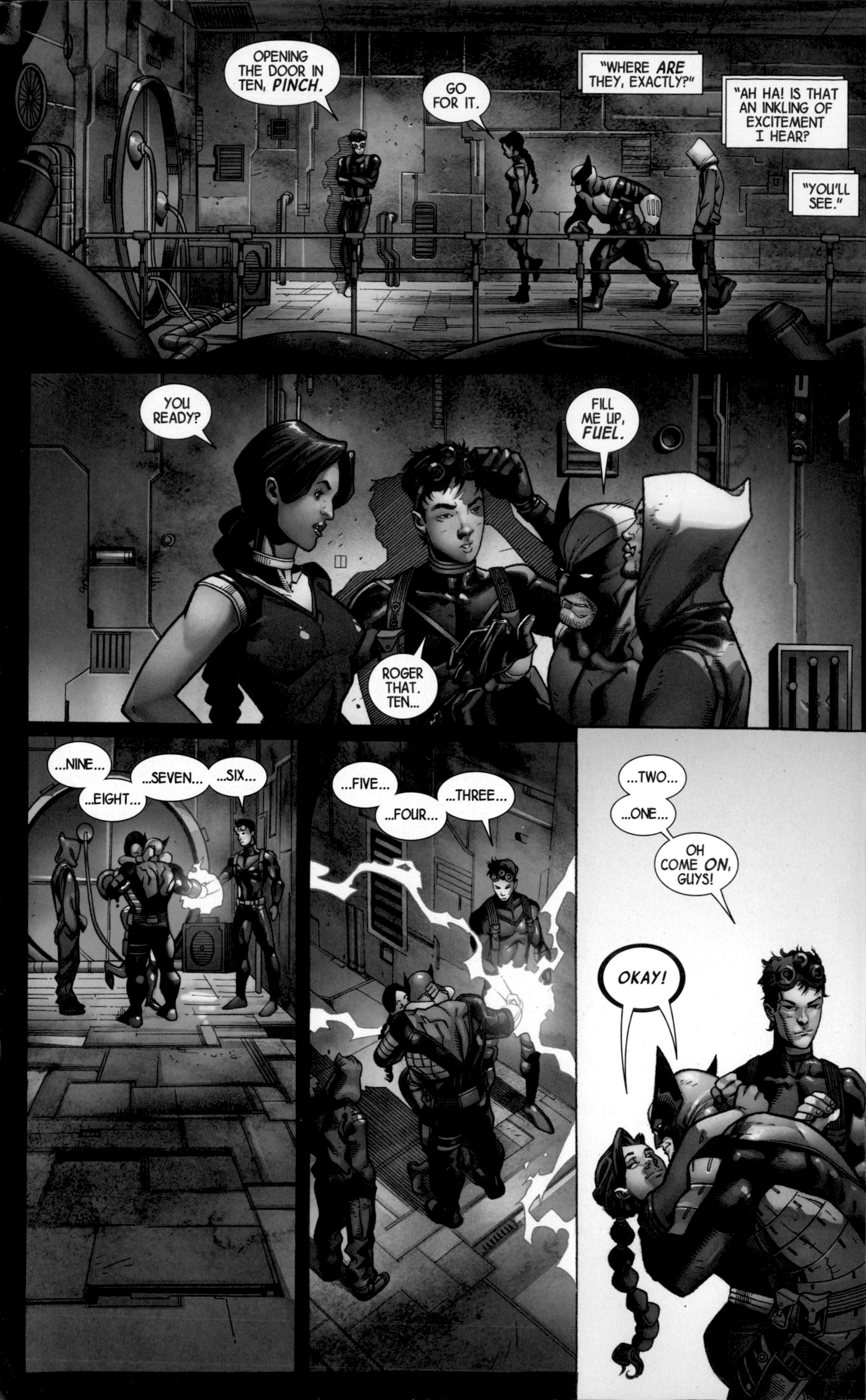
OPENING THE DOOR IN TEN, PINCH.
GO FOR IT.
"WHERE ARE THEY, EXACTLY?"
"AH HA! IS THAT AN INKLING OF EXCITEMENT I HEAR?
"YOU'LL SEE."
YOU READY?
FILL ME UP, FUEL.
ROGER THAT. TEN...
...NINE...
...EIGHT...
...SEVEN...
...SIX...
...FIVE...
...FOUR...
...THREE...
...TWO...
...ONE...
OH COME ON, GUYS!
OKAY!

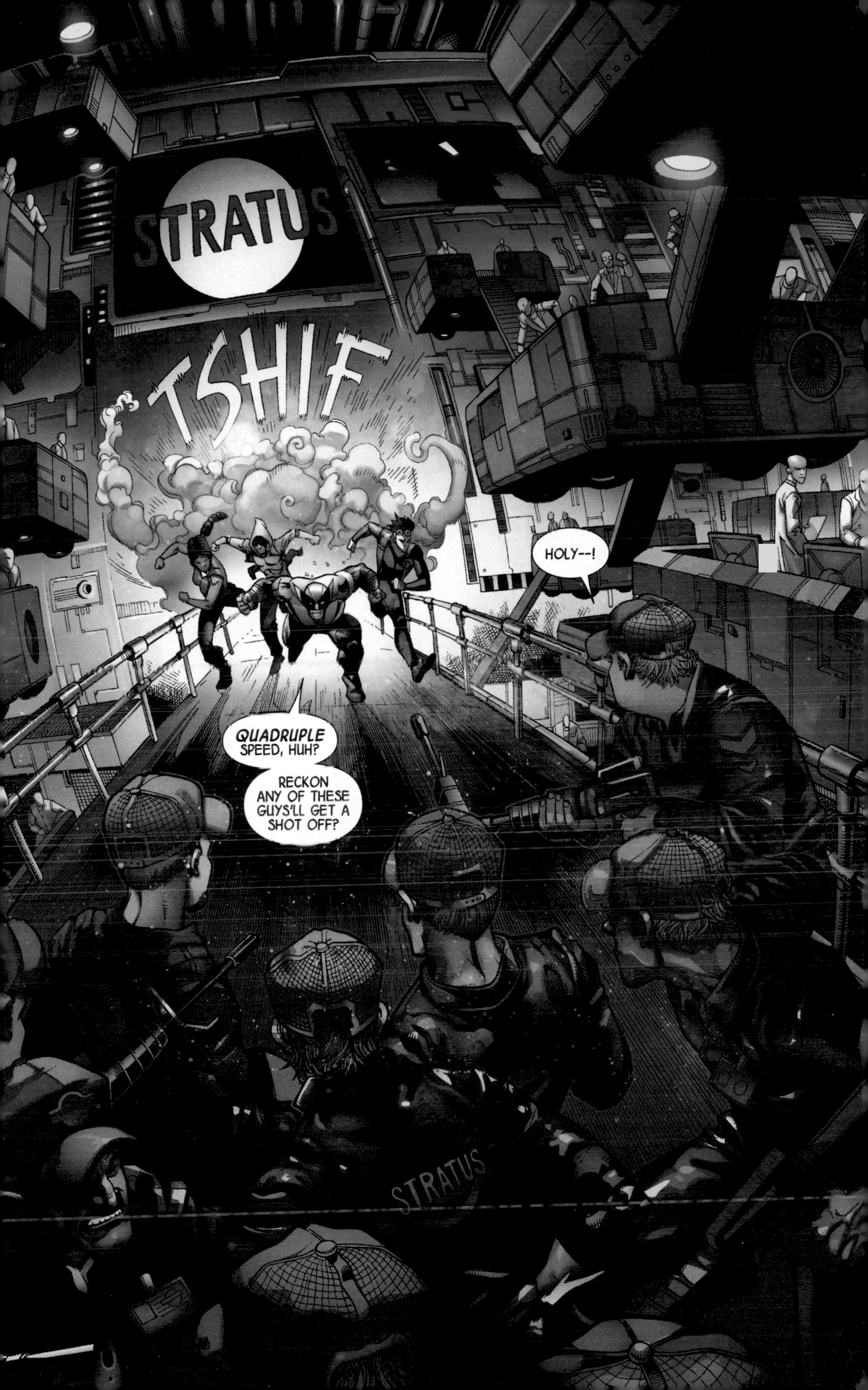
STRATUS
TSHIF
HOLY--!
QUADRUPLE SPEED, HUH?
RECKON ANY OF THESE GUYS'LL GET A SHOT OFF?
STRATUS

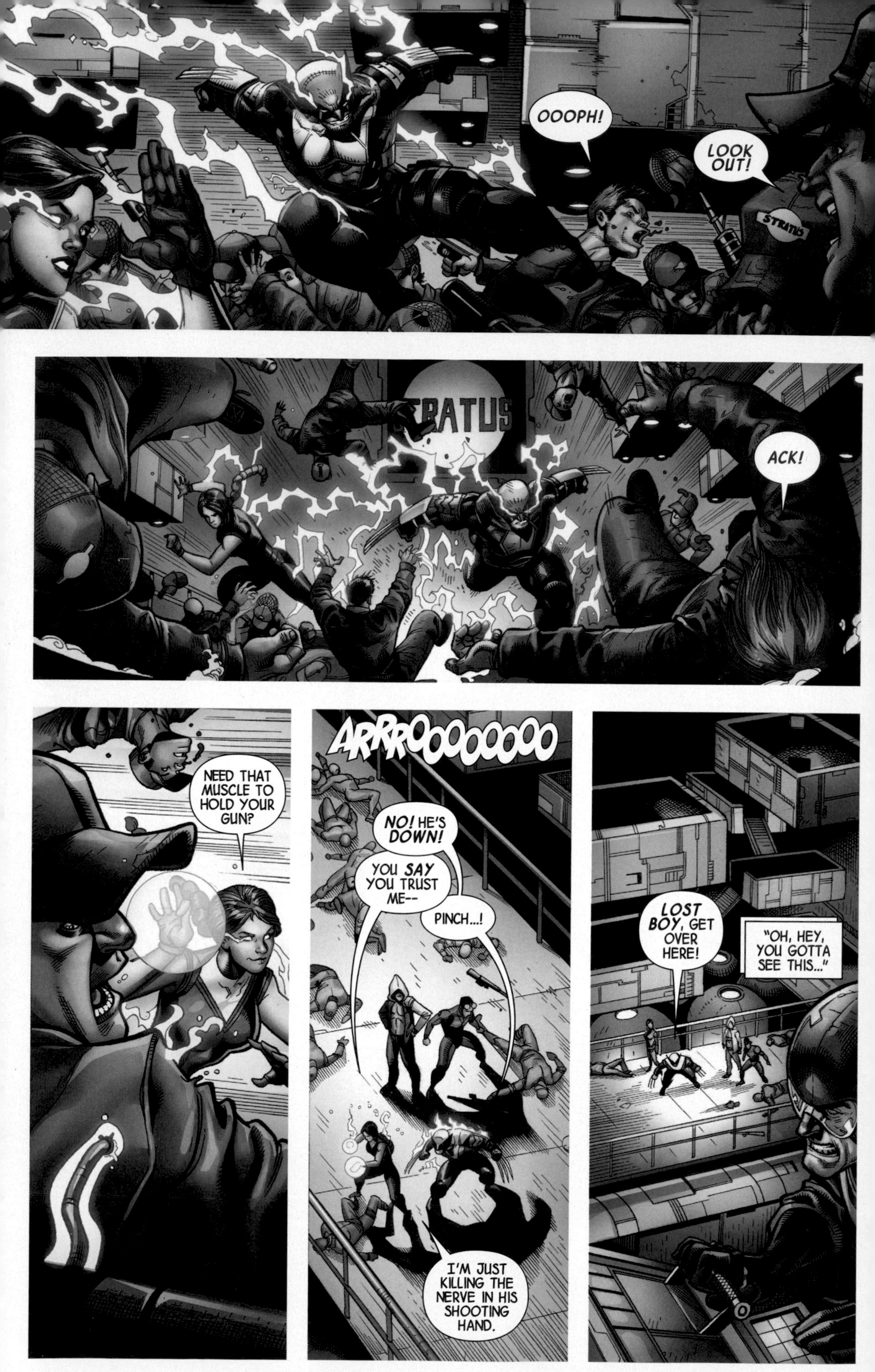
OOOPH!
LOOK OUT!
STRATUS
STRATUS
ACK!
NEED THAT MUSCLE TO HOLD YOUR GUN?
ARRROOOOOOOO
NO! HE'S DOWN!
YOU SAY YOU TRUST ME--
PINCH...!
I'M JUST KILLING THE NERVE IN HIS SHOOTING HAND.
LOST BOY, GET OVER HERE!
"OH, HEY, YOU GOTTA SEE THIS..."

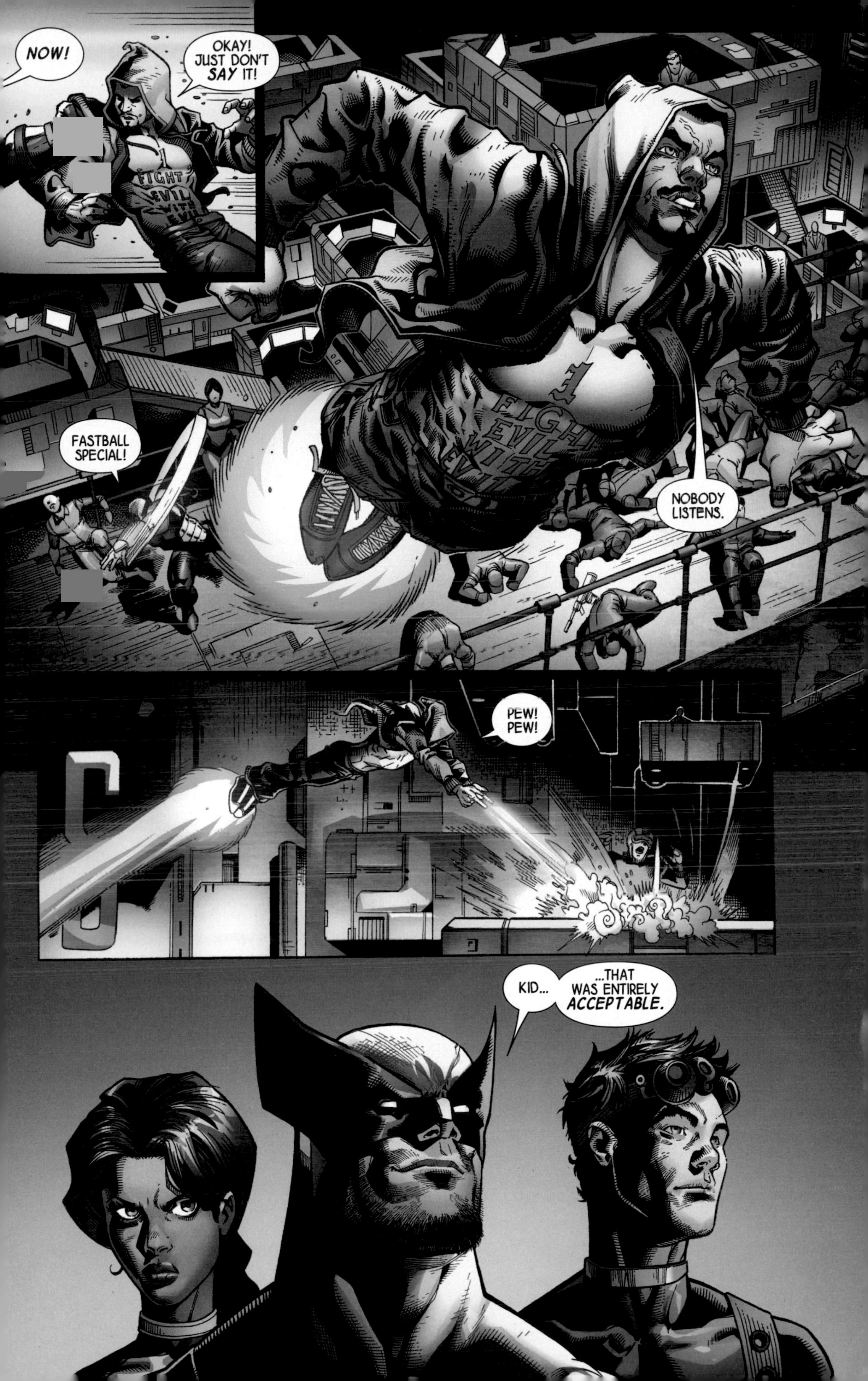
NOW!
OKAY! JUST DON'T SAY IT!
FASTBALL SPECIAL!
NOBODY LISTENS.
PEW! PEW!
KID...
...THAT WAS ENTIRELY ACCEPTABLE.

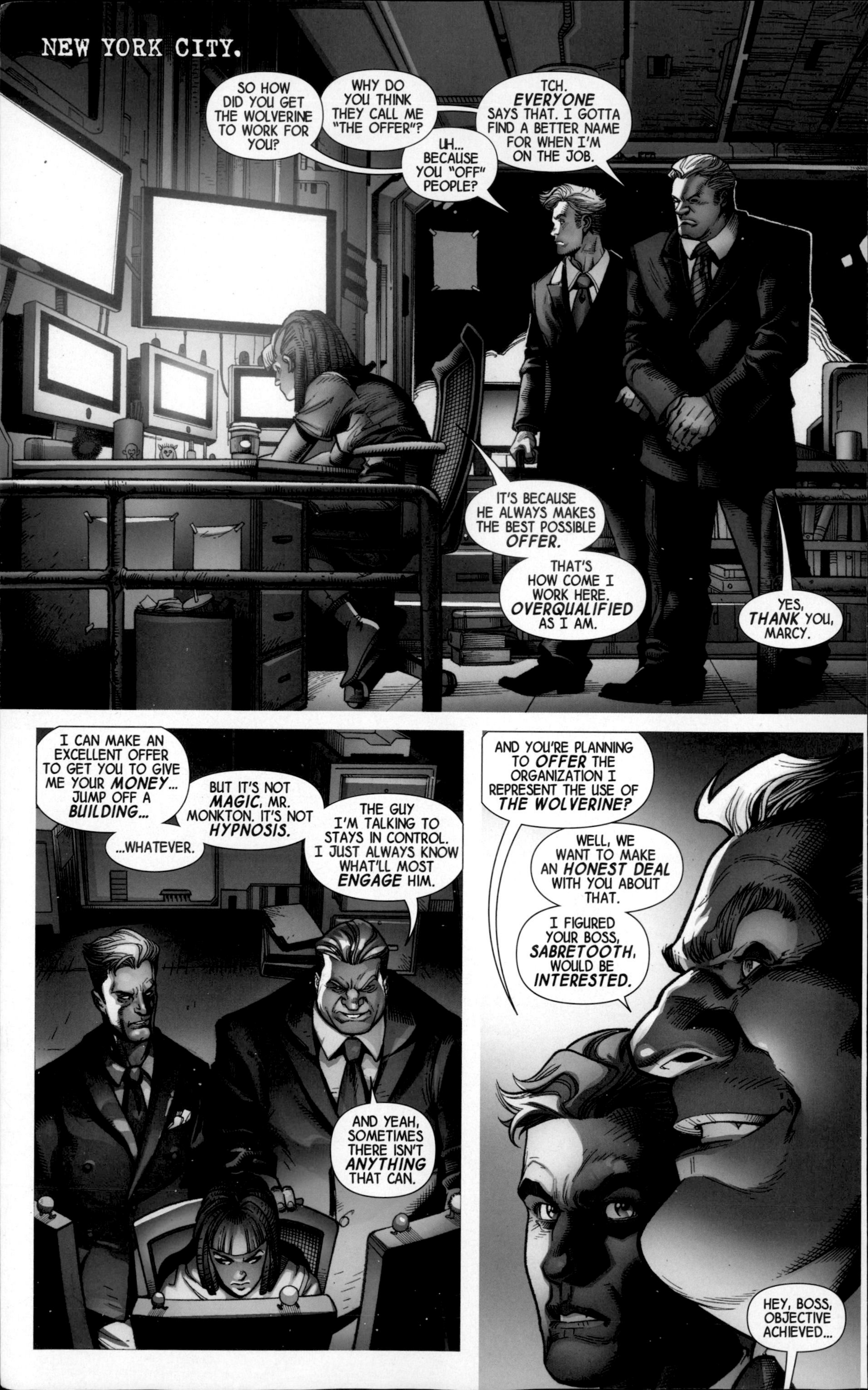
NEW YORK CITY.
SO HOW DID YOU GET THE WOLVERINE TO WORK FOR YOU?
WHY DO YOU THINK THEY CALL ME "THE OFFER"?
UH... BECAUSE YOU "OFF" PEOPLE?
TCH. EVERYONE SAYS THAT. I GOTTA FIND A BETTER NAME FOR WHEN I'M ON THE JOB.
IT'S BECAUSE HE ALWAYS MAKES THE BEST POSSIBLE OFFER.
THAT'S HOW COME I WORK HERE. OVERQUALIFIED AS I AM.
YES, THANK YOU, MARCY.
I CAN MAKE AN EXCELLENT OFFER TO GET YOU TO GIVE ME YOUR MONEY... JUMP OFF A BUILDING...
...WHATEVER.
BUT IT'S NOT MAGIC, MR. MONKTON. IT'S NOT HYPNOSIS.
THE GUY I'M TALKING TO STAYS IN CONTROL. I JUST ALWAYS KNOW WHAT'LL MOST ENGAGE HIM.
AND YEAH, SOMETIMES THERE ISN'T ANYTHING THAT CAN.
AND YOU'RE PLANNING TO OFFER THE ORGANIZATION I REPRESENT THE USE OF THE WOLVERINE?
WELL, WE WANT TO MAKE AN HONEST DEAL WITH YOU ABOUT THAT.
I FIGURED YOUR BOSS, SABRETOOTH, WOULD BE INTERESTED.
HEY, BOSS, OBJECTIVE ACHIEVED...

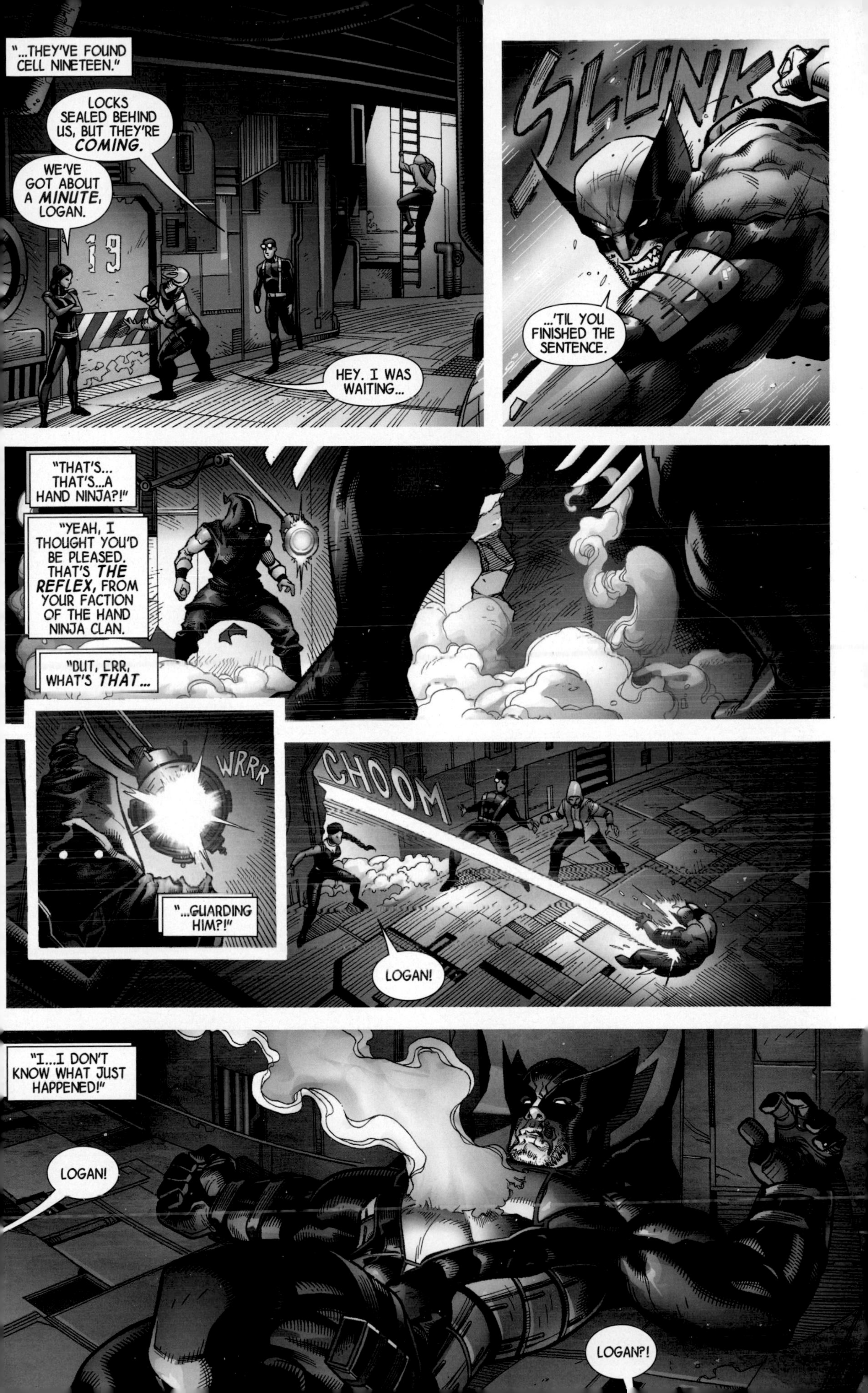
"...THEY'VE FOUND CELL NINETEEN."
LOCKS SEALED BEHIND US, BUT THEY'RE COMING.
WE'VE GOT ABOUT A MINUTE, LOGAN.
19
HEY. I WAS WAITING...
SLUNK
...'TIL YOU FINISHED THE SENTENCE.
"THAT'S... THAT'S...A HAND NINJA?!"
"YEAH, I THOUGHT YOU'D BE PLEASED. THAT'S THE REFLEX, FROM YOUR FACTION OF THE HAND NINJA CLAN.
"BUT, ERR, WHAT'S THAT...
WRRR
"...GUARDING HIM?!"
CHOOM
LOGAN!
"I...I DON'T KNOW WHAT JUST HAPPENED!"
LOGAN!
LOGAN?!

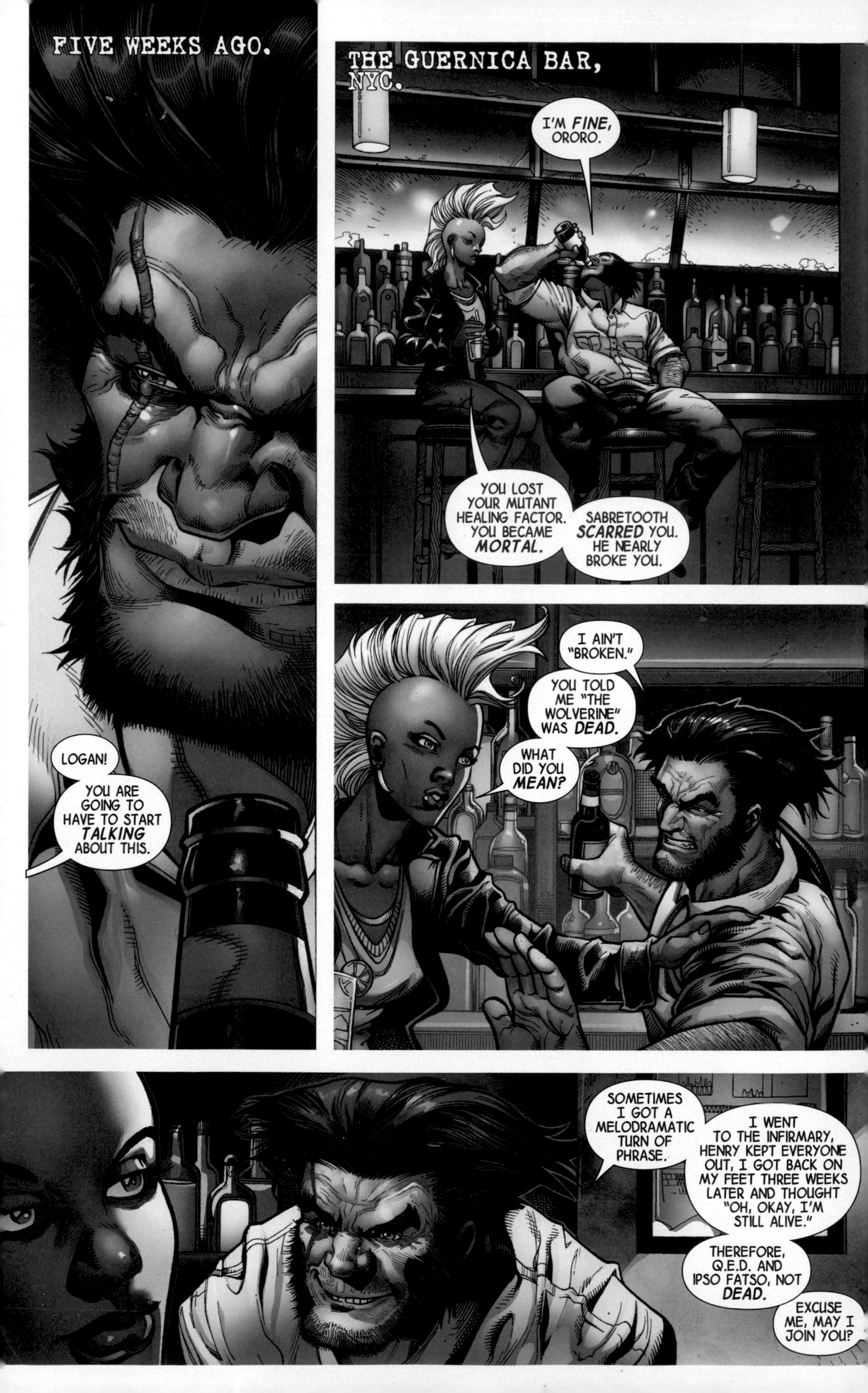
FIVE WEEKS AGO.
THE GUERNICA BAR, NYC.
I'M FINE, ORORO.
YOU LOST YOUR MUTANT HEALING FACTOR. YOU BECAME MORTAL.
SABRETOOTH SCARRED YOU. HE NEARLY BROKE YOU.
LOGAN!
YOU ARE GOING TO HAVE TO START TALKING ABOUT THIS.
I AIN'T "BROKEN."
YOU TOLD ME "THE WOLVERINE" WAS DEAD.
WHAT DID YOU MEAN?
SOMETIMES I GOT A MELODRAMATIC TURN OF PHRASE.
I WENT TO THE INFIRMARY, HENRY KEPT EVERYONE OUT, I GOT BACK ON MY FEET THREE WEEKS LATER AND THOUGHT "OH, OKAY, I'M STILL ALIVE."
THEREFORE, Q.E.D. AND IPSO FATSO, NOT DEAD.
EXCUSE ME, MAY I JOIN YOU?

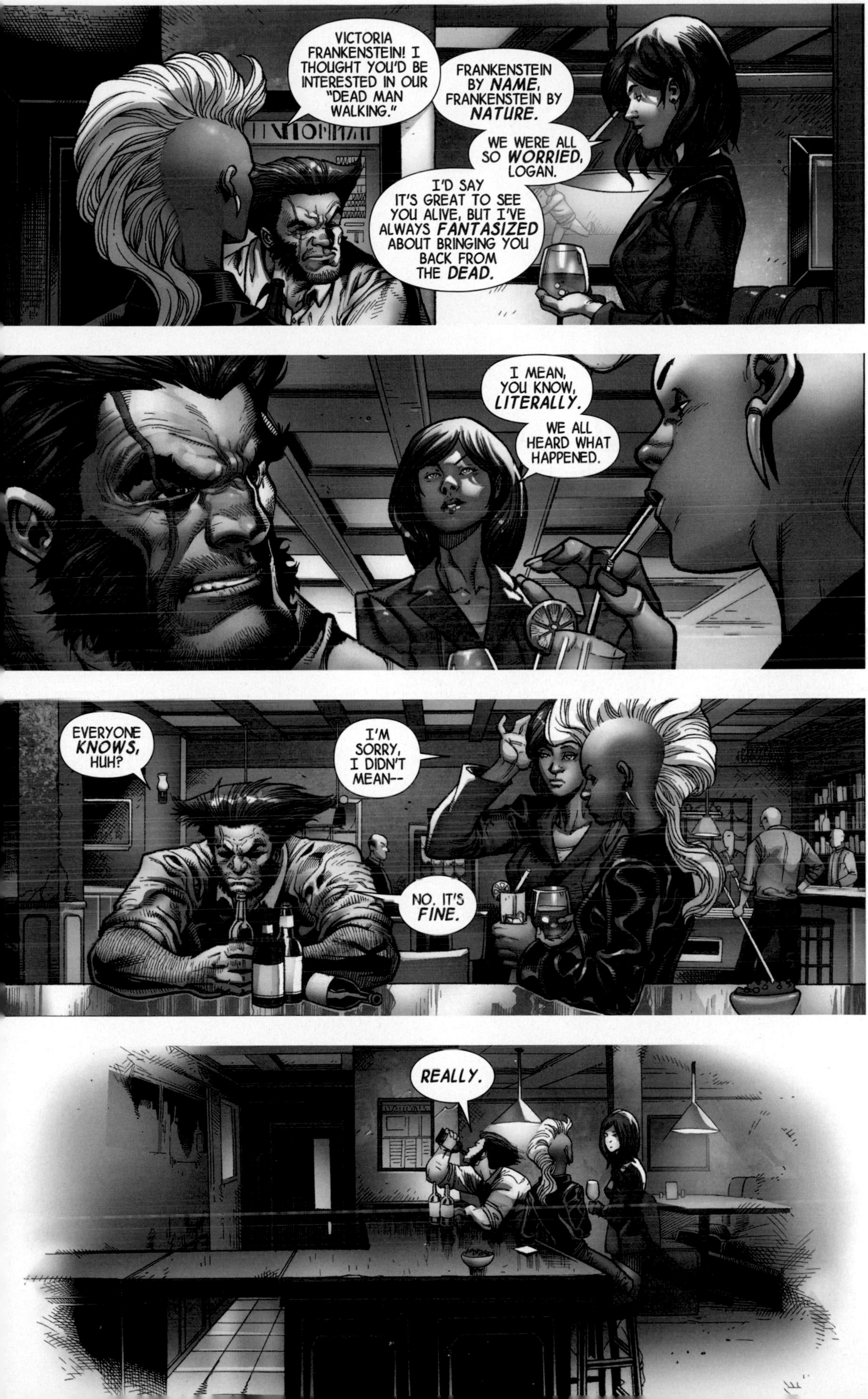
VICTORIA FRANKENSTEIN! I THOUGHT YOU'D BE INTERESTED IN OUR "DEAD MAN WALKING."
FRANKENSTEIN BY NAME, FRANKENSTEIN BY NATURE.
WE WERE ALL SO WORRIED, LOGAN.
I'D SAY IT'S GREAT TO SEE YOU ALIVE, BUT I'VE ALWAYS FANTASIZED ABOUT BRINGING YOU BACK FROM THE DEAD.
I MEAN, YOU KNOW, LITERALLY.
WE ALL HEARD WHAT HAPPENED.
EVERYONE KNOWS, HUH?
I'M SORRY, I DIDN'T MEAN--
NO. IT'S FINE.
REALLY.

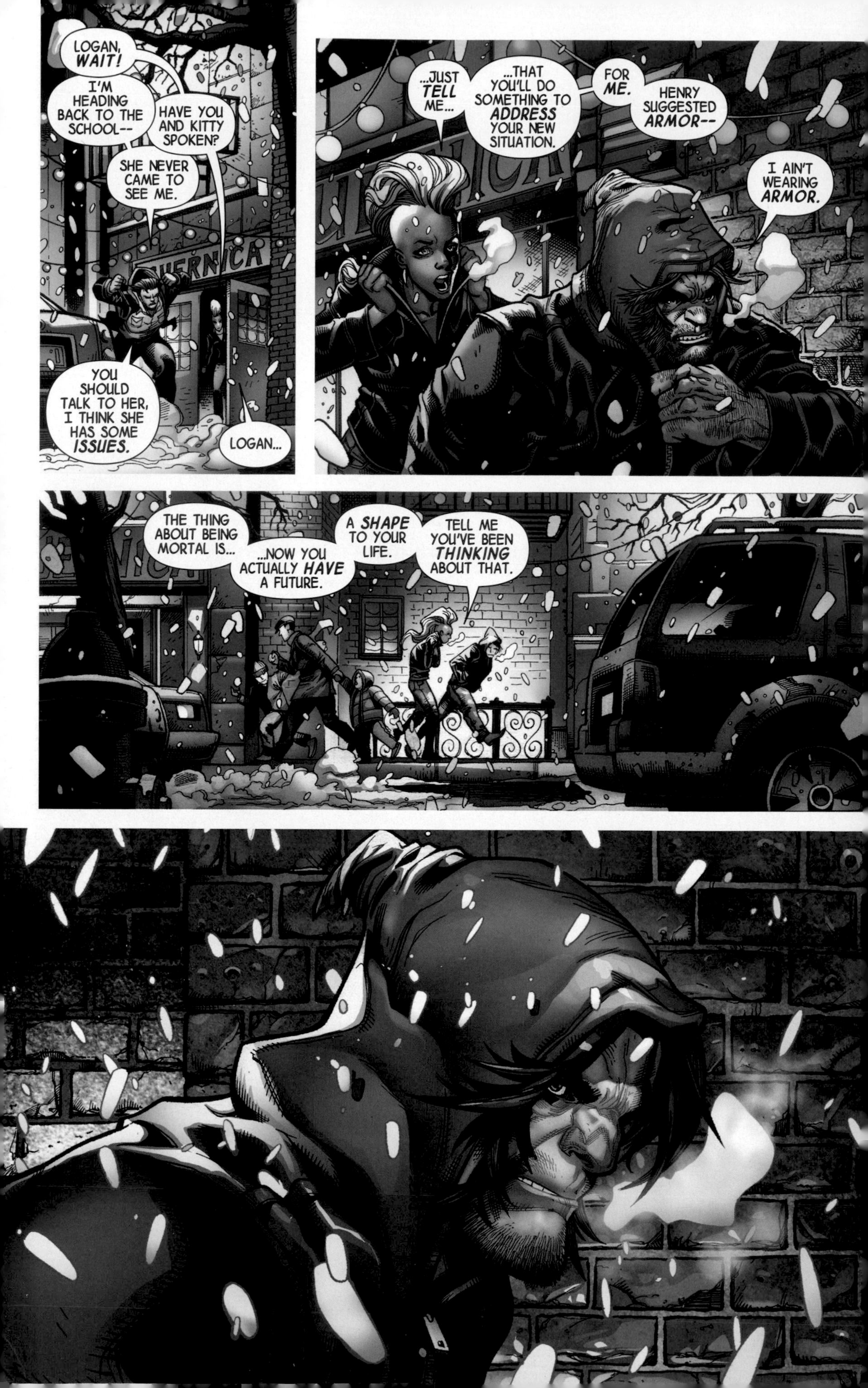
LOGAN, WAIT!
I'M HEADING BACK TO THE SCHOOL--
HAVE YOU AND KITTY SPOKEN?
SHE NEVER CAME TO SEE ME.
YOU SHOULD TALK TO HER, I THINK SHE HAS SOME ISSUES.
LOGAN...
...JUST TELL ME...
...THAT YOU'LL DO SOMETHING TO ADDRESS YOUR NEW SITUATION.
FOR ME.
HENRY SUGGESTED ARMOR--
I AIN'T WEARING ARMOR.
THE THING ABOUT BEING MORTAL IS...
...NOW YOU ACTUALLY HAVE A FUTURE.
A SHAPE TO YOUR LIFE.
TELL ME YOU'VE BEEN THINKING ABOUT THAT.

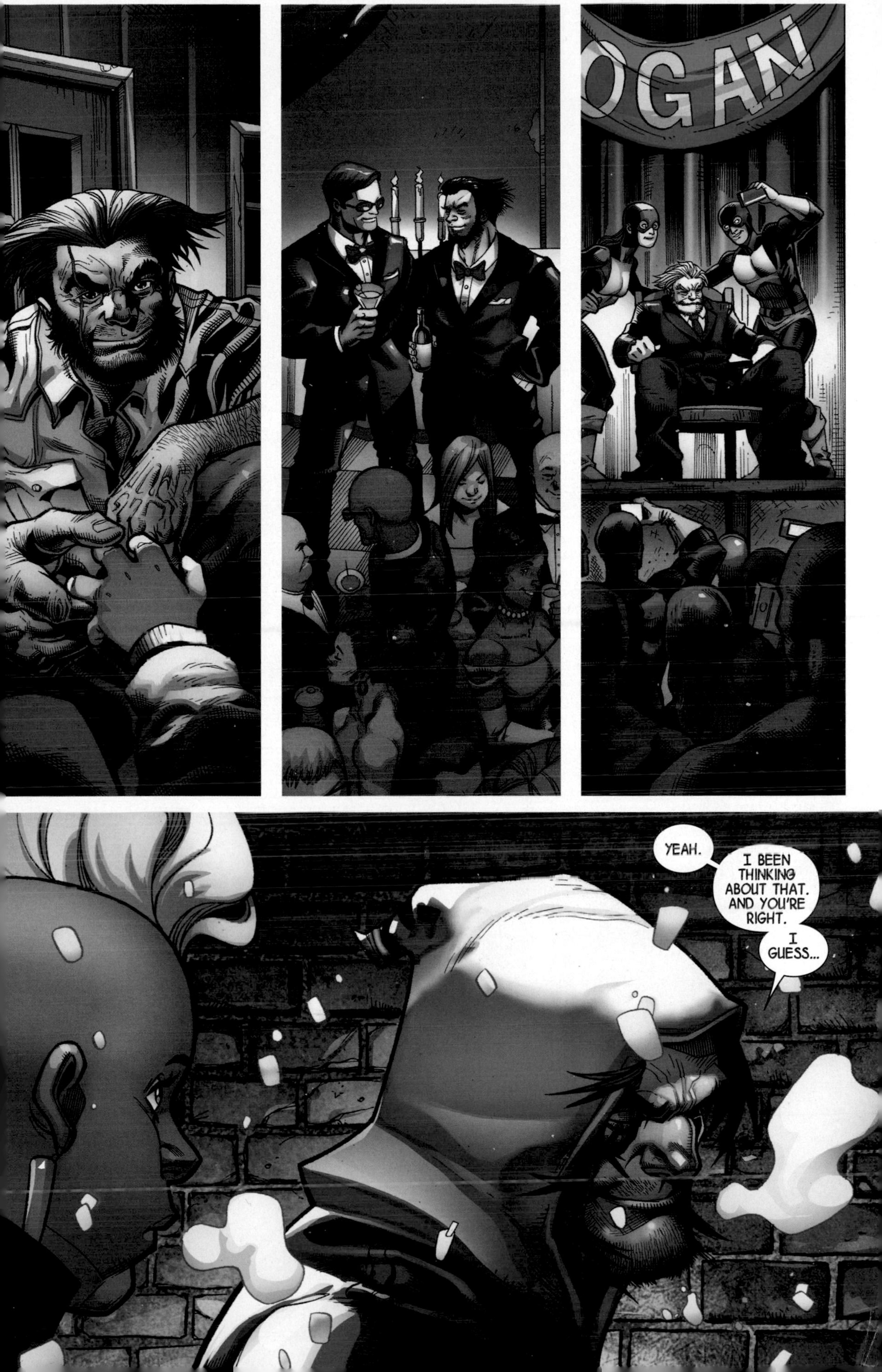
OGAN
YEAH.
I BEEN THINKING ABOUT THAT. AND YOU'RE RIGHT.
I GUESS...

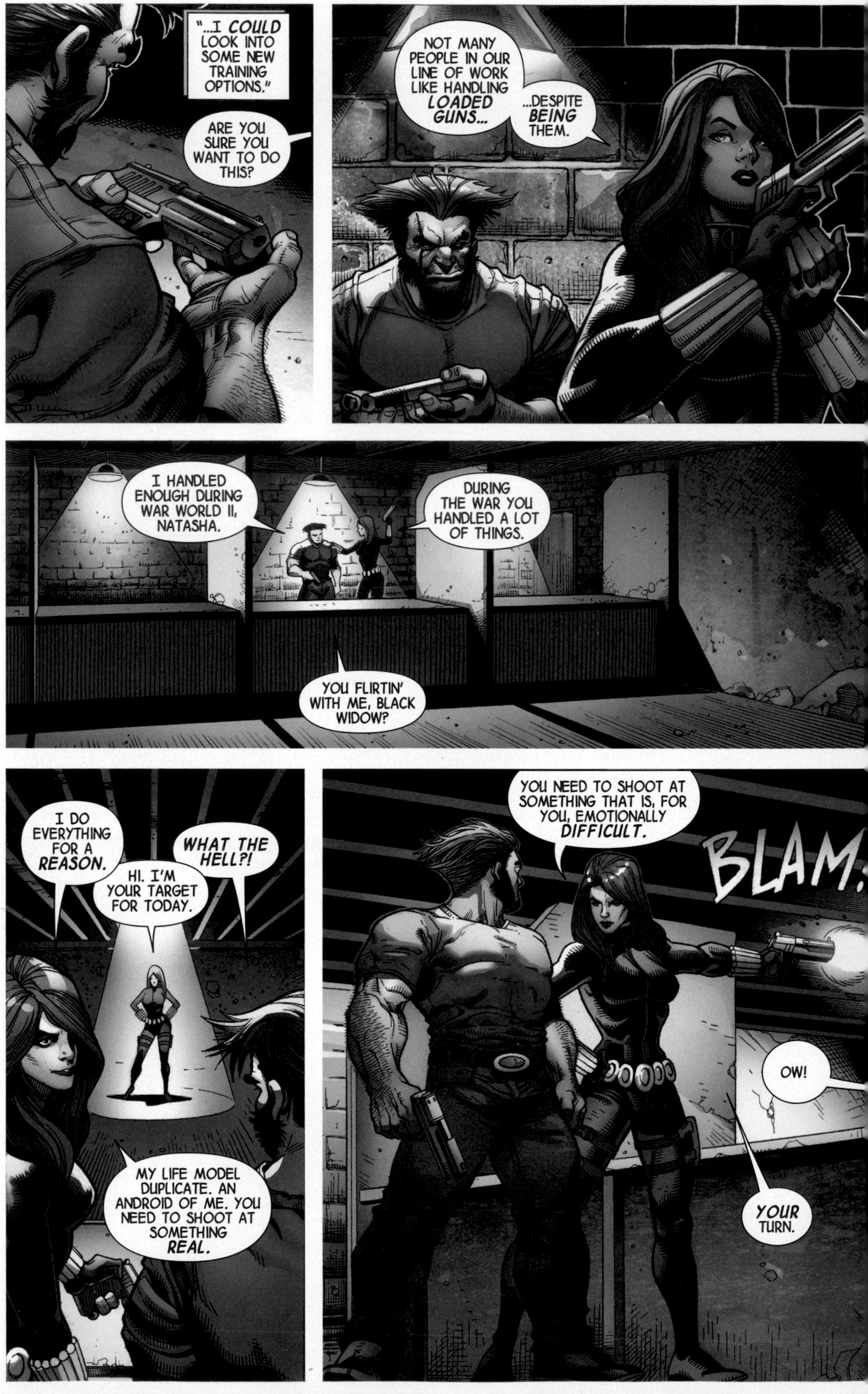
"...I COULD LOOK INTO SOME NEW TRAINING OPTIONS."
ARE YOU SURE YOU WANT TO DO THIS?
NOT MANY PEOPLE IN OUR LINE OF WORK LIKE HANDLING LOADED GUNS...
...DESPITE BEING THEM.
I HANDLED ENOUGH DURING WAR WORLD II, NATASHA.
DURING THE WAR YOU HANDLED A LOT OF THINGS.
YOU FLIRTIN' WITH ME, BLACK WIDOW?
I DO EVERYTHING FOR A REASON.
HI. I'M YOUR TARGET FOR TODAY.
WHAT THE HELL?!
MY LIFE MODEL DUPLICATE. AN ANDROID OF ME. YOU NEED TO SHOOT AT SOMETHING REAL.
YOU NEED TO SHOOT AT SOMETHING THAT IS, FOR YOU, EMOTIONALLY DIFFICULT.
BLAM
OW!
YOUR TURN.

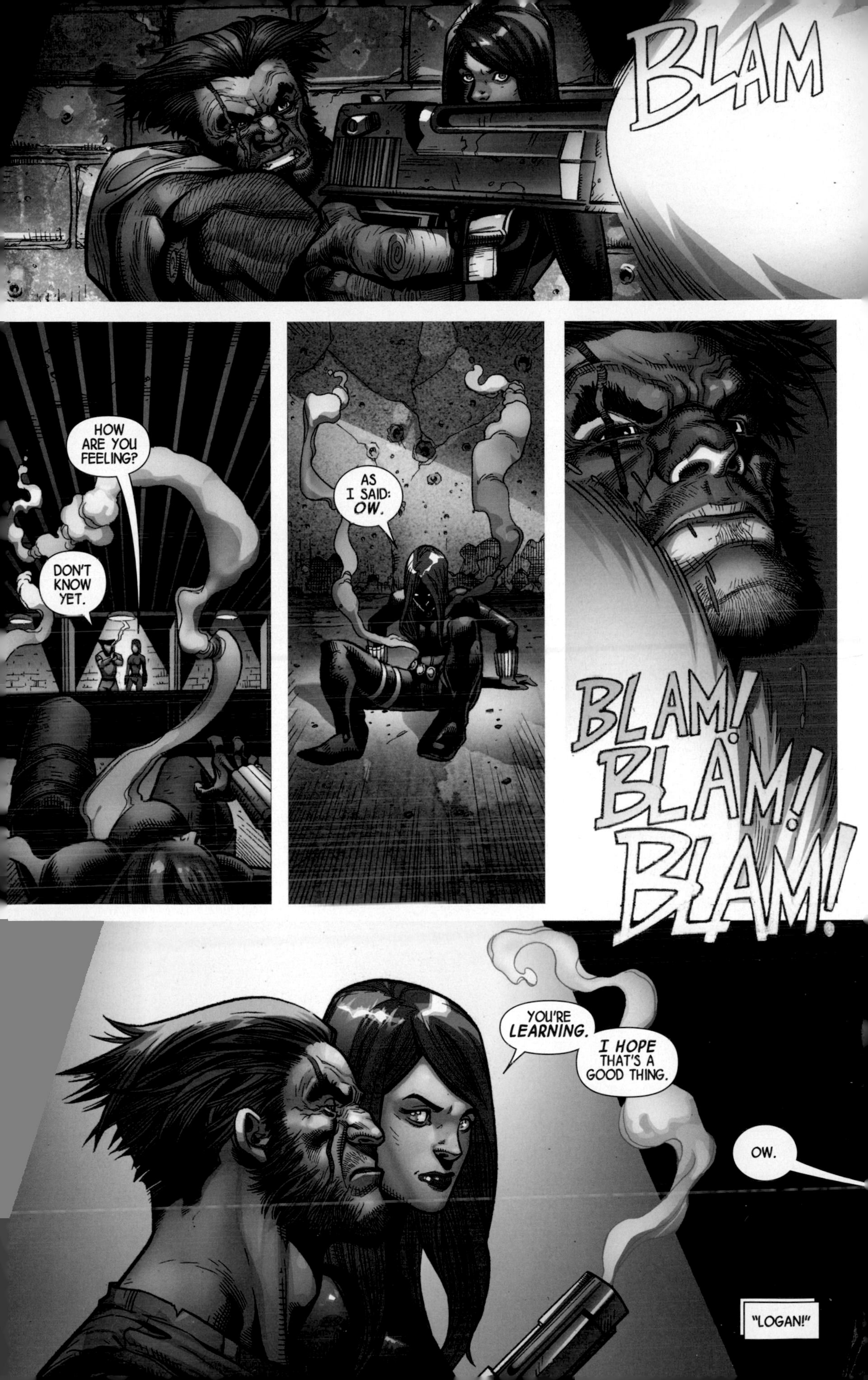

BLAM
HOW ARE YOU FEELING?
DON'T KNOW YET.
AS I SAID: OW.
BLAM! BLAM! BLAM!
YOU'RE LEARNING.
I HOPE THAT'S A GOOD THING.
OW.
"LOGAN!"

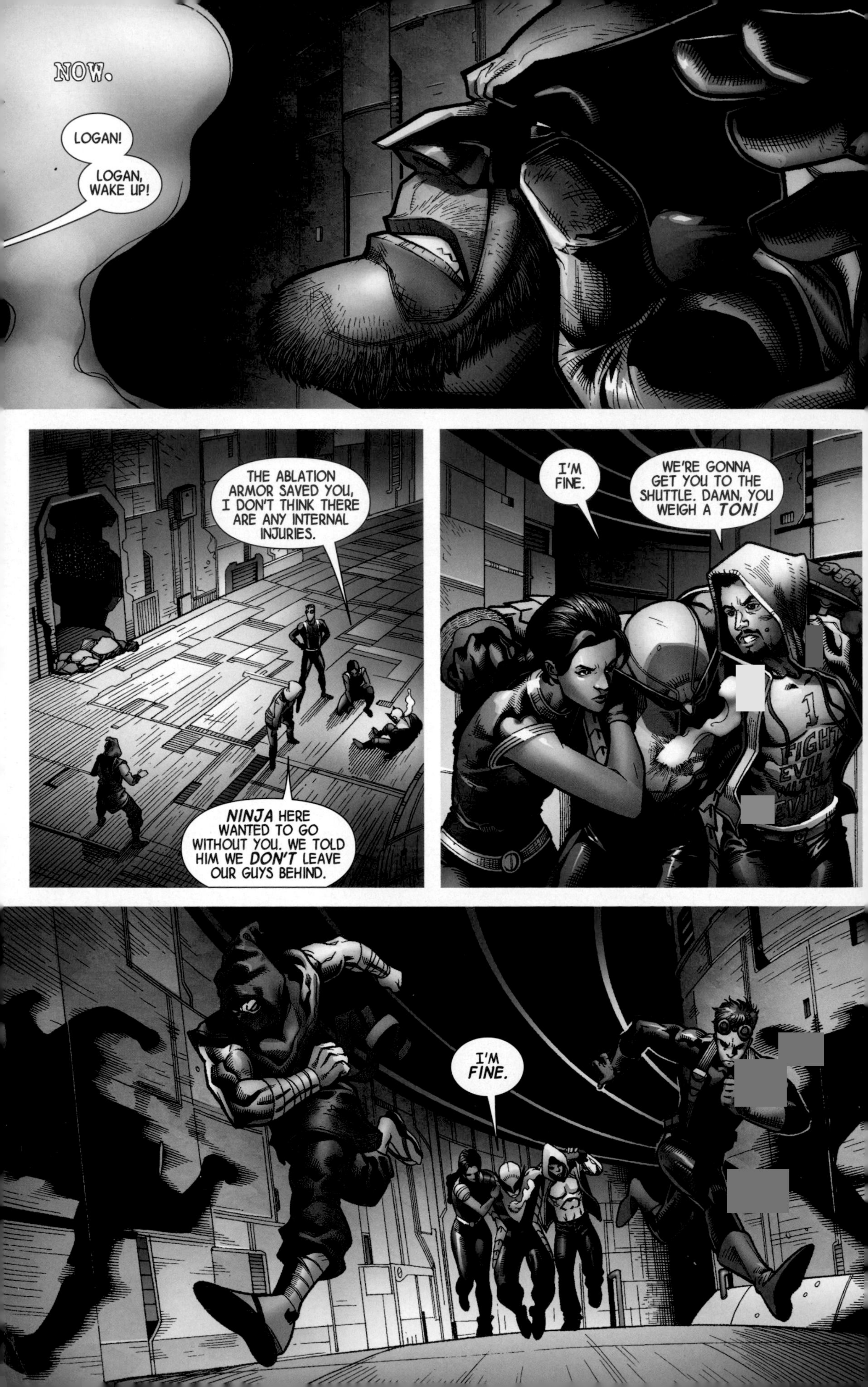
NOW.
LOGAN!
LOGAN, WAKE UP!
THE ABLATION ARMOR SAVED YOU, I DON'T THINK THERE ARE ANY INTERNAL INJURIES.
NINJA HERE WANTED TO GO WITHOUT YOU. WE TOLD HIM WE DON'T LEAVE OUR GUYS BEHIND.
I'M FINE.
WE'RE GONNA GET YOU TO THE SHUTTLE. DAMN, YOU WEIGH A TON!
FIGHT EVIL WITH EVIL
I'M FINE.

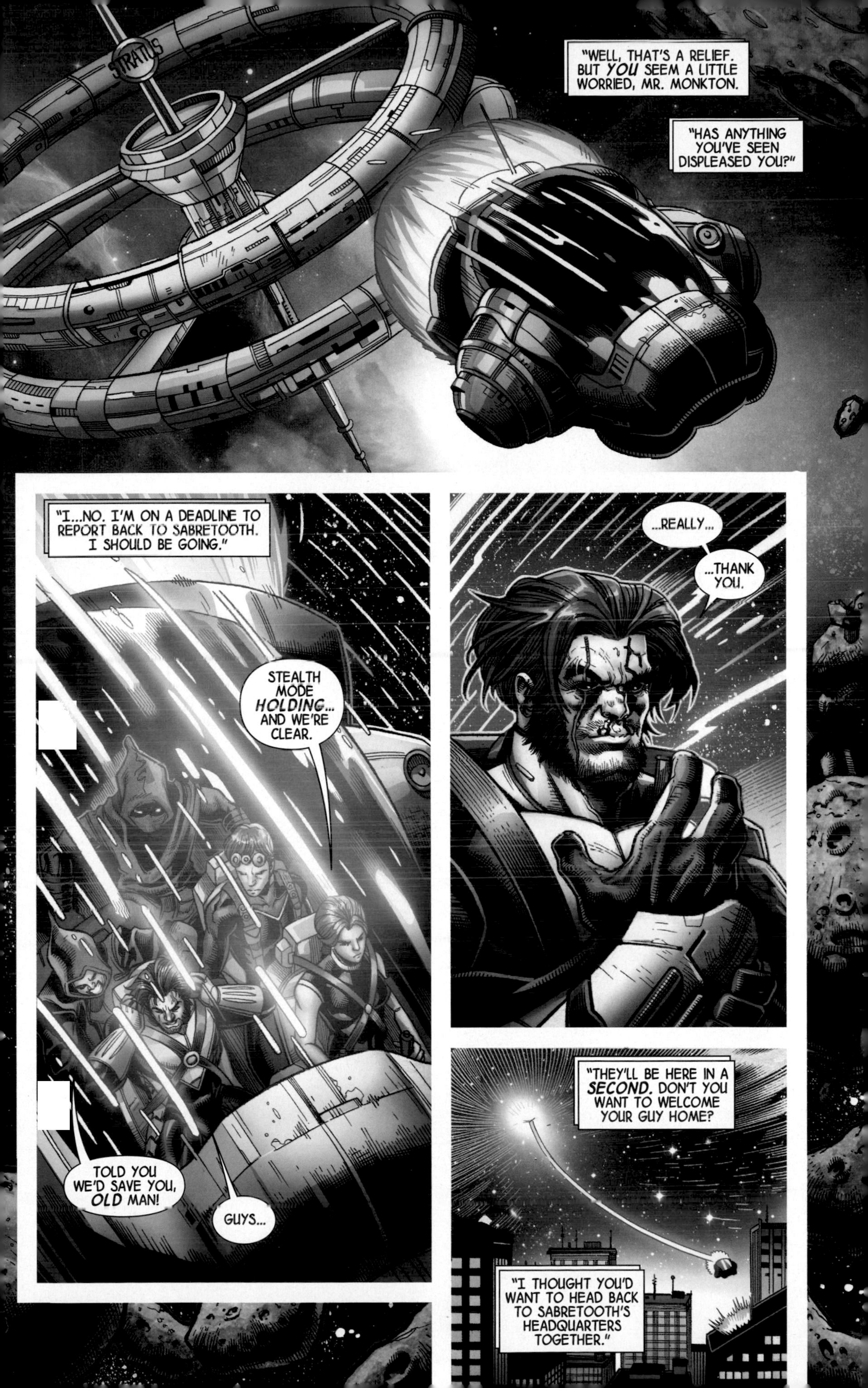
"WELL, THAT'S A RELIEF. BUT YOU SEEM A LITTLE WORRIED, MR. MONKTON.
"HAS ANYTHING YOU'VE SEEN DISPLEASED YOU?"
STRATUS
"I...NO. I'M ON A DEADLINE TO REPORT BACK TO SABRETOOTH. I SHOULD BE GOING."
STEALTH MODE HOLDING... AND WE'RE CLEAR.
TOLD YOU WE'D SAVE YOU, OLD MAN!
GUYS...
...REALLY...
...THANK YOU.
"THEY'LL BE HERE IN A SECOND. DON'T YOU WANT TO WELCOME YOUR GUY HOME?
"I THOUGHT YOU'D WANT TO HEAD BACK TO SABRETOOTH'S HEADQUARTERS TOGETHER."

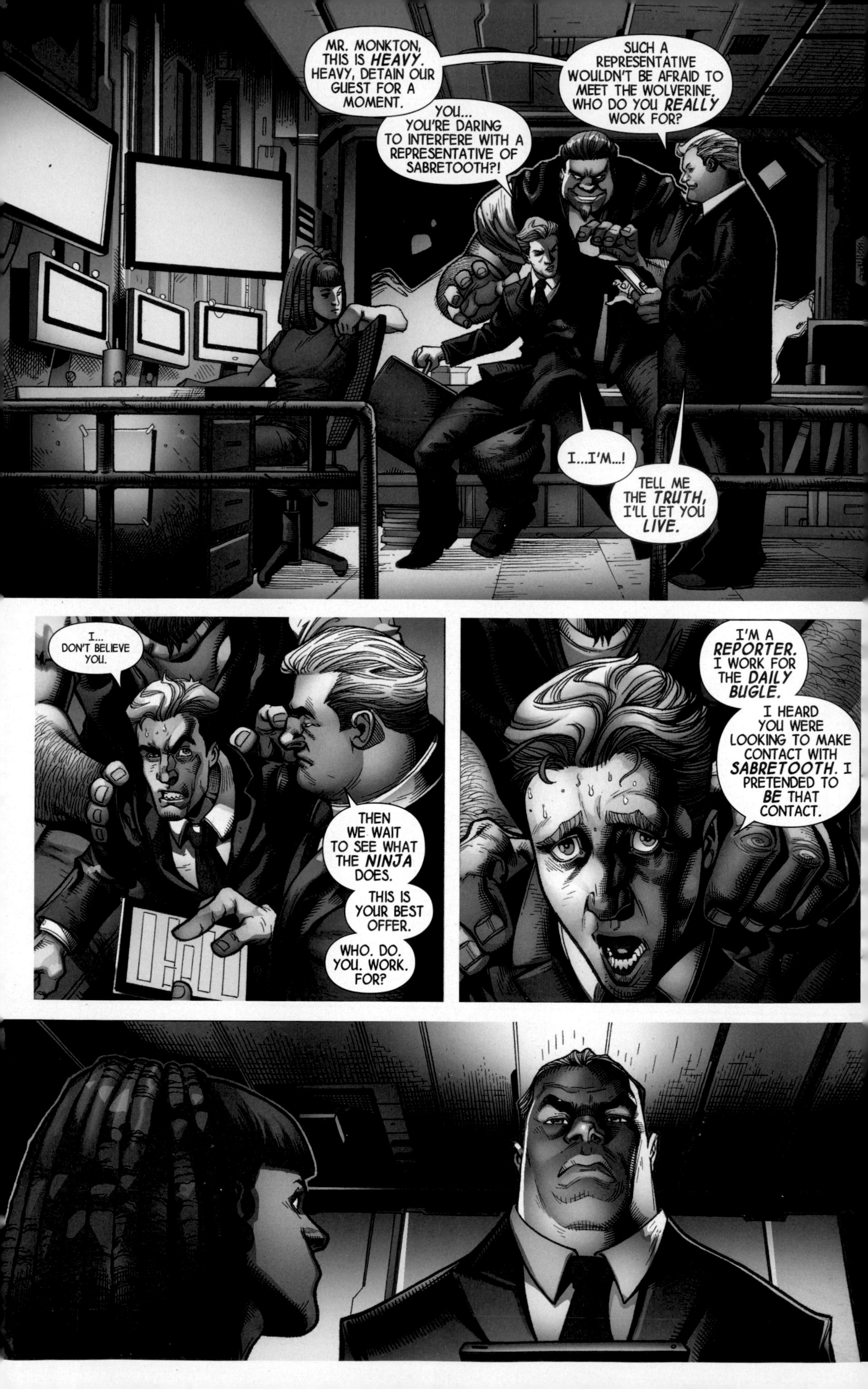

MR. MONKTON, THIS IS HEAVY. HEAVY, DETAIN OUR GUEST FOR A MOMENT.
YOU... YOU'RE DARING TO INTERFERE WITH A REPRESENTATIVE OF SABRETOOTH?!
SUCH A REPRESENTATIVE WOULDN'T BE AFRAID TO MEET THE WOLVERINE. WHO DO YOU REALLY WORK FOR?
I...I'M...!
TELL ME THE TRUTH, I'LL LET YOU LIVE.
I... DON'T BELIEVE YOU.
THEN WE WAIT TO SEE WHAT THE NINJA DOES.
THIS IS YOUR BEST OFFER.
WHO. DO. YOU. WORK. FOR?
I'M A REPORTER. I WORK FOR THE DAILY BUGLE.
I HEARD YOU WERE LOOKING TO MAKE CONTACT WITH SABRETOOTH. I PRETENDED TO BE THAT CONTACT.

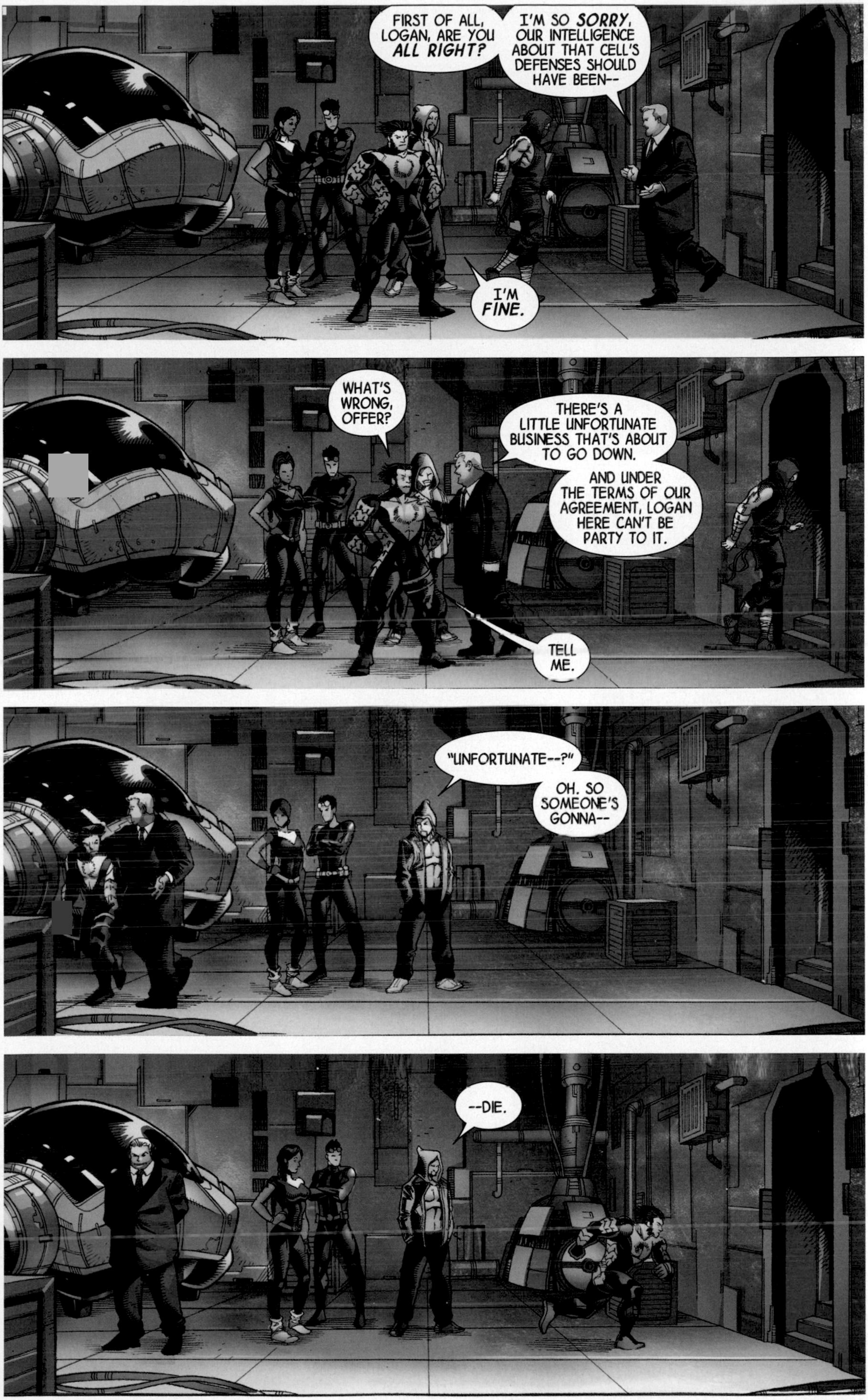
FIRST OF ALL, LOGAN, ARE YOU ALL RIGHT?
I'M SO SORRY, OUR INTELLIGENCE ABOUT THAT CELL'S DEFENSES SHOULD HAVE BEEN--
I'M FINE.
WHAT'S WRONG, OFFER?
THERE'S A LITTLE UNFORTUNATE BUSINESS THAT'S ABOUT TO GO DOWN.
AND UNDER THE TERMS OF OUR AGREEMENT, LOGAN HERE CAN'T BE PARTY TO IT.
TELL ME.
"UNFORTUNATE--?"
OH. SO SOMEONE'S GONNA--
--DIE.

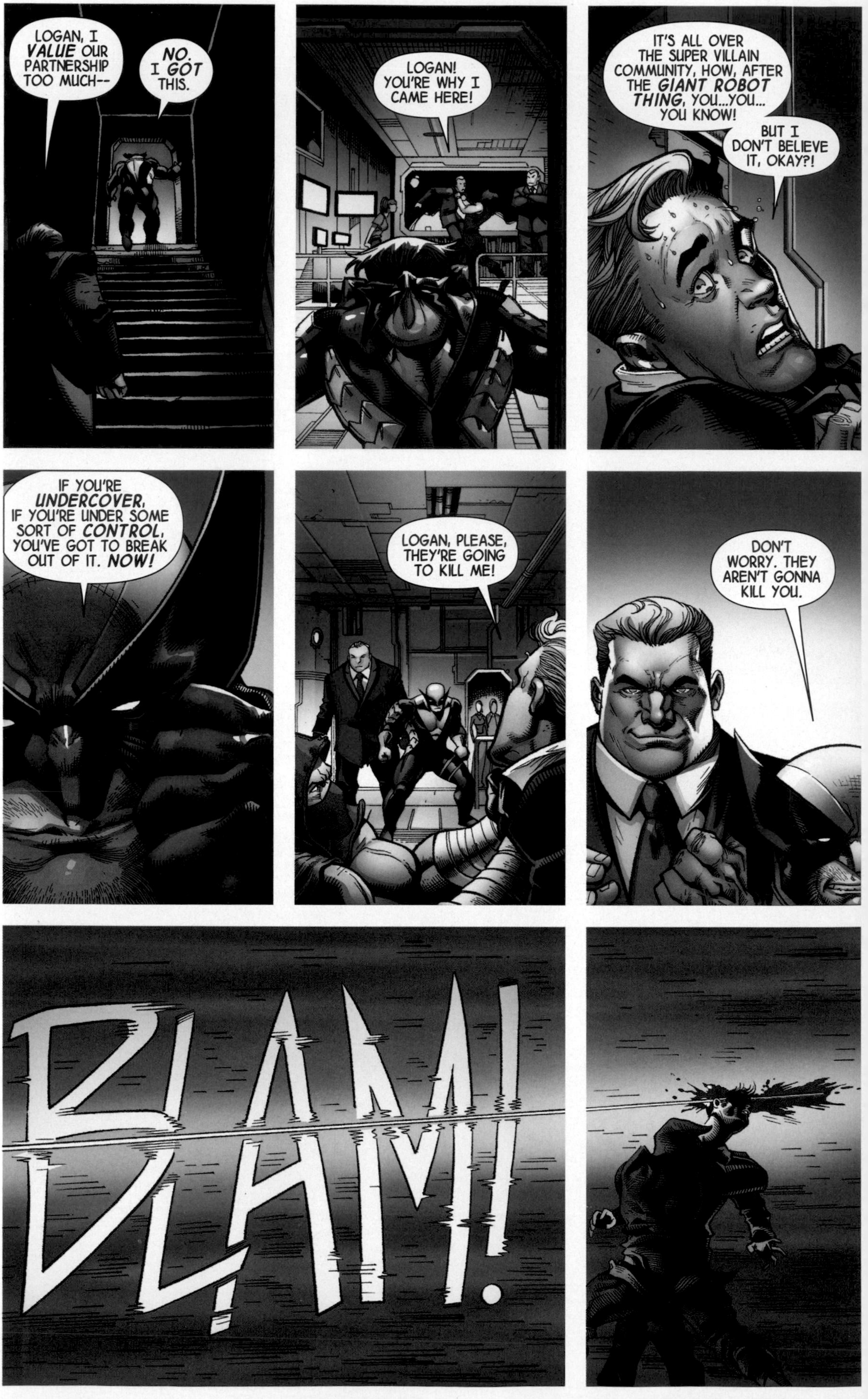

LOGAN, I VALUE OUR PARTNERSHIP TOO MUCH--
NO. I GOT THIS.
LOGAN! YOU'RE WHY I CAME HERE!
IT'S ALL OVER THE SUPER VILLAIN COMMUNITY, HOW, AFTER THE GIANT ROBOT THING, YOU...YOU... YOU KNOW!
BUT I DON'T BELIEVE IT, OKAY?!
IF YOU'RE UNDERCOVER, IF YOU'RE UNDER SOME SORT OF CONTROL, YOU'VE GOT TO BREAK OUT OF IT. NOW!
LOGAN, PLEASE, THEY'RE GOING TO KILL ME!
DON'T WORRY. THEY AREN'T GONNA KILL YOU.
BLAM!

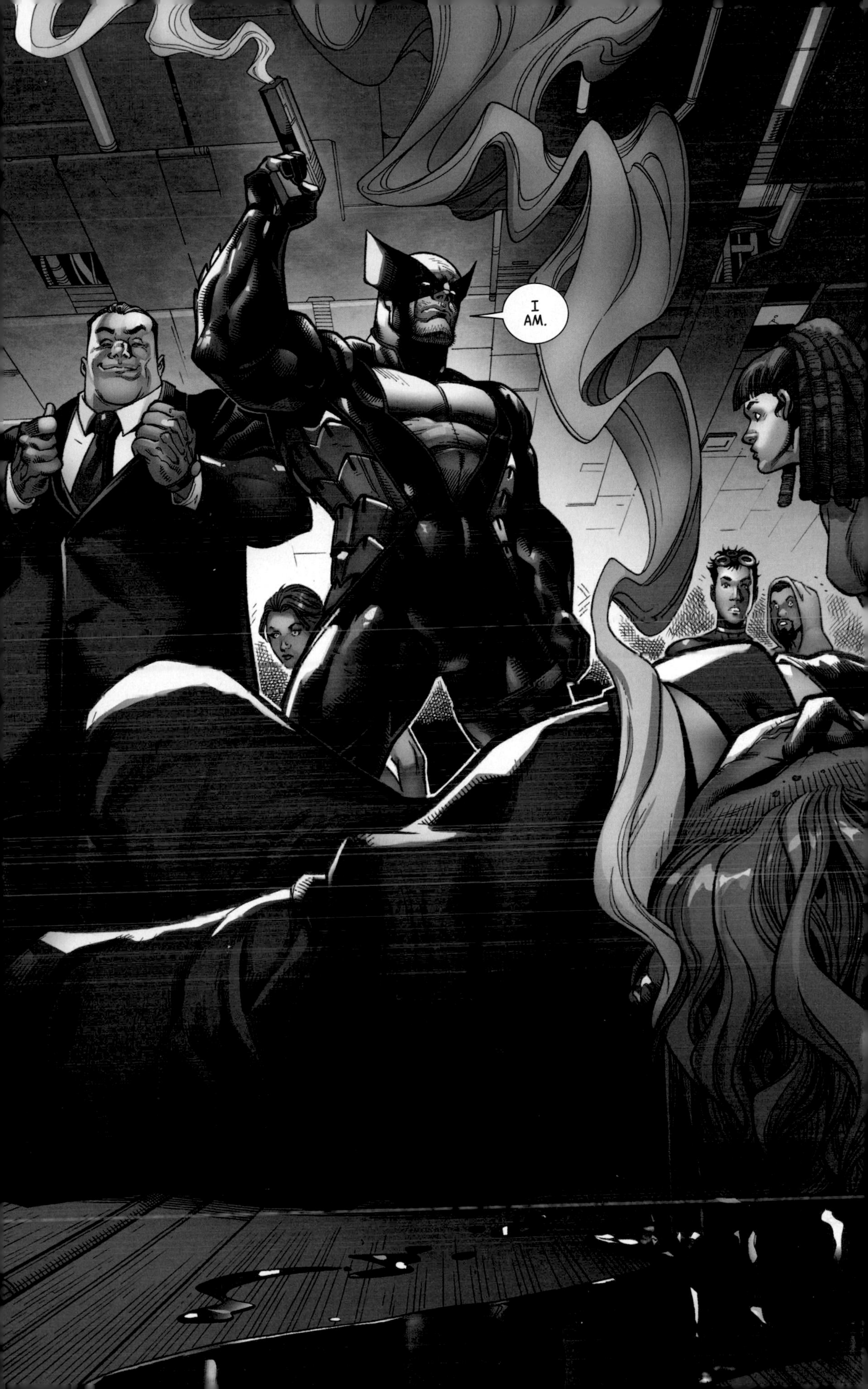
I AM.

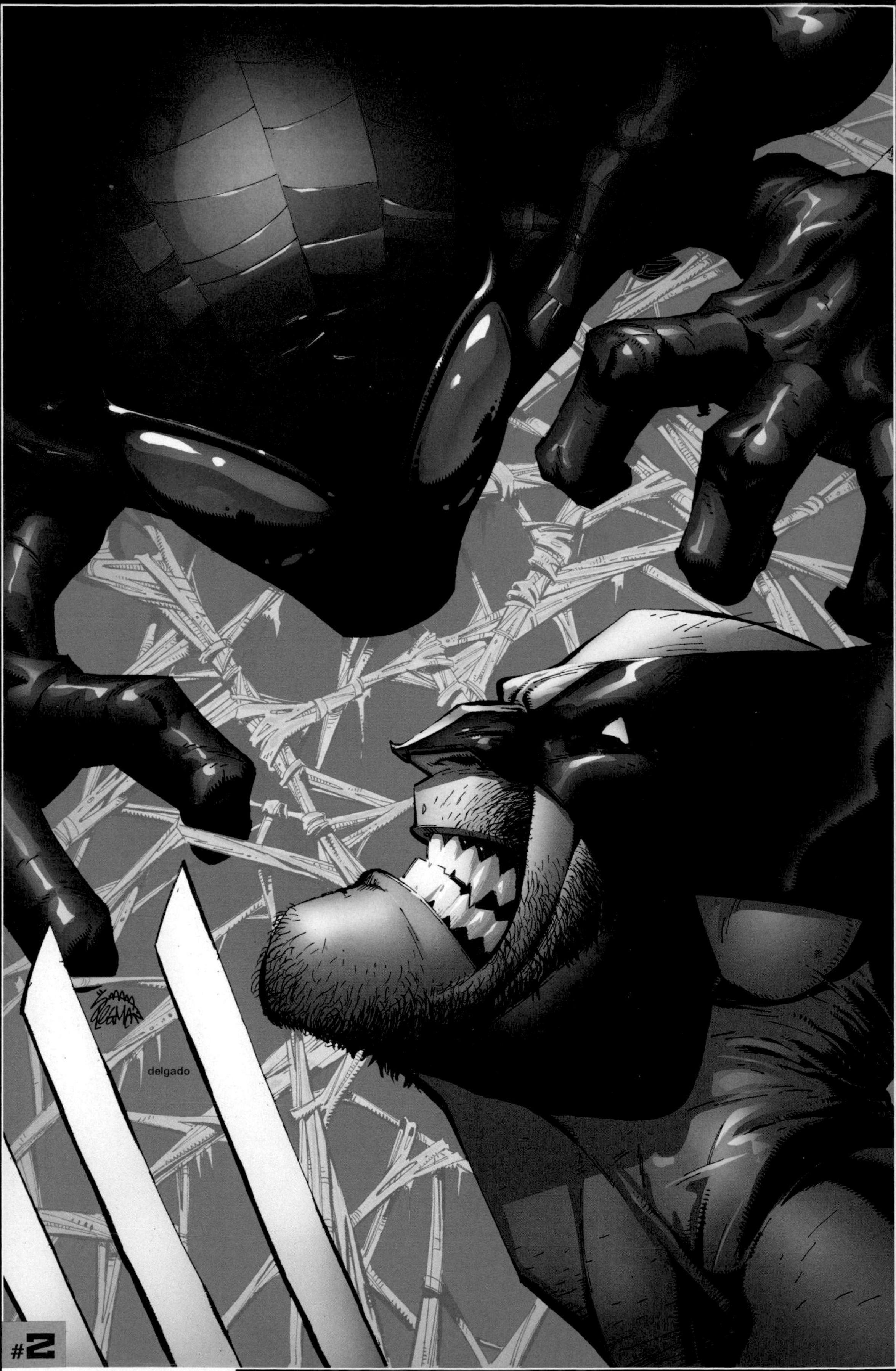
delgado
#2

ROGUE LOGAN PART 2

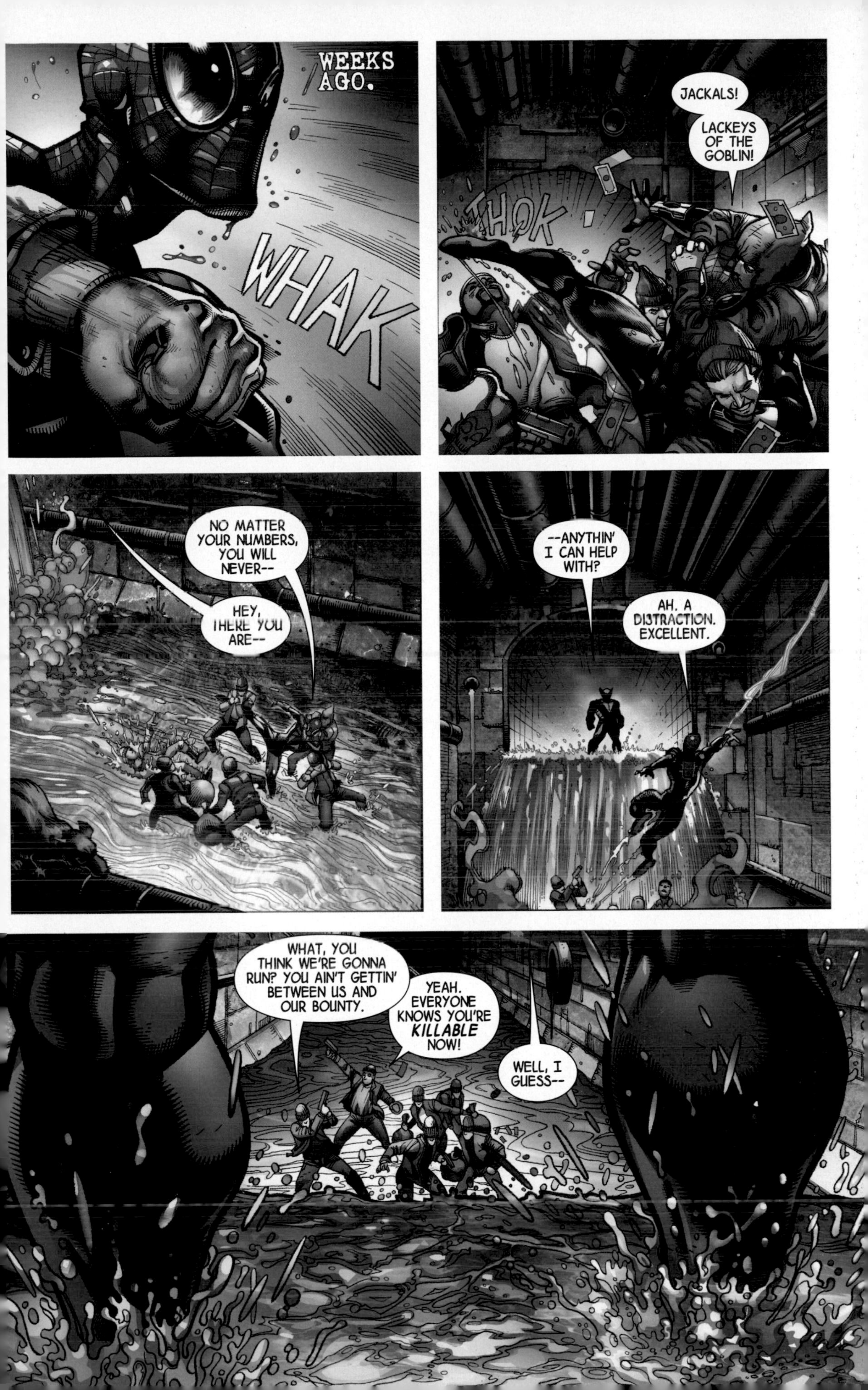
WEEKS AGO.
WHAK
JACKALS!
LACKEYS OF THE GOBLIN!
THOK
NO MATTER YOUR NUMBERS, YOU WILL NEVER--
HEY, THERE YOU ARE--
--ANYTHIN' I CAN HELP WITH?
AH. A DISTRACTION. EXCELLENT.
WHAT, YOU THINK WE'RE GONNA RUN? YOU AIN'T GETTIN' BETWEEN US AND OUR BOUNTY.
YEAH. EVERYONE KNOWS YOU'RE *KILLABLE* NOW!
WELL, I GUESS--

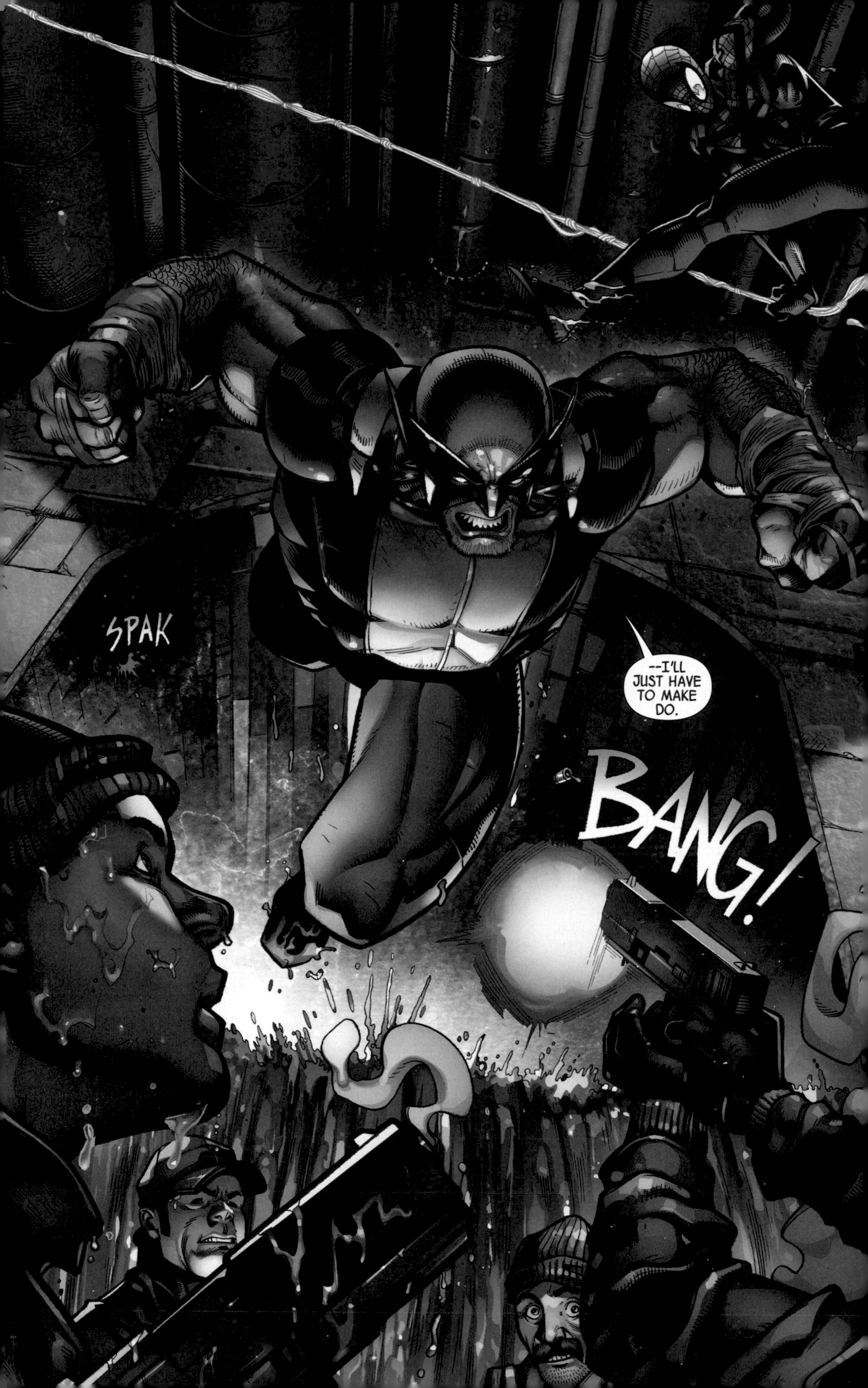
SPAK
--I'LL JUST HAVE TO MAKE DO.
BANG!

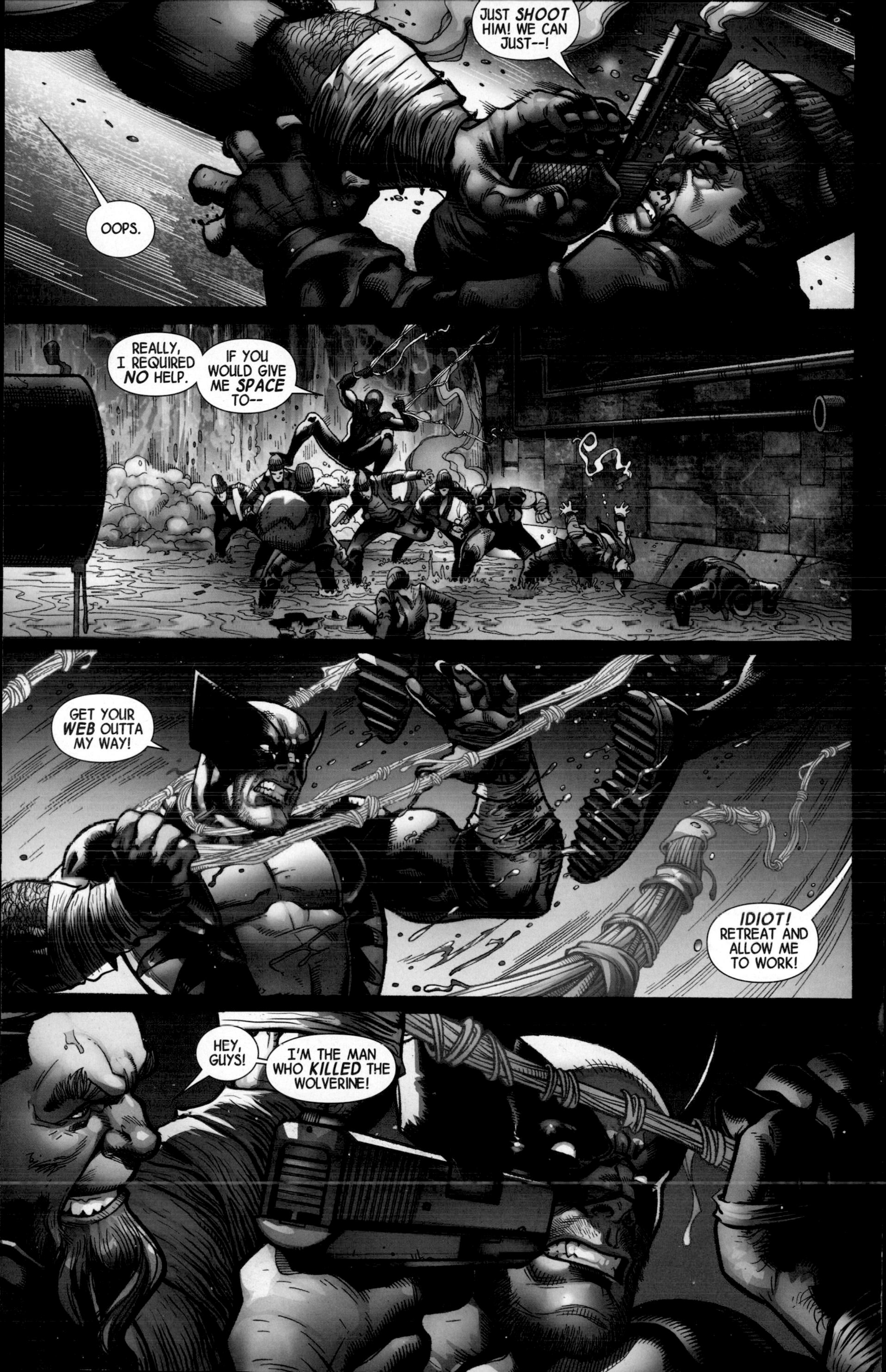

JUST SHOOT HIM! WE CAN JUST--!
OOPS.
REALLY, I REQUIRED NO HELP.
IF YOU WOULD GIVE ME SPACE TO--
GET YOUR WEB OUTTA MY WAY!
IDIOT! RETREAT AND ALLOW ME TO WORK!
HEY, GUYS!
I'M THE MAN WHO KILLED THE WOLVERINE!

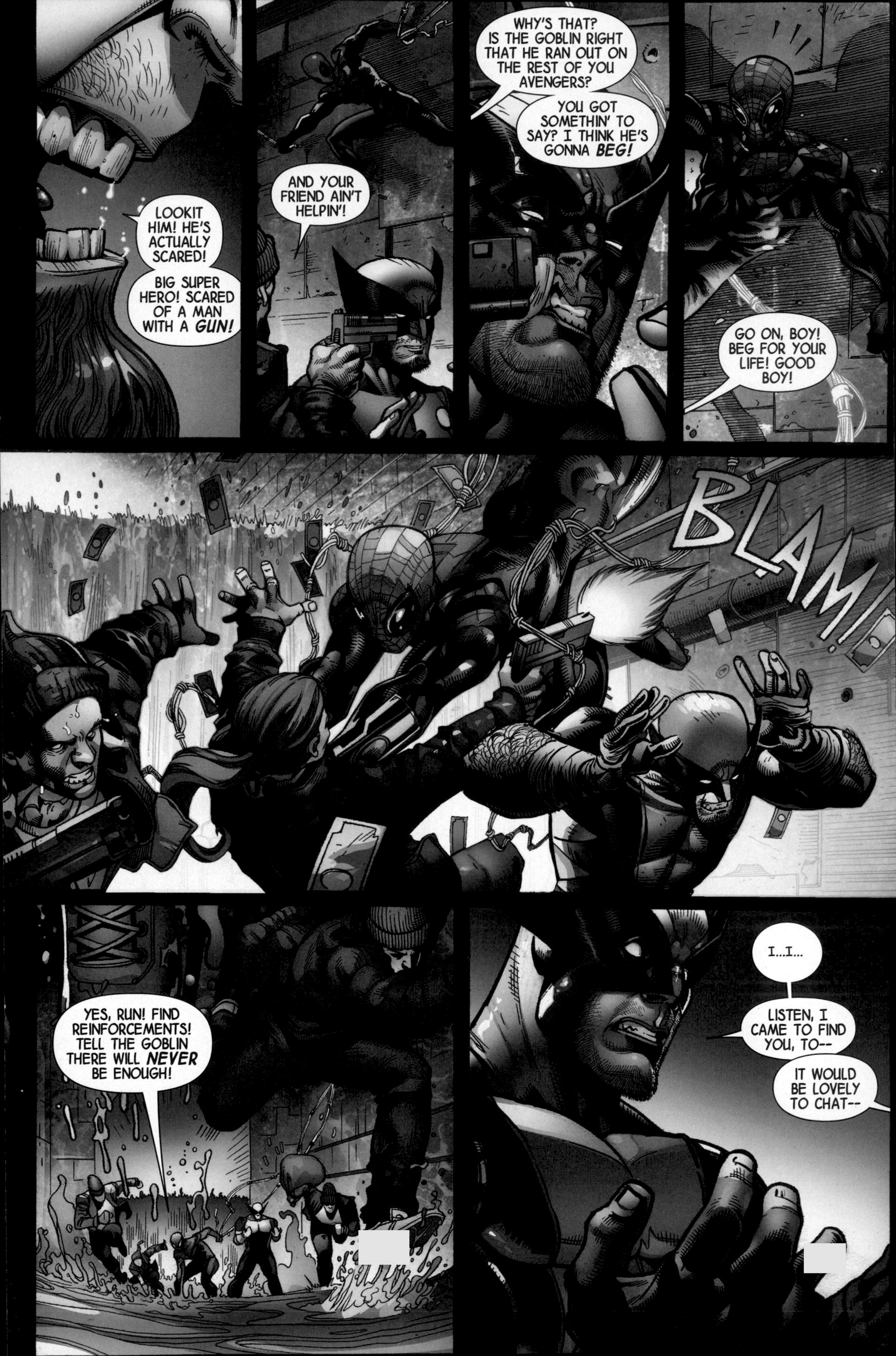
LOOKIT HIM! HE'S ACTUALLY SCARED!
BIG SUPER HERO! SCARED OF A MAN WITH A *GUN!*
AND YOUR FRIEND AIN'T HELPIN'!
WHY'S THAT? IS THE GOBLIN RIGHT THAT HE RAN OUT ON THE REST OF YOU AVENGERS?
YOU GOT SOMETHIN' TO SAY? I THINK HE'S GONNA *BEG!*
GO ON, BOY! BEG FOR YOUR LIFE! GOOD BOY!
BLAM!
YES, RUN! FIND REINFORCEMENTS! TELL THE GOBLIN THERE WILL *NEVER* BE ENOUGH!
I...I...
LISTEN, I CAME TO FIND YOU, TO--
IT WOULD BE LOVELY TO CHAT--

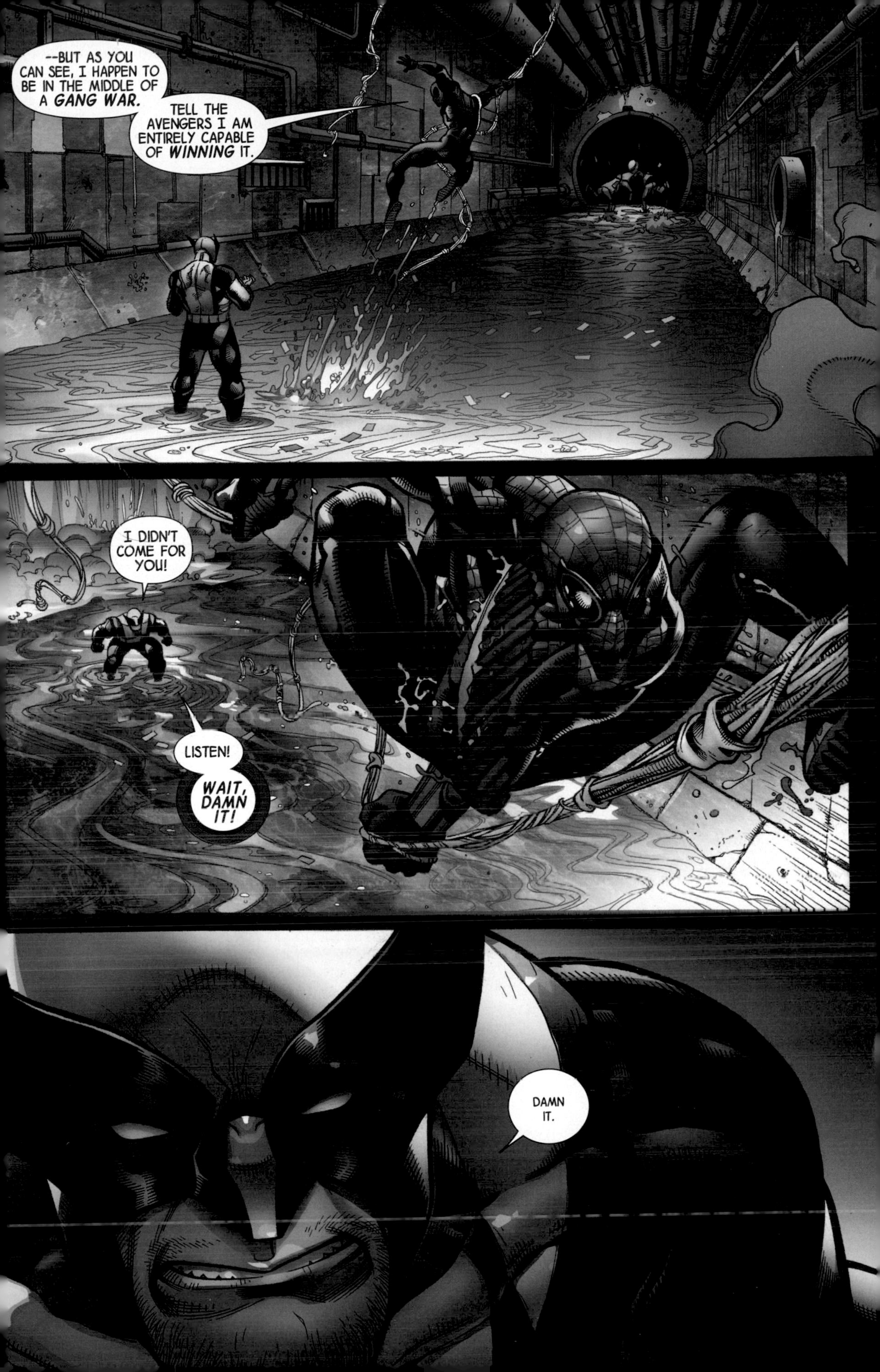
--BUT AS YOU CAN SEE, I HAPPEN TO BE IN THE MIDDLE OF A GANG WAR.
TELL THE AVENGERS I AM ENTIRELY CAPABLE OF WINNING IT.
I DIDN'T COME FOR YOU!
LISTEN!
WAIT, DAMN IT!
DAMN IT.

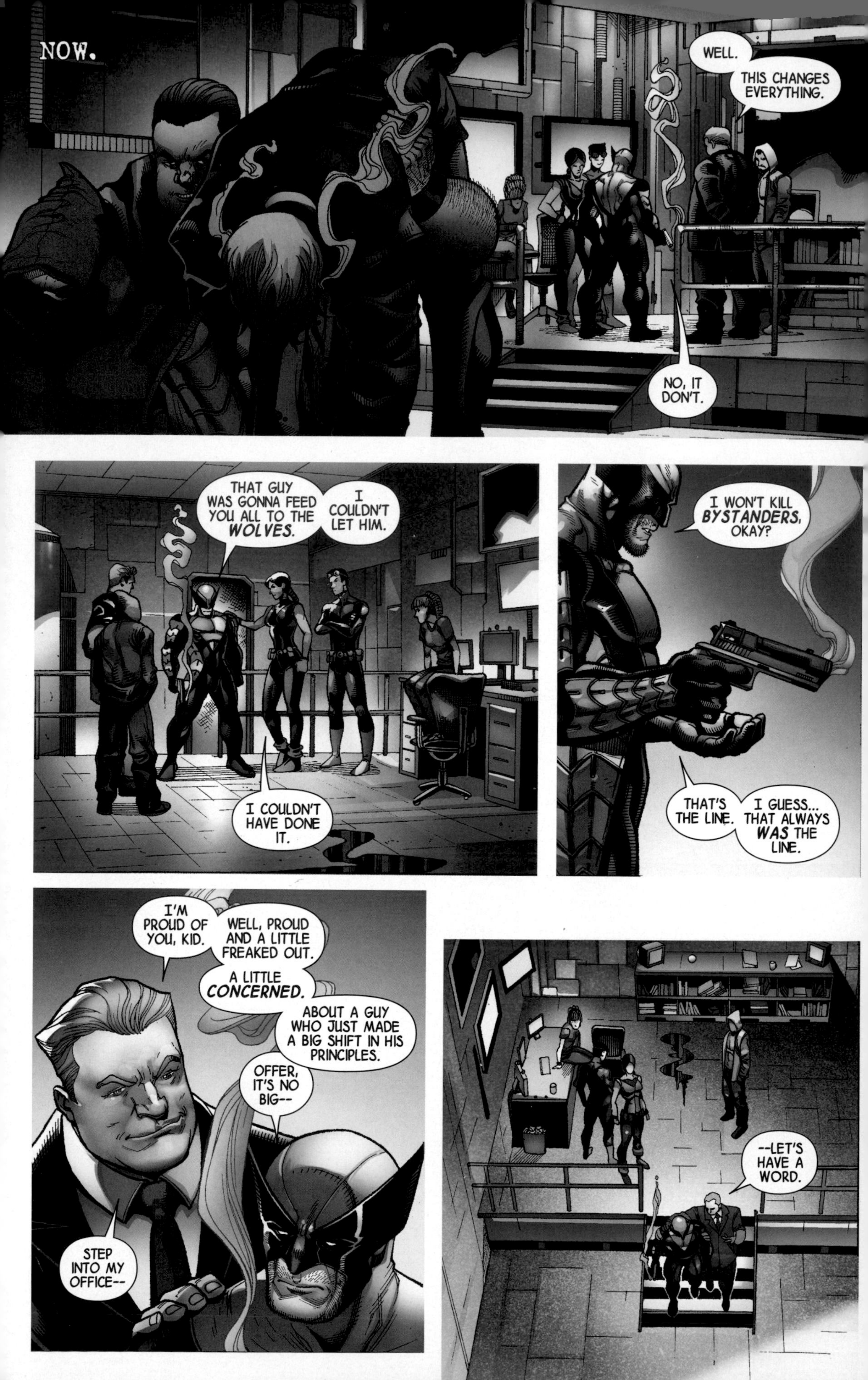
NOW.
WELL.
THIS CHANGES EVERYTHING.
NO, IT DON'T.
THAT GUY WAS GONNA FEED YOU ALL TO THE WOLVES.
I COULDN'T LET HIM.
I COULDN'T HAVE DONE IT.
I WON'T KILL BYSTANDERS, OKAY?
THAT'S THE LINE.
I GUESS... THAT ALWAYS WAS THE LINE.
I'M PROUD OF YOU, KID.
WELL, PROUD AND A LITTLE FREAKED OUT.
A LITTLE CONCERNED.
ABOUT A GUY WHO JUST MADE A BIG SHIFT IN HIS PRINCIPLES.
OFFER, IT'S NO BIG--
STEP INTO MY OFFICE--
--LET'S HAVE A WORD.

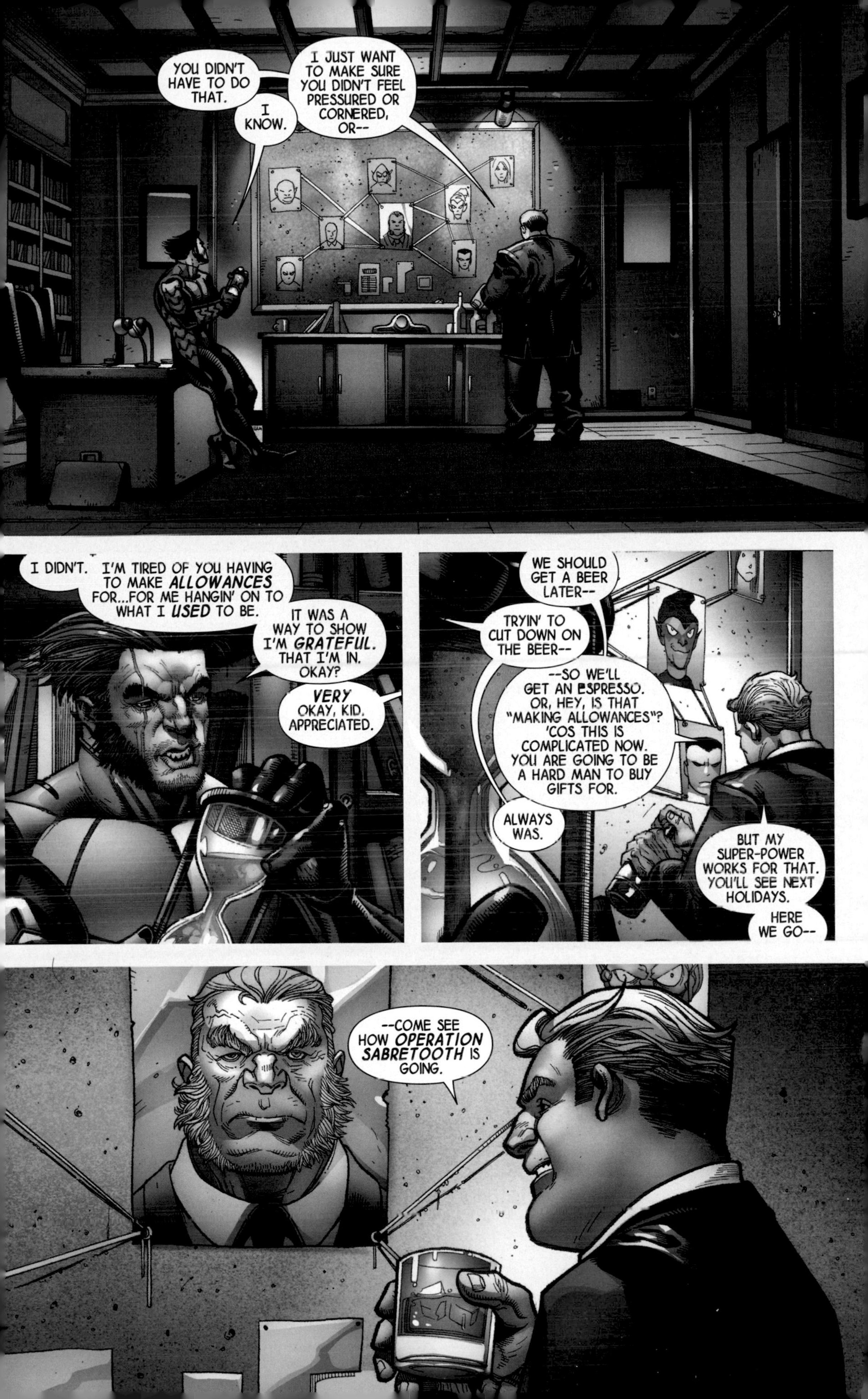

YOU DIDN'T HAVE TO DO THAT.
I JUST WANT TO MAKE SURE YOU DIDN'T FEEL PRESSURED OR CORNERED, OR--
I KNOW.
I DIDN'T.
I'M TIRED OF YOU HAVING TO MAKE ALLOWANCES FOR...FOR ME HANGIN' ON TO WHAT I USED TO BE.
IT WAS A WAY TO SHOW I'M GRATEFUL. THAT I'M IN. OKAY?
VERY OKAY, KID. APPRECIATED.
WE SHOULD GET A BEER LATER--
TRYIN' TO CUT DOWN ON THE BEER--
--SO WE'LL GET AN ESPRESSO. OR, HEY, IS THAT "MAKING ALLOWANCES"? 'COS THIS IS COMPLICATED NOW. YOU ARE GOING TO BE A HARD MAN TO BUY GIFTS FOR.
ALWAYS WAS.
BUT MY SUPER-POWER WORKS FOR THAT. YOU'LL SEE NEXT HOLIDAYS.
HERE WE GO--
--COME SEE HOW OPERATION SABRETOOTH IS GOING.

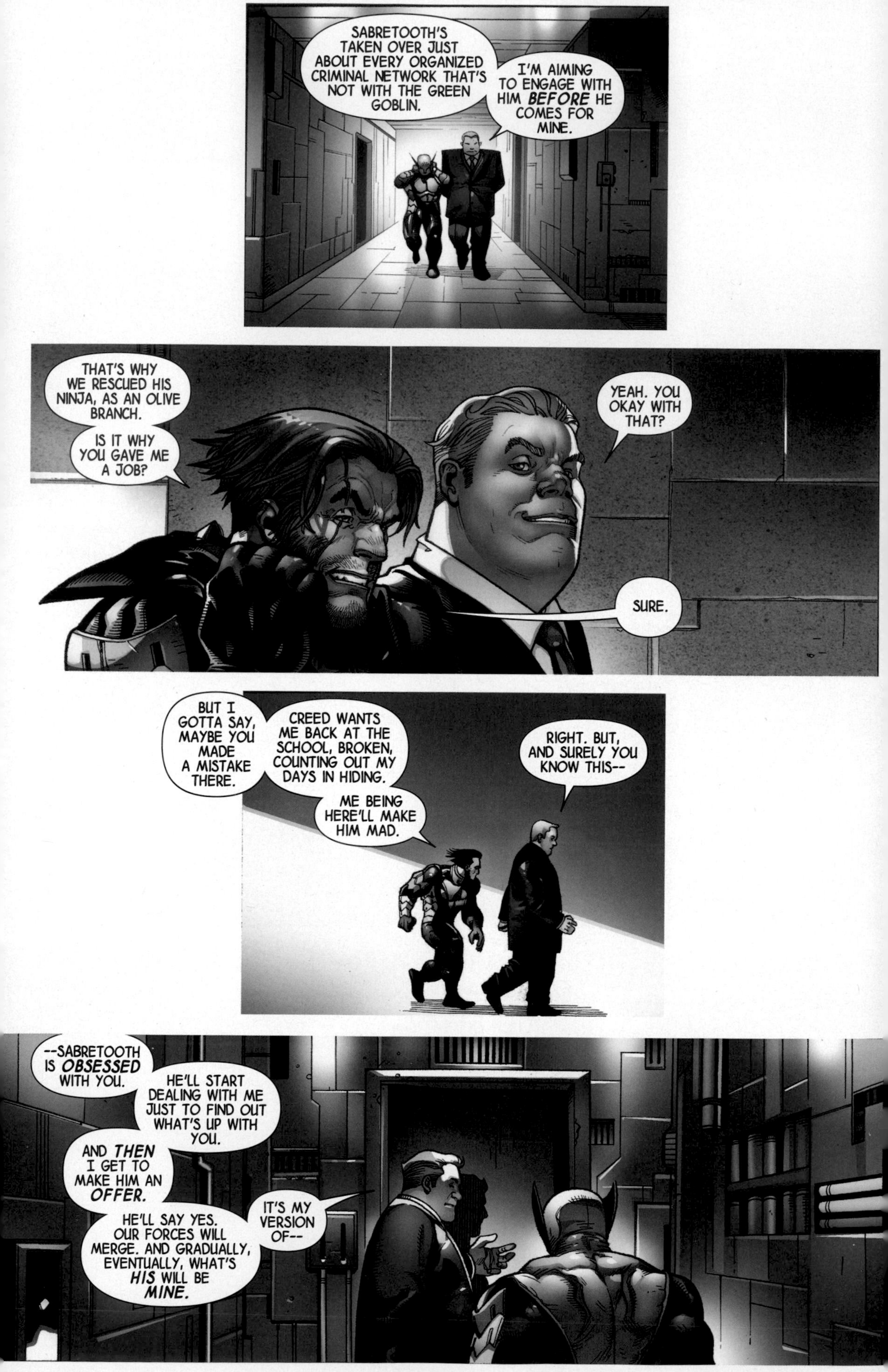
SABRETOOTH'S TAKEN OVER JUST ABOUT EVERY ORGANIZED CRIMINAL NETWORK THAT'S NOT WITH THE GREEN GOBLIN.
I'M AIMING TO ENGAGE WITH HIM BEFORE HE COMES FOR MINE.
THAT'S WHY WE RESCUED HIS NINJA, AS AN OLIVE BRANCH.
IS IT WHY YOU GAVE ME A JOB?
YEAH. YOU OKAY WITH THAT?
SURE.
BUT I GOTTA SAY, MAYBE YOU MADE A MISTAKE THERE.
CREED WANTS ME BACK AT THE SCHOOL, BROKEN, COUNTING OUT MY DAYS IN HIDING.
ME BEING HERE'LL MAKE HIM MAD.
RIGHT. BUT, AND SURELY YOU KNOW THIS--
--SABRETOOTH IS OBSESSED WITH YOU.
HE'LL START DEALING WITH ME JUST TO FIND OUT WHAT'S UP WITH YOU.
AND THEN I GET TO MAKE HIM AN OFFER.
HE'LL SAY YES. OUR FORCES WILL MERGE. AND GRADUALLY, EVENTUALLY, WHAT'S HIS WILL BE MINE.
IT'S MY VERSION OF--

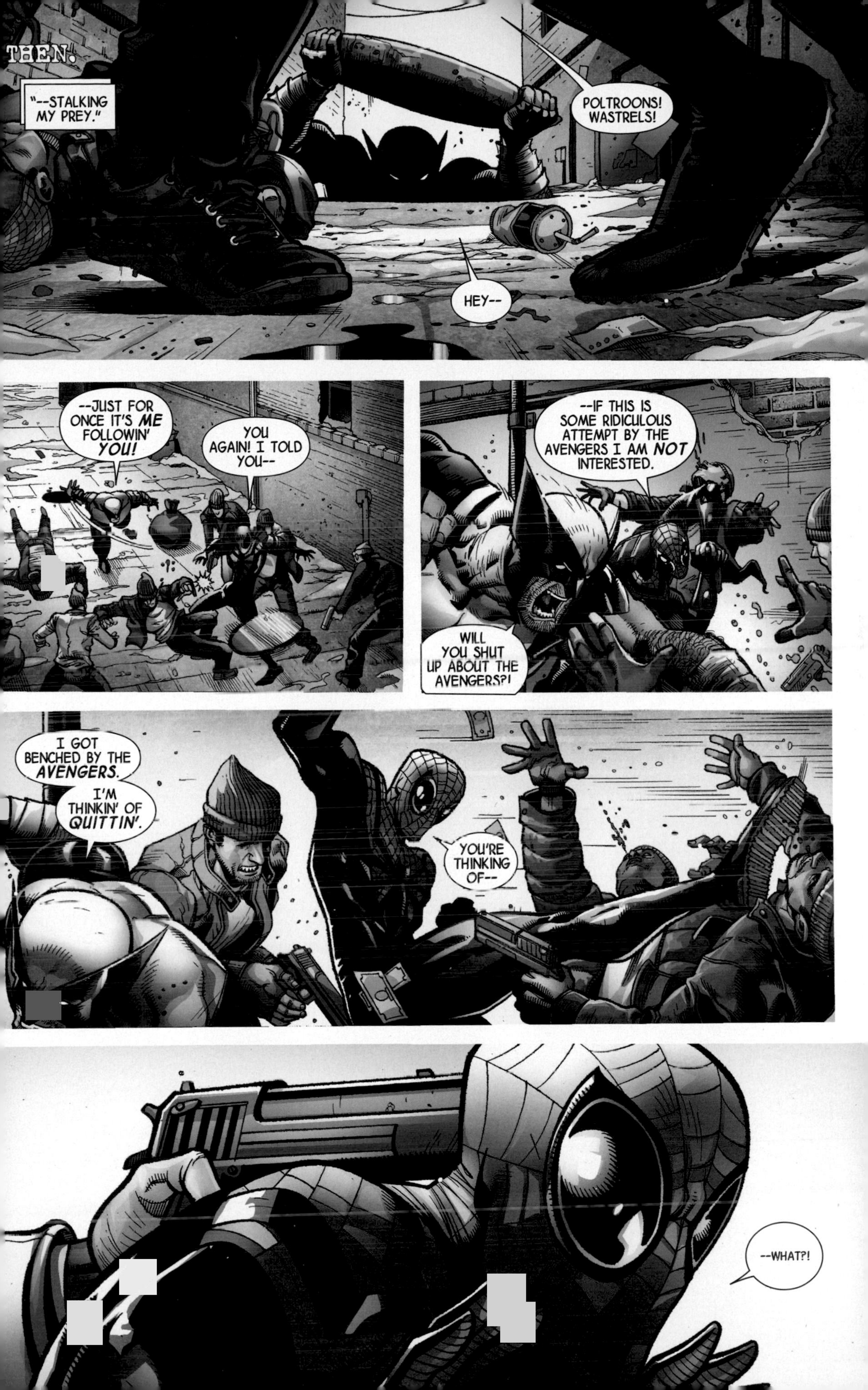
THEN.
"--STALKING MY PREY."
POLTROONS! WASTRELS!
HEY--
--JUST FOR ONCE IT'S ME FOLLOWIN' YOU!
YOU AGAIN! I TOLD YOU--
--IF THIS IS SOME RIDICULOUS ATTEMPT BY THE AVENGERS I AM NOT INTERESTED.
WILL YOU SHUT UP ABOUT THE AVENGERS?!
I GOT BENCHED BY THE AVENGERS.
I'M THINKIN' OF QUITTIN'.
YOU'RE THINKING OF--
--WHAT?!

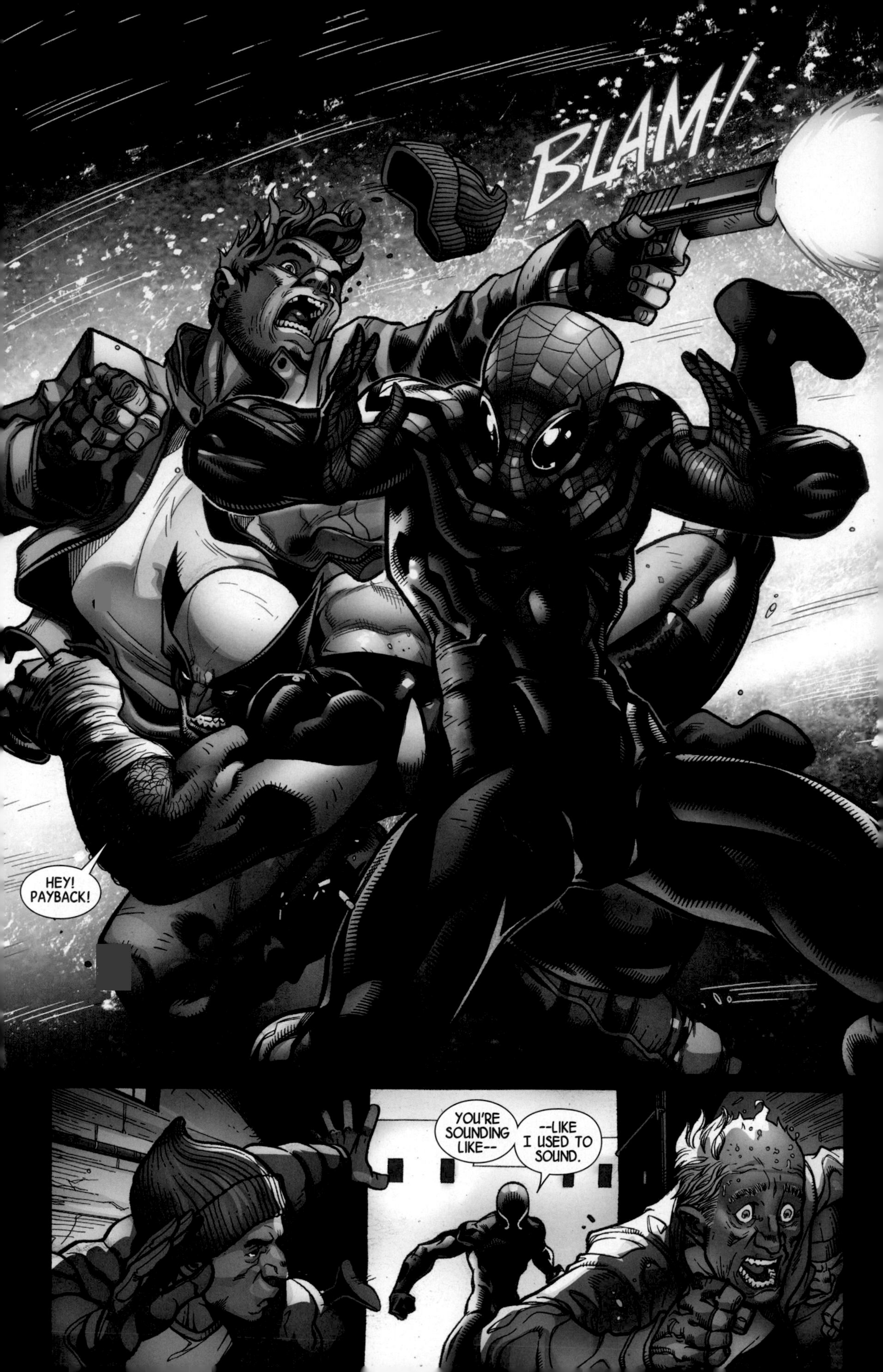
BLAM!
HEY! PAYBACK!
YOU'RE SOUNDING LIKE--
--LIKE I USED TO SOUND.

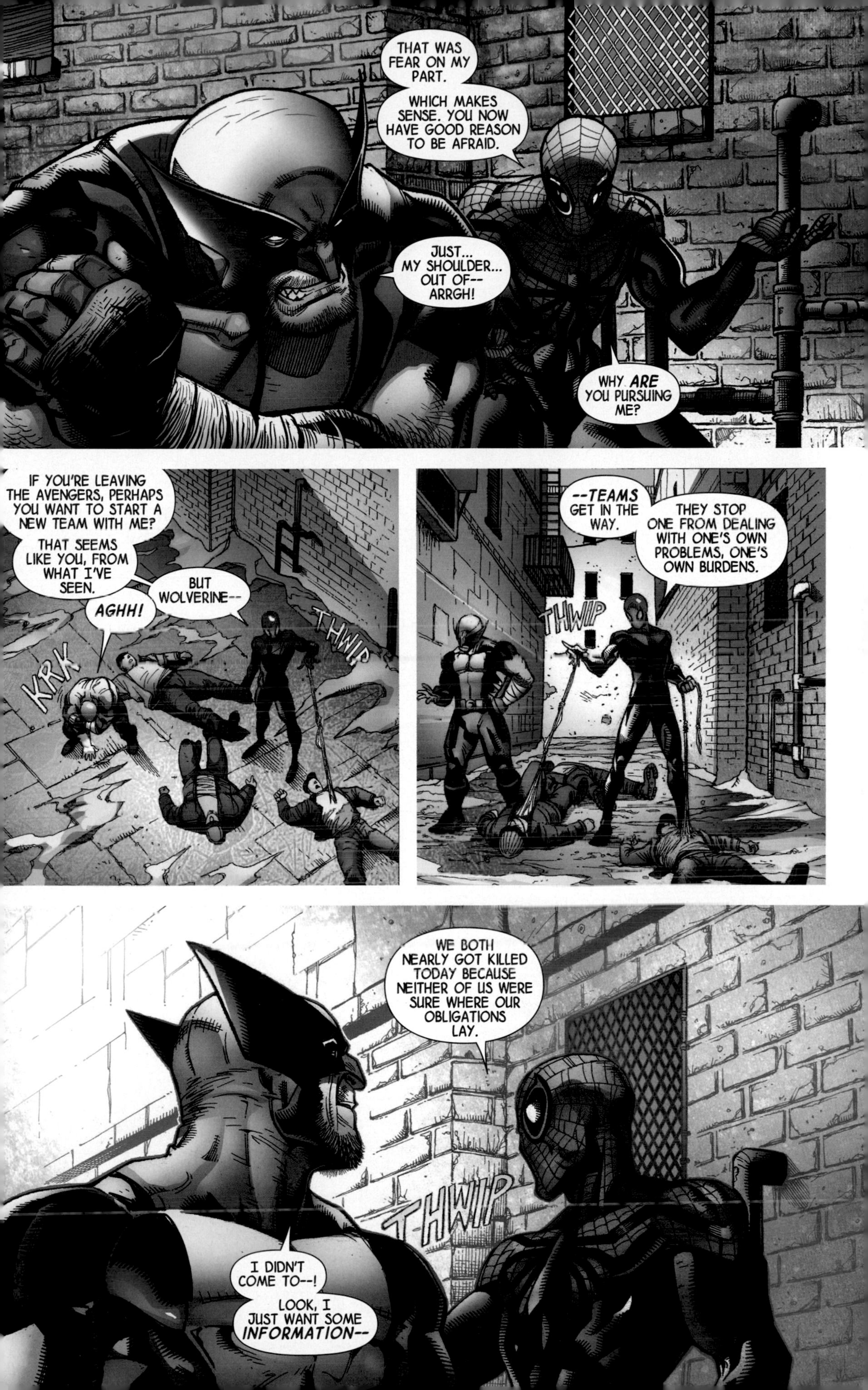
THAT WAS FEAR ON MY PART.
WHICH MAKES SENSE. YOU NOW HAVE GOOD REASON TO BE AFRAID.
JUST... MY SHOULDER... OUT OF-- ARRGH!
WHY ARE YOU PURSUING ME?
IF YOU'RE LEAVING THE AVENGERS, PERHAPS YOU WANT TO START A NEW TEAM WITH ME?
THAT SEEMS LIKE YOU, FROM WHAT I'VE SEEN.
BUT WOLVERINE--
AGHH!
KRK
THWIP
--TEAMS GET IN THE WAY.
THEY STOP ONE FROM DEALING WITH ONE'S OWN PROBLEMS, ONE'S OWN BURDENS.
THWIP
WE BOTH NEARLY GOT KILLED TODAY BECAUSE NEITHER OF US WERE SURE WHERE OUR OBLIGATIONS LAY.
THWIP
I DIDN'T COME TO--!
LOOK, I JUST WANT SOME INFORMATION--

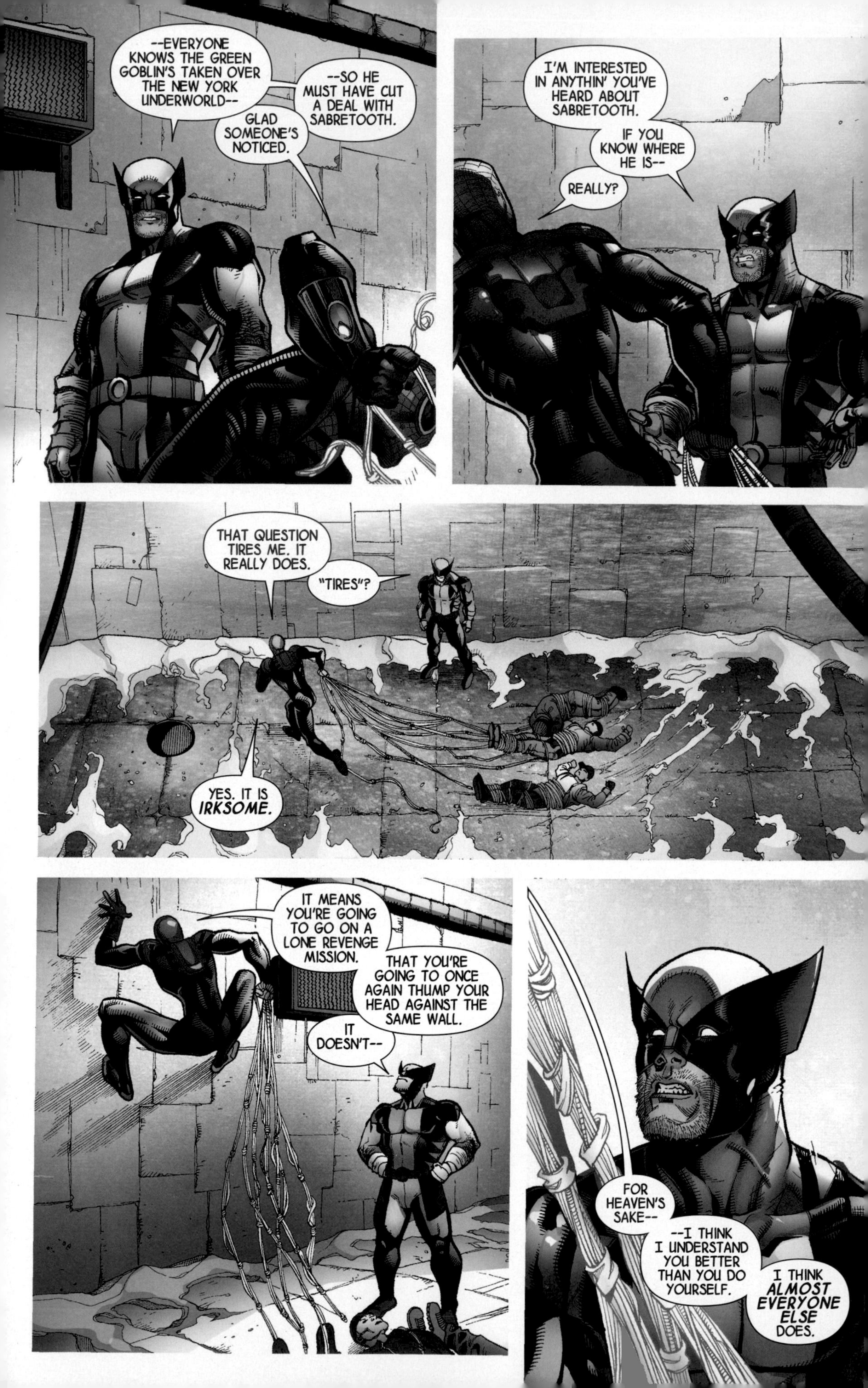
--EVERYONE KNOWS THE GREEN GOBLIN'S TAKEN OVER THE NEW YORK UNDERWORLD--
--SO HE MUST HAVE CUT A DEAL WITH SABRETOOTH.
GLAD SOMEONE'S NOTICED.
I'M INTERESTED IN ANYTHIN' YOU'VE HEARD ABOUT SABRETOOTH.
IF YOU KNOW WHERE HE IS--
REALLY?
THAT QUESTION TIRES ME. IT REALLY DOES.
"TIRES"?
YES. IT IS IRKSOME.
IT MEANS YOU'RE GOING TO GO ON A LONE REVENGE MISSION.
THAT YOU'RE GOING TO ONCE AGAIN THUMP YOUR HEAD AGAINST THE SAME WALL.
IT DOESN'T--
FOR HEAVEN'S SAKE--
--I THINK I UNDERSTAND YOU BETTER THAN YOU DO YOURSELF.
I THINK ALMOST EVERYONE ELSE DOES.

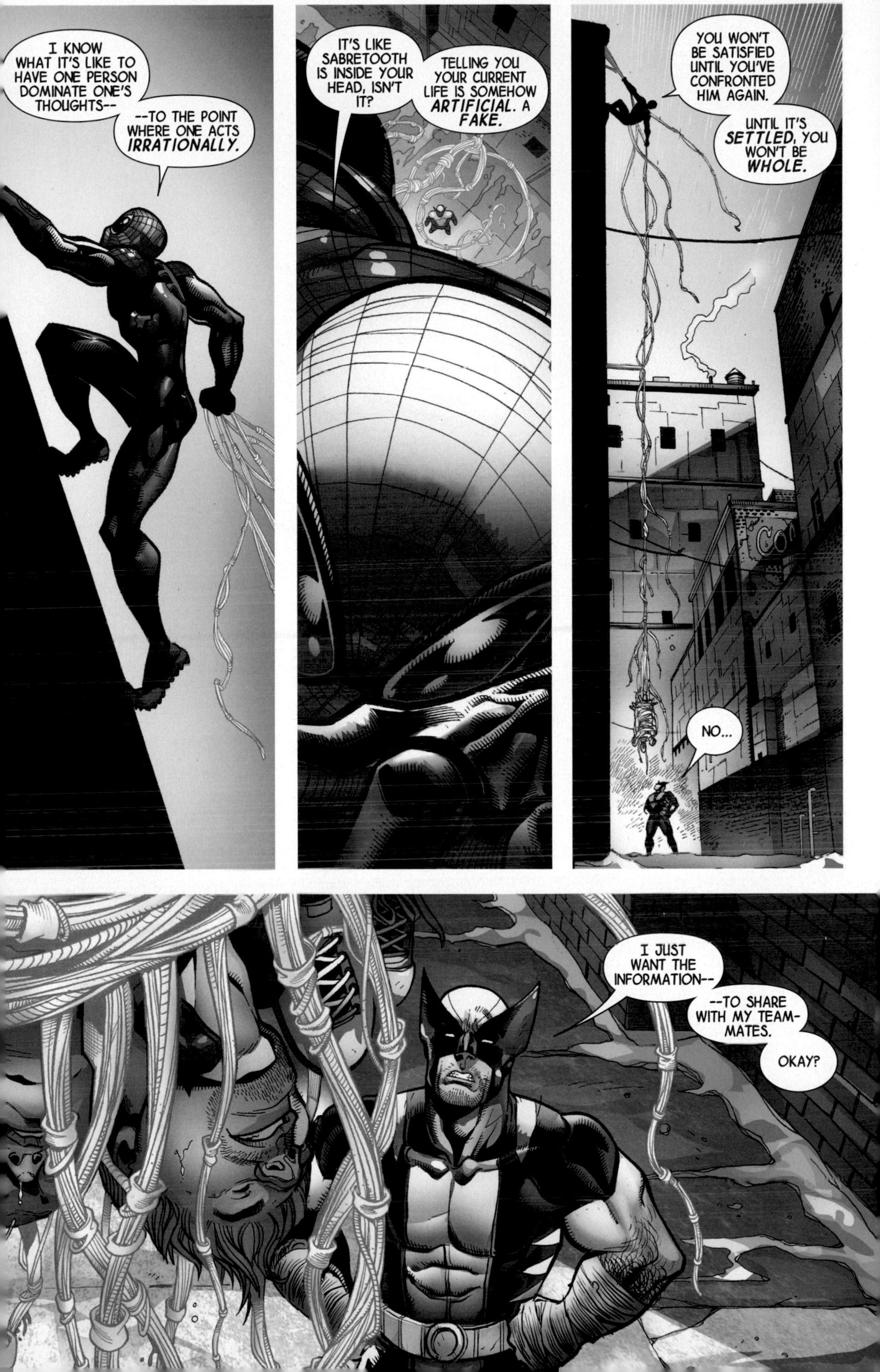
I KNOW WHAT IT'S LIKE TO HAVE ONE PERSON DOMINATE ONE'S THOUGHTS--
--TO THE POINT WHERE ONE ACTS *IRRATIONALLY.*
IT'S LIKE SABRETOOTH IS INSIDE YOUR HEAD, ISN'T IT?
TELLING YOU YOUR CURRENT LIFE IS SOMEHOW *ARTIFICIAL.* A *FAKE.*
YOU WON'T BE SATISFIED UNTIL YOU'VE CONFRONTED HIM AGAIN.
UNTIL IT'S *SETTLED,* YOU WON'T BE *WHOLE.*
NO...
I JUST WANT THE INFORMATION--
--TO SHARE WITH MY TEAM-MATES.
OKAY?

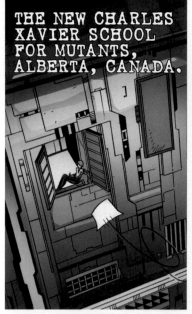

THE NEW CHARLES XAVIER SCHOOL FOR MUTANTS, ALBERTA, CANADA.

THAT LOOKS LIKE A VERY *DIRECTED* BREEZE, LOCKHEED.

YEP...

...SHE'S GOOD.

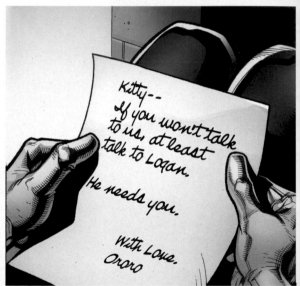

Kitty--
If you won't talk to us, at least talk to Logan.

He needs you.

With Love,
Ororo

WHAT'S THAT?

NOTHING I WANT TO DEAL WITH RIGHT NOW, SCOTT.

CRMPLE

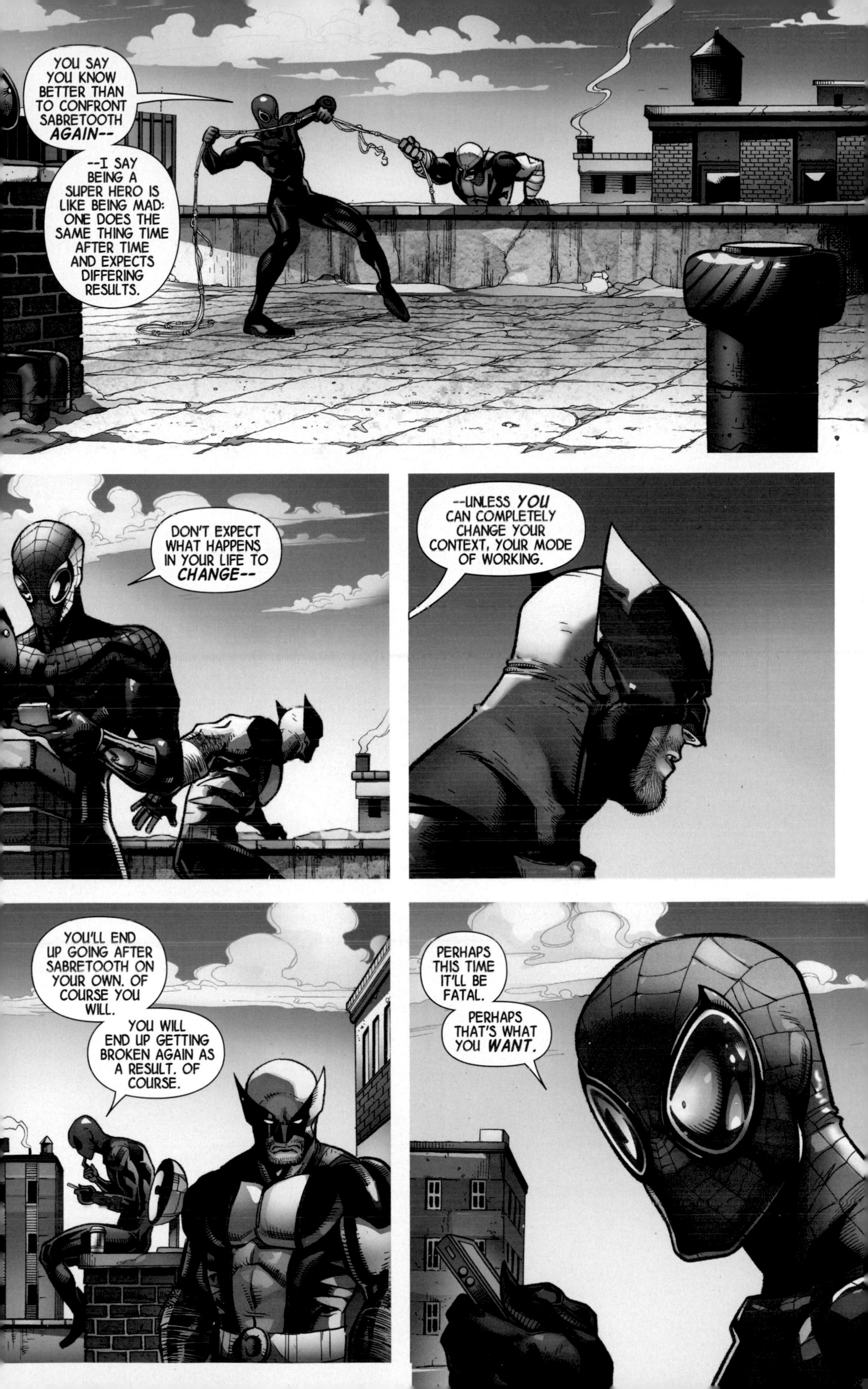
YOU SAY YOU KNOW BETTER THAN TO CONFRONT SABRETOOTH AGAIN--
--I SAY BEING A SUPER HERO IS LIKE BEING MAD: ONE DOES THE SAME THING TIME AFTER TIME AND EXPECTS DIFFERING RESULTS.
DON'T EXPECT WHAT HAPPENS IN YOUR LIFE TO CHANGE--
--UNLESS YOU CAN COMPLETELY CHANGE YOUR CONTEXT, YOUR MODE OF WORKING.
YOU'LL END UP GOING AFTER SABRETOOTH ON YOUR OWN. OF COURSE YOU WILL.
YOU WILL END UP GETTING BROKEN AGAIN AS A RESULT. OF COURSE.
PERHAPS THIS TIME IT'LL BE FATAL.
PERHAPS THAT'S WHAT YOU WANT.

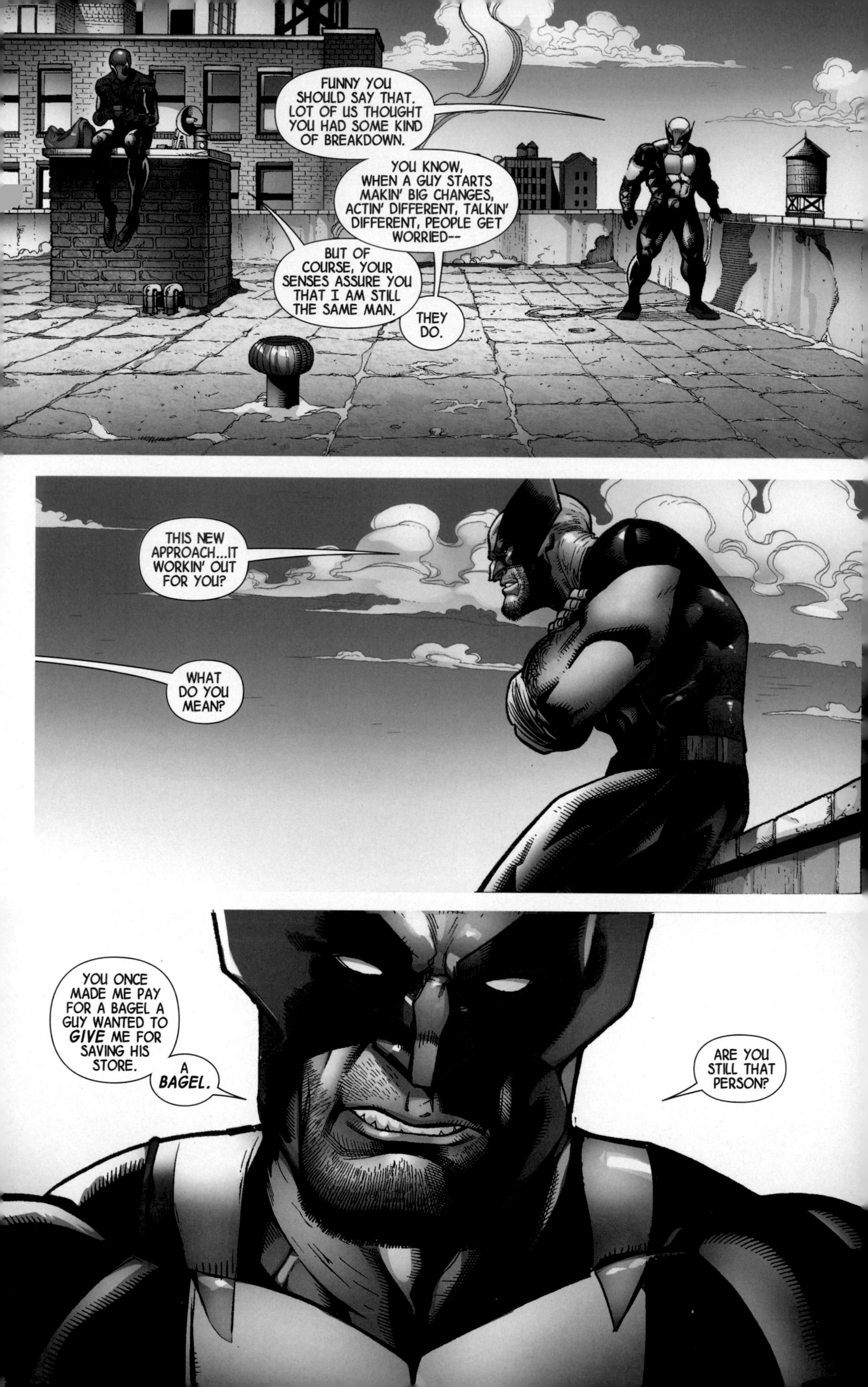
FUNNY YOU SHOULD SAY THAT. LOT OF US THOUGHT YOU HAD SOME KIND OF BREAKDOWN.
YOU KNOW, WHEN A GUY STARTS MAKIN' BIG CHANGES, ACTIN' DIFFERENT, TALKIN' DIFFERENT, PEOPLE GET WORRIED--
BUT OF COURSE, YOUR SENSES ASSURE YOU THAT I AM STILL THE SAME MAN.
THEY DO.
THIS NEW APPROACH...IT WORKIN' OUT FOR YOU?
WHAT DO YOU MEAN?
YOU ONCE MADE ME PAY FOR A BAGEL A GUY WANTED TO **GIVE** ME FOR SAVING HIS STORE.
A **BAGEL.**
ARE YOU STILL THAT PERSON?

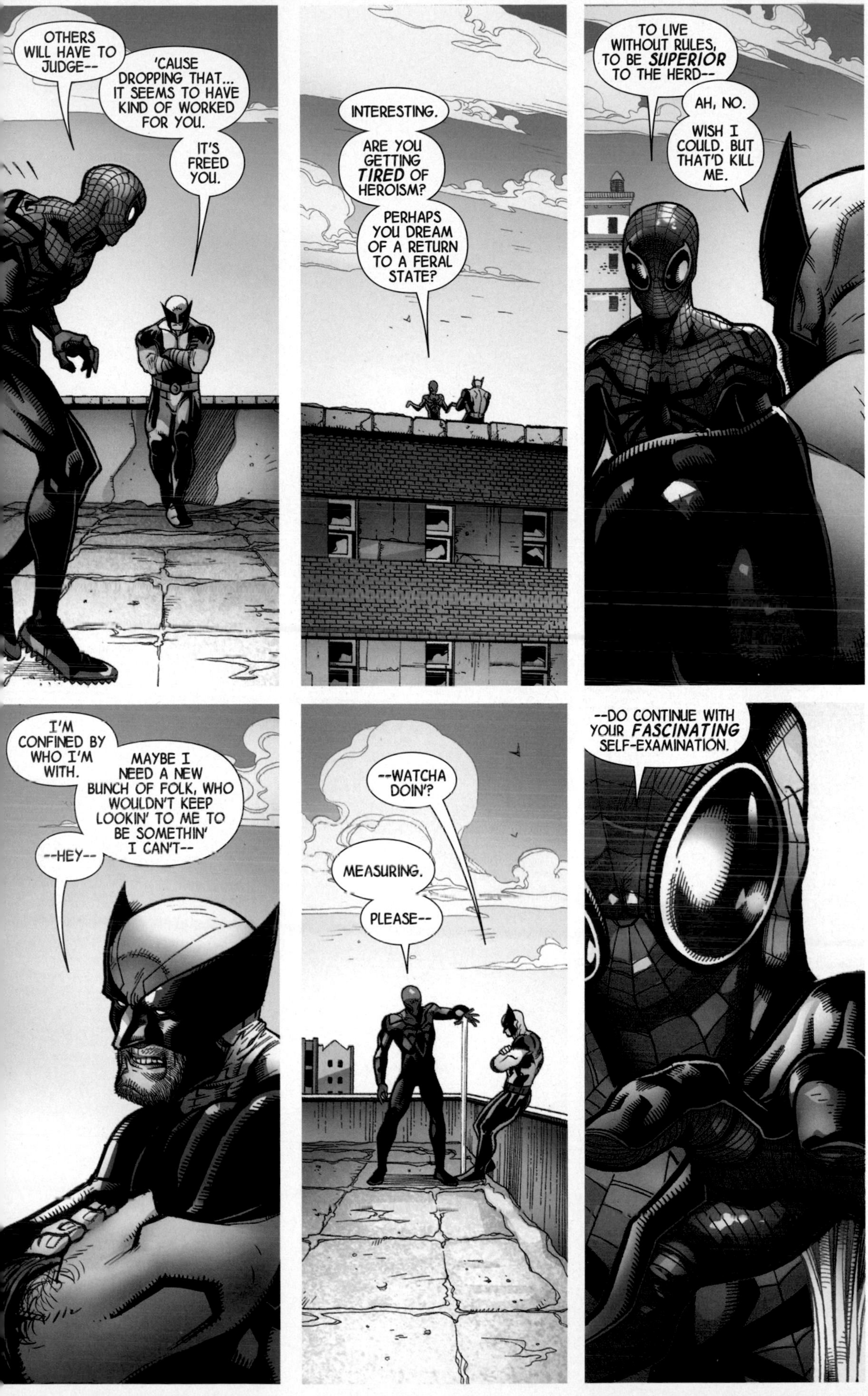
OTHERS WILL HAVE TO JUDGE--
'CAUSE DROPPING THAT... IT SEEMS TO HAVE KIND OF WORKED FOR YOU.
IT'S FREED YOU.
INTERESTING.
ARE YOU GETTING TIRED OF HEROISM?
PERHAPS YOU DREAM OF A RETURN TO A FERAL STATE?
TO LIVE WITHOUT RULES, TO BE SUPERIOR TO THE HERD--
AH, NO.
WISH I COULD. BUT THAT'D KILL ME.
I'M CONFINED BY WHO I'M WITH.
MAYBE I NEED A NEW BUNCH OF FOLK, WHO WOULDN'T KEEP LOOKIN' TO ME TO BE SOMETHIN' I CAN'T--
--HEY--
--WATCHA DOIN'?
MEASURING.
PLEASE--
--DO CONTINUE WITH YOUR FASCINATING SELF-EXAMINATION.

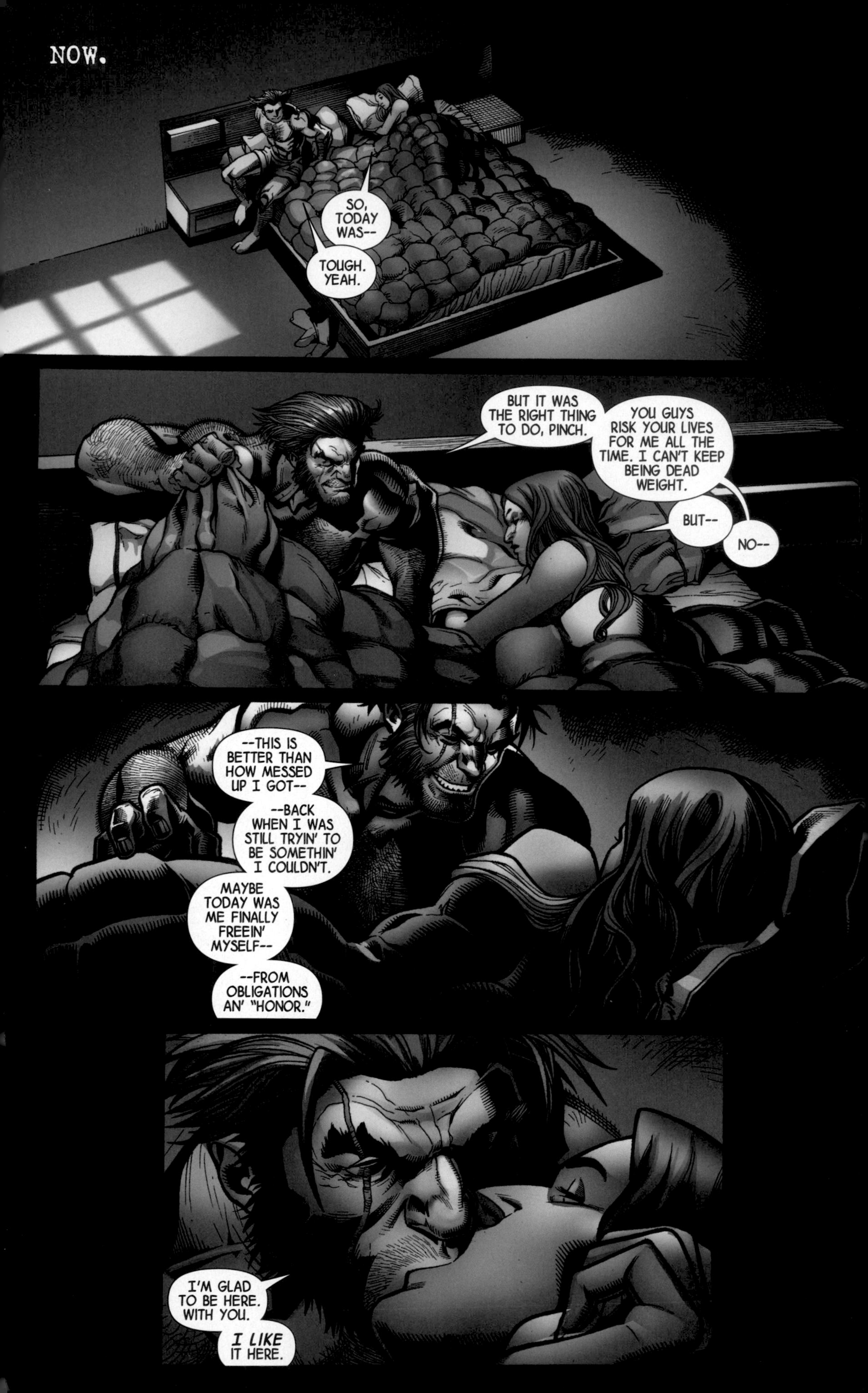
NOW.
SO, TODAY WAS--
TOUGH. YEAH.
BUT IT WAS THE RIGHT THING TO DO, PINCH.
YOU GUYS RISK YOUR LIVES FOR ME ALL THE TIME. I CAN'T KEEP BEING DEAD WEIGHT.
BUT--
NO--
--THIS IS BETTER THAN HOW MESSED UP I GOT--
--BACK WHEN I WAS STILL TRYIN' TO BE SOMETHIN' I COULDN'T.
MAYBE TODAY WAS ME FINALLY FREEIN' MYSELF--
--FROM OBLIGATIONS AN' "HONOR."
I'M GLAD TO BE HERE. WITH YOU.
I LIKE IT HERE.

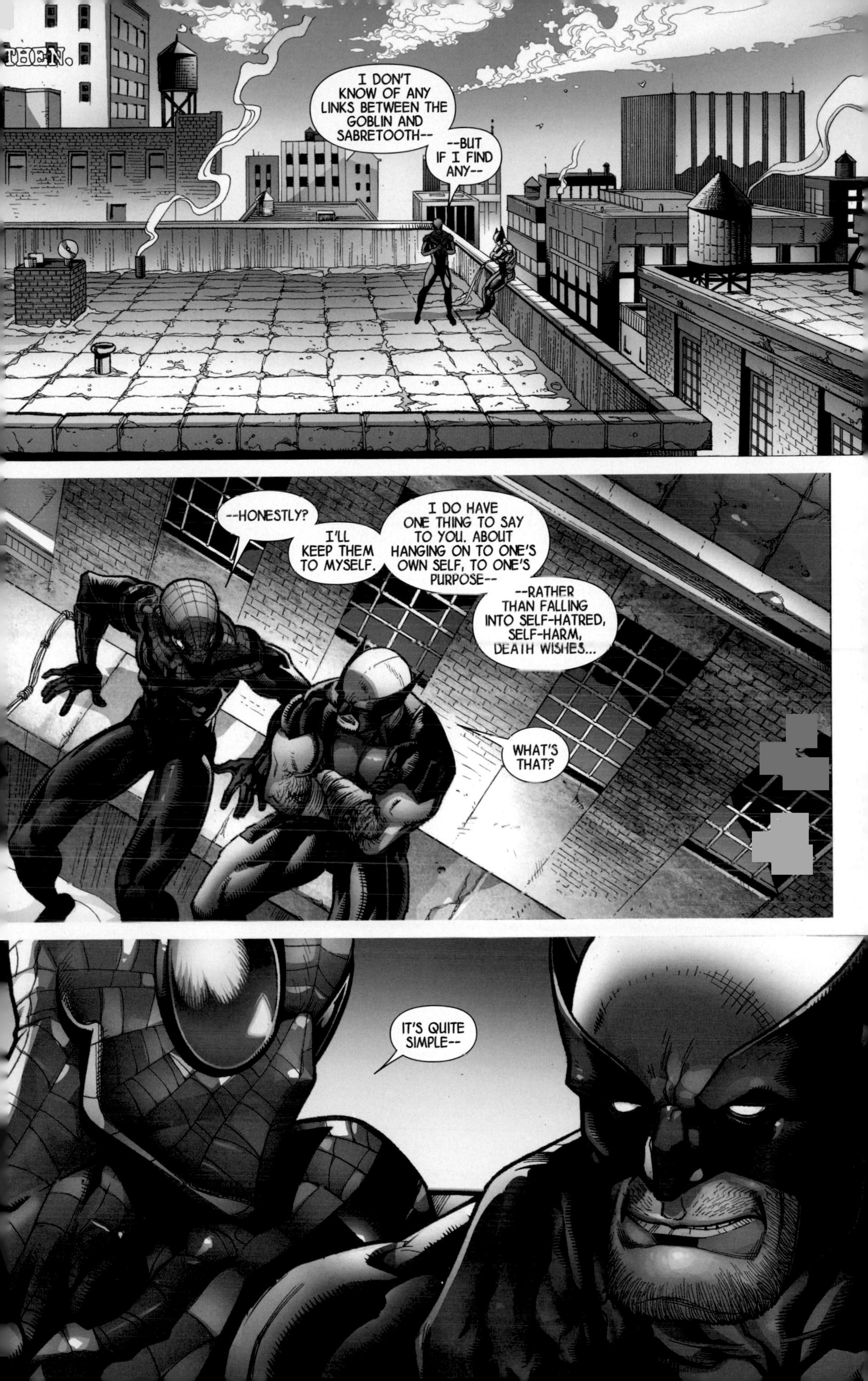
THEN.
I DON'T KNOW OF ANY LINKS BETWEEN THE GOBLIN AND SABRETOOTH--
--BUT IF I FIND ANY--
--HONESTLY?
I'LL KEEP THEM TO MYSELF.
I DO HAVE ONE THING TO SAY TO YOU. ABOUT HANGING ON TO ONE'S OWN SELF, TO ONE'S PURPOSE--
--RATHER THAN FALLING INTO SELF-HATRED, SELF-HARM, DEATH WISHES...
WHAT'S THAT?
IT'S QUITE SIMPLE--

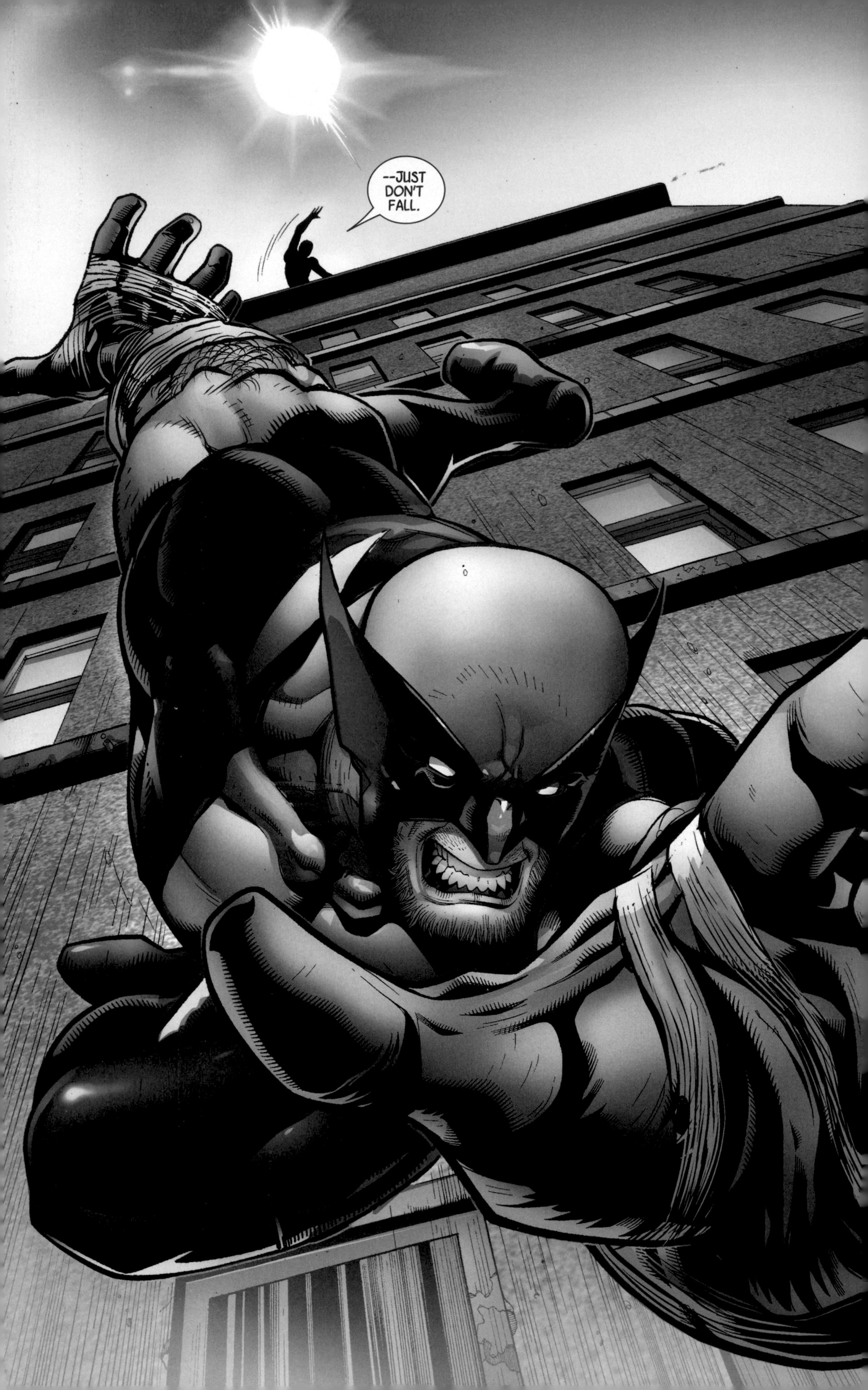
--JUST DON'T FALL.

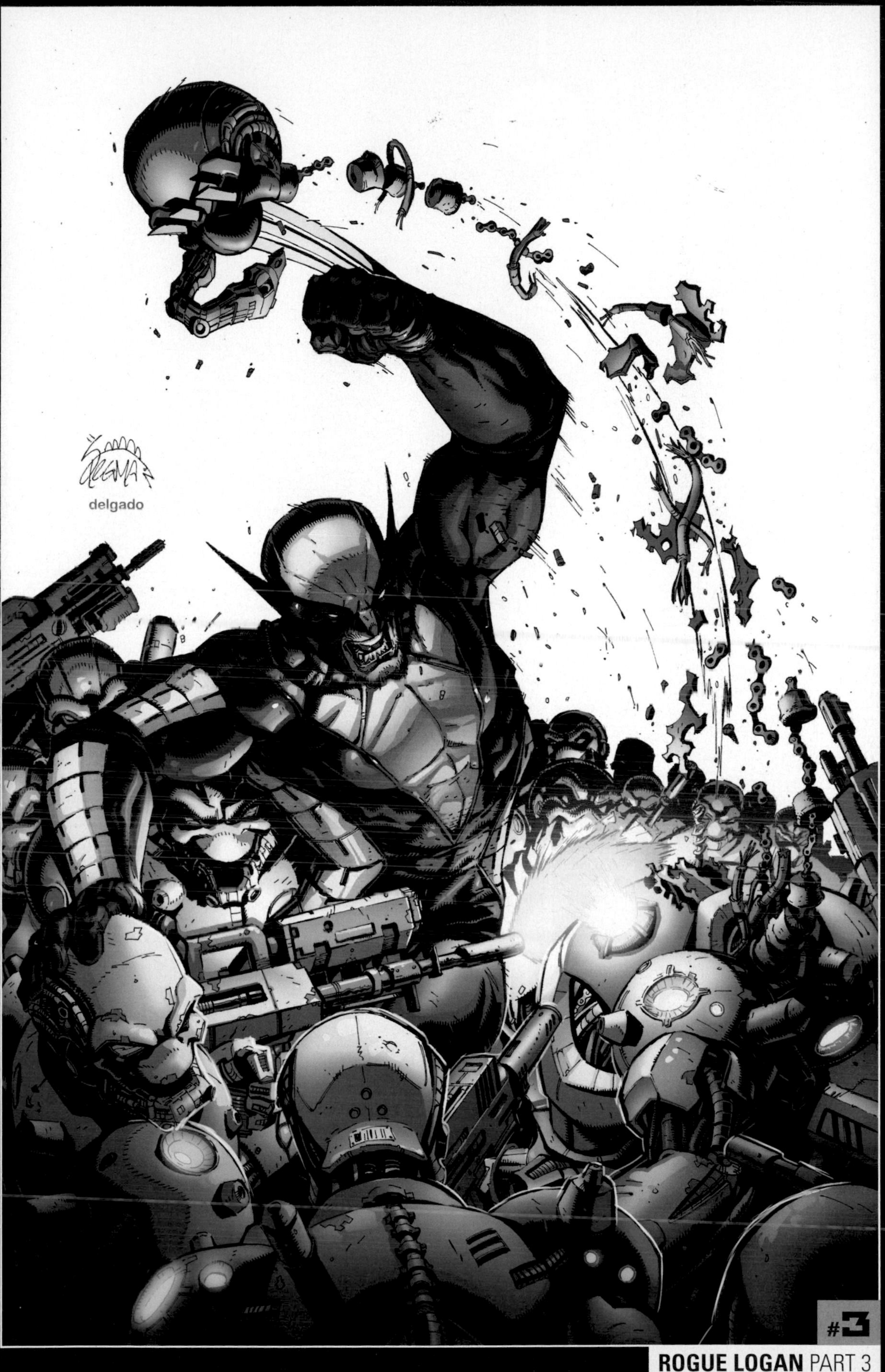
delgado
#3

ROGUE LOGAN PART 3

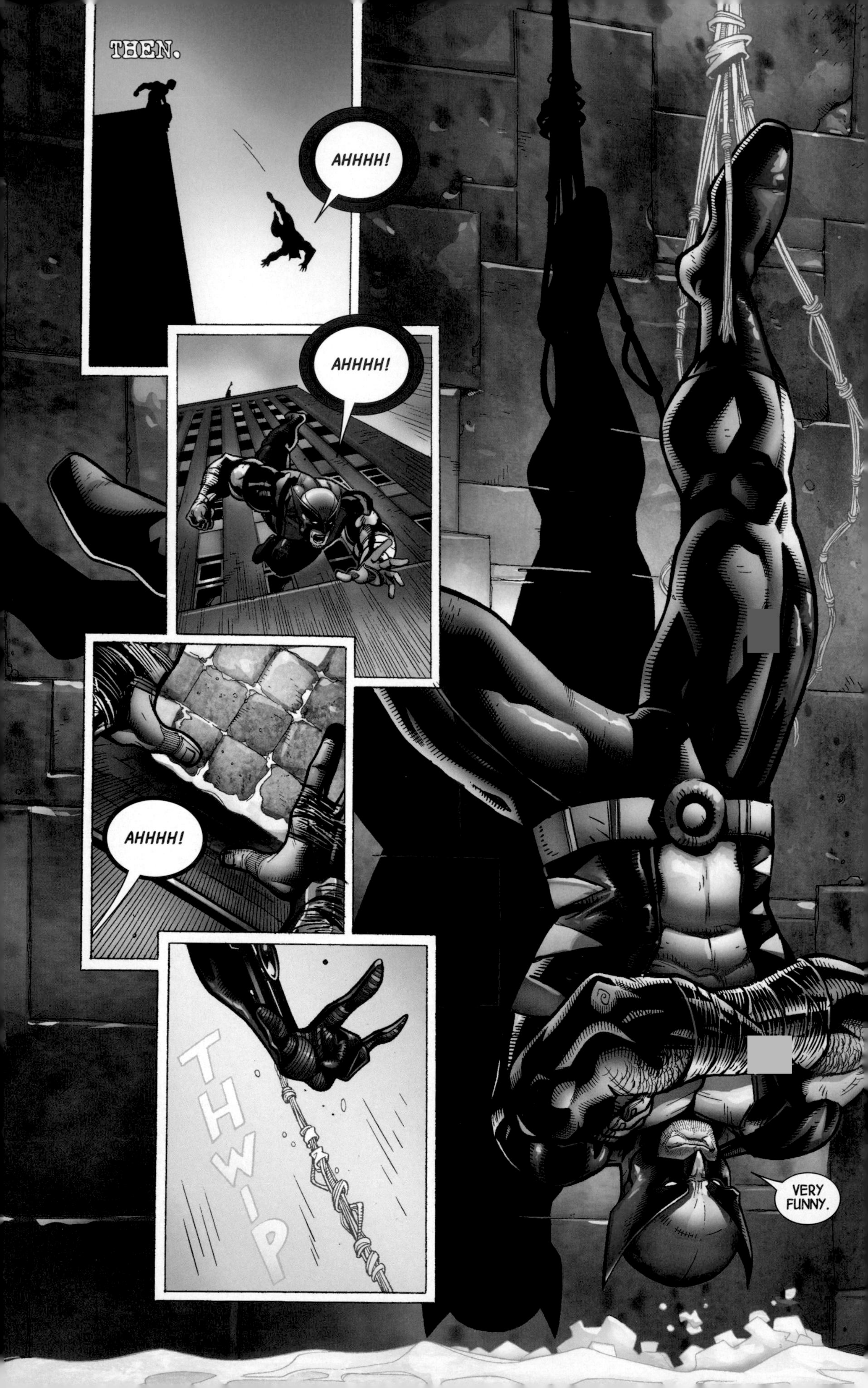
THEN.
AHHHH!
AHHHH!
AHHHH!
THWIP
VERY FUNNY.

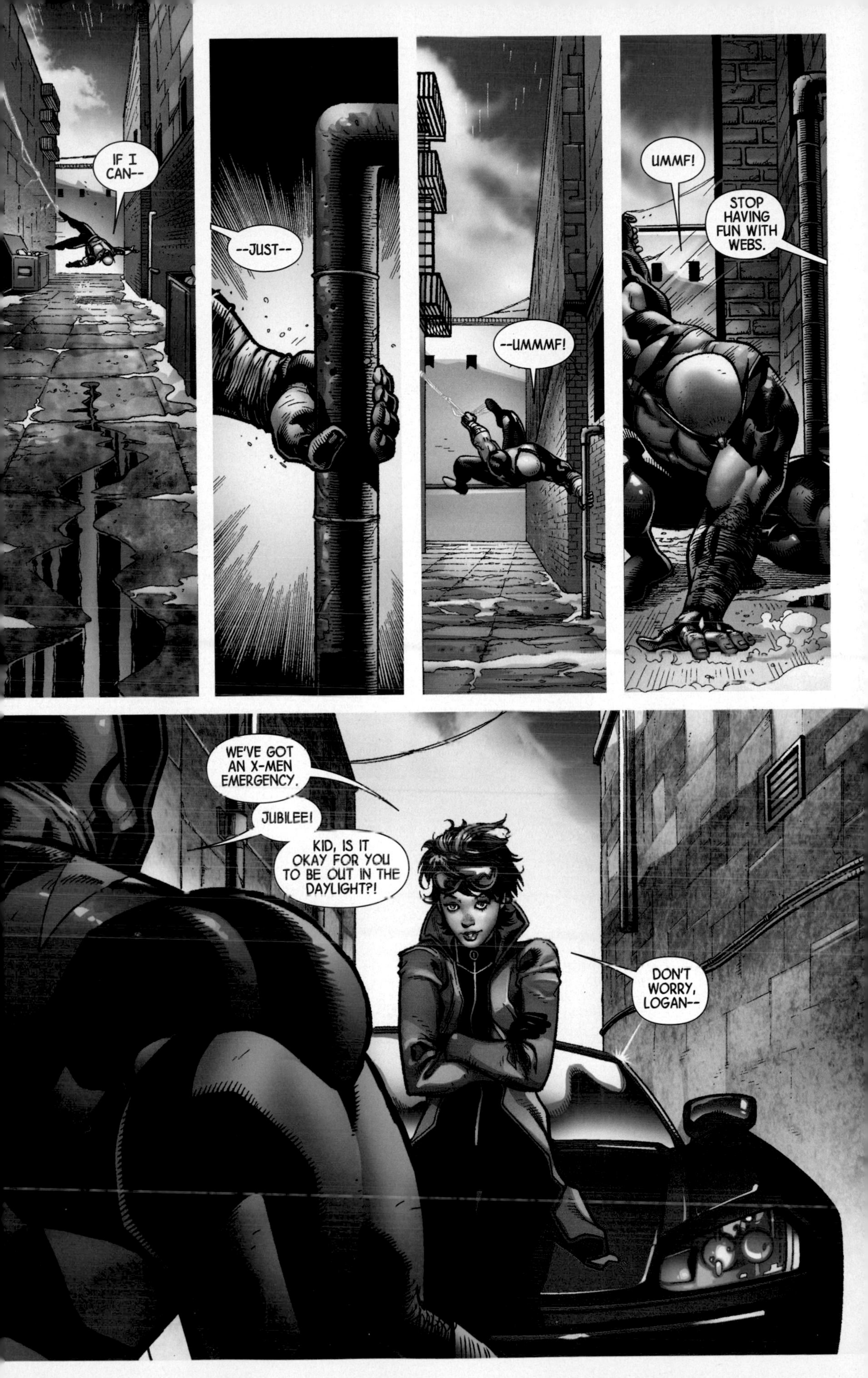
IF I CAN--
--JUST--
--UMMMF!
UMMF!
STOP HAVING FUN WITH WEBS.
WE'VE GOT AN X-MEN EMERGENCY.
JUBILEE!
KID, IS IT OKAY FOR YOU TO BE OUT IN THE DAYLIGHT?!
DON'T WORRY, LOGAN--

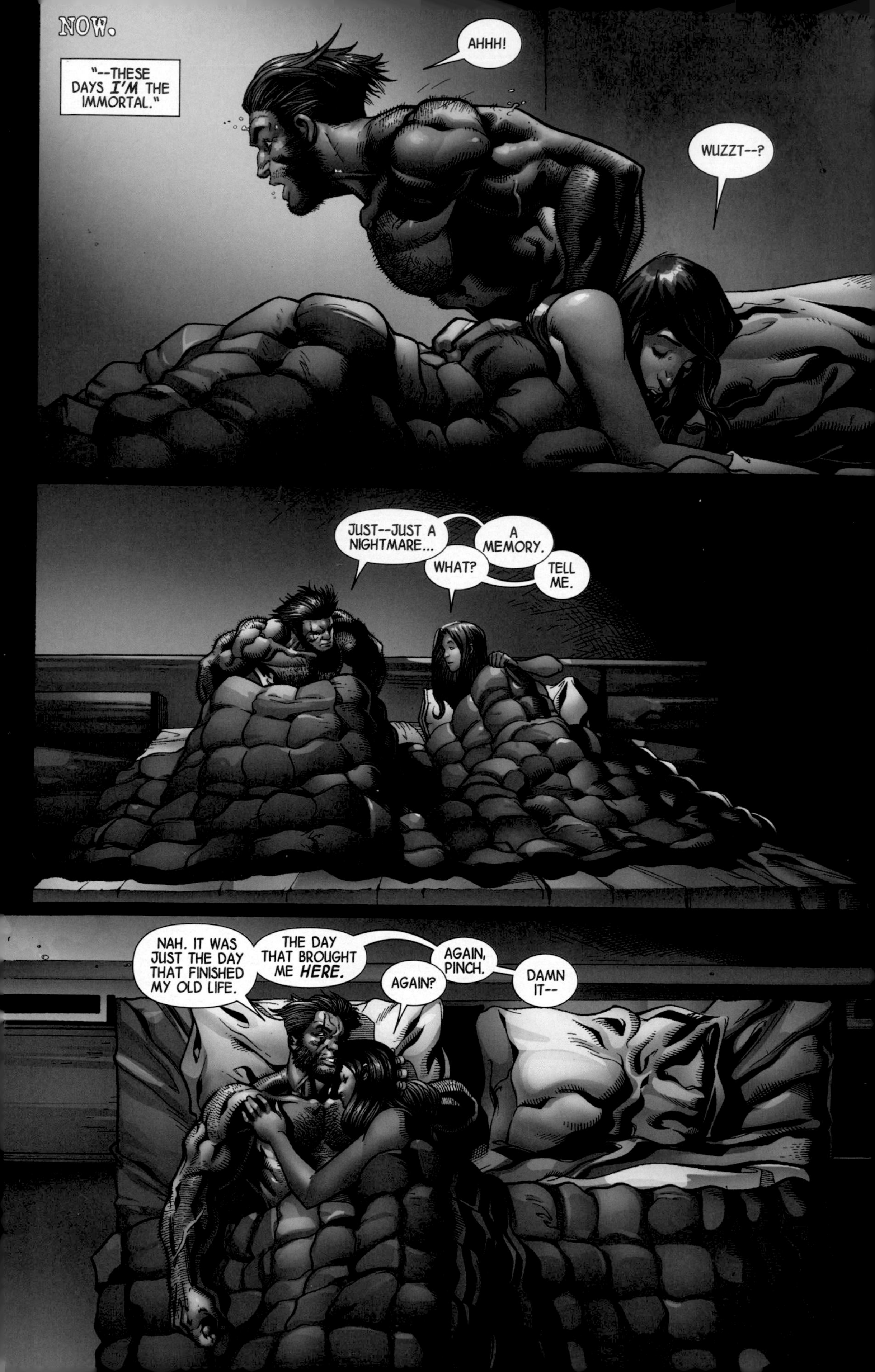
NOW.
"--THESE DAYS I'M THE IMMORTAL."
AHHH!
WUZZT--?
JUST--JUST A NIGHTMARE...
WHAT?
A MEMORY.
TELL ME.
NAH. IT WAS JUST THE DAY THAT FINISHED MY OLD LIFE.
THE DAY THAT BROUGHT ME HERE.
AGAIN?
AGAIN, PINCH.
DAMN IT--

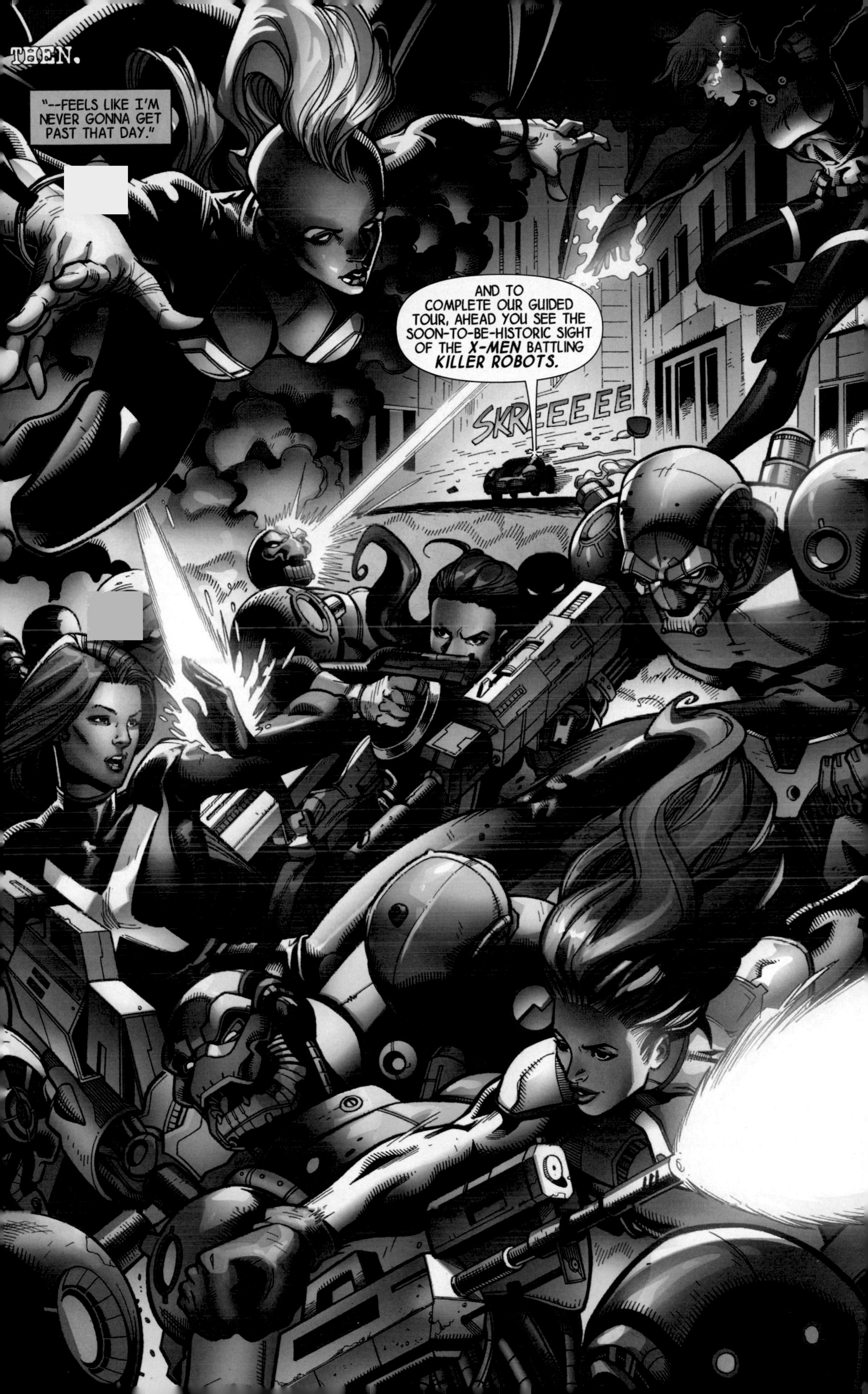
THEN.
"--FEELS LIKE I'M NEVER GONNA GET PAST THAT DAY."
AND TO COMPLETE OUR GUIDED TOUR, AHEAD YOU SEE THE SOON-TO-BE-HISTORIC SIGHT OF THE X-MEN BATTLING KILLER ROBOTS.
SKREEEEEE

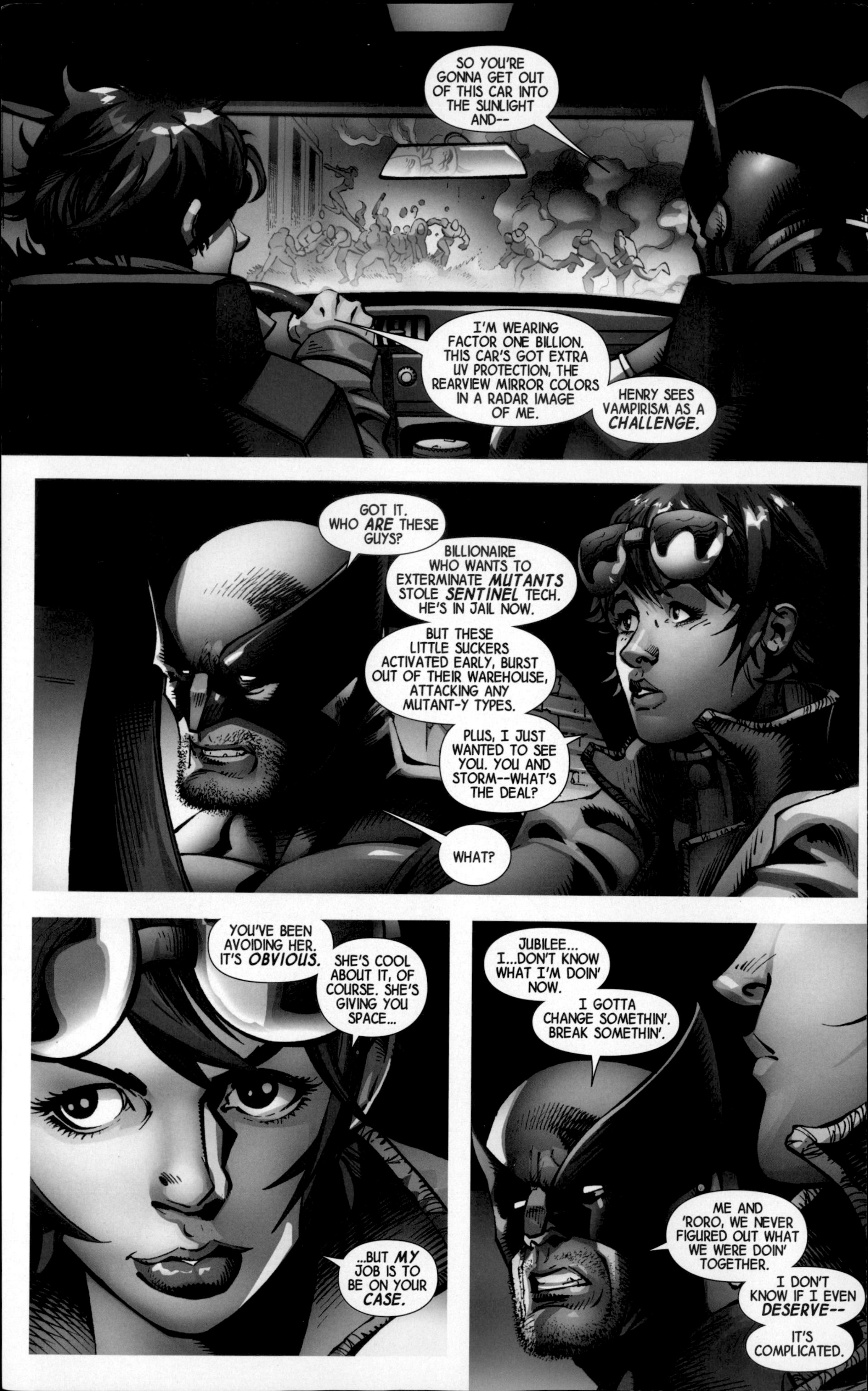
SO YOU'RE GONNA GET OUT OF THIS CAR INTO THE SUNLIGHT AND--
I'M WEARING FACTOR ONE BILLION. THIS CAR'S GOT EXTRA UV PROTECTION, THE REARVIEW MIRROR COLORS IN A RADAR IMAGE OF ME.
HENRY SEES VAMPIRISM AS A *CHALLENGE.*
GOT IT. WHO *ARE* THESE GUYS?
BILLIONAIRE WHO WANTS TO EXTERMINATE *MUTANTS* STOLE *SENTINEL* TECH. HE'S IN JAIL NOW.
BUT THESE LITTLE SUCKERS ACTIVATED EARLY, BURST OUT OF THEIR WAREHOUSE, ATTACKING ANY MUTANT-Y TYPES.
PLUS, I JUST WANTED TO SEE YOU. YOU AND STORM--WHAT'S THE DEAL?
WHAT?
YOU'VE BEEN AVOIDING HER. IT'S *OBVIOUS.*
SHE'S COOL ABOUT IT, OF COURSE. SHE'S GIVING YOU SPACE...
...BUT *MY* JOB IS TO BE ON YOUR *CASE.*
JUBILEE... I...DON'T KNOW WHAT I'M DOIN' NOW.
I GOTTA CHANGE SOMETHIN'. BREAK SOMETHIN'.
ME AND 'RORO, WE NEVER FIGURED OUT WHAT WE WERE DOIN' TOGETHER.
I DON'T KNOW IF I EVEN *DESERVE--*
IT'S COMPLICATED.

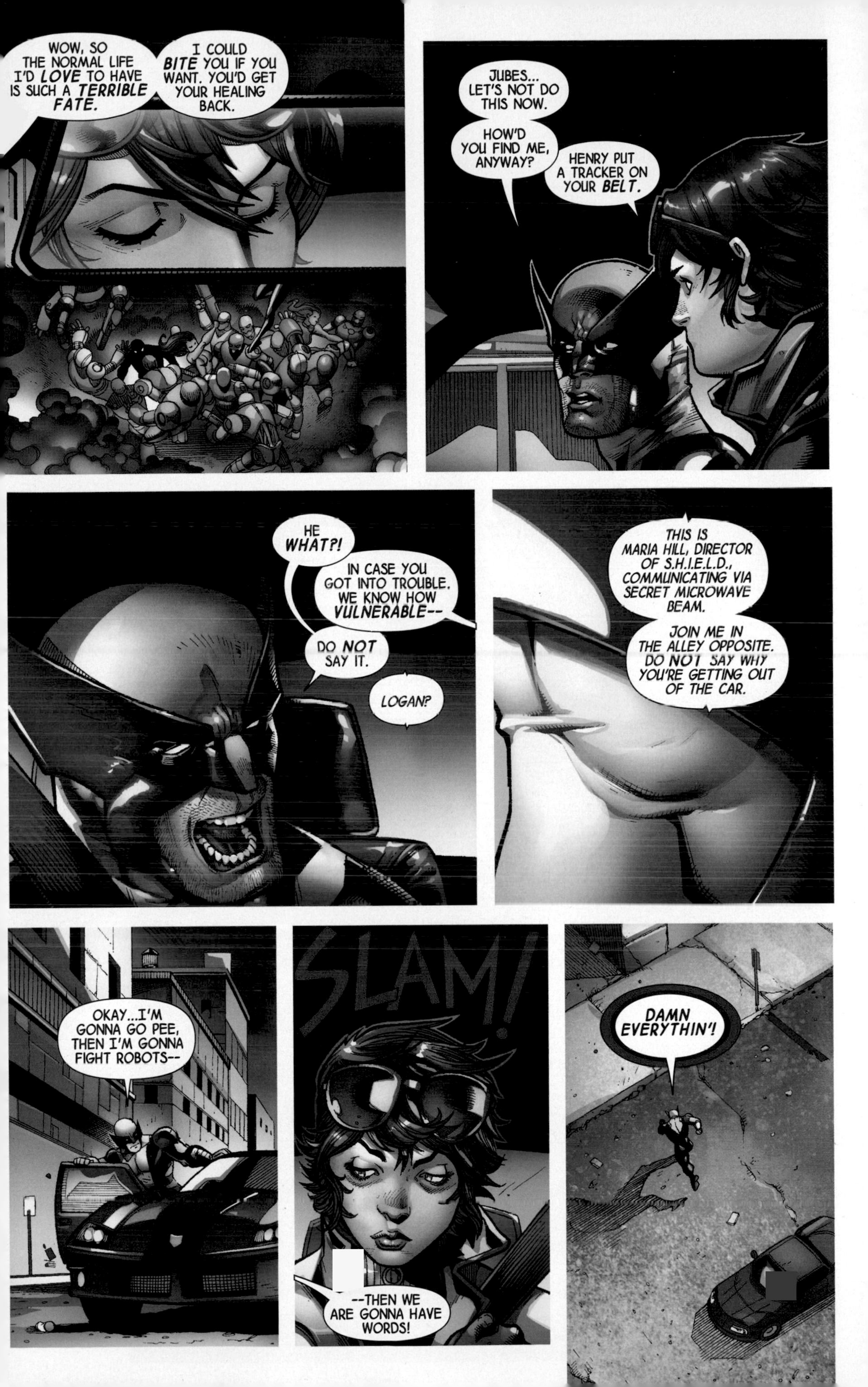
WOW, SO THE NORMAL LIFE I'D LOVE TO HAVE IS SUCH A TERRIBLE FATE.
I COULD BITE YOU IF YOU WANT. YOU'D GET YOUR HEALING BACK.
JUBES... LET'S NOT DO THIS NOW.
HOW'D YOU FIND ME, ANYWAY?
HENRY PUT A TRACKER ON YOUR BELT.
HE WHAT?!
IN CASE YOU GOT INTO TROUBLE. WE KNOW HOW VULNERABLE--
DO NOT SAY IT.
LOGAN?
THIS IS MARIA HILL, DIRECTOR OF S.H.I.E.L.D., COMMUNICATING VIA SECRET MICROWAVE BEAM.
JOIN ME IN THE ALLEY OPPOSITE. DO NOT SAY WHY YOU'RE GETTING OUT OF THE CAR.
OKAY...I'M GONNA GO PEE, THEN I'M GONNA FIGHT ROBOTS--
SLAM!
--THEN WE ARE GONNA HAVE WORDS!
DAMN EVERYTHIN'!

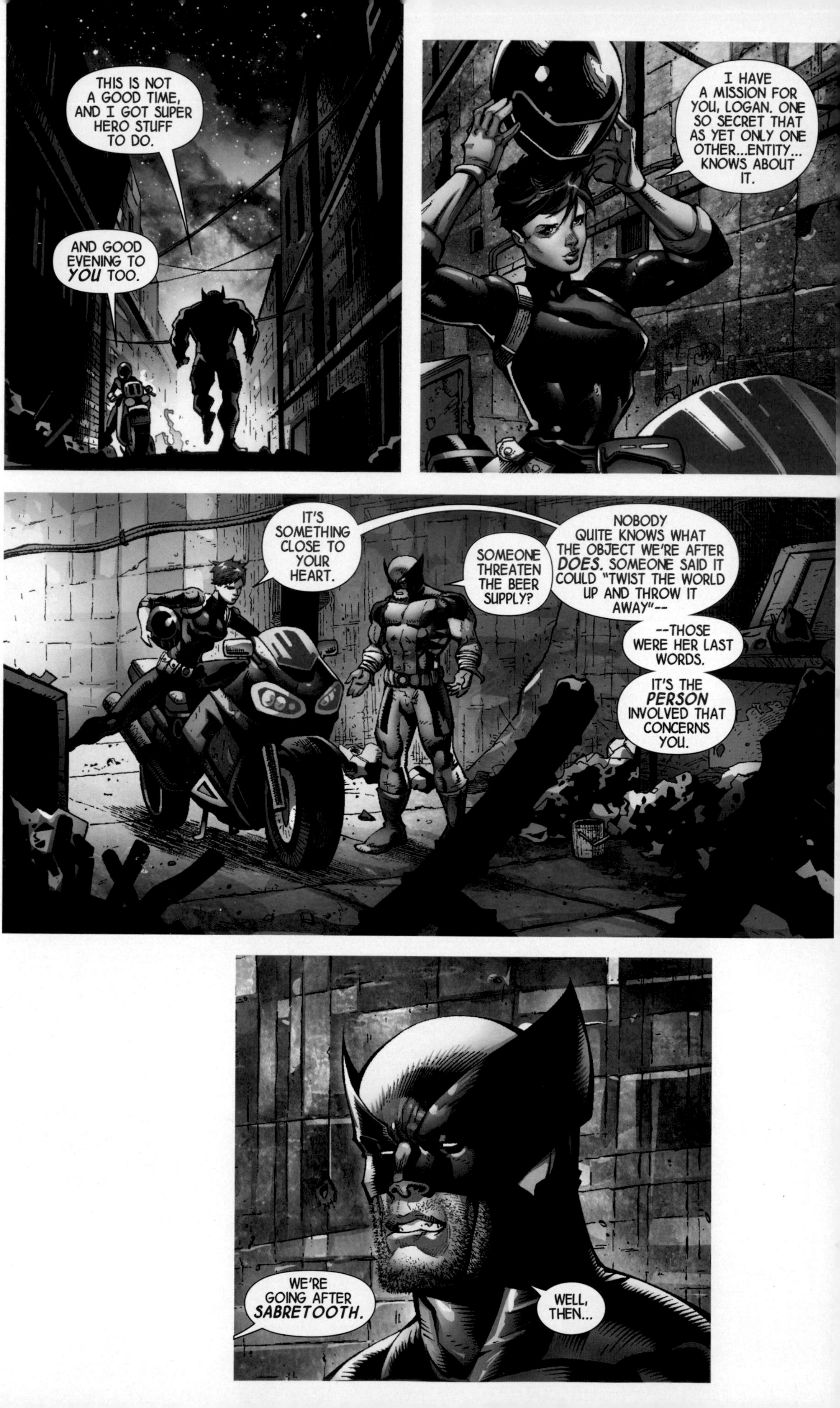
THIS IS NOT A GOOD TIME, AND I GOT SUPER HERO STUFF TO DO.
AND GOOD EVENING TO YOU TOO.
I HAVE A MISSION FOR YOU, LOGAN. ONE SO SECRET THAT AS YET ONLY ONE OTHER...ENTITY... KNOWS ABOUT IT.
IT'S SOMETHING CLOSE TO YOUR HEART.
SOMEONE THREATEN THE BEER SUPPLY?
NOBODY QUITE KNOWS WHAT THE OBJECT WE'RE AFTER DOES. SOMEONE SAID IT COULD "TWIST THE WORLD UP AND THROW IT AWAY"--
--THOSE WERE HER LAST WORDS.
IT'S THE PERSON INVOLVED THAT CONCERNS YOU.
WE'RE GOING AFTER SABRETOOTH.
WELL, THEN...

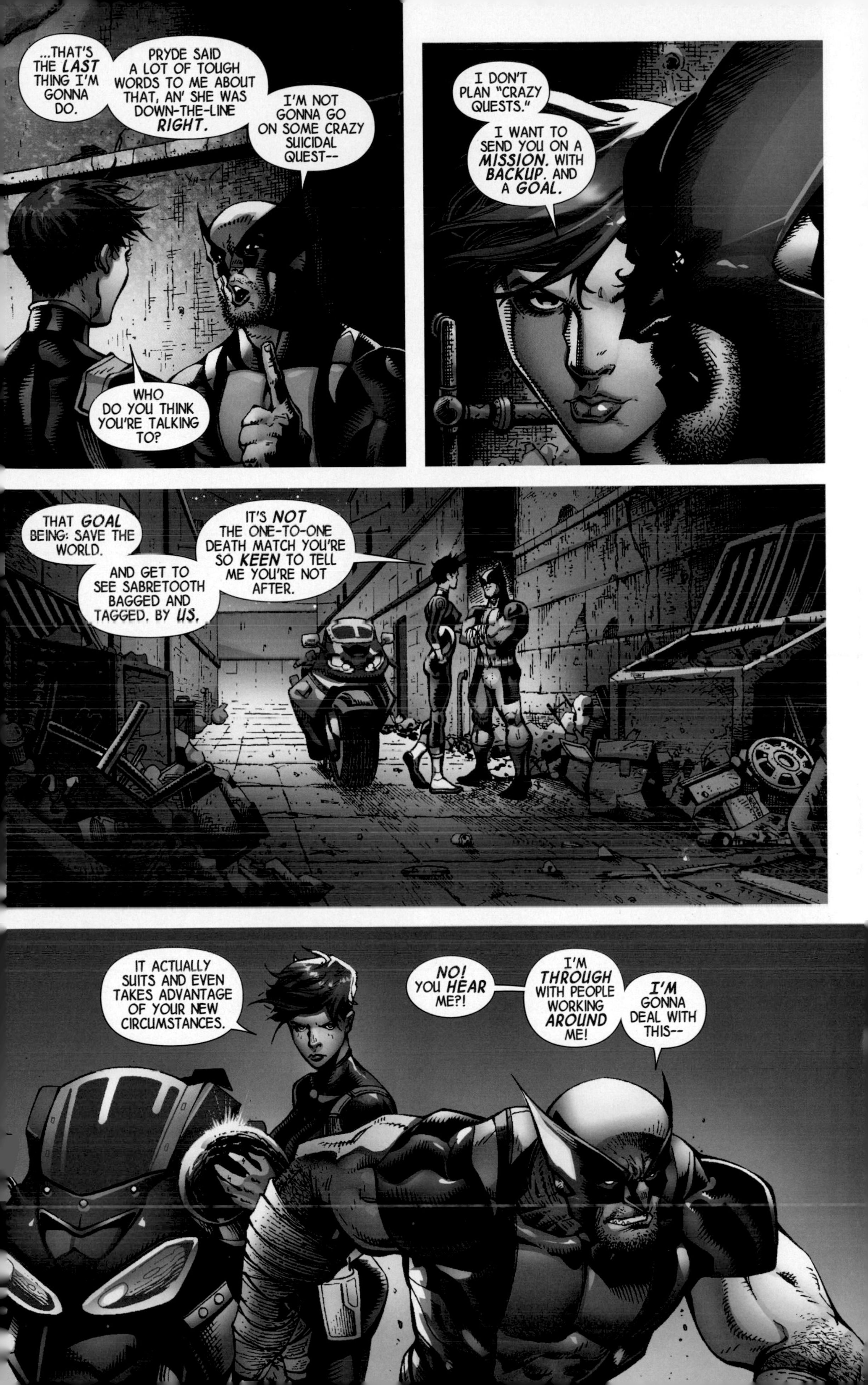
...THAT'S THE LAST THING I'M GONNA DO.
PRYDE SAID A LOT OF TOUGH WORDS TO ME ABOUT THAT, AN' SHE WAS DOWN-THE-LINE RIGHT.
I'M NOT GONNA GO ON SOME CRAZY SUICIDAL QUEST--
WHO DO YOU THINK YOU'RE TALKING TO?
I DON'T PLAN "CRAZY QUESTS."
I WANT TO SEND YOU ON A MISSION. WITH BACKUP. AND A GOAL.
THAT GOAL BEING: SAVE THE WORLD.
AND GET TO SEE SABRETOOTH BAGGED AND TAGGED. BY US.
IT'S NOT THE ONE-TO-ONE DEATH MATCH YOU'RE SO KEEN TO TELL ME YOU'RE NOT AFTER.
IT ACTUALLY SUITS AND EVEN TAKES ADVANTAGE OF YOUR NEW CIRCUMSTANCES.
NO! YOU HEAR ME?!
I'M THROUGH WITH PEOPLE WORKING AROUND ME!
I'M GONNA DEAL WITH THIS--

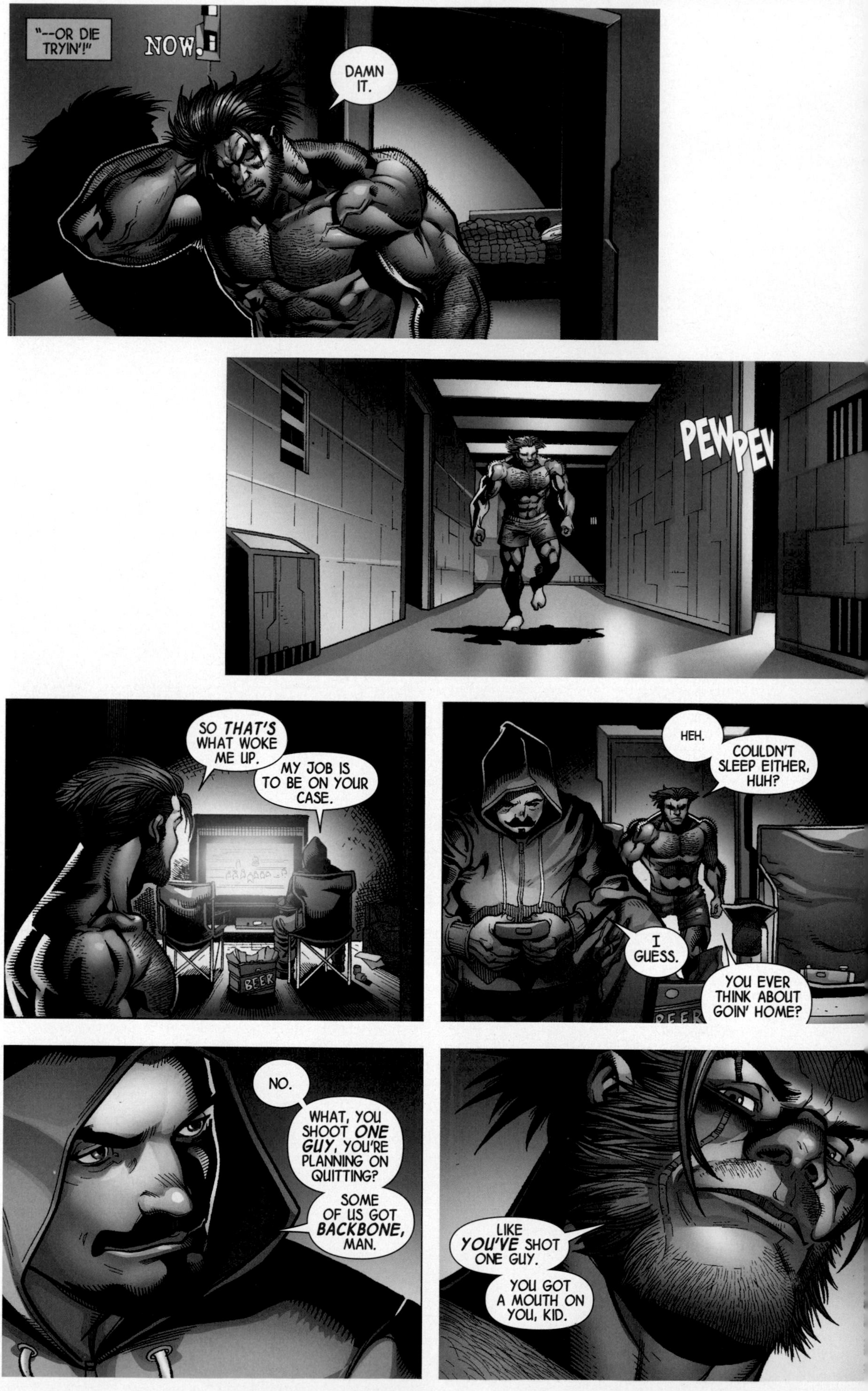

"--OR DIE TRYIN'!"
NOW.
DAMN IT.
PEWPEW
SO THAT'S WHAT WOKE ME UP.
MY JOB IS TO BE ON YOUR CASE.
HEH.
COULDN'T SLEEP EITHER, HUH?
I GUESS.
YOU EVER THINK ABOUT GOIN' HOME?
BEER
NO.
WHAT, YOU SHOOT ONE GUY, YOU'RE PLANNING ON QUITTING?
SOME OF US GOT BACKBONE, MAN.
LIKE YOU'VE SHOT ONE GUY.
YOU GOT A MOUTH ON YOU, KID.

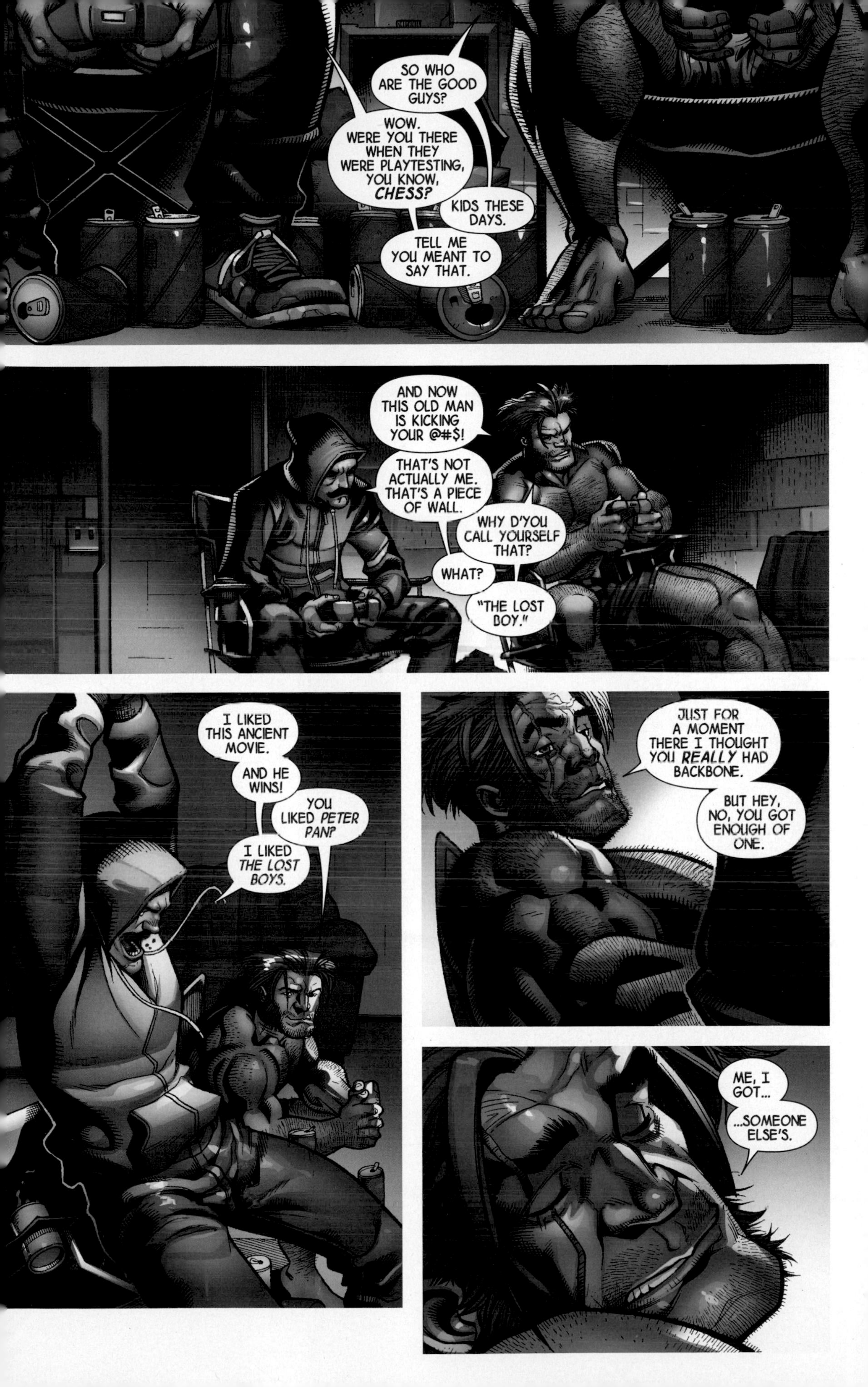
SO WHO ARE THE GOOD GUYS?
WOW. WERE YOU THERE WHEN THEY WERE PLAYTESTING, YOU KNOW, *CHESS?*
KIDS THESE DAYS.
TELL ME YOU MEANT TO SAY THAT.
AND NOW THIS OLD MAN IS KICKING YOUR @#$!
THAT'S NOT ACTUALLY ME. THAT'S A PIECE OF WALL.
WHY D'YOU CALL YOURSELF THAT?
WHAT?
"THE LOST BOY."
I LIKED THIS ANCIENT MOVIE.
AND HE WINS!
YOU LIKED *PETER PAN?*
I LIKED *THE LOST BOYS.*
JUST FOR A MOMENT THERE I THOUGHT YOU *REALLY* HAD BACKBONE.
BUT HEY, NO, YOU GOT ENOUGH OF ONE.
ME, I GOT...
...SOMEONE ELSE'S.

THEN.

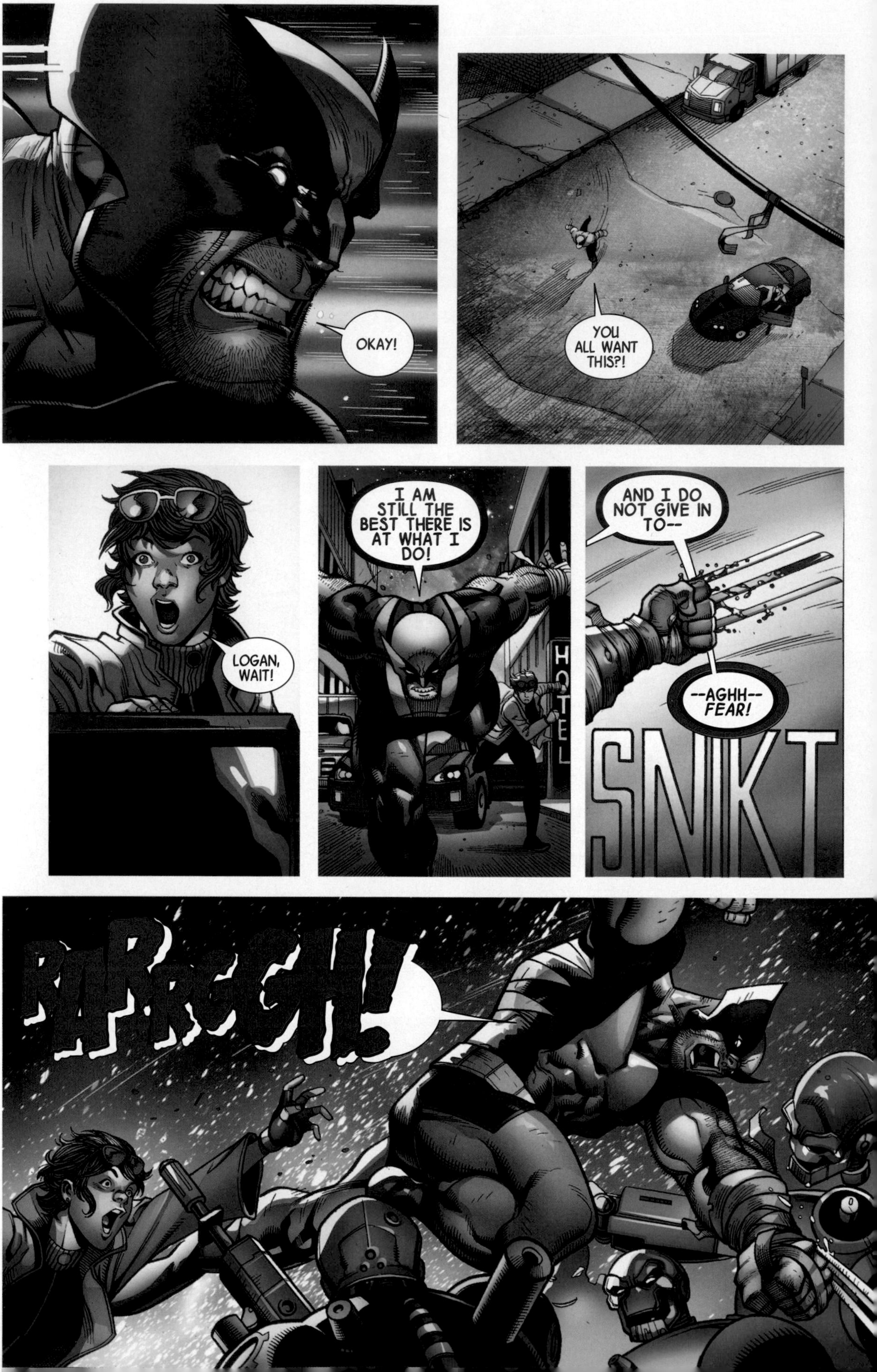
OKAY!
YOU ALL WANT THIS?!
LOGAN, WAIT!
I AM STILL THE BEST THERE IS AT WHAT I DO!
AND I DO NOT GIVE IN TO--
--AGHH-- FEAR!
SNIKT
RARRGGH!

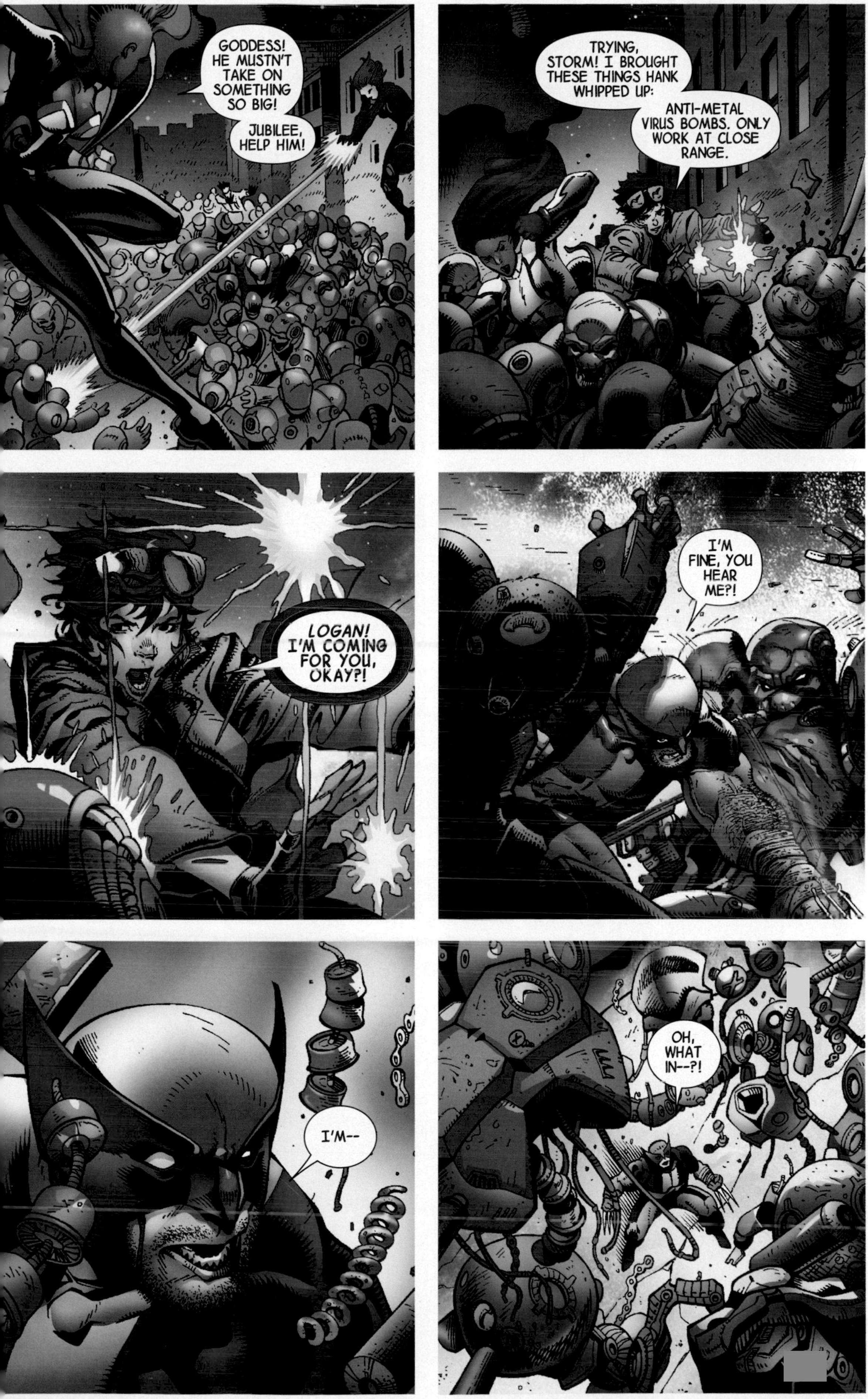
GODDESS! HE MUSTN'T TAKE ON SOMETHING SO BIG!
JUBILEE, HELP HIM!
TRYING, STORM! I BROUGHT THESE THINGS HANK WHIPPED UP:
ANTI-METAL VIRUS BOMBS. ONLY WORK AT CLOSE RANGE.
LOGAN! I'M COMING FOR YOU, OKAY?!
I'M FINE, YOU HEAR ME?!
I'M--
OH, WHAT IN--?!

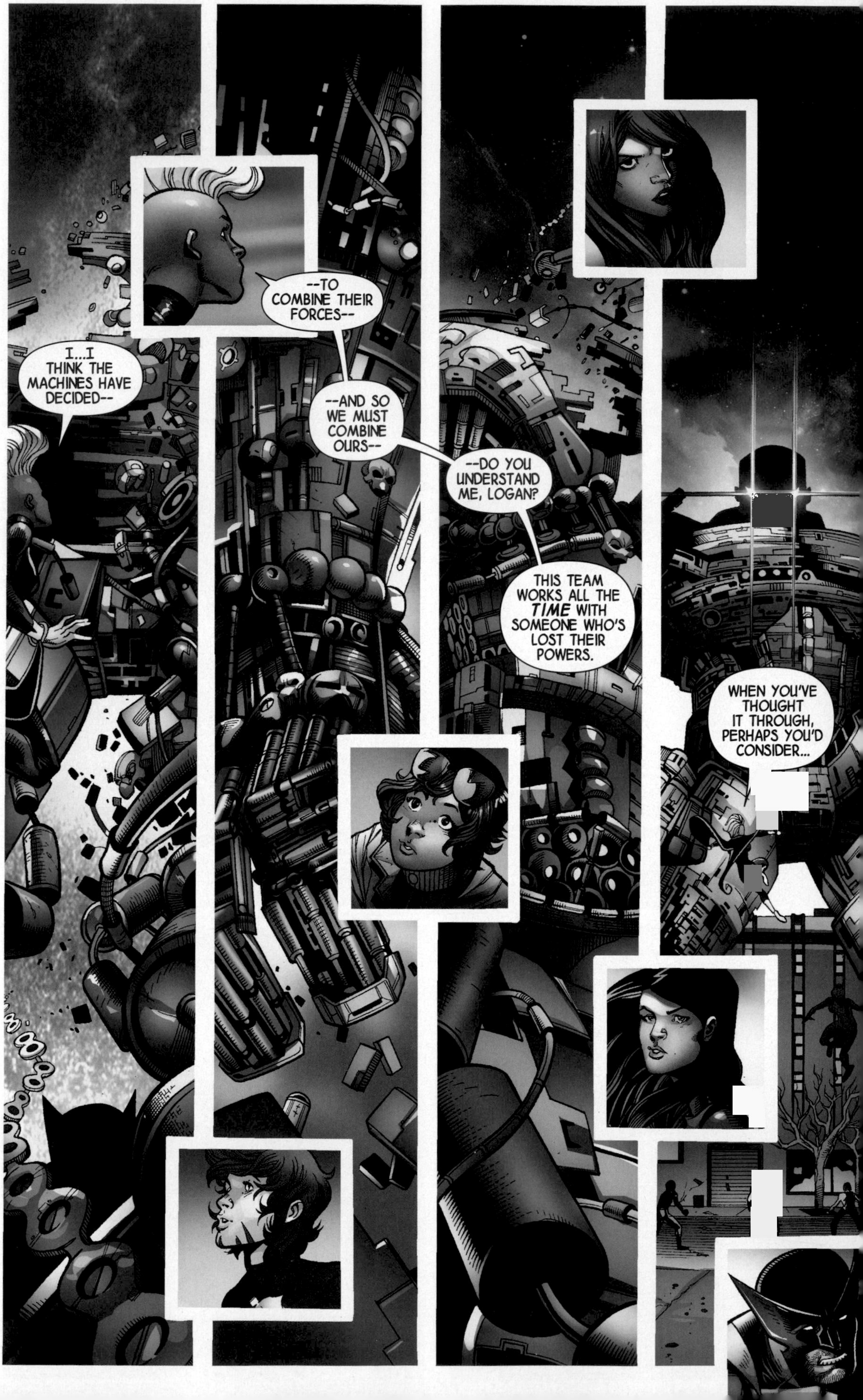
--TO COMBINE THEIR FORCES--
I...I THINK THE MACHINES HAVE DECIDED--
--AND SO WE MUST COMBINE OURS--
--DO YOU UNDERSTAND ME, LOGAN?
THIS TEAM WORKS ALL THE TIME WITH SOMEONE WHO'S LOST THEIR POWERS.
WHEN YOU'VE THOUGHT IT THROUGH, PERHAPS YOU'D CONSIDER...

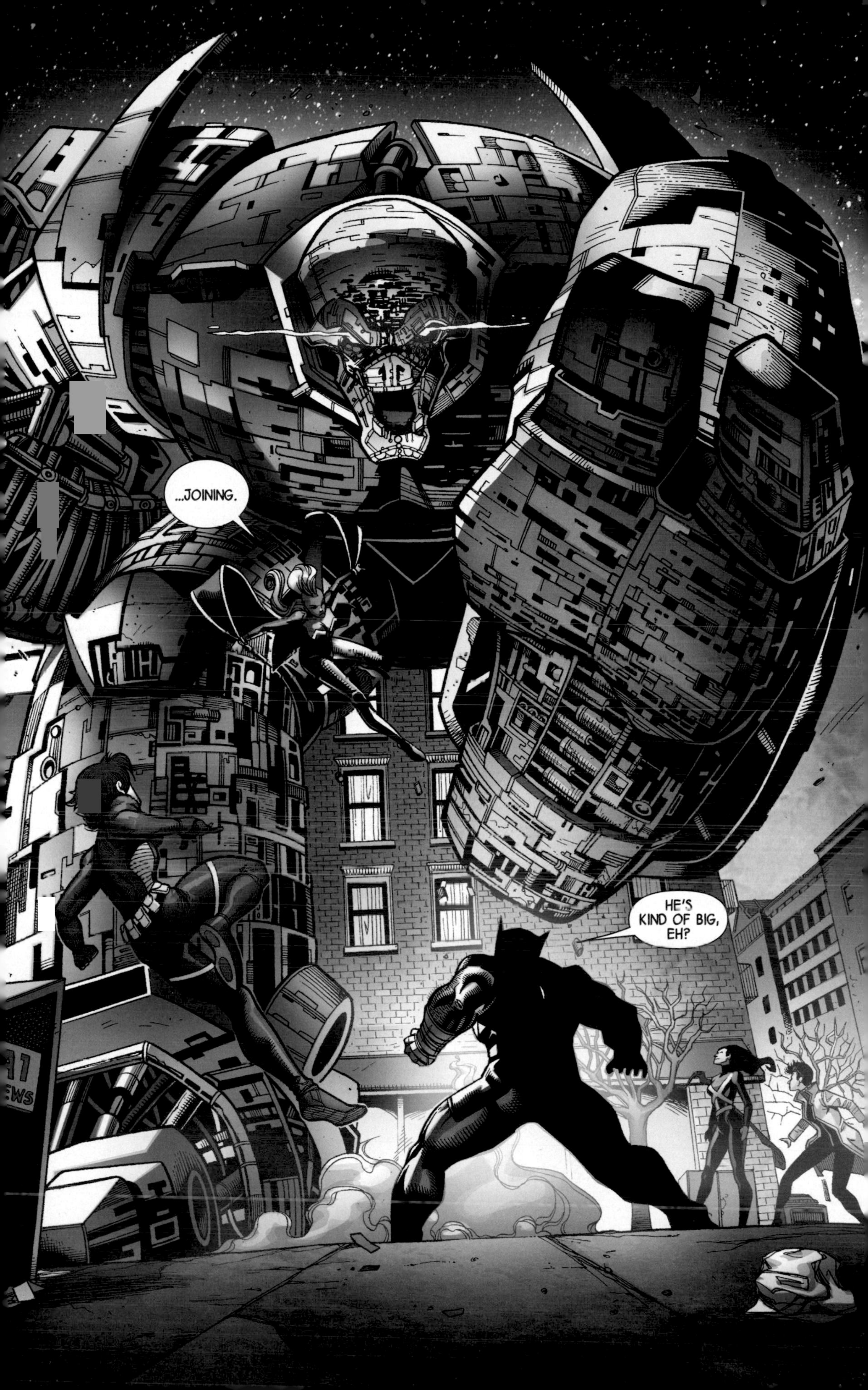

...JOINING.
HE'S KIND OF BIG, EH?

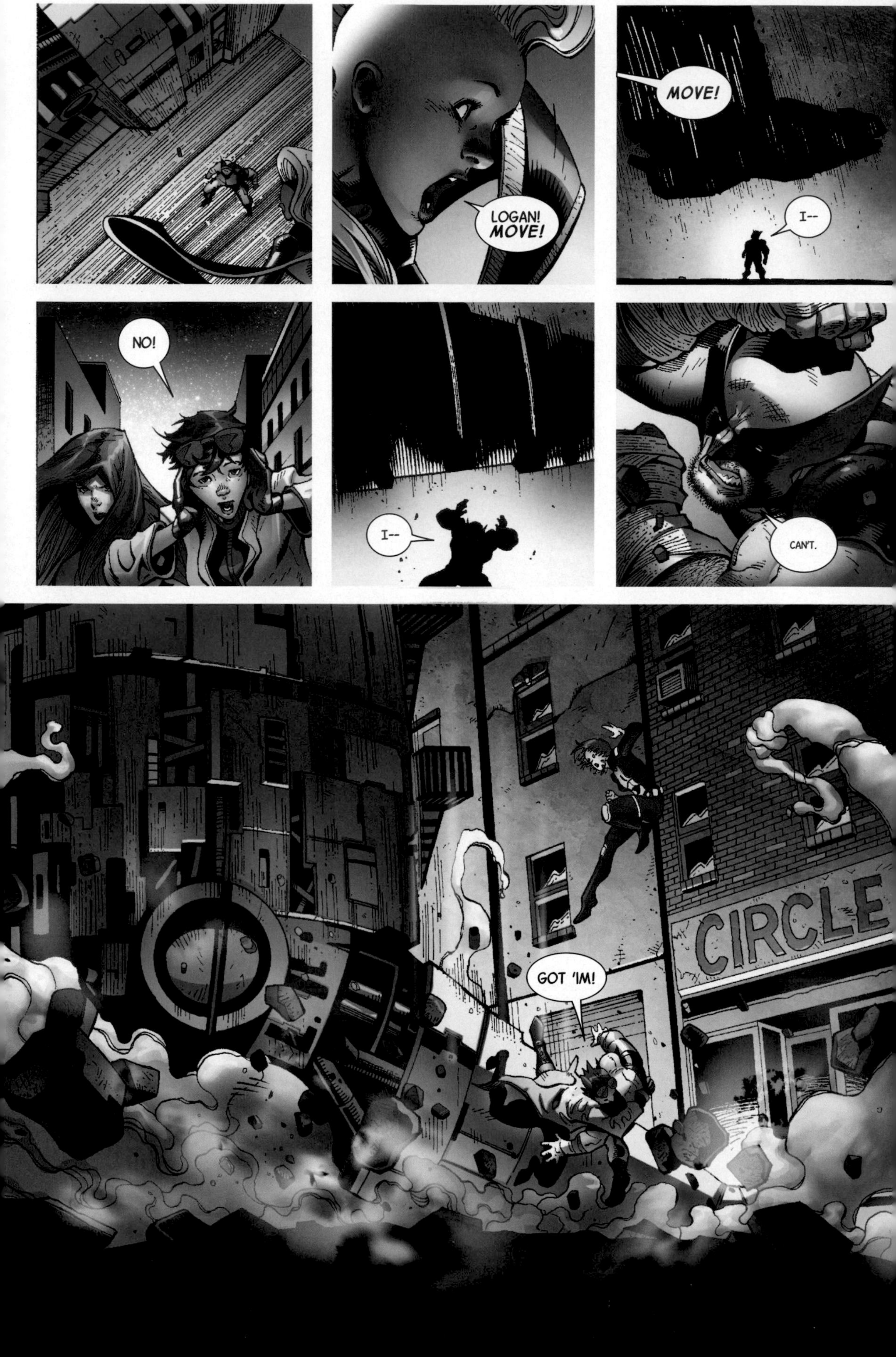
LOGAN! MOVE!
MOVE!
I--
NO!
I--
CAN'T.
CIRCLE
GOT 'IM!

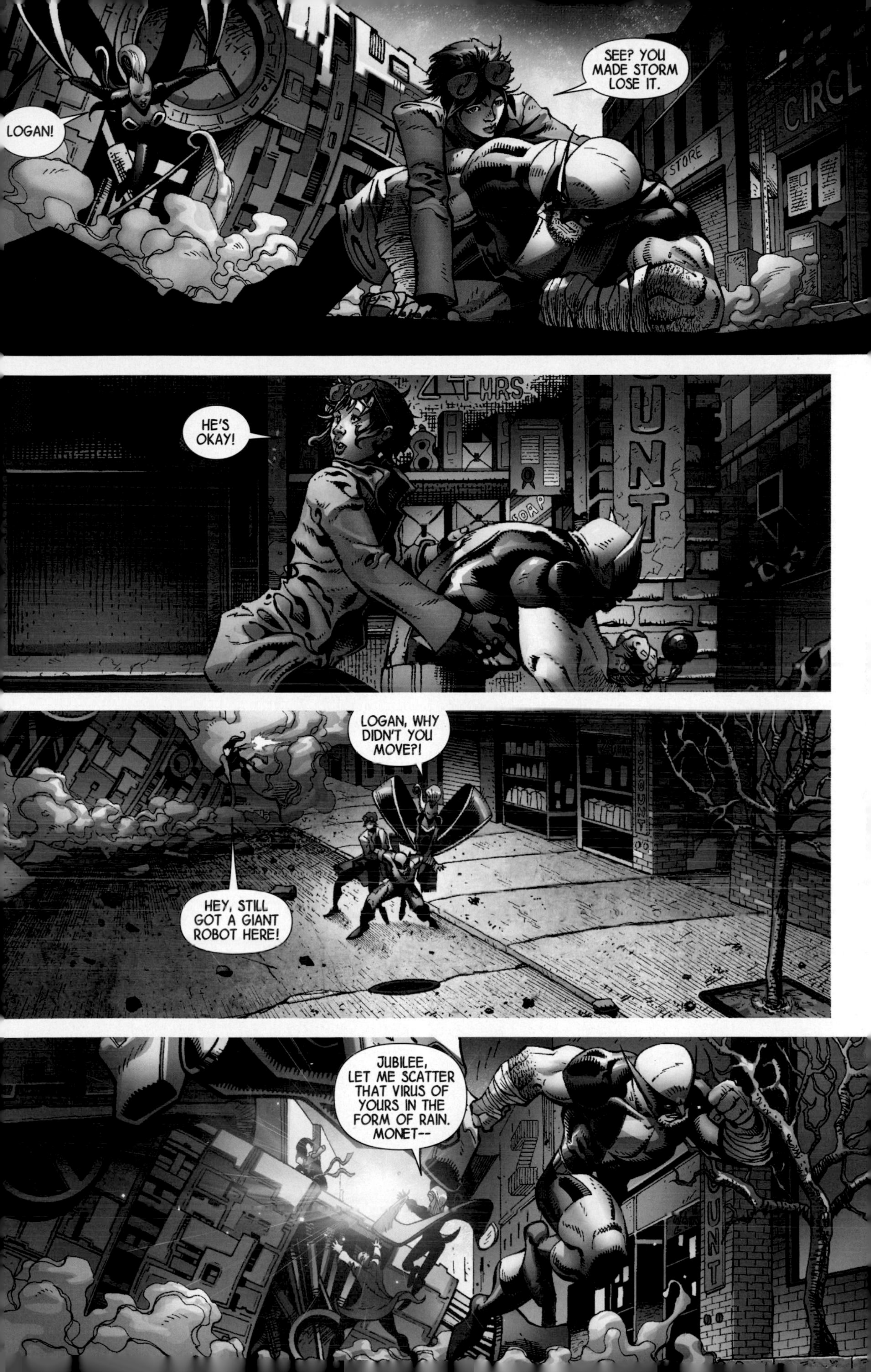
LOGAN!
SEE? YOU MADE STORM LOSE IT.
HE'S OKAY!
LOGAN, WHY DIDN'T YOU MOVE?!
HEY, STILL GOT A GIANT ROBOT HERE!
JUBILEE, LET ME SCATTER THAT VIRUS OF YOURS IN THE FORM OF RAIN. MONET--

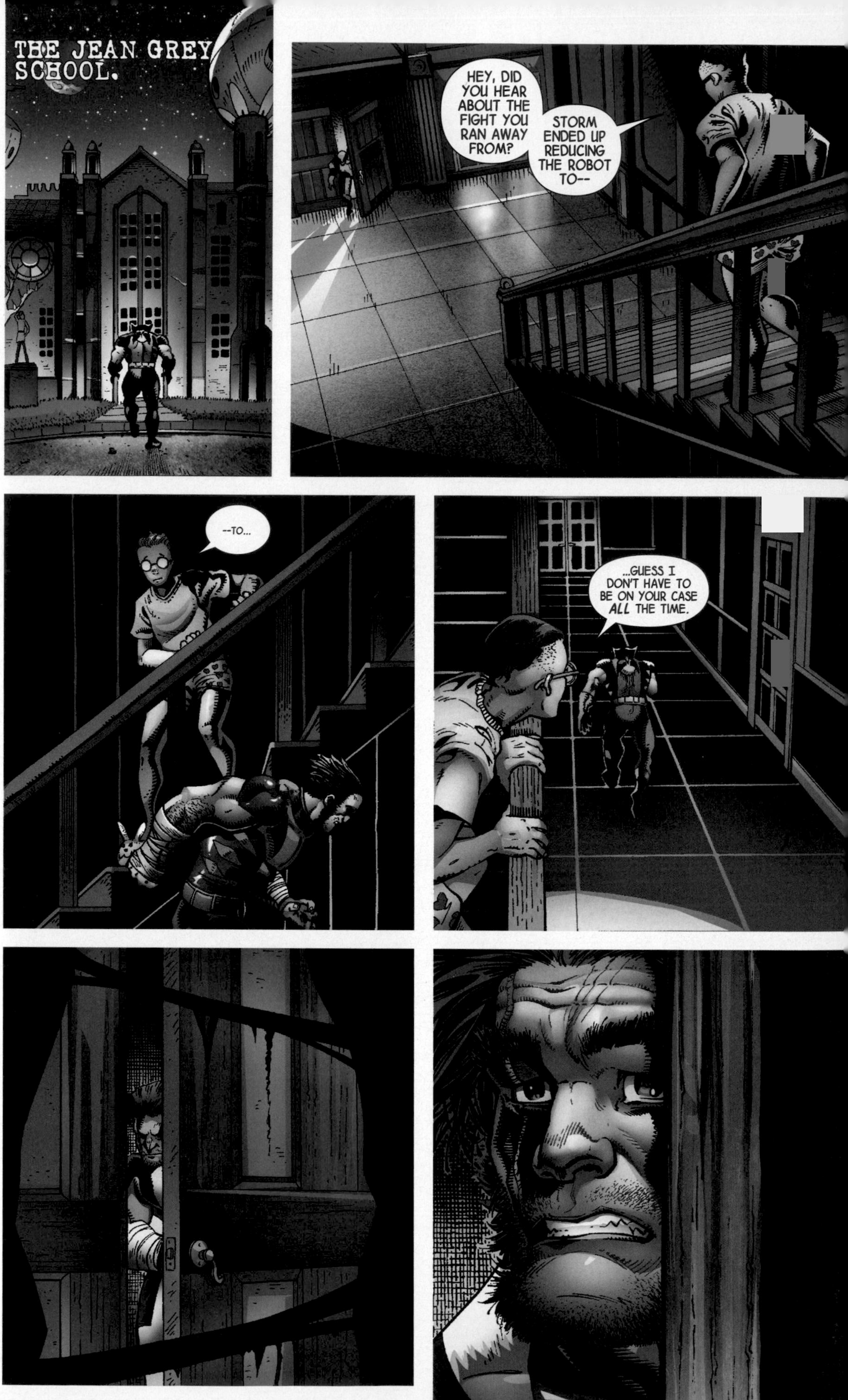
THE JEAN GREY SCHOOL.
HEY, DID YOU HEAR ABOUT THE FIGHT YOU RAN AWAY FROM?
STORM ENDED UP REDUCING THE ROBOT TO--
--TO...
...GUESS I DON'T HAVE TO BE ON YOUR CASE ALL THE TIME.

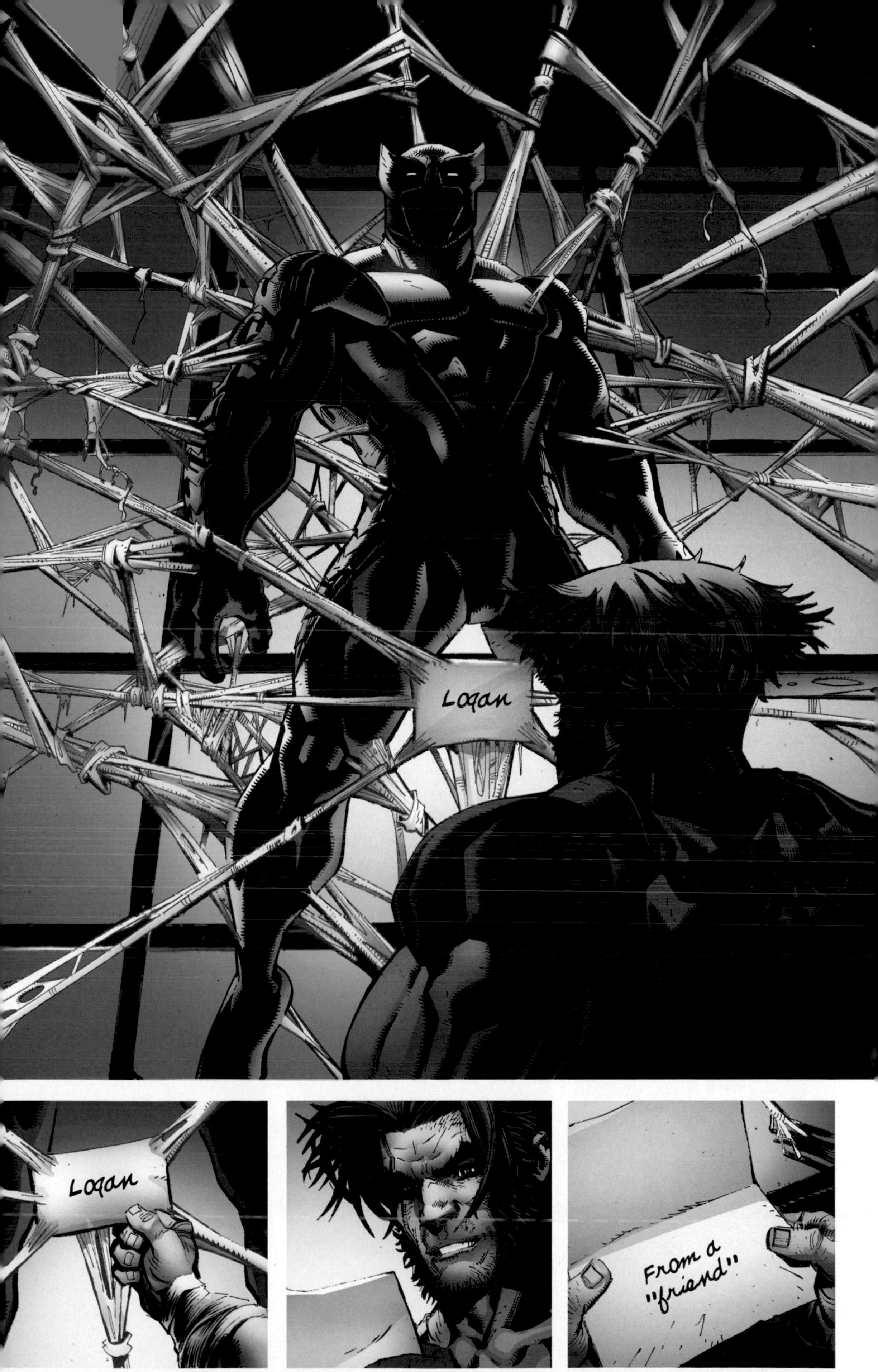
Logan
Logan
From a "friend"

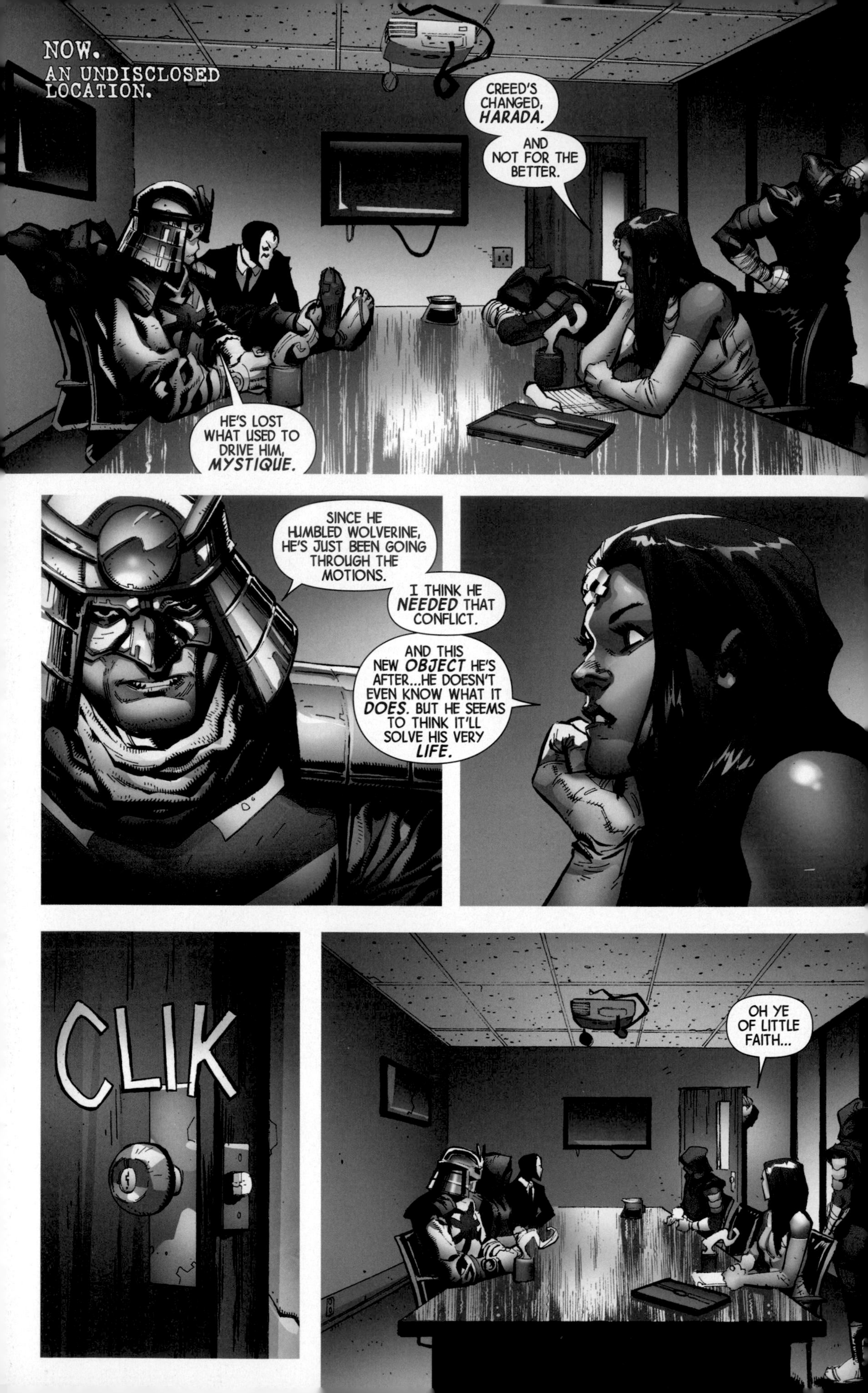
NOW.
AN UNDISCLOSED LOCATION.
CREED'S CHANGED, HARADA.
AND NOT FOR THE BETTER.
HE'S LOST WHAT USED TO DRIVE HIM, MYSTIQUE.
SINCE HE HUMBLED WOLVERINE, HE'S JUST BEEN GOING THROUGH THE MOTIONS.
I THINK HE NEEDED THAT CONFLICT.
AND THIS NEW OBJECT HE'S AFTER...HE DOESN'T EVEN KNOW WHAT IT DOES. BUT HE SEEMS TO THINK IT'LL SOLVE HIS VERY LIFE.
CLIK
OH YE OF LITTLE FAITH...

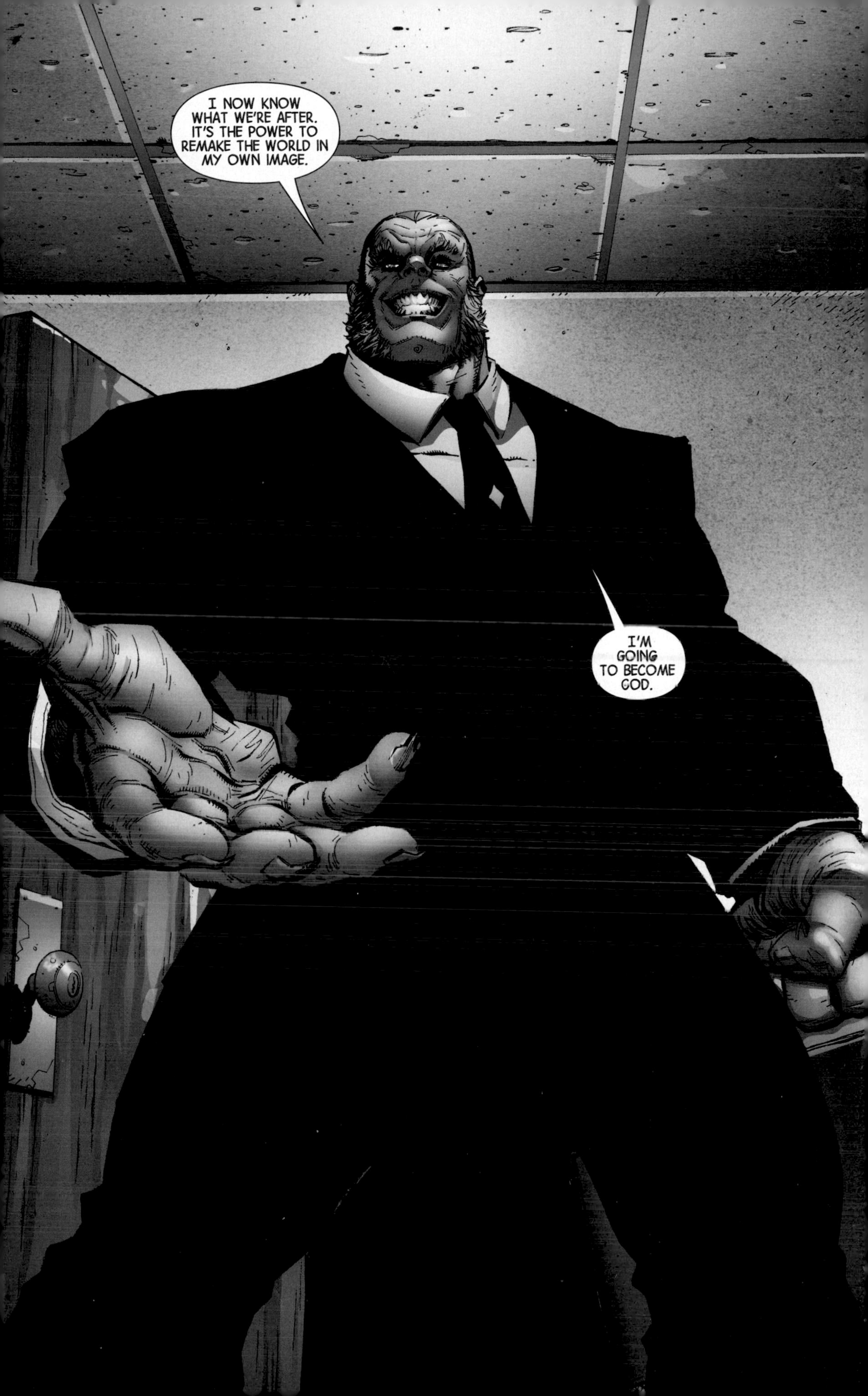
I NOW KNOW WHAT WE'RE AFTER. IT'S THE POWER TO REMAKE THE WORLD IN MY OWN IMAGE.
I'M GOING TO BECOME GOD.

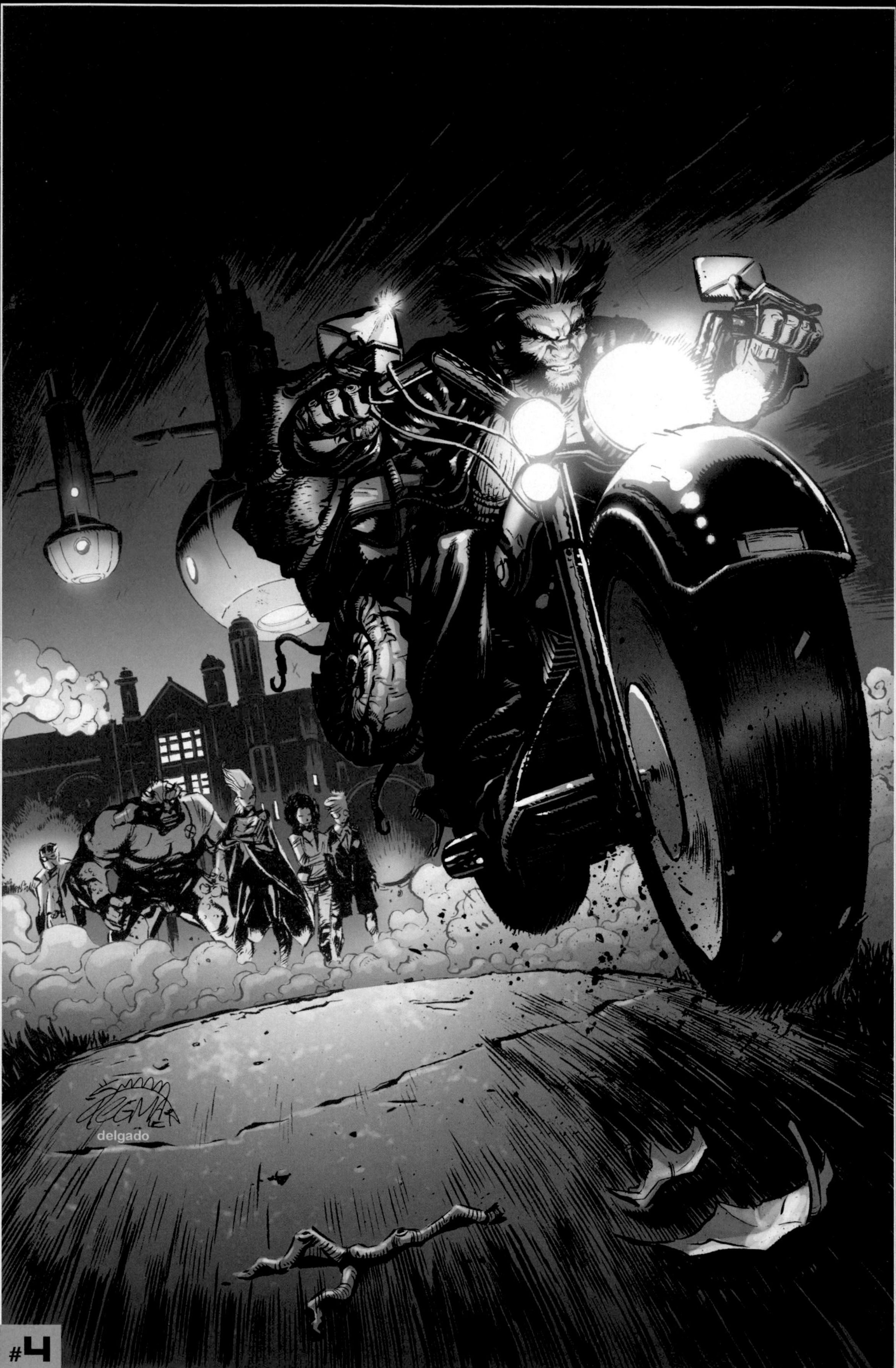
delgado

#4

ROGUE LOGAN PART 4

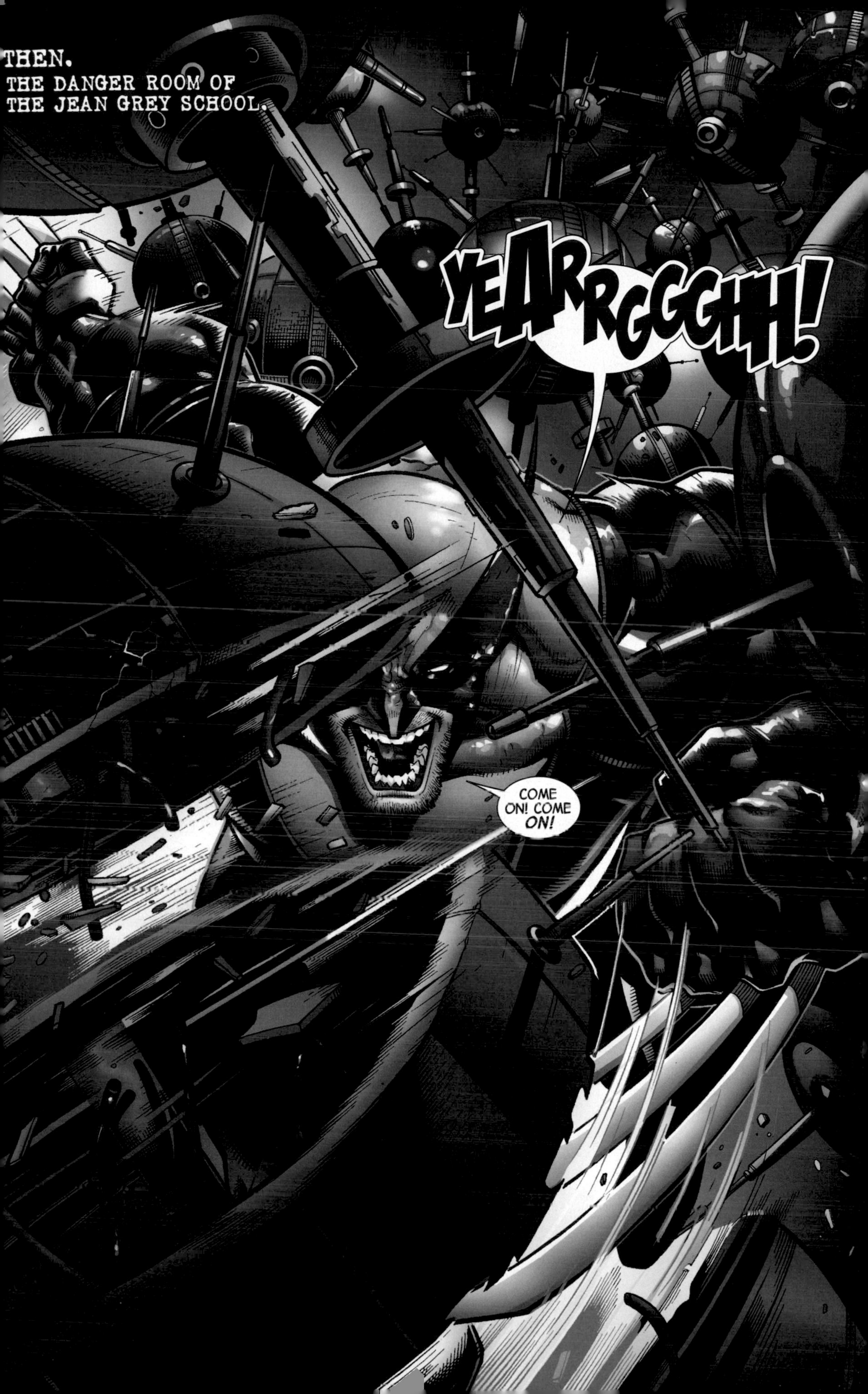
THEN.
THE DANGER ROOM OF THE JEAN GREY SCHOOL.
YEARRGGGHH!
COME ON! COME ON!

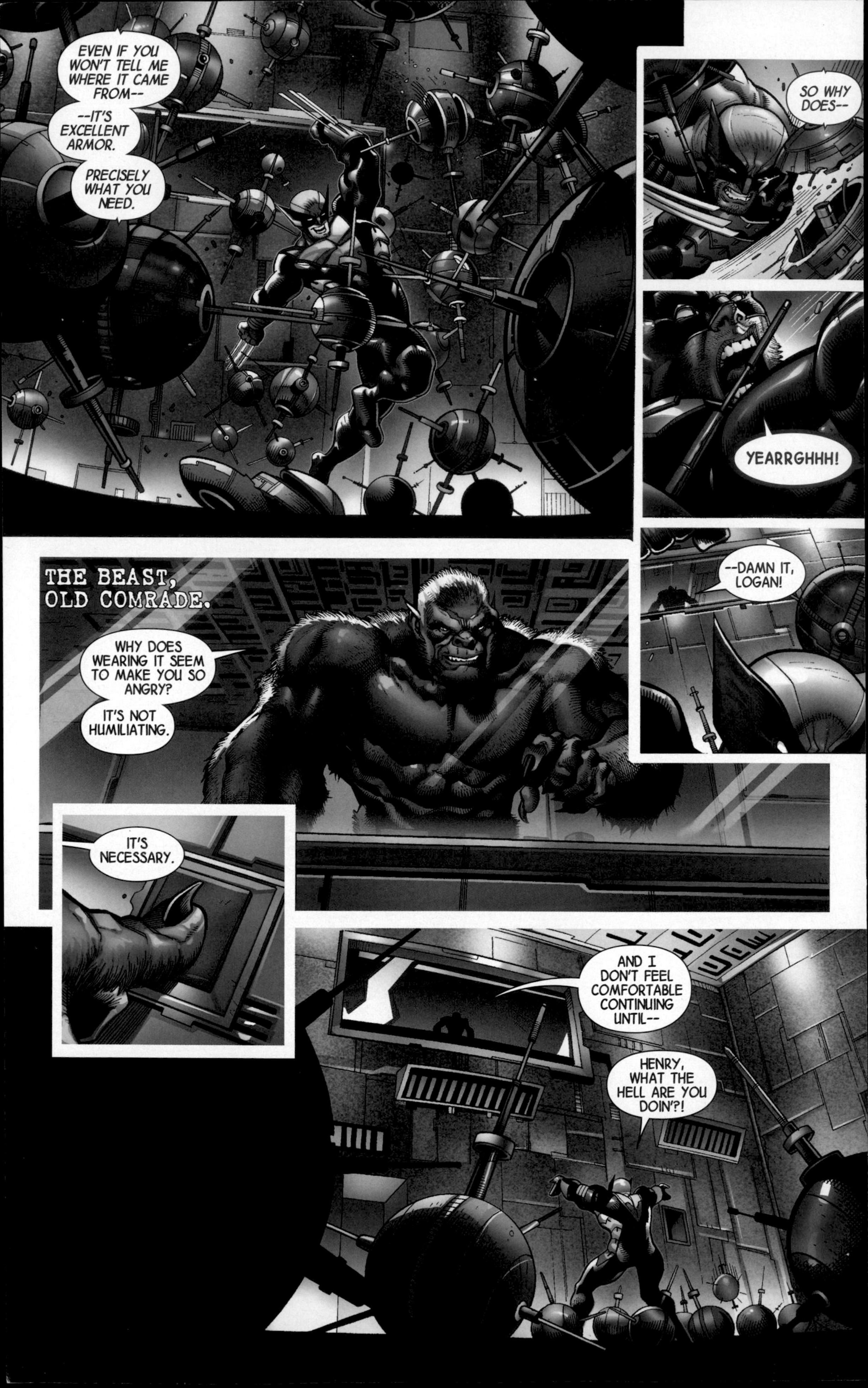
EVEN IF YOU WON'T TELL ME WHERE IT CAME FROM--
--IT'S EXCELLENT ARMOR.
PRECISELY WHAT YOU NEED.
SO WHY DOES--
YEARRGHHH!
THE BEAST, OLD COMRADE.
WHY DOES WEARING IT SEEM TO MAKE YOU SO ANGRY?
IT'S NOT HUMILIATING.
--DAMN IT, LOGAN!
IT'S NECESSARY.
AND I DON'T FEEL COMFORTABLE CONTINUING UNTIL--
HENRY, WHAT THE HELL ARE YOU DOIN'?!

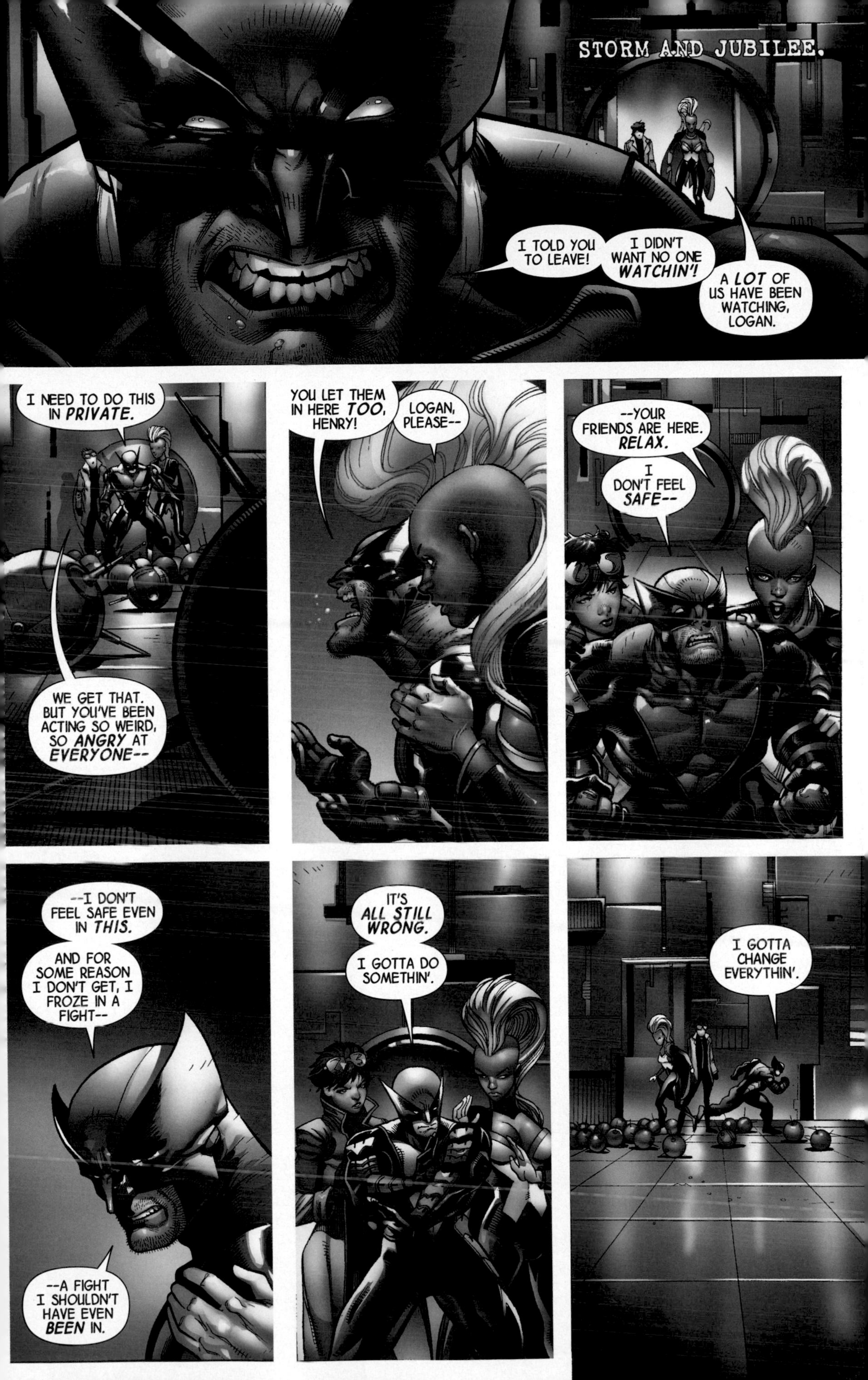
STORM AND JUBILEE.
I TOLD YOU TO LEAVE!
I DIDN'T WANT NO ONE WATCHIN'!
A LOT OF US HAVE BEEN WATCHING, LOGAN.
I NEED TO DO THIS IN PRIVATE.
WE GET THAT. BUT YOU'VE BEEN ACTING SO WEIRD, SO ANGRY AT EVERYONE--
YOU LET THEM IN HERE TOO, HENRY!
LOGAN, PLEASE--
--YOUR FRIENDS ARE HERE. RELAX.
I DON'T FEEL SAFE--
--I DON'T FEEL SAFE EVEN IN THIS.
AND FOR SOME REASON I DON'T GET, I FROZE IN A FIGHT--
--A FIGHT I SHOULDN'T HAVE EVEN BEEN IN.
IT'S ALL STILL WRONG.
I GOTTA DO SOMETHIN'.
I GOTTA CHANGE EVERYTHIN'.

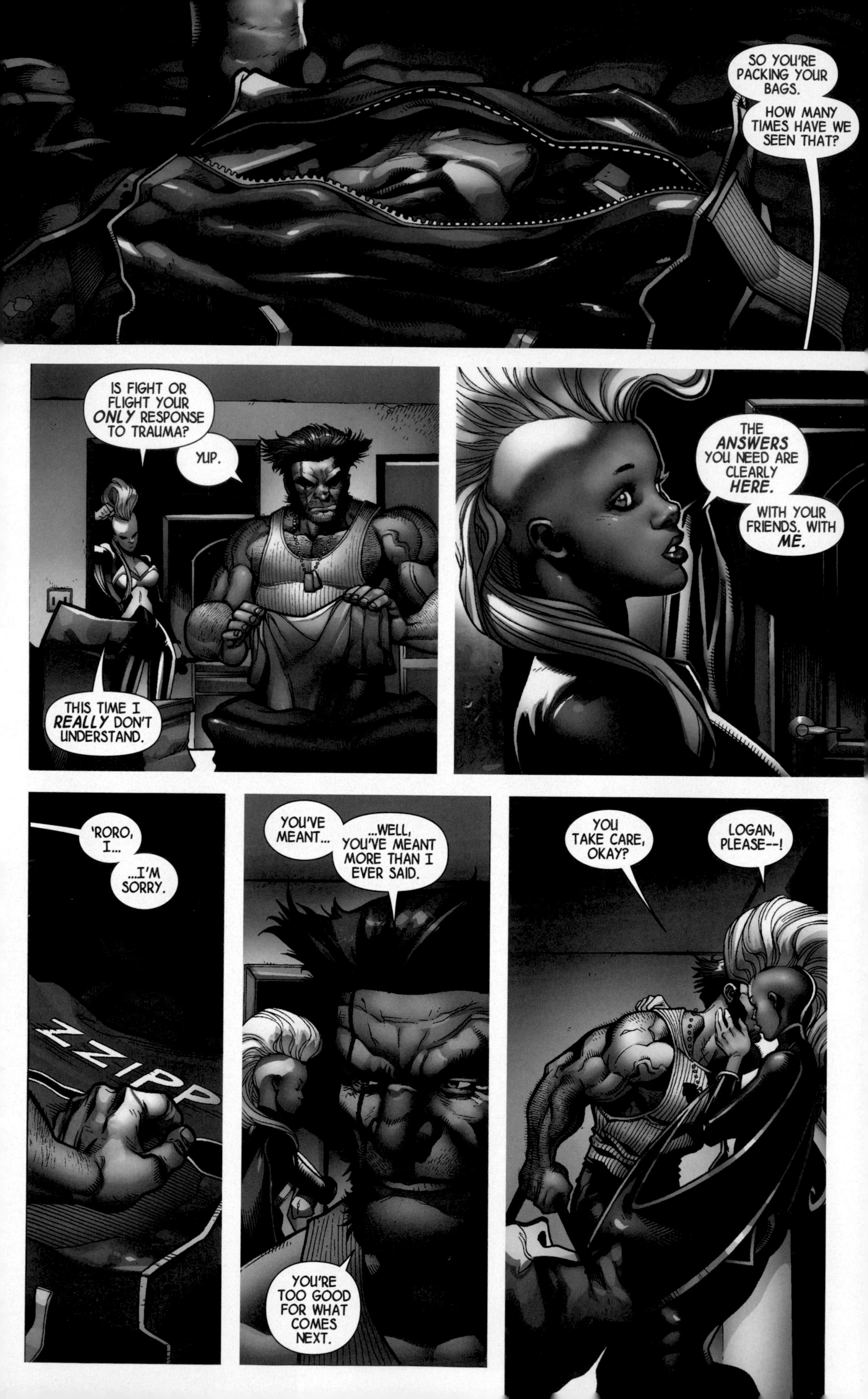
SO YOU'RE PACKING YOUR BAGS.
HOW MANY TIMES HAVE WE SEEN THAT?
IS FIGHT OR FLIGHT YOUR ONLY RESPONSE TO TRAUMA?
YUP.
THIS TIME I REALLY DON'T UNDERSTAND.
THE ANSWERS YOU NEED ARE CLEARLY HERE.
WITH YOUR FRIENDS. WITH ME.
'RORO, I...
...I'M SORRY.
ZZIPP
YOU'VE MEANT...
...WELL, YOU'VE MEANT MORE THAN I EVER SAID.
YOU'RE TOO GOOD FOR WHAT COMES NEXT.
YOU TAKE CARE, OKAY?
LOGAN, PLEASE--!

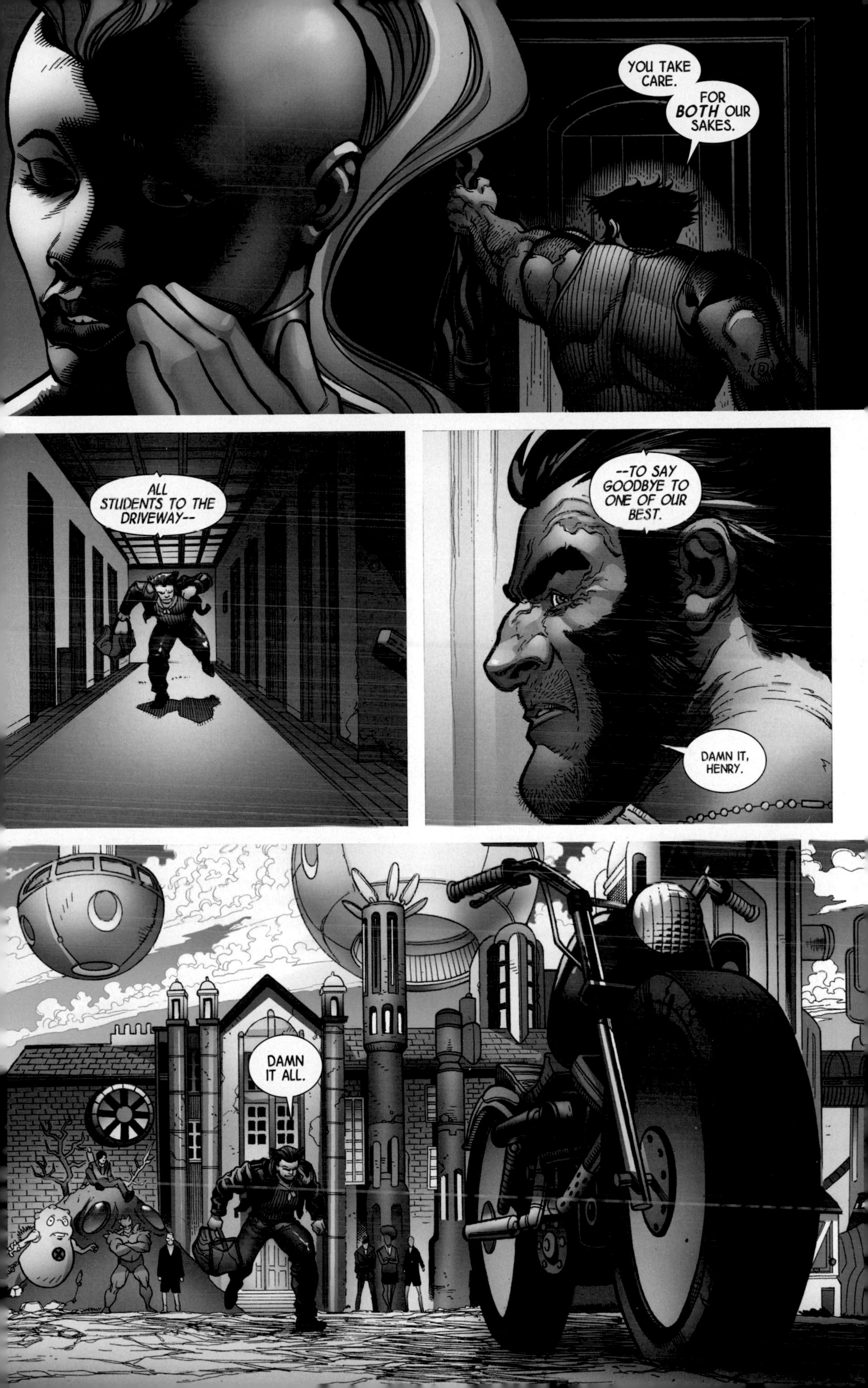
YOU TAKE CARE.
FOR *BOTH* OUR SAKES.
ALL STUDENTS TO THE DRIVEWAY--
--TO SAY GOODBYE TO ONE OF OUR BEST.
DAMN IT, HENRY.
DAMN IT ALL.

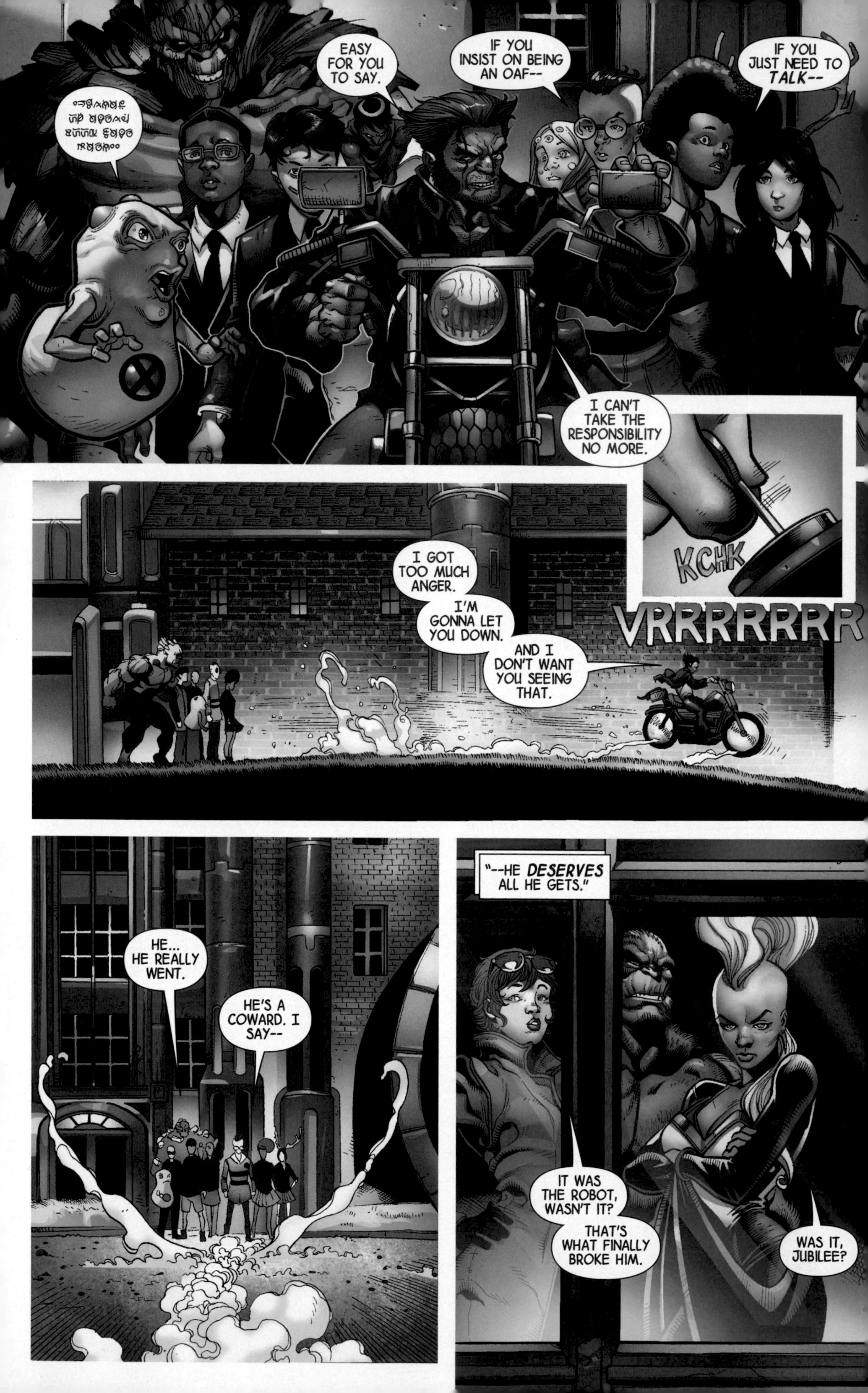
EASY FOR YOU TO SAY.
IF YOU INSIST ON BEING AN OAF--
IF YOU JUST NEED TO TALK--
I CAN'T TAKE THE RESPONSIBILITY NO MORE.
KCHK
I GOT TOO MUCH ANGER.
I'M GONNA LET YOU DOWN.
AND I DON'T WANT YOU SEEING THAT.
VRRRRRRR
HE... HE REALLY WENT.
HE'S A COWARD. I SAY--
"--HE DESERVES ALL HE GETS."
IT WAS THE ROBOT, WASN'T IT?
THAT'S WHAT FINALLY BROKE HIM.
WAS IT, JUBILEE?

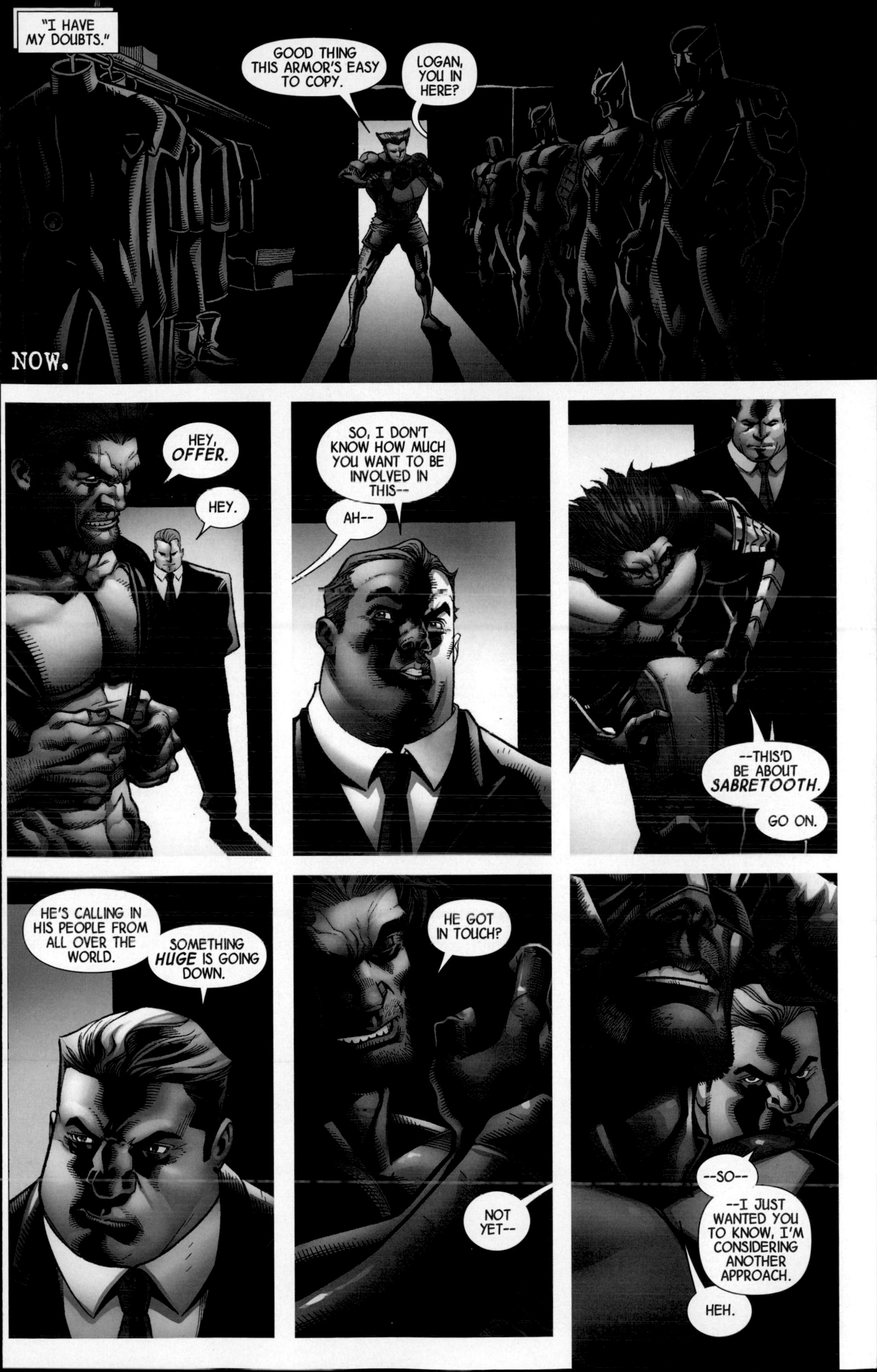
"I HAVE MY DOUBTS."
GOOD THING THIS ARMOR'S EASY TO COPY.
LOGAN, YOU IN HERE?
NOW.
HEY, OFFER.
HEY.
SO, I DON'T KNOW HOW MUCH YOU WANT TO BE INVOLVED IN THIS--
AH--
--THIS'D BE ABOUT SABRETOOTH.
GO ON.
HE'S CALLING IN HIS PEOPLE FROM ALL OVER THE WORLD.
SOMETHING HUGE IS GOING DOWN.
HE GOT IN TOUCH?
NOT YET--
--SO--
--I JUST WANTED YOU TO KNOW, I'M CONSIDERING ANOTHER APPROACH.
HEH.

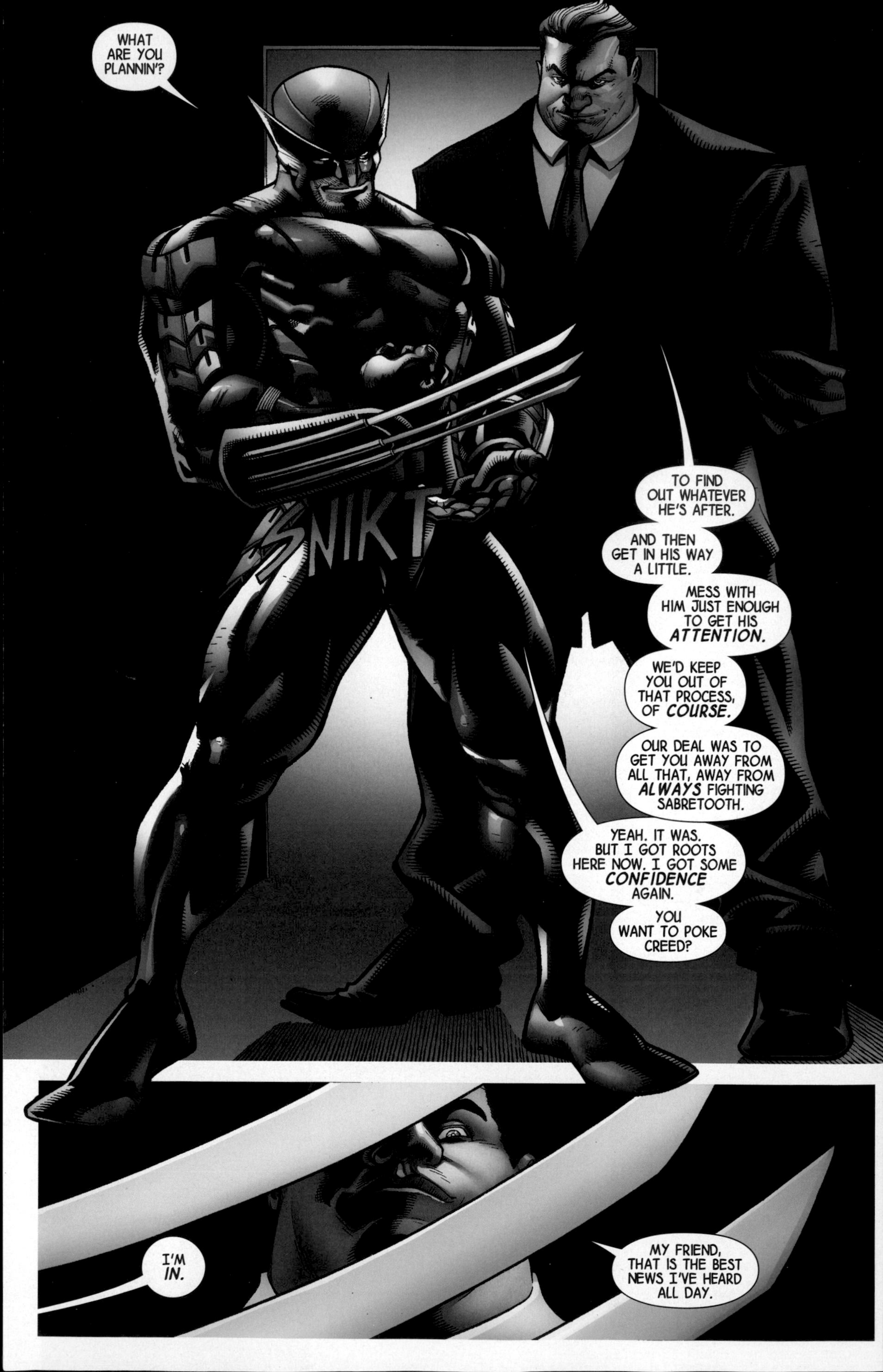
WHAT ARE YOU PLANNIN'?
SNIKT
TO FIND OUT WHATEVER HE'S AFTER.
AND THEN GET IN HIS WAY A LITTLE.
MESS WITH HIM JUST ENOUGH TO GET HIS ATTENTION.
WE'D KEEP YOU OUT OF THAT PROCESS, OF COURSE.
OUR DEAL WAS TO GET YOU AWAY FROM ALL THAT, AWAY FROM ALWAYS FIGHTING SABRETOOTH.
YEAH. IT WAS. BUT I GOT ROOTS HERE NOW. I GOT SOME CONFIDENCE AGAIN.
YOU WANT TO POKE CREED?
I'M IN.
MY FRIEND, THAT IS THE BEST NEWS I'VE HEARD ALL DAY.

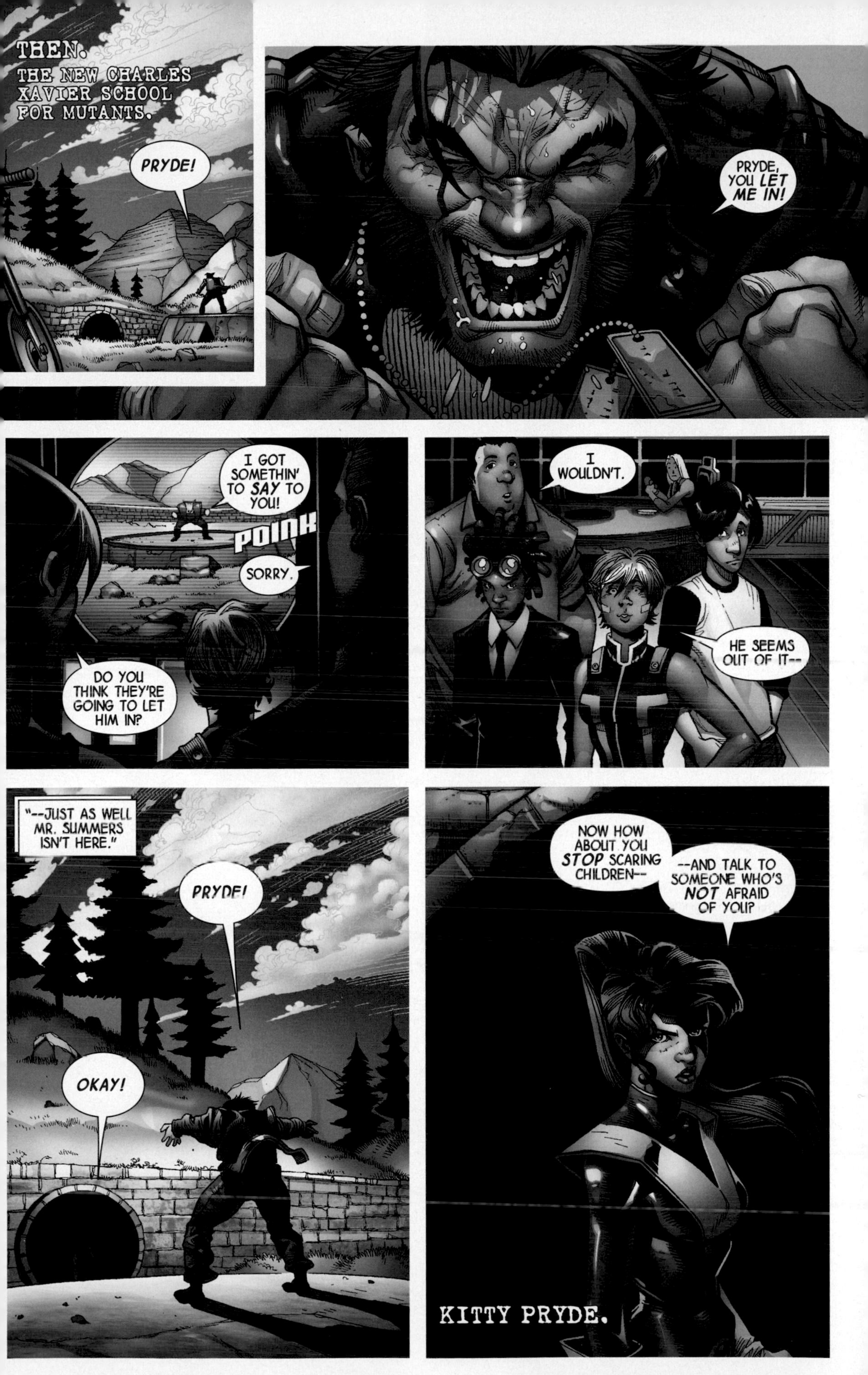
THEN.
THE NEW CHARLES XAVIER SCHOOL FOR MUTANTS.
PRYDE!
PRYDE, YOU LET ME IN!
I GOT SOMETHIN' TO SAY TO YOU!
POINK
SORRY.
DO YOU THINK THEY'RE GOING TO LET HIM IN?
I WOULDN'T.
HE SEEMS OUT OF IT--
"--JUST AS WELL MR. SUMMERS ISN'T HERE."
PRYDE!
OKAY!
NOW HOW ABOUT YOU STOP SCARING CHILDREN--
--AND TALK TO SOMEONE WHO'S NOT AFRAID OF YOU?
KITTY PRYDE.

YOU NEVER WANTED TO TALK TO ME *BEFORE* YOU LEFT 'BOUT WHAT HAPPENED WITH CREED.

GREAT. I'M INTERESTED IN HAVING THAT CONVERSATION IF YOU'VE THOUGHT ABOUT IT--

--AND WANT TO APOLOGIZE.

APOLOGIZE?

YOU KNEW SABRETOOTH HAD SET *SOME* SORT OF TRAP. YOU *COULD* HAVE GOTTEN *HELP*.

BUT YOU MADE IT ALL ABOUT YOU. AND *TWELVE PEOPLE* WERE KILLED.

I CAME HERE TO SEE IF YOU'D *UNDERSTAND!*

I HEARD YOU *WALKED OUT!*

YOU THREW IT ALL AWAY! *AGAIN!*

YOU WANT IT ALL TO BE OVER, TO GO OUT IN A BLAZE OF GLORY?!

WE LEAD THE KIDS HERE *AWAY* FROM MUTANT SELF-HATRED.

SNIKT

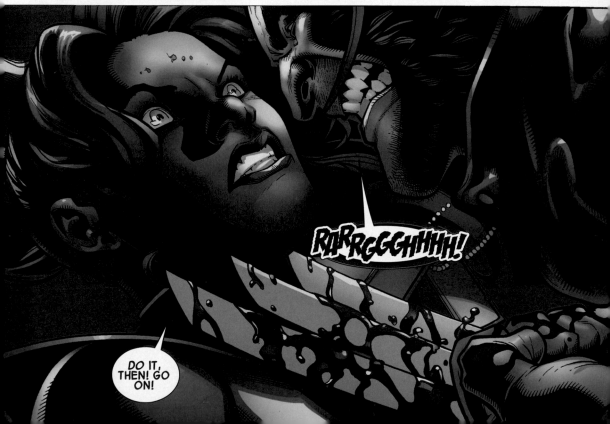

RARRGGCHHHH!

DO IT, THEN! GO ON!

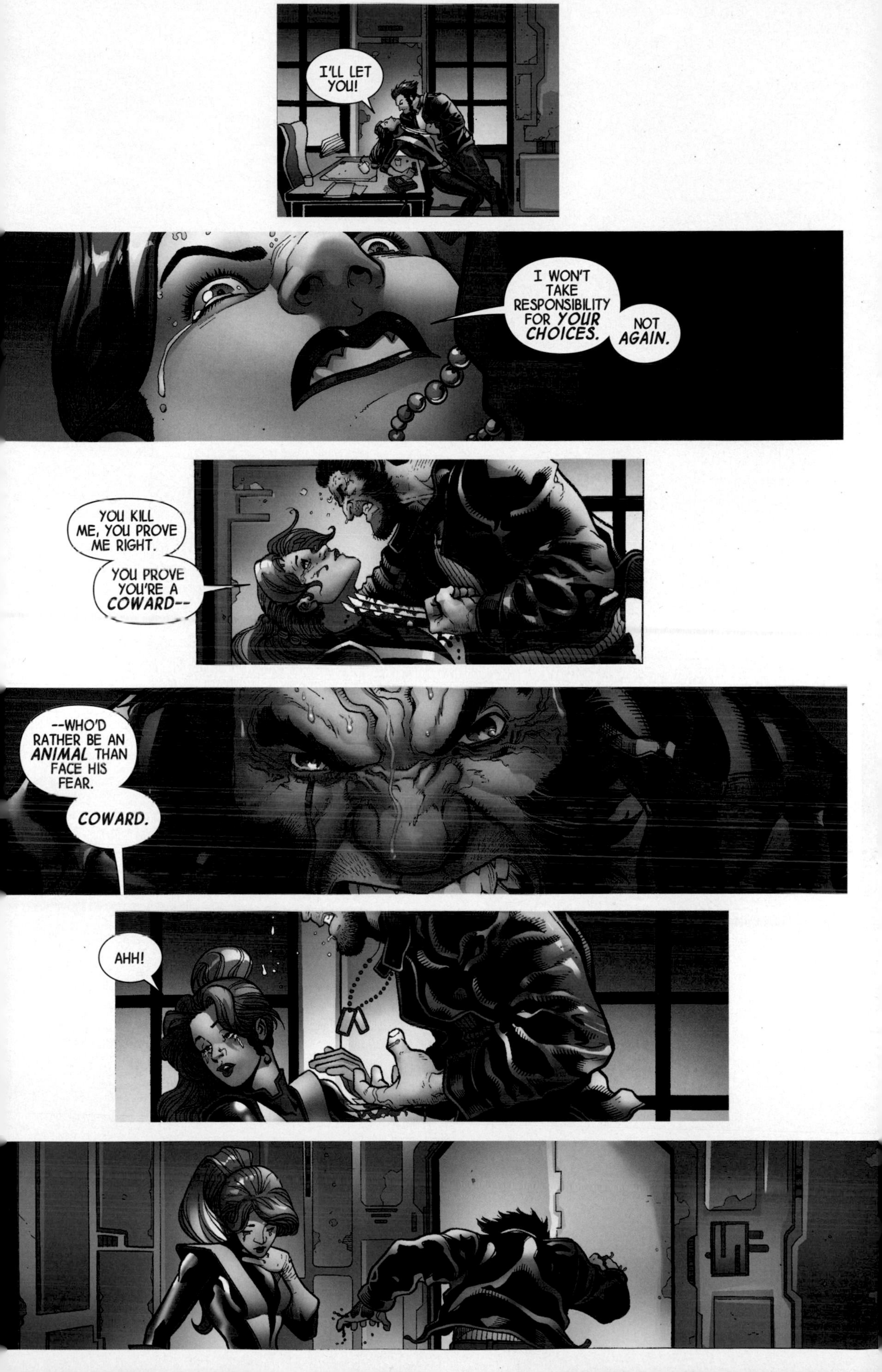
I'LL LET YOU!
I WON'T TAKE RESPONSIBILITY FOR YOUR CHOICES.
NOT AGAIN.
YOU KILL ME, YOU PROVE ME RIGHT.
YOU PROVE YOU'RE A COWARD--
--WHO'D RATHER BE AN ANIMAL THAN FACE HIS FEAR.
COWARD.
AHH!

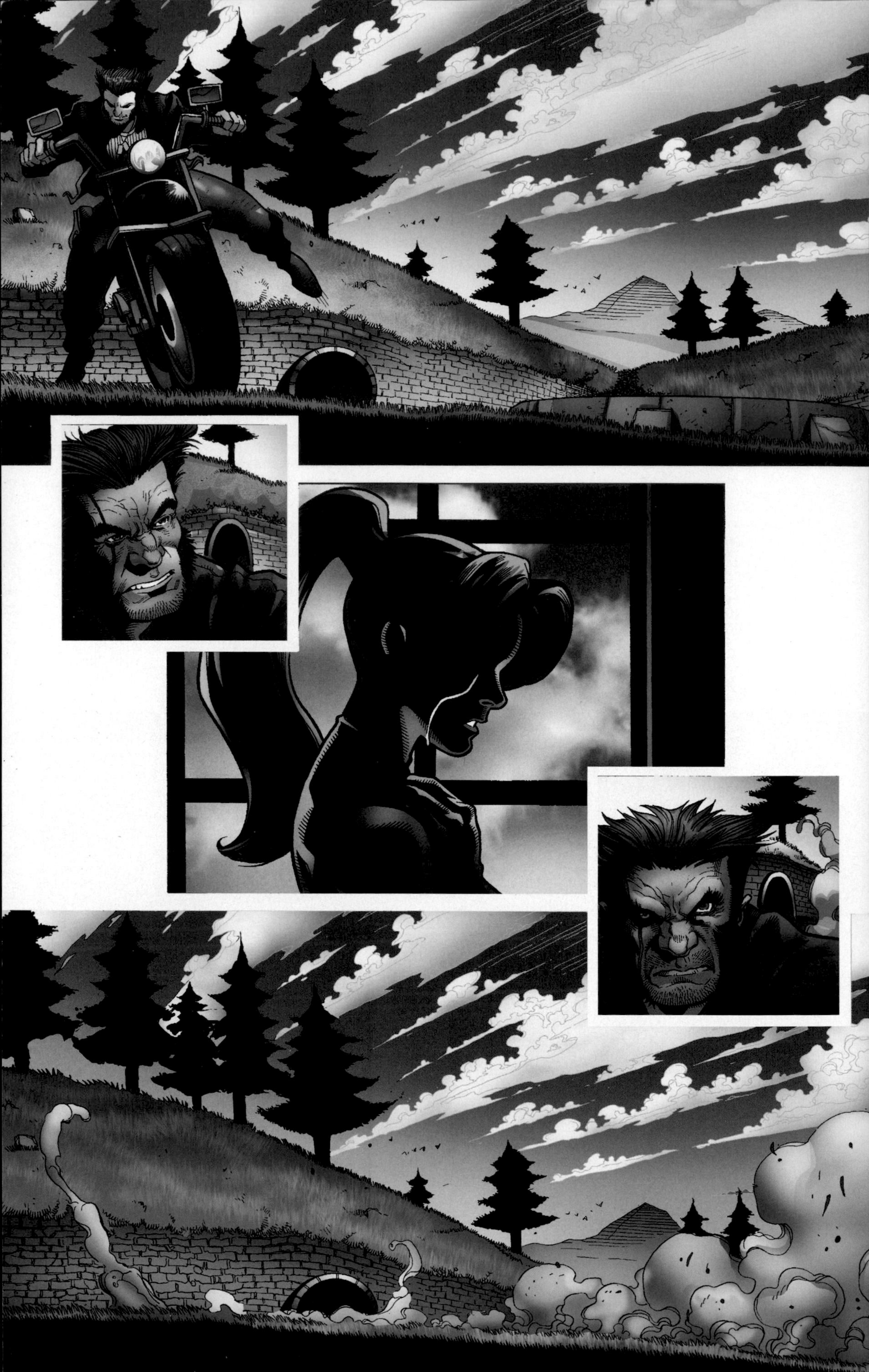

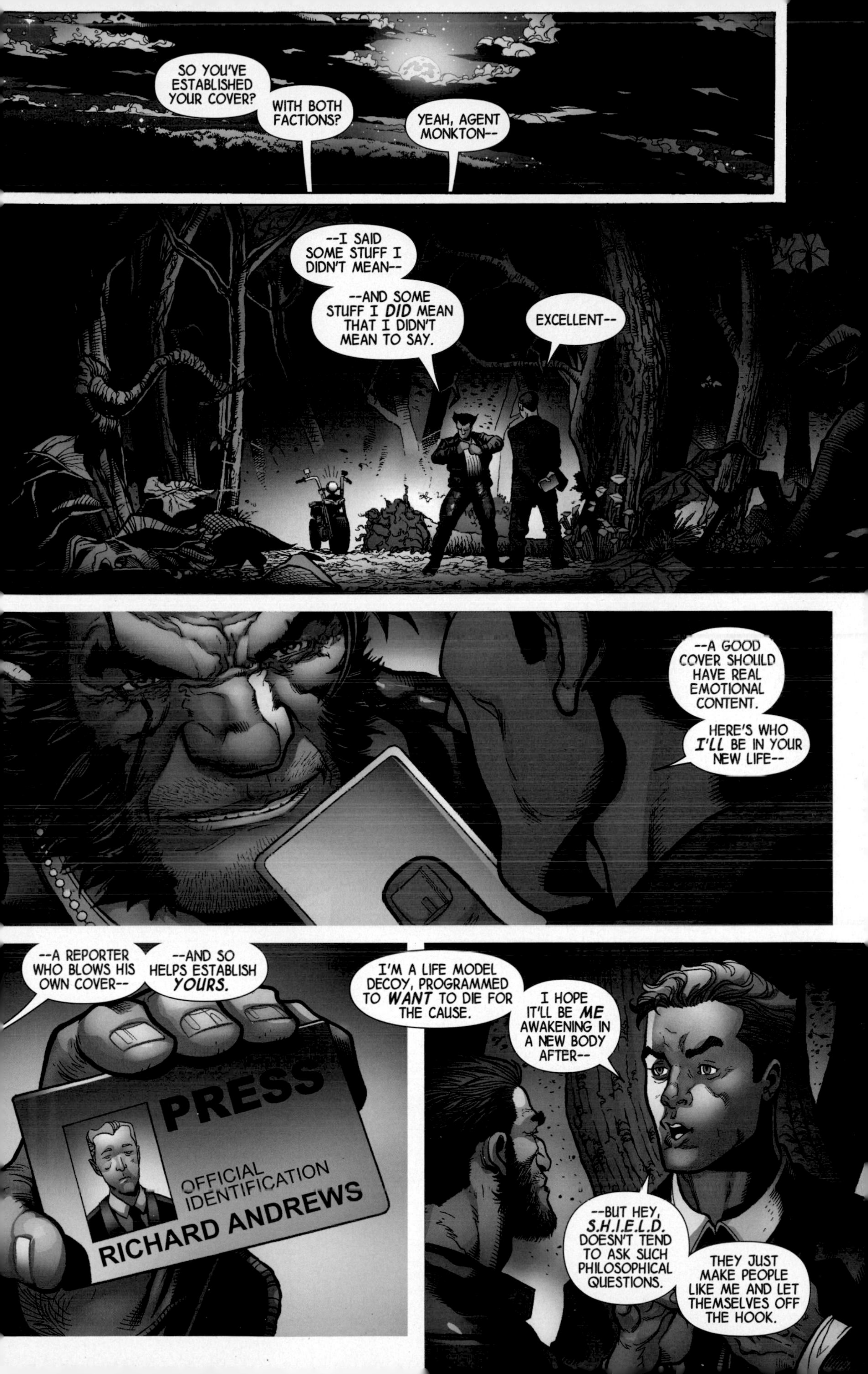
SO YOU'VE ESTABLISHED YOUR COVER?
WITH BOTH FACTIONS?
YEAH, AGENT MONKTON--
--I SAID SOME STUFF I DIDN'T MEAN--
--AND SOME STUFF I DID MEAN THAT I DIDN'T MEAN TO SAY.
EXCELLENT--
--A GOOD COVER SHOULD HAVE REAL EMOTIONAL CONTENT.
HERE'S WHO I'LL BE IN YOUR NEW LIFE--
--A REPORTER WHO BLOWS HIS OWN COVER--
--AND SO HELPS ESTABLISH YOURS.
PRESS
OFFICIAL IDENTIFICATION
RICHARD ANDREWS
I'M A LIFE MODEL DECOY, PROGRAMMED TO WANT TO DIE FOR THE CAUSE.
I HOPE IT'LL BE ME AWAKENING IN A NEW BODY AFTER--
--BUT HEY, S.H.I.E.L.D. DOESN'T TEND TO ASK SUCH PHILOSOPHICAL QUESTIONS.
THEY JUST MAKE PEOPLE LIKE ME AND LET THEMSELVES OFF THE HOOK.

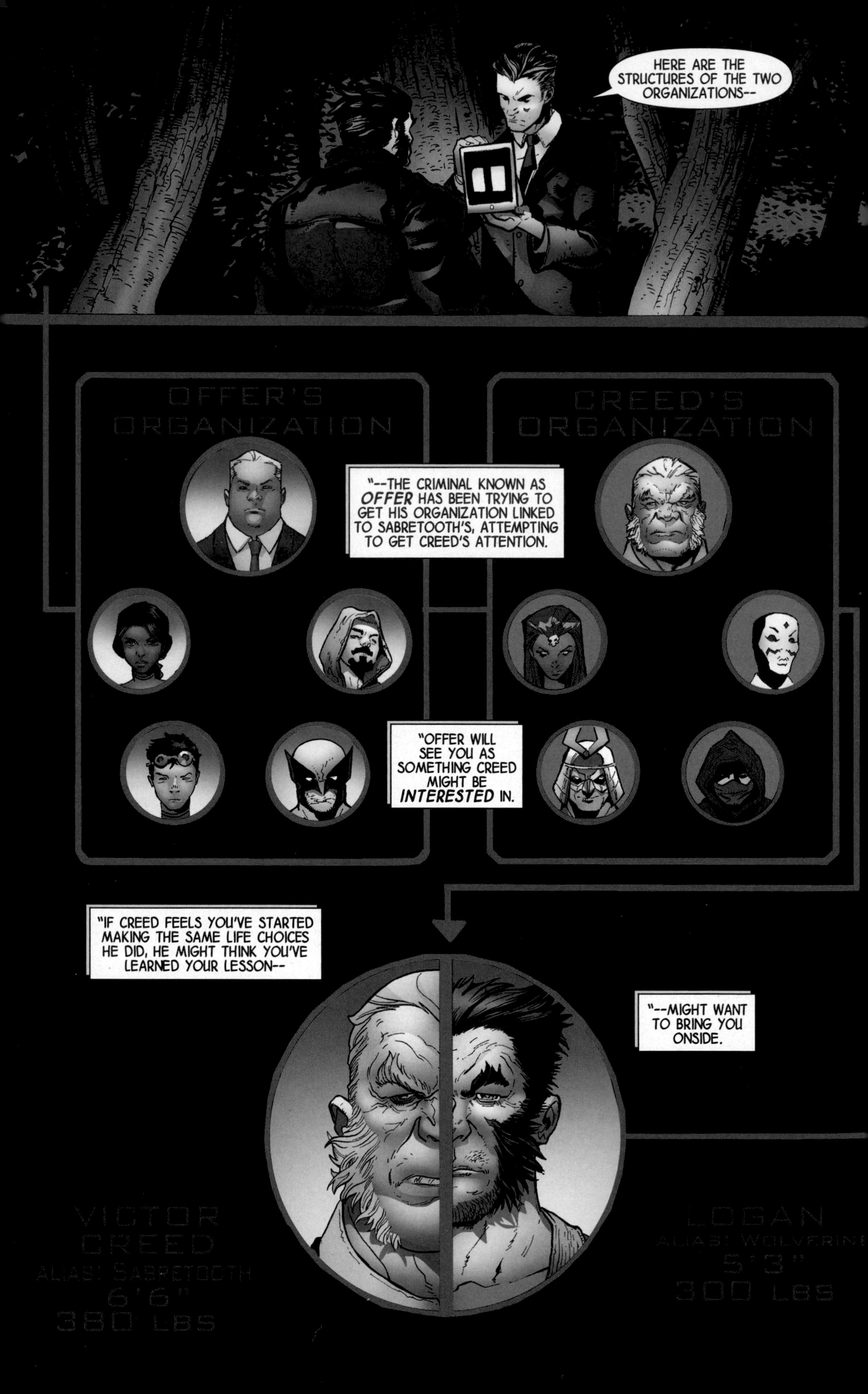
HERE ARE THE STRUCTURES OF THE TWO ORGANIZATIONS--
OFFER'S ORGANIZATION
CREED'S ORGANIZATION
"--THE CRIMINAL KNOWN AS OFFER HAS BEEN TRYING TO GET HIS ORGANIZATION LINKED TO SABRETOOTH'S, ATTEMPTING TO GET CREED'S ATTENTION.
"OFFER WILL SEE YOU AS SOMETHING CREED MIGHT BE INTERESTED IN.
"IF CREED FEELS YOU'VE STARTED MAKING THE SAME LIFE CHOICES HE DID, HE MIGHT THINK YOU'VE LEARNED YOUR LESSON--
"--MIGHT WANT TO BRING YOU ONSIDE.
VICTOR CREED
ALIAS: SABRETOOTH
6'6"
380 LBS
LOGAN
ALIAS: WOLVERINE
5'3"
300 LBS

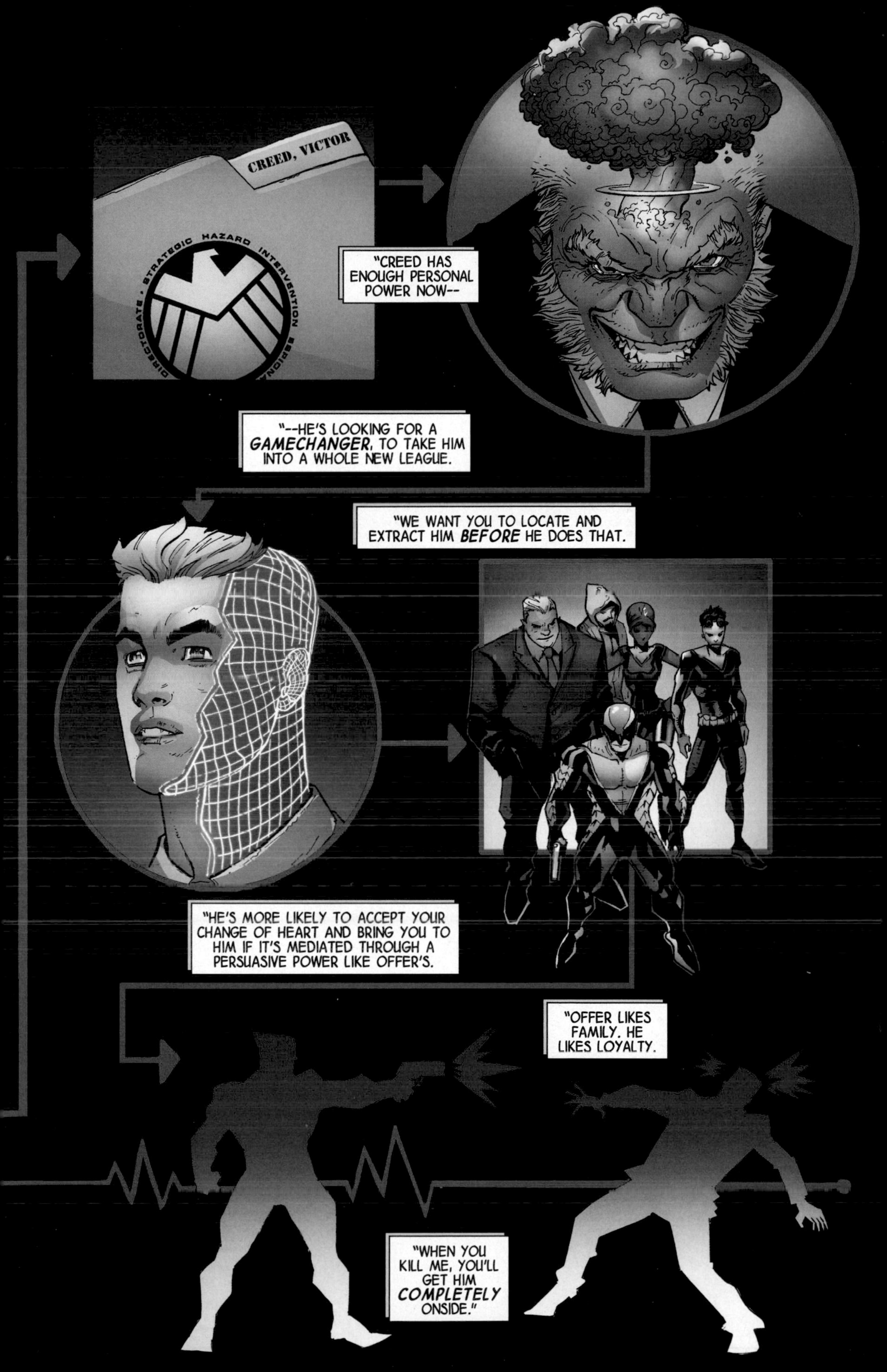
CREED, VICTOR
STRATEGIC HAZARD INTERVENTION ESPIONAGE DIRECTORATE
"CREED HAS ENOUGH PERSONAL POWER NOW--
"--HE'S LOOKING FOR A GAMECHANGER, TO TAKE HIM INTO A WHOLE NEW LEAGUE.
"WE WANT YOU TO LOCATE AND EXTRACT HIM BEFORE HE DOES THAT.
"HE'S MORE LIKELY TO ACCEPT YOUR CHANGE OF HEART AND BRING YOU TO HIM IF IT'S MEDIATED THROUGH A PERSUASIVE POWER LIKE OFFER'S.
"OFFER LIKES FAMILY. HE LIKES LOYALTY.
"WHEN YOU KILL ME, YOU'LL GET HIM COMPLETELY ONSIDE."

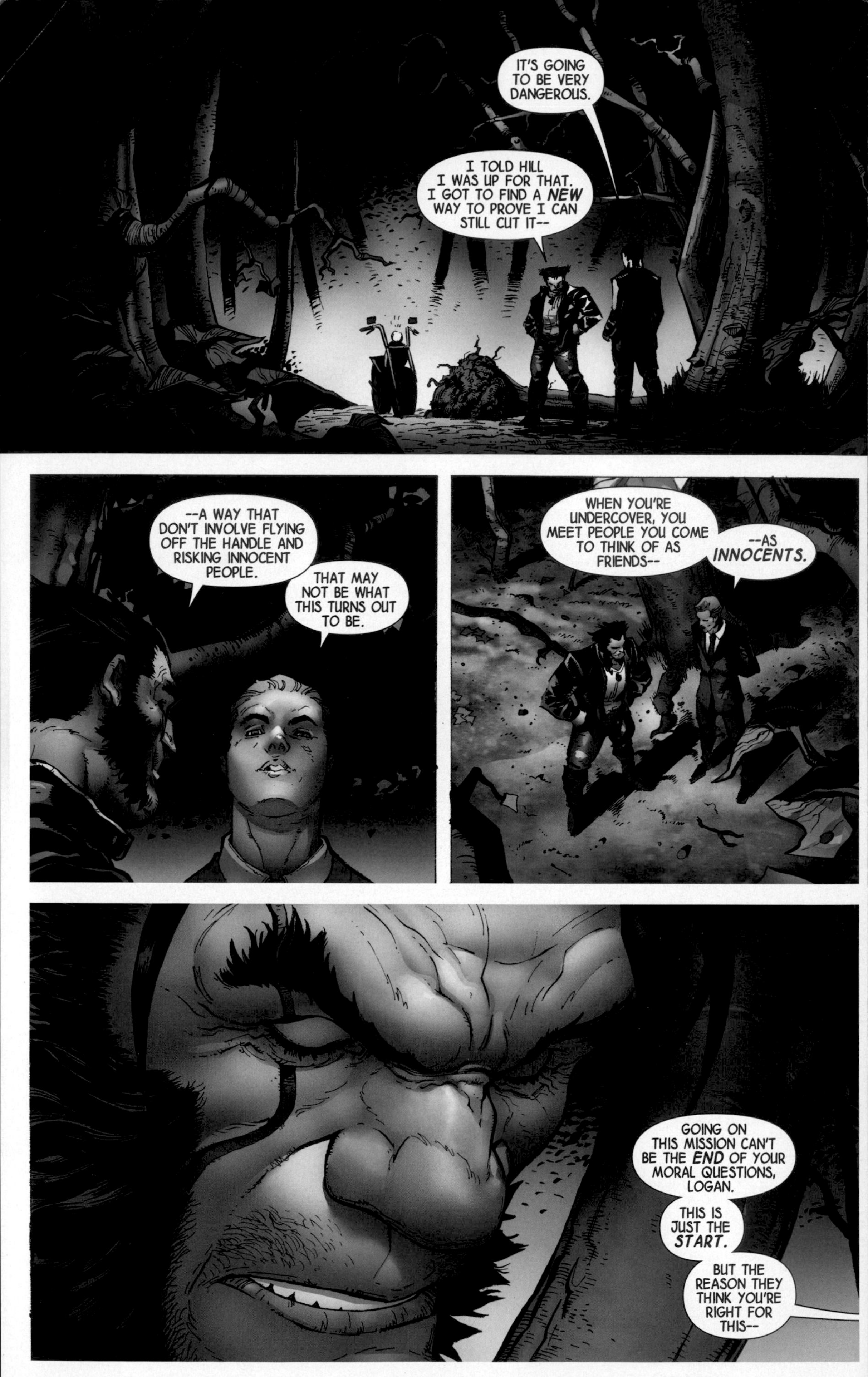
IT'S GOING TO BE VERY DANGEROUS.
I TOLD HILL I WAS UP FOR THAT. I GOT TO FIND A NEW WAY TO PROVE I CAN STILL CUT IT--
--A WAY THAT DON'T INVOLVE FLYING OFF THE HANDLE AND RISKING INNOCENT PEOPLE.
THAT MAY NOT BE WHAT THIS TURNS OUT TO BE.
WHEN YOU'RE UNDERCOVER, YOU MEET PEOPLE YOU COME TO THINK OF AS FRIENDS--
--AS INNOCENTS.
GOING ON THIS MISSION CAN'T BE THE END OF YOUR MORAL QUESTIONS, LOGAN.
THIS IS JUST THE START.
BUT THE REASON THEY THINK YOU'RE RIGHT FOR THIS--

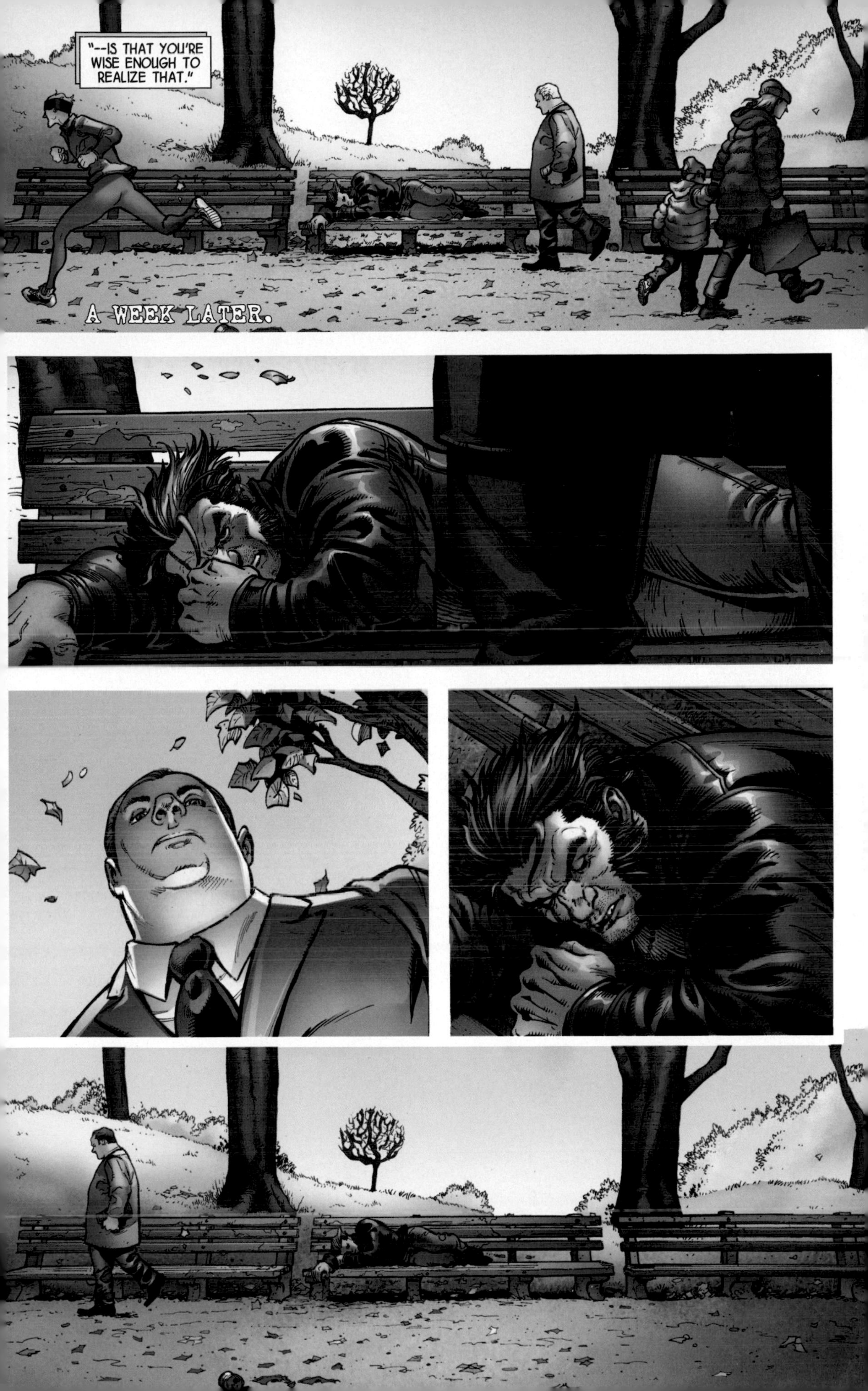
"--IS THAT YOU'RE WISE ENOUGH TO REALIZE THAT."
A WEEK LATER.

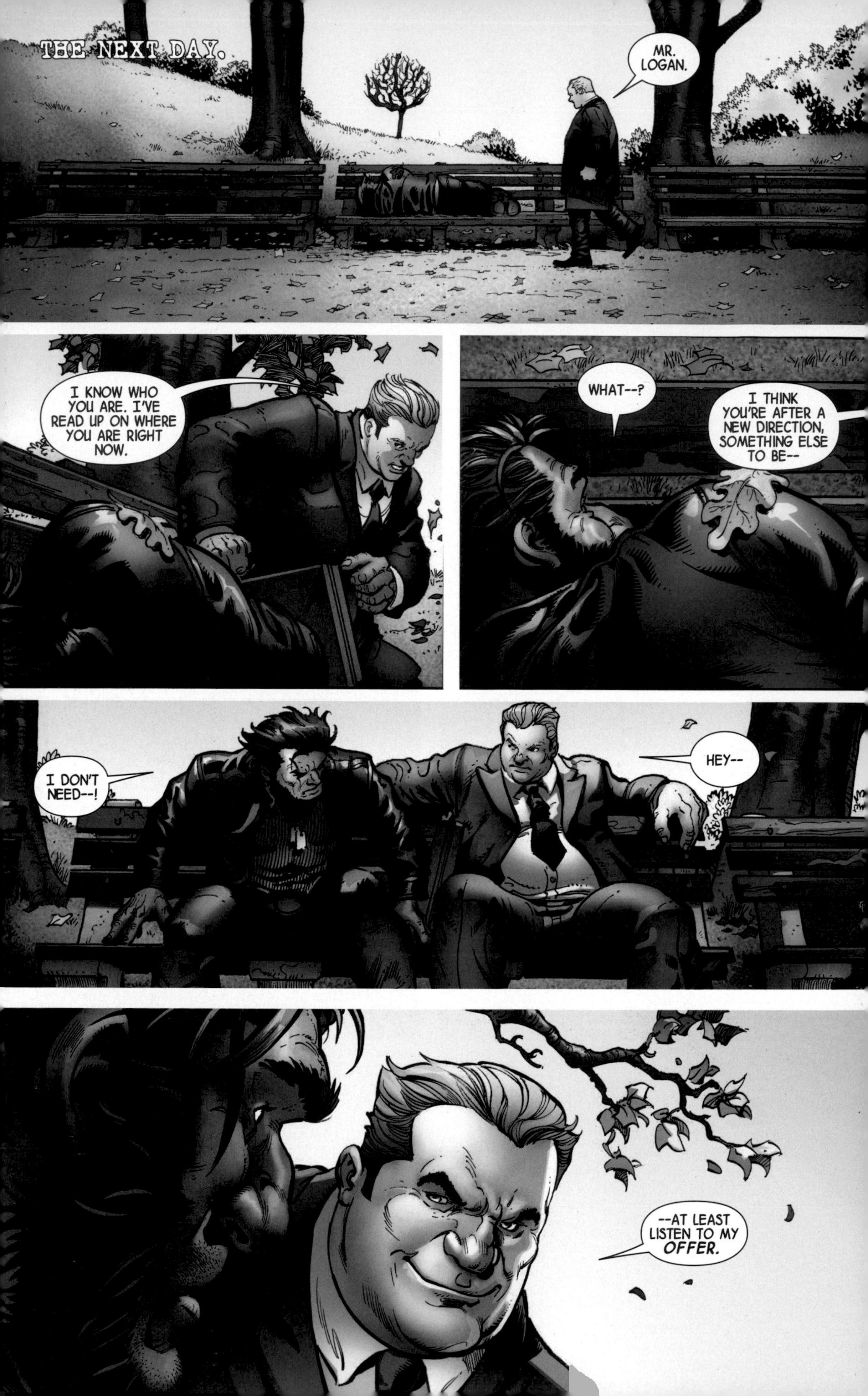
THE NEXT DAY.
MR. LOGAN.
I KNOW WHO YOU ARE. I'VE READ UP ON WHERE YOU ARE RIGHT NOW.
WHAT--?
I THINK YOU'RE AFTER A NEW DIRECTION, SOMETHING ELSE TO BE--
I DON'T NEED--!
HEY--
--AT LEAST LISTEN TO MY *OFFER.*

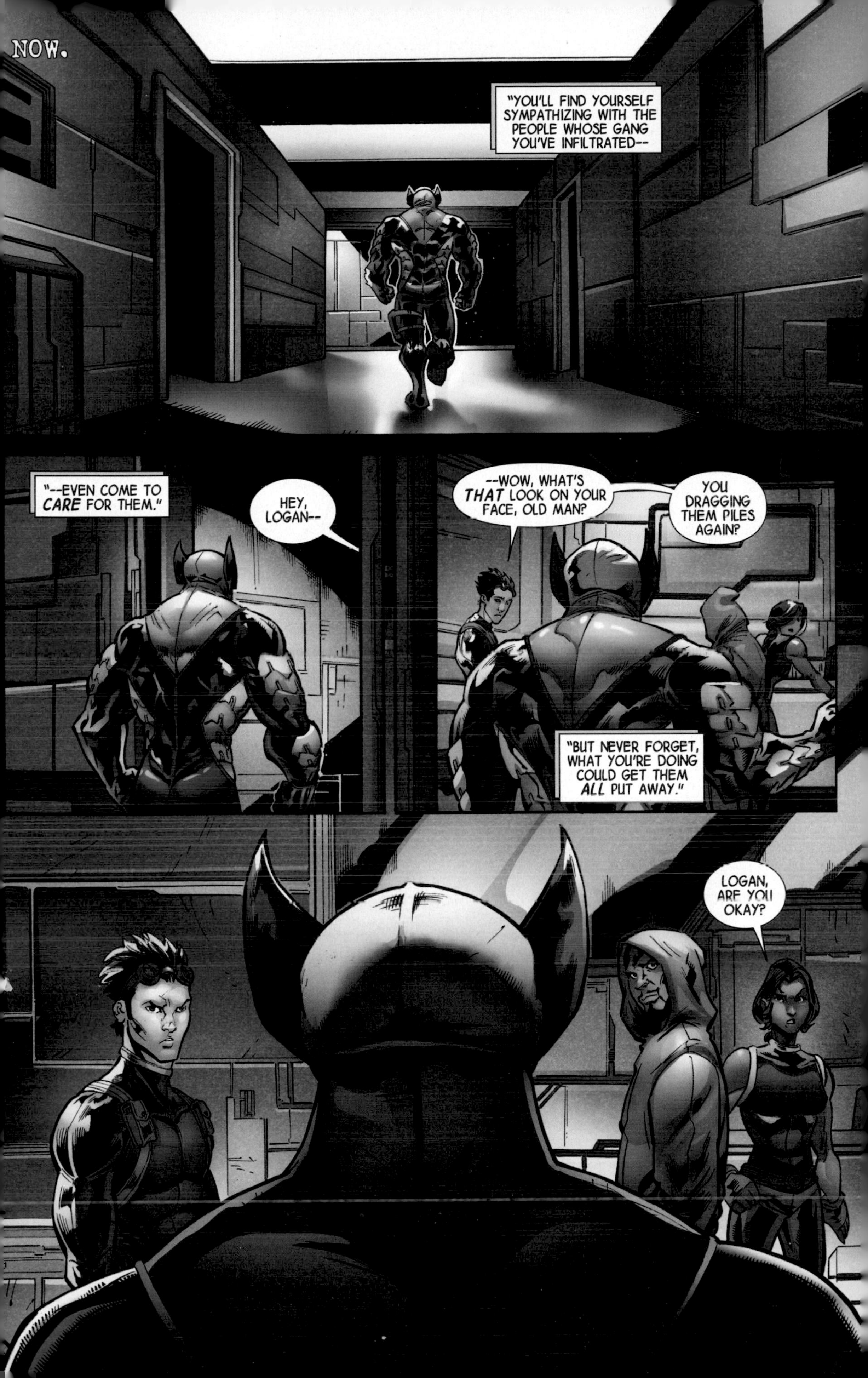
NOW.
"YOU'LL FIND YOURSELF SYMPATHIZING WITH THE PEOPLE WHOSE GANG YOU'VE INFILTRATED--
"--EVEN COME TO CARE FOR THEM."
HEY, LOGAN--
--WOW, WHAT'S THAT LOOK ON YOUR FACE, OLD MAN?
YOU DRAGGING THEM PILES AGAIN?
"BUT NEVER FORGET, WHAT YOU'RE DOING COULD GET THEM ALL PUT AWAY."
LOGAN, ARE YOU OKAY?

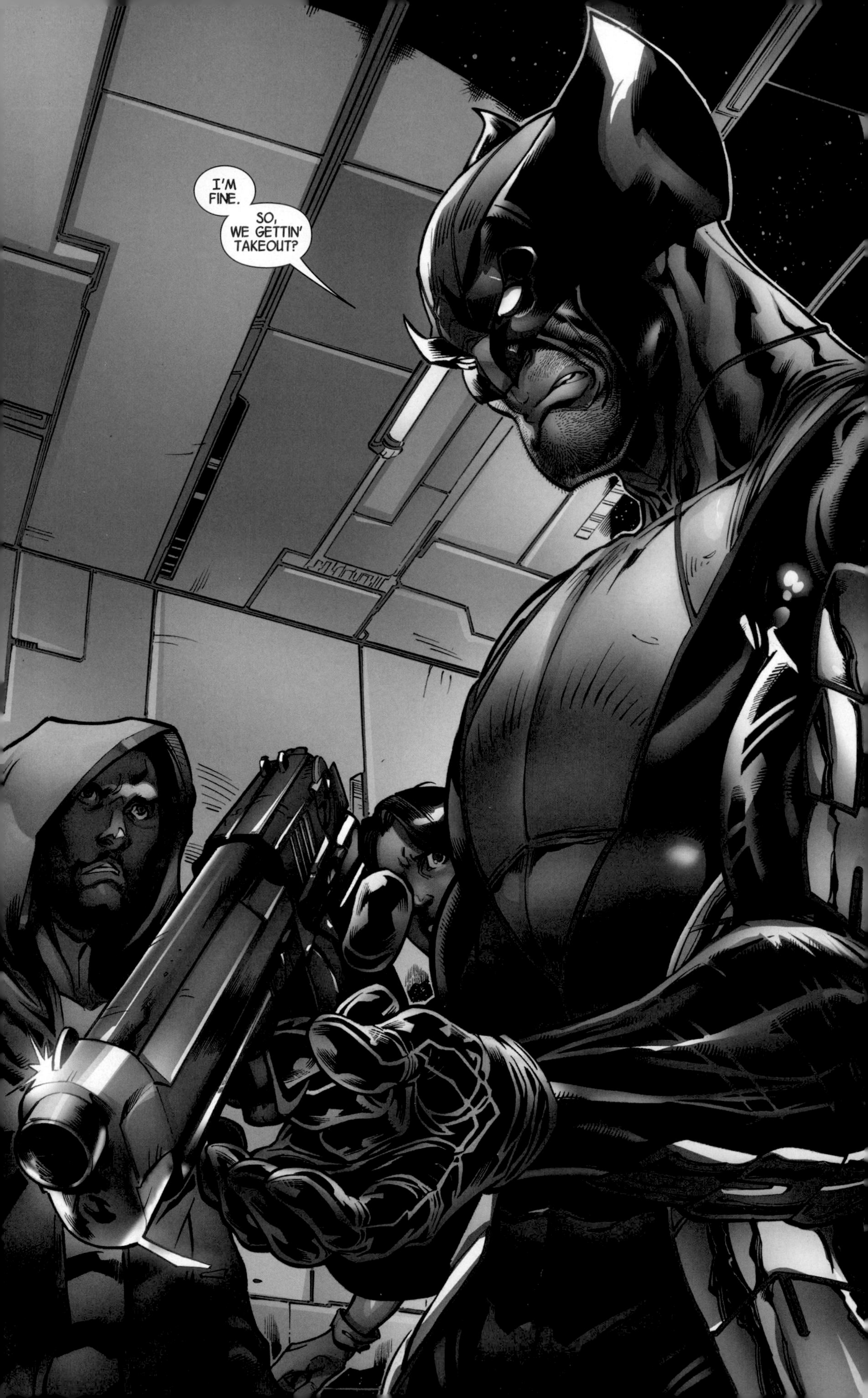
I'M FINE.
SO, WE GETTIN' TAKEOUT?

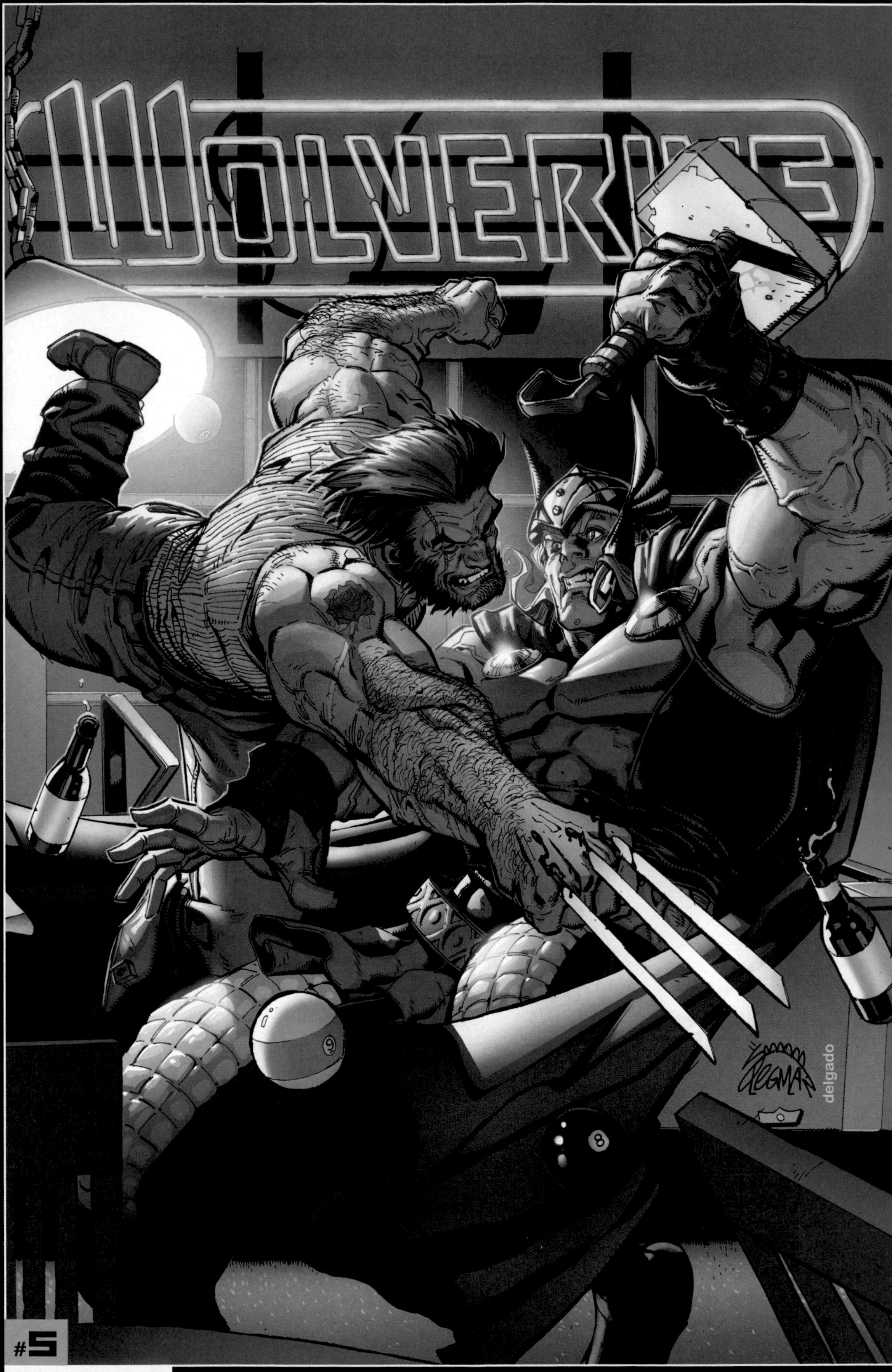
WOLVERINE
delgado

#5

HIS OWN SKIN

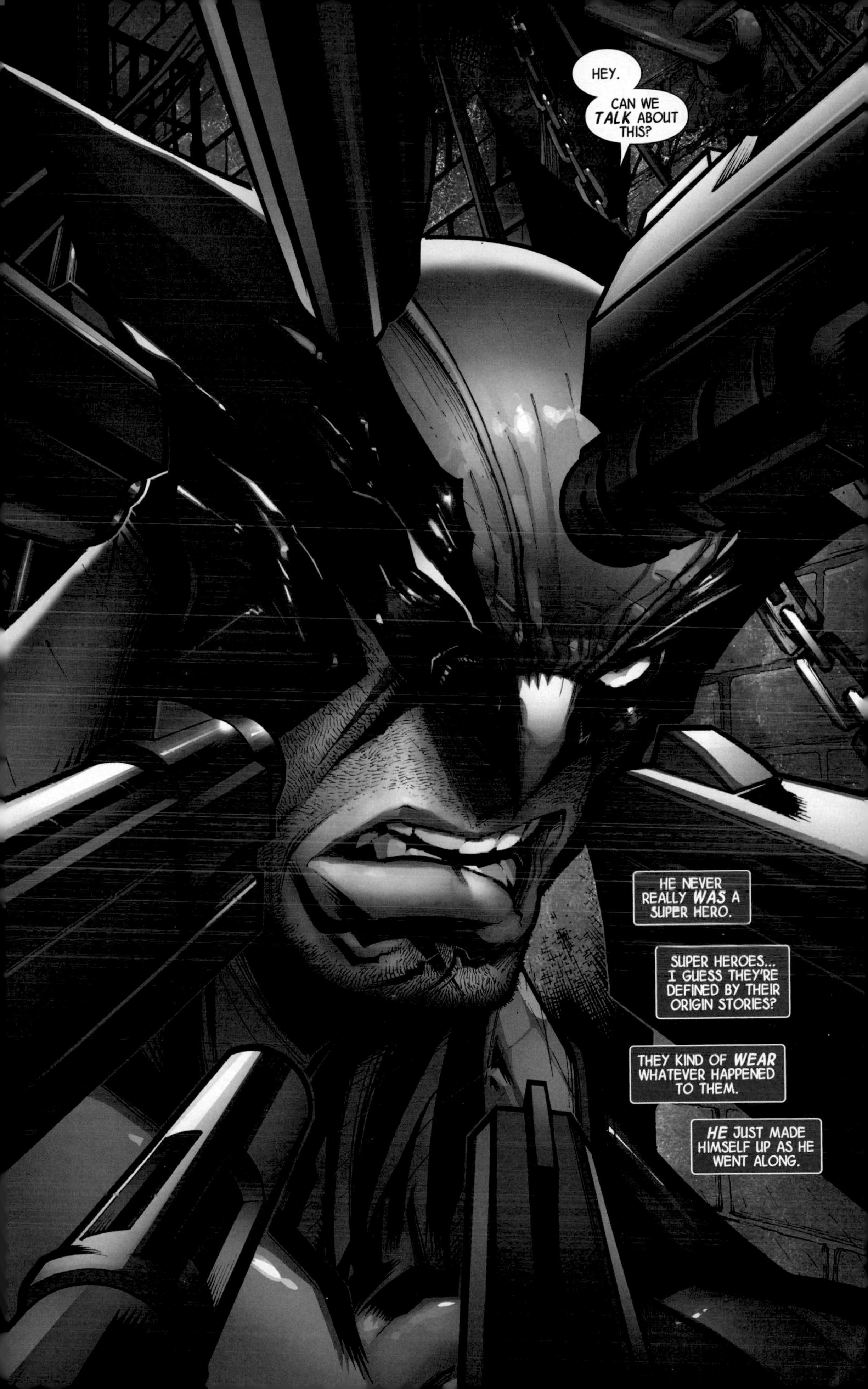
HEY.
CAN WE TALK ABOUT THIS?
HE NEVER REALLY WAS A SUPER HERO.
SUPER HEROES... I GUESS THEY'RE DEFINED BY THEIR ORIGIN STORIES?
THEY KIND OF WEAR WHATEVER HAPPENED TO THEM.
HE JUST MADE HIMSELF UP AS HE WENT ALONG.

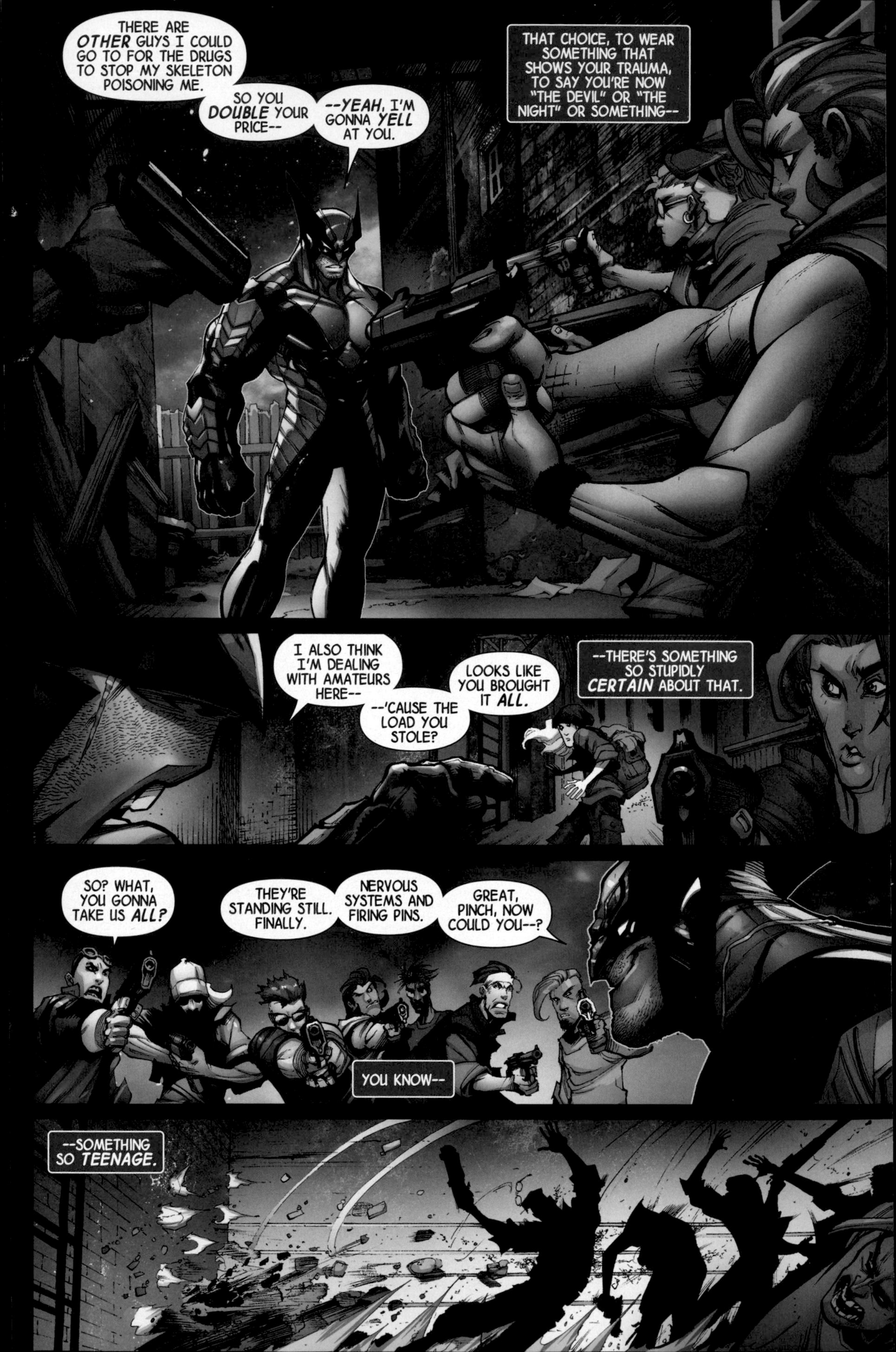

THERE ARE OTHER GUYS I COULD GO TO FOR THE DRUGS TO STOP MY SKELETON POISONING ME.
SO YOU DOUBLE YOUR PRICE--
--YEAH, I'M GONNA YELL AT YOU.
THAT CHOICE, TO WEAR SOMETHING THAT SHOWS YOUR TRAUMA, TO SAY YOU'RE NOW "THE DEVIL" OR "THE NIGHT" OR SOMETHING--
I ALSO THINK I'M DEALING WITH AMATEURS HERE--
--'CAUSE THE LOAD YOU STOLE?
LOOKS LIKE YOU BROUGHT IT ALL.
--THERE'S SOMETHING SO STUPIDLY CERTAIN ABOUT THAT.
SO? WHAT, YOU GONNA TAKE US ALL?
THEY'RE STANDING STILL. FINALLY.
NERVOUS SYSTEMS AND FIRING PINS.
GREAT, PINCH, NOW COULD YOU--?
YOU KNOW--
--SOMETHING SO TEENAGE.

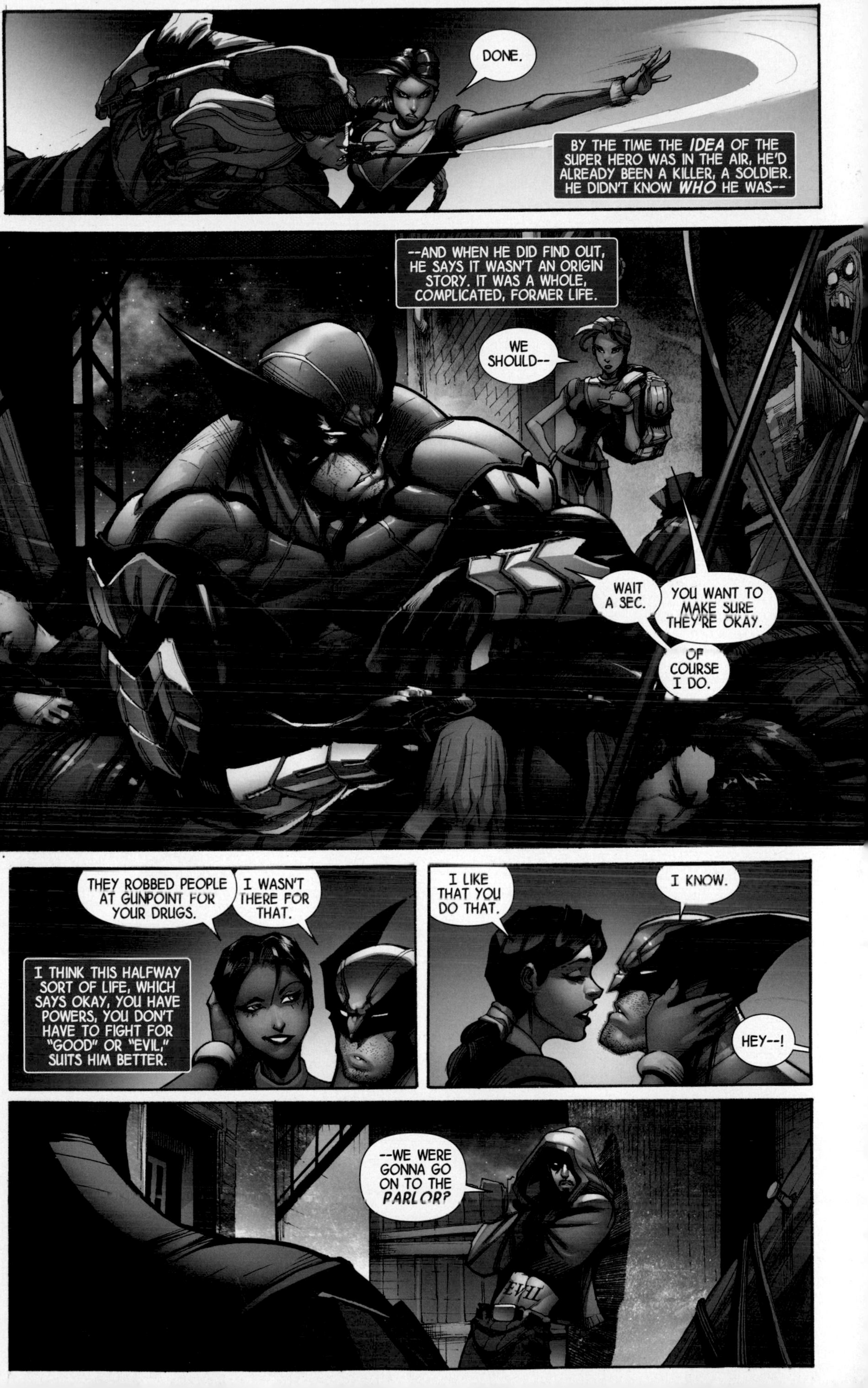
DONE.
BY THE TIME THE IDEA OF THE SUPER HERO WAS IN THE AIR, HE'D ALREADY BEEN A KILLER, A SOLDIER. HE DIDN'T KNOW WHO HE WAS--
--AND WHEN HE DID FIND OUT, HE SAYS IT WASN'T AN ORIGIN STORY. IT WAS A WHOLE, COMPLICATED, FORMER LIFE.
WE SHOULD--
WAIT A SEC.
YOU WANT TO MAKE SURE THEY'RE OKAY.
OF COURSE I DO.
THEY ROBBED PEOPLE AT GUNPOINT FOR YOUR DRUGS.
I WASN'T THERE FOR THAT.
I THINK THIS HALFWAY SORT OF LIFE, WHICH SAYS OKAY, YOU HAVE POWERS, YOU DON'T HAVE TO FIGHT FOR "GOOD" OR "EVIL," SUITS HIM BETTER.
I LIKE THAT YOU DO THAT.
I KNOW.
HEY--!
--WE WERE GONNA GO ON TO THE PARLOR?
EVIL

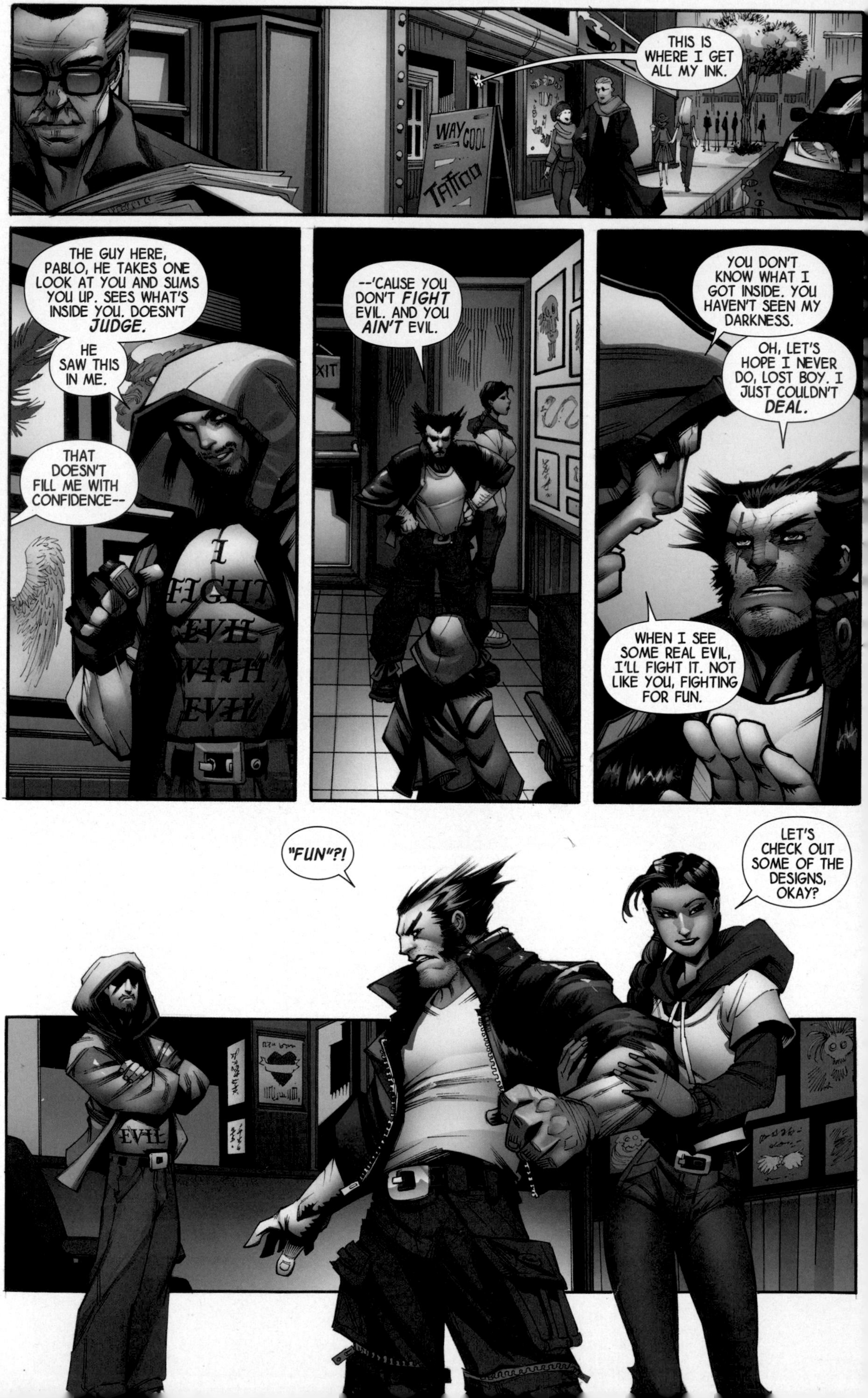

WAY COOL
TATTOO
THIS IS WHERE I GET ALL MY INK.
THE GUY HERE, PABLO, HE TAKES ONE LOOK AT YOU AND SUMS YOU UP. SEES WHAT'S INSIDE YOU. DOESN'T JUDGE.
HE SAW THIS IN ME.
I FIGHT EVIL WITH EVIL
THAT DOESN'T FILL ME WITH CONFIDENCE--
--'CAUSE YOU DON'T FIGHT EVIL. AND YOU AIN'T EVIL.
YOU DON'T KNOW WHAT I GOT INSIDE. YOU HAVEN'T SEEN MY DARKNESS.
OH, LET'S HOPE I NEVER DO, LOST BOY. I JUST COULDN'T DEAL.
WHEN I SEE SOME REAL EVIL, I'LL FIGHT IT. NOT LIKE YOU, FIGHTING FOR FUN.
"FUN"?!
LET'S CHECK OUT SOME OF THE DESIGNS, OKAY?
EVIL

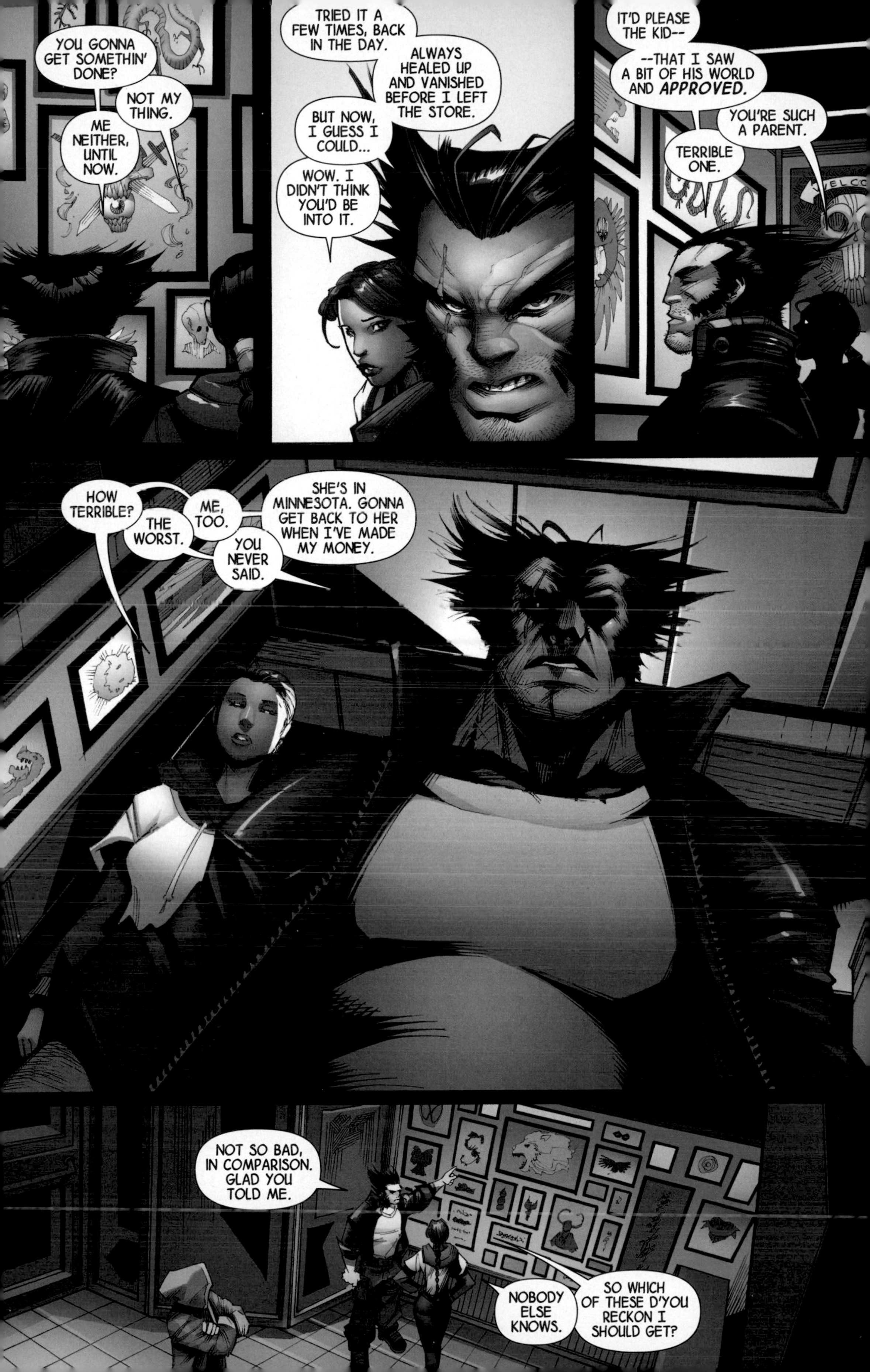
YOU GONNA GET SOMETHIN' DONE?
NOT MY THING.
ME NEITHER, UNTIL NOW.
TRIED IT A FEW TIMES, BACK IN THE DAY.
ALWAYS HEALED UP AND VANISHED BEFORE I LEFT THE STORE.
BUT NOW, I GUESS I COULD...
WOW. I DIDN'T THINK YOU'D BE INTO IT.
IT'D PLEASE THE KID--
--THAT I SAW A BIT OF HIS WORLD AND APPROVED.
YOU'RE SUCH A PARENT.
TERRIBLE ONE.
HOW TERRIBLE?
THE WORST.
ME, TOO.
YOU NEVER SAID.
SHE'S IN MINNESOTA. GONNA GET BACK TO HER WHEN I'VE MADE MY MONEY.
NOT SO BAD, IN COMPARISON. GLAD YOU TOLD ME.
NOBODY ELSE KNOWS.
SO WHICH OF THESE D'YOU RECKON I SHOULD GET?

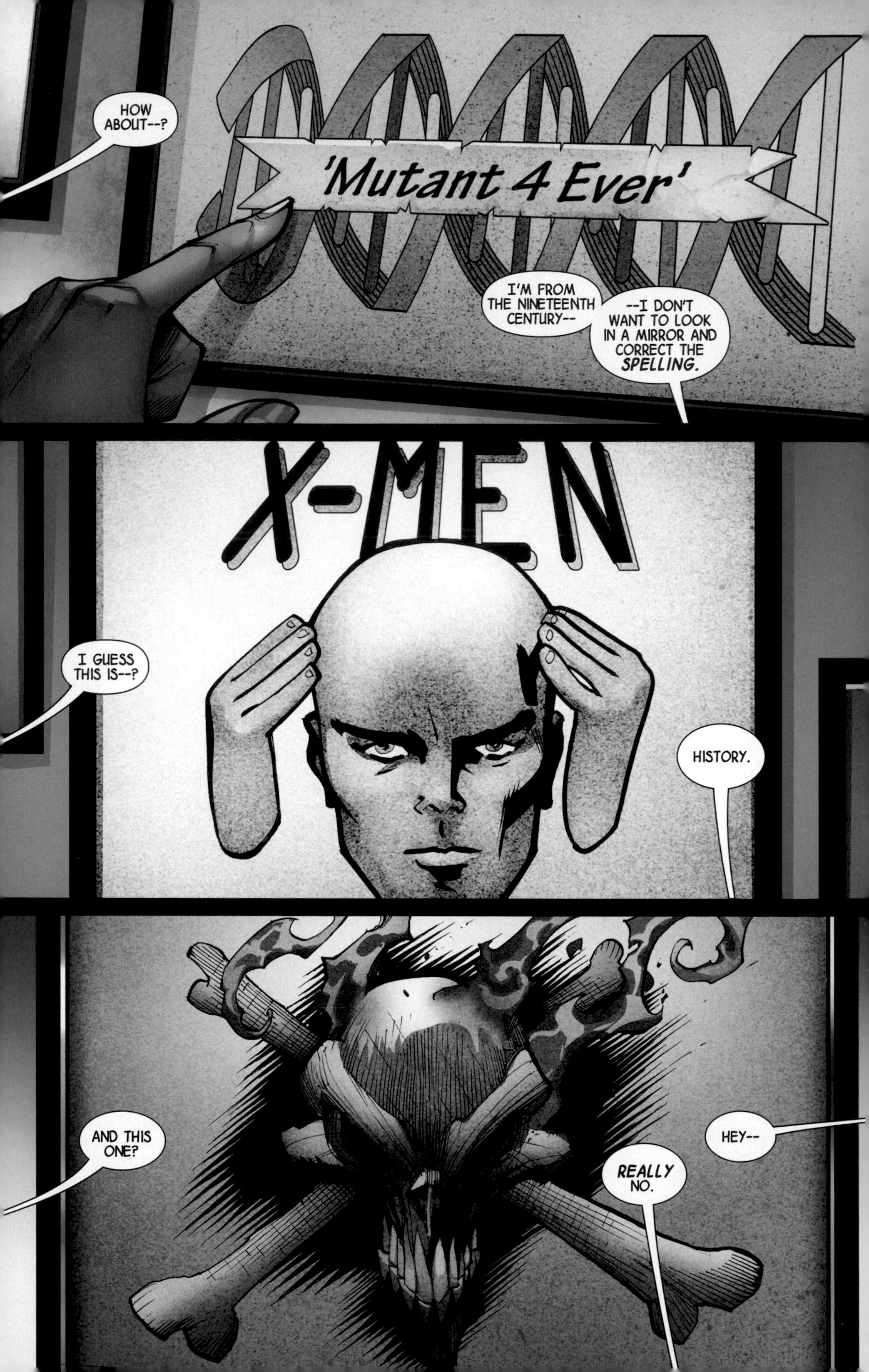
HOW ABOUT--?
'Mutant 4 Ever'
I'M FROM THE NINETEENTH CENTURY--
--I DON'T WANT TO LOOK IN A MIRROR AND CORRECT THE SPELLING.
X-MEN
I GUESS THIS IS--?
HISTORY.
AND THIS ONE?
HEY--
REALLY NO.

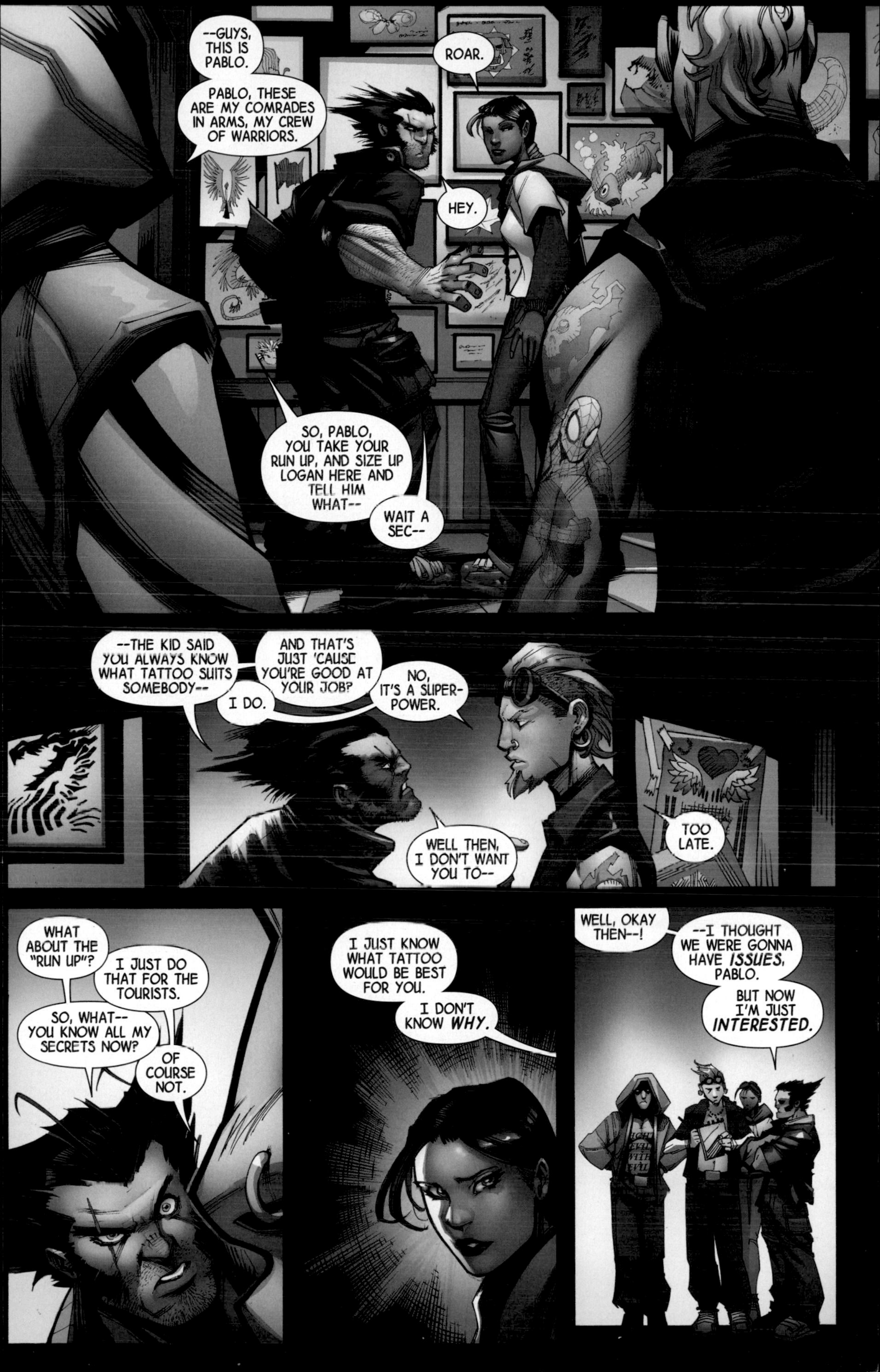
--GUYS, THIS IS PABLO.
PABLO, THESE ARE MY COMRADES IN ARMS, MY CREW OF WARRIORS.
ROAR.
HEY.
SO, PABLO, YOU TAKE YOUR RUN UP, AND SIZE UP LOGAN HERE AND TELL HIM WHAT--
WAIT A SEC--
--THE KID SAID YOU ALWAYS KNOW WHAT TATTOO SUITS SOMEBODY--
I DO.
AND THAT'S JUST 'CAUSE YOU'RE GOOD AT YOUR JOB?
NO, IT'S A SUPER-POWER.
WELL THEN, I DON'T WANT YOU TO--
TOO LATE.
WHAT ABOUT THE "RUN UP"?
I JUST DO THAT FOR THE TOURISTS.
SO, WHAT-- YOU KNOW ALL MY SECRETS NOW?
OF COURSE NOT.
I JUST KNOW WHAT TATTOO WOULD BE BEST FOR YOU.
I DON'T KNOW WHY.
WELL, OKAY THEN--!
--I THOUGHT WE WERE GONNA HAVE ISSUES, PABLO.
BUT NOW I'M JUST INTERESTED.

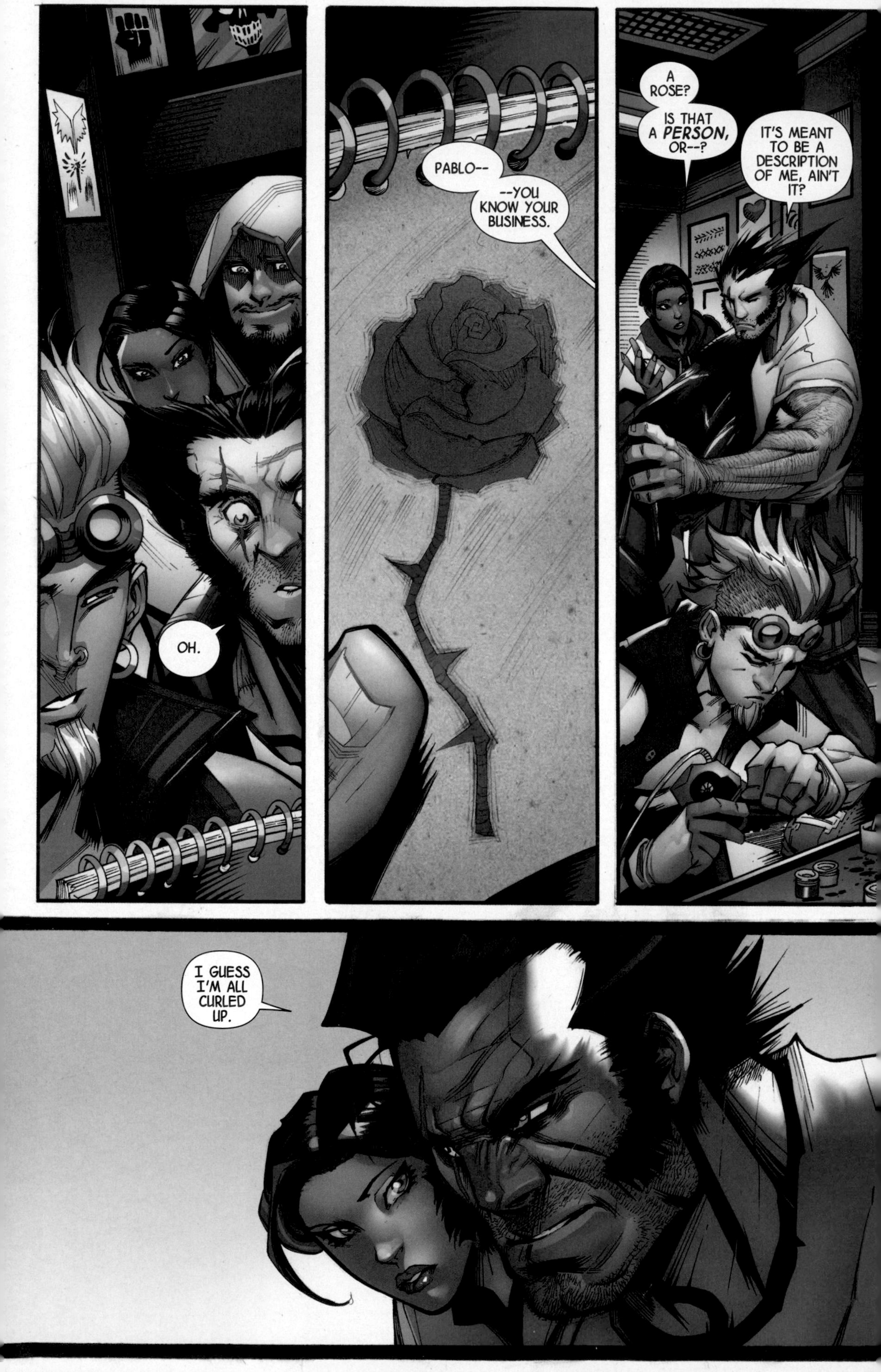
OH.
PABLO--
--YOU KNOW YOUR BUSINESS.
A ROSE?
IS THAT A PERSON, OR--?
IT'S MEANT TO BE A DESCRIPTION OF ME, AIN'T IT?
I GUESS I'M ALL CURLED UP.

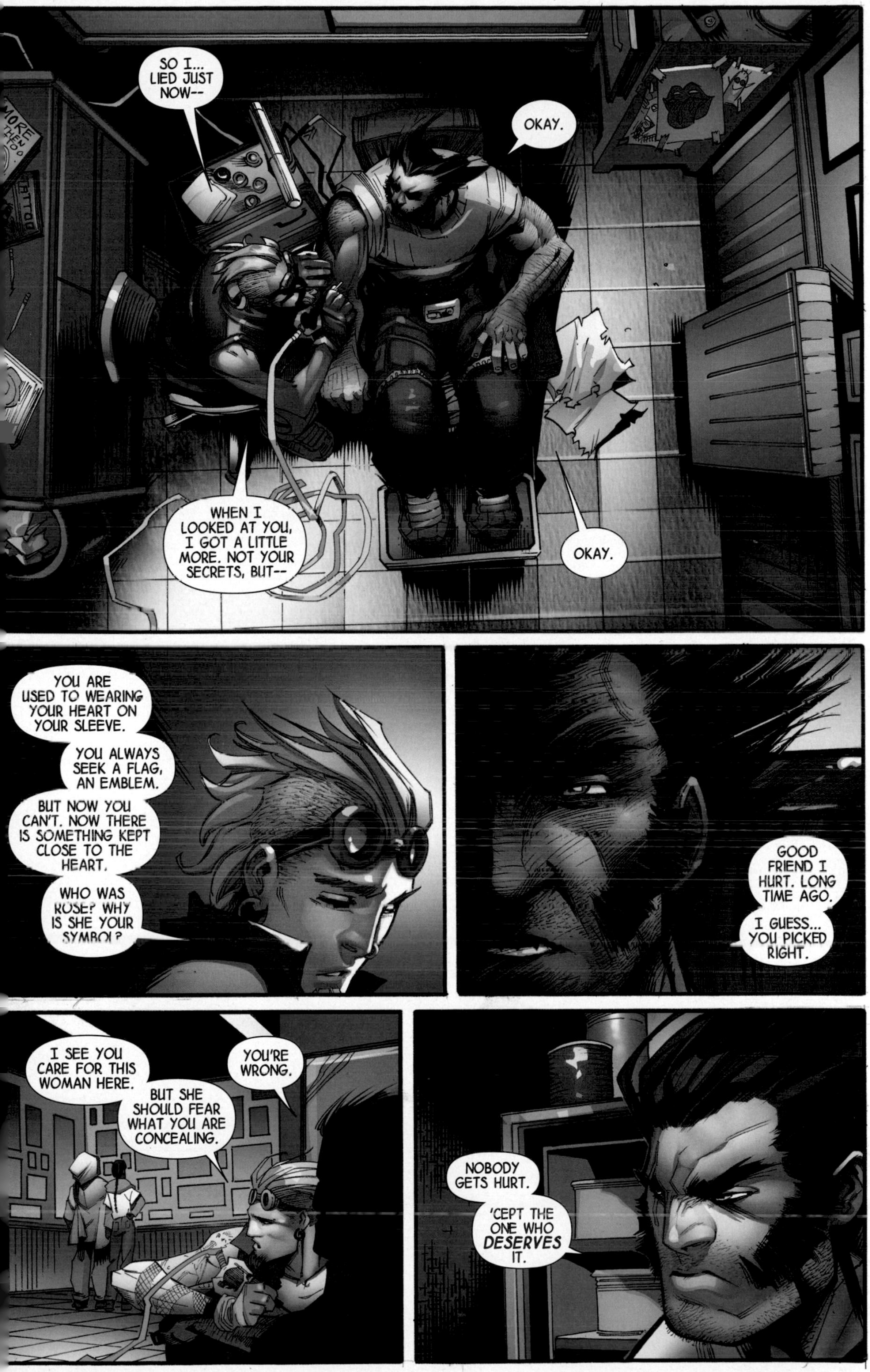
SO I... LIED JUST NOW--
OKAY.
WHEN I LOOKED AT YOU, I GOT A LITTLE MORE. NOT YOUR SECRETS, BUT--
OKAY.
YOU ARE USED TO WEARING YOUR HEART ON YOUR SLEEVE.
YOU ALWAYS SEEK A FLAG, AN EMBLEM.
BUT NOW YOU CAN'T. NOW THERE IS SOMETHING KEPT CLOSE TO THE HEART.
WHO WAS ROSE? WHY IS SHE YOUR SYMBOL?
GOOD FRIEND I HURT. LONG TIME AGO.
I GUESS... YOU PICKED RIGHT.
I SEE YOU CARE FOR THIS WOMAN HERE.
BUT SHE SHOULD FEAR WHAT YOU ARE CONCEALING.
YOU'RE WRONG.
NOBODY GETS HURT.
'CEPT THE ONE WHO DESERVES IT.

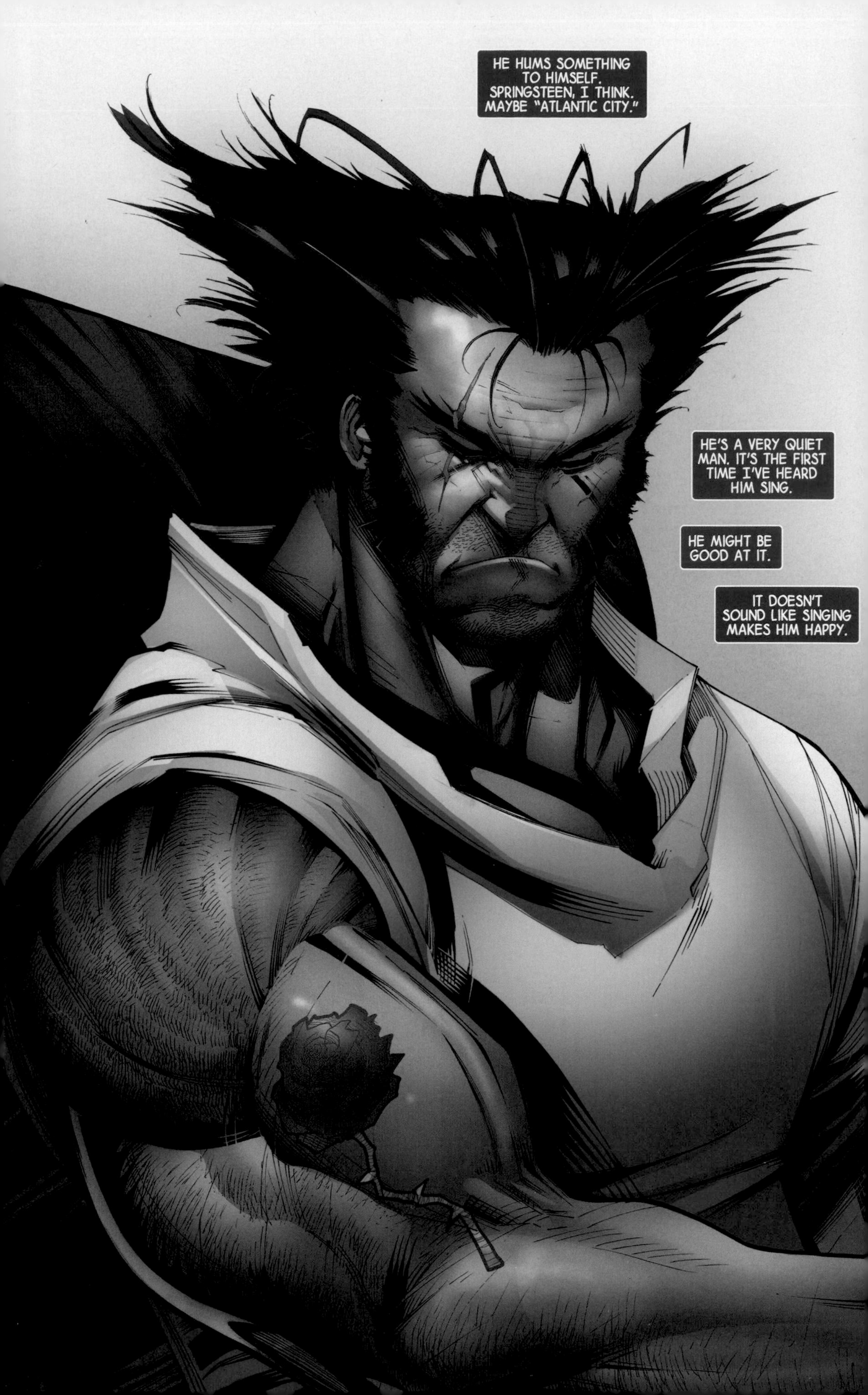
HE HUMS SOMETHING TO HIMSELF. SPRINGSTEEN, I THINK. MAYBE "ATLANTIC CITY."
HE'S A VERY QUIET MAN. IT'S THE FIRST TIME I'VE HEARD HIM SING.
HE MIGHT BE GOOD AT IT.
IT DOESN'T SOUND LIKE SINGING MAKES HIM HAPPY.

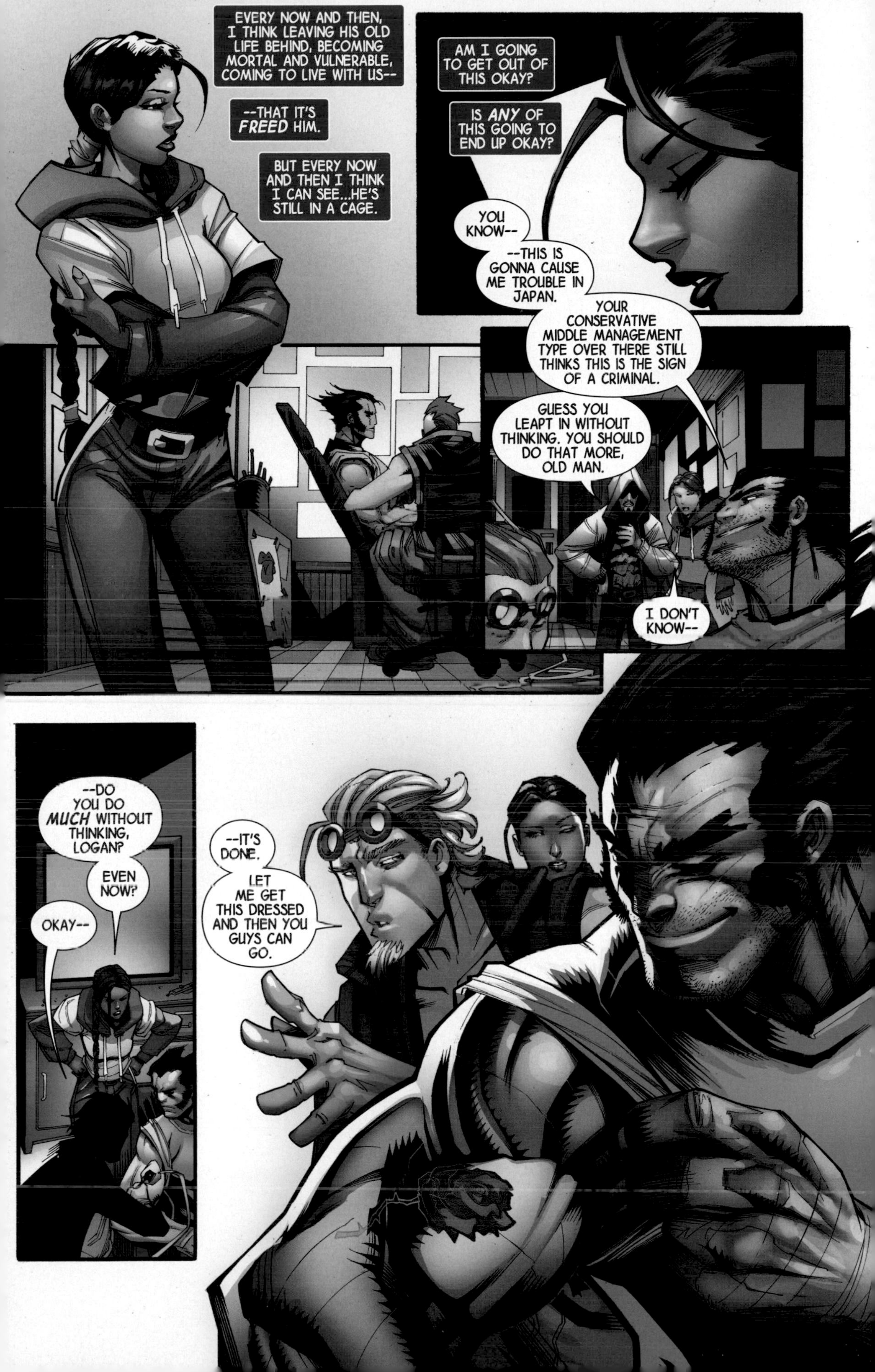
EVERY NOW AND THEN, I THINK LEAVING HIS OLD LIFE BEHIND, BECOMING MORTAL AND VULNERABLE, COMING TO LIVE WITH US--
--THAT IT'S FREED HIM.
BUT EVERY NOW AND THEN I THINK I CAN SEE...HE'S STILL IN A CAGE.
AM I GOING TO GET OUT OF THIS OKAY?
IS ANY OF THIS GOING TO END UP OKAY?
YOU KNOW--
--THIS IS GONNA CAUSE ME TROUBLE IN JAPAN.
YOUR CONSERVATIVE MIDDLE MANAGEMENT TYPE OVER THERE STILL THINKS THIS IS THE SIGN OF A CRIMINAL.
GUESS YOU LEAPT IN WITHOUT THINKING. YOU SHOULD DO THAT MORE, OLD MAN.
I DON'T KNOW--
--DO YOU DO MUCH WITHOUT THINKING, LOGAN?
EVEN NOW?
OKAY--
--IT'S DONE.
LET ME GET THIS DRESSED AND THEN YOU GUYS CAN GO.

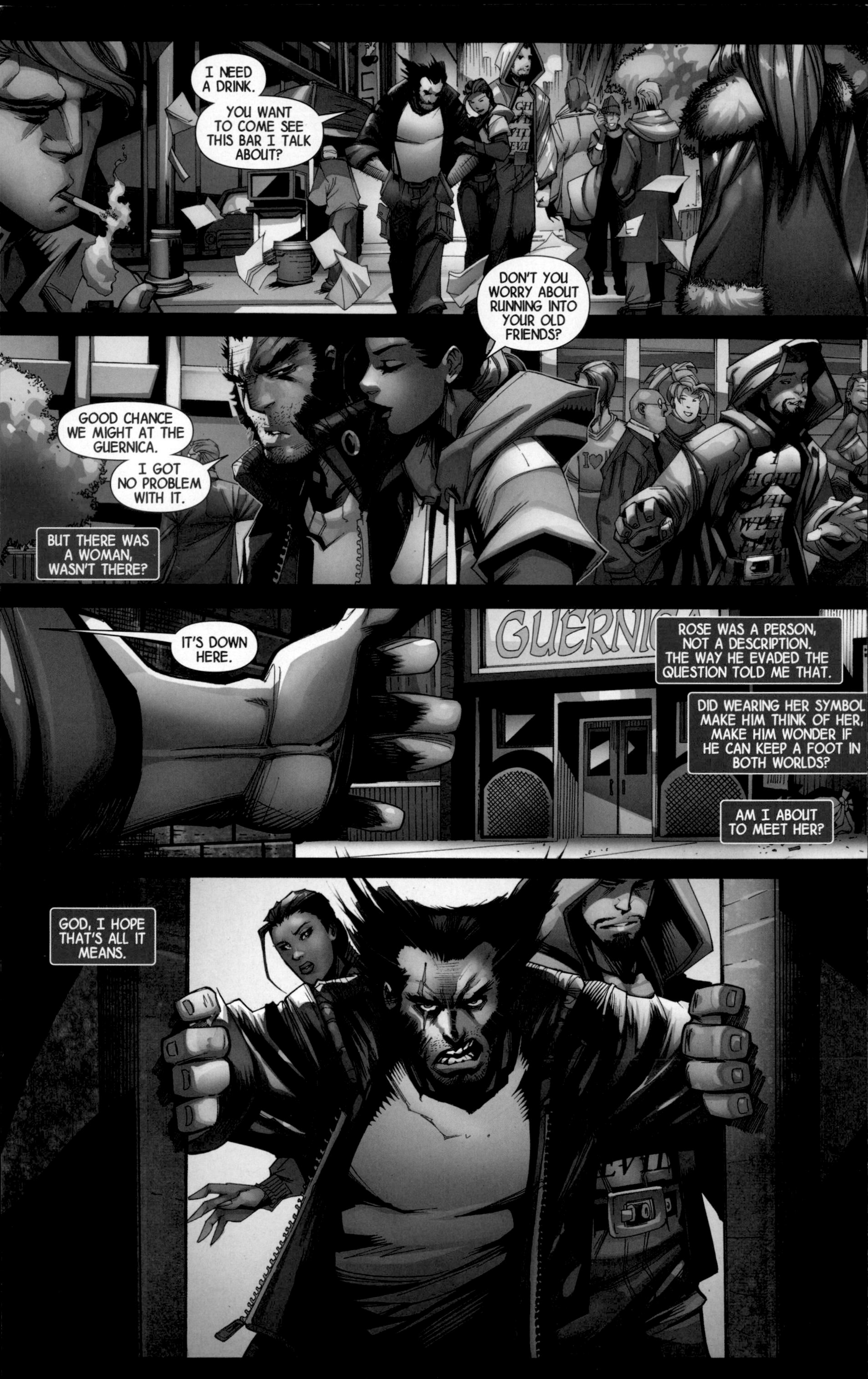

I NEED A DRINK.
YOU WANT TO COME SEE THIS BAR I TALK ABOUT?
DON'T YOU WORRY ABOUT RUNNING INTO YOUR OLD FRIENDS?
GOOD CHANCE WE MIGHT AT THE GUERNICA.
I GOT NO PROBLEM WITH IT.
BUT THERE WAS A WOMAN, WASN'T THERE?
IT'S DOWN HERE.
GUERNIC
ROSE WAS A PERSON, NOT A DESCRIPTION. THE WAY HE EVADED THE QUESTION TOLD ME THAT.
DID WEARING HER SYMBOL MAKE HIM THINK OF HER, MAKE HIM WONDER IF HE CAN KEEP A FOOT IN BOTH WORLDS?
AM I ABOUT TO MEET HER?
GOD, I HOPE THAT'S ALL IT MEANS.

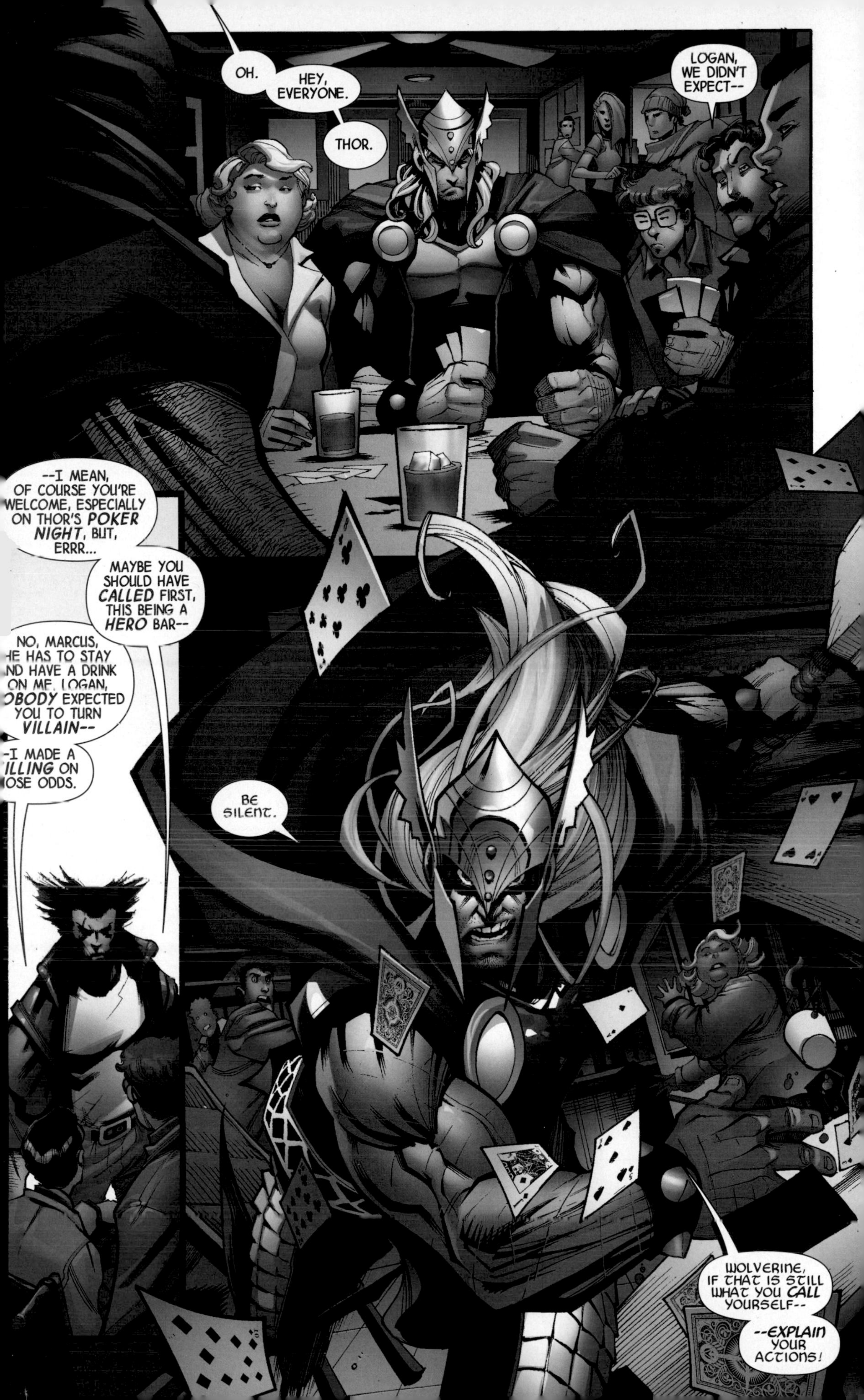

OH.
HEY, EVERYONE.
THOR.
LOGAN, WE DIDN'T EXPECT--
--I MEAN, OF COURSE YOU'RE WELCOME, ESPECIALLY ON THOR'S POKER NIGHT, BUT, ERRR...
MAYBE YOU SHOULD HAVE CALLED FIRST, THIS BEING A HERO BAR--
NO, MARCUS, HE HAS TO STAY AND HAVE A DRINK ON ME. LOGAN, NOBODY EXPECTED YOU TO TURN VILLAIN--
--I MADE A KILLING ON THOSE ODDS.
BE SILENT.
WOLVERINE, IF THAT IS STILL WHAT YOU CALL YOURSELF--
--EXPLAIN YOUR ACTIONS!

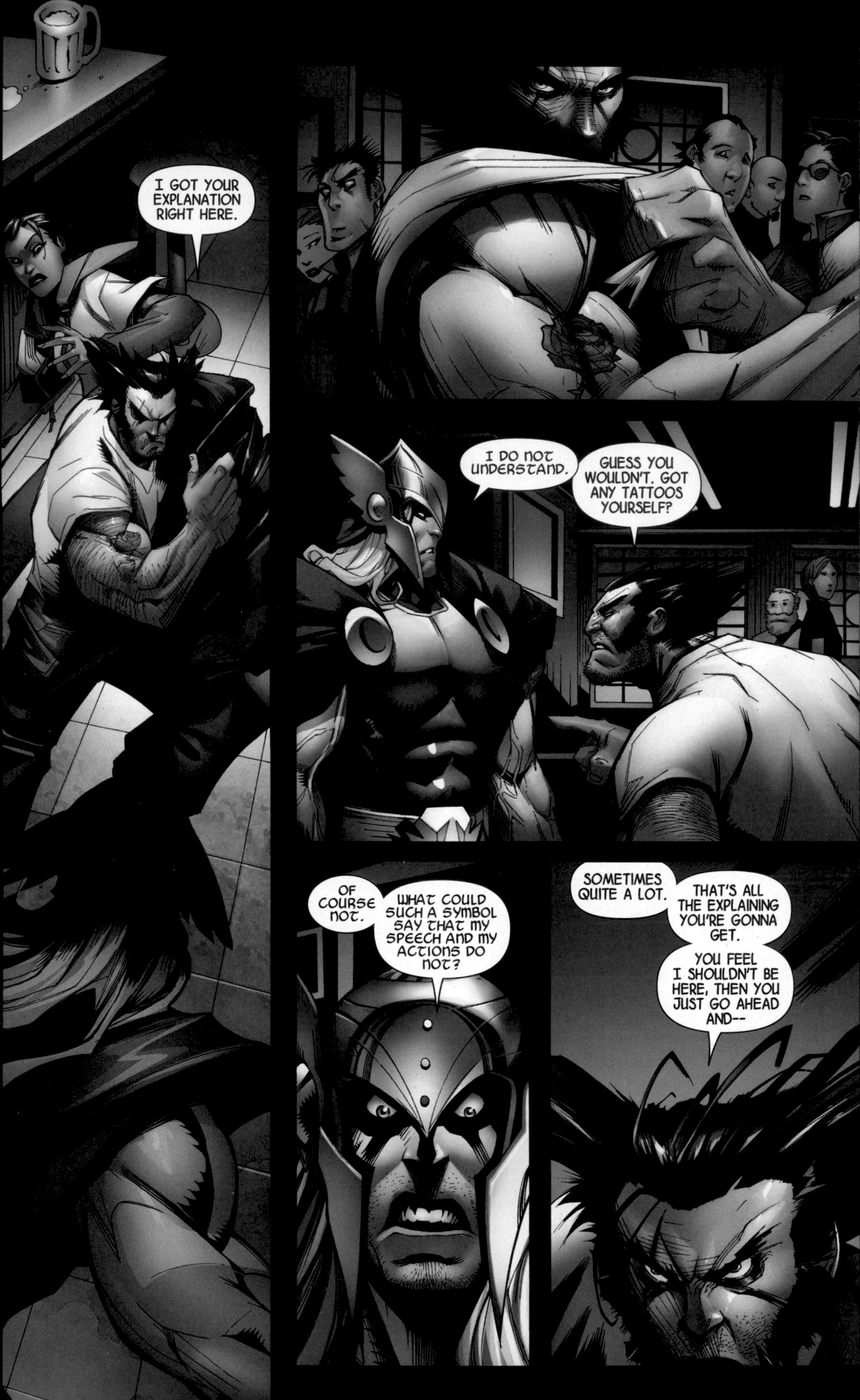
I GOT YOUR EXPLANATION RIGHT HERE.
I DO NOT UNDERSTAND.
GUESS YOU WOULDN'T. GOT ANY TATTOOS YOURSELF?
OF COURSE NOT.
WHAT COULD SUCH A SYMBOL SAY THAT MY SPEECH AND MY ACTIONS DO NOT?
SOMETIMES QUITE A LOT.
THAT'S ALL THE EXPLAINING YOU'RE GONNA GET.
YOU FEEL I SHOULDN'T BE HERE, THEN YOU JUST GO AHEAD AND--

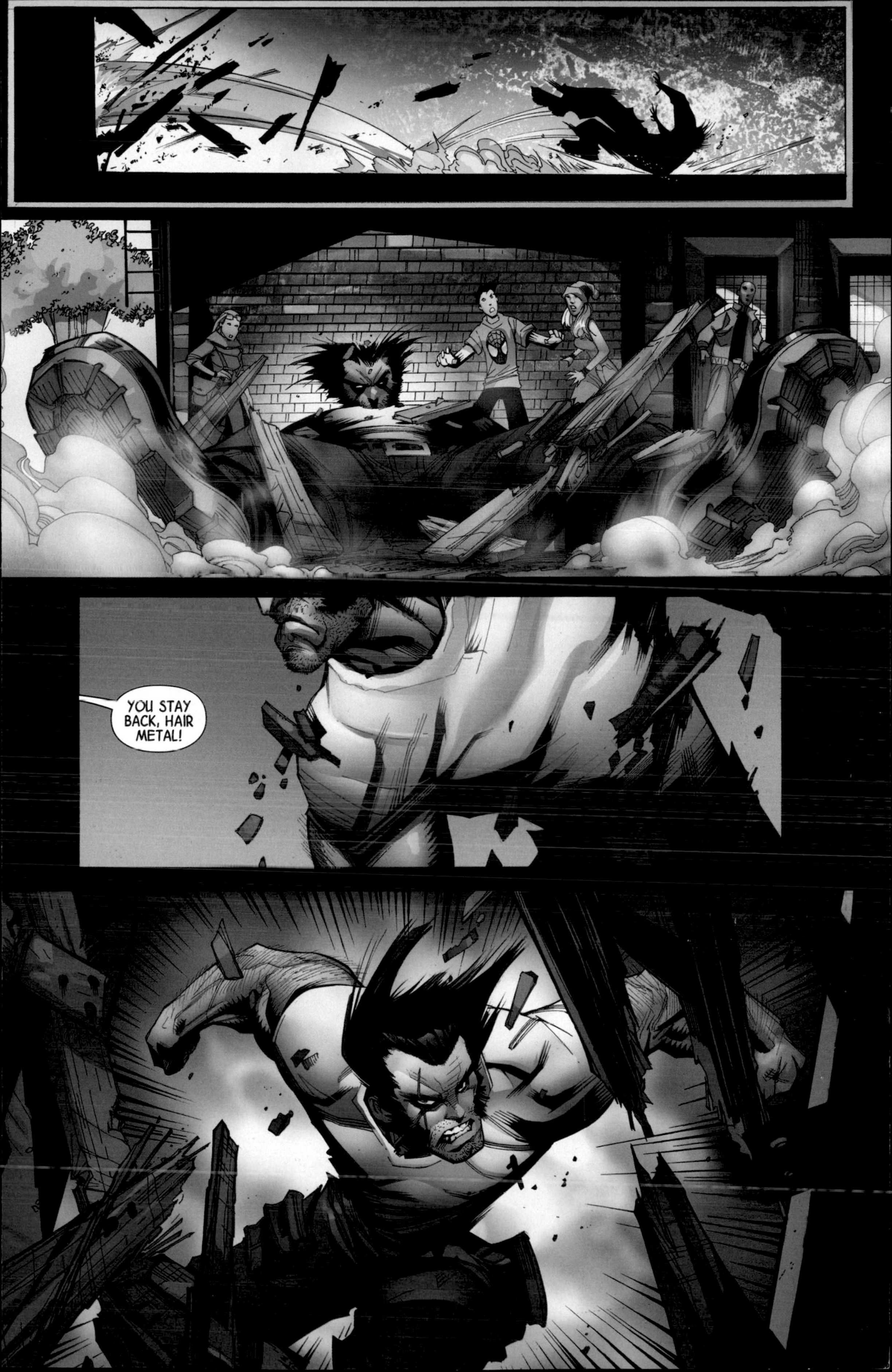
YOU STAY BACK, HAIR METAL!

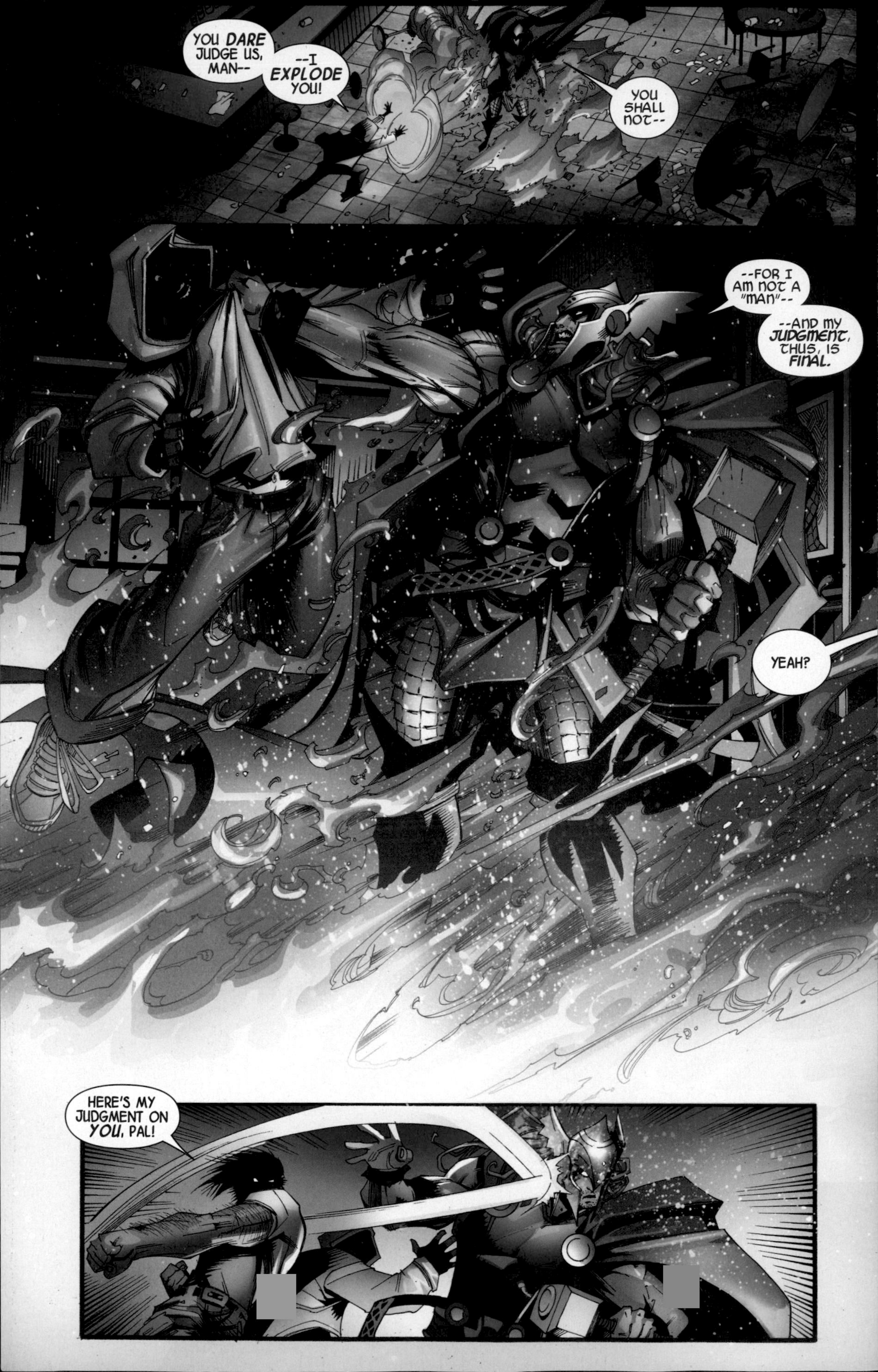
YOU DARE JUDGE US, MAN--
--I EXPLODE YOU!
YOU SHALL NOT--
--FOR I AM NOT A "MAN"--
--AND MY JUDGMENT, THUS, IS FINAL.
YEAH?
HERE'S MY JUDGMENT ON YOU, PAL!

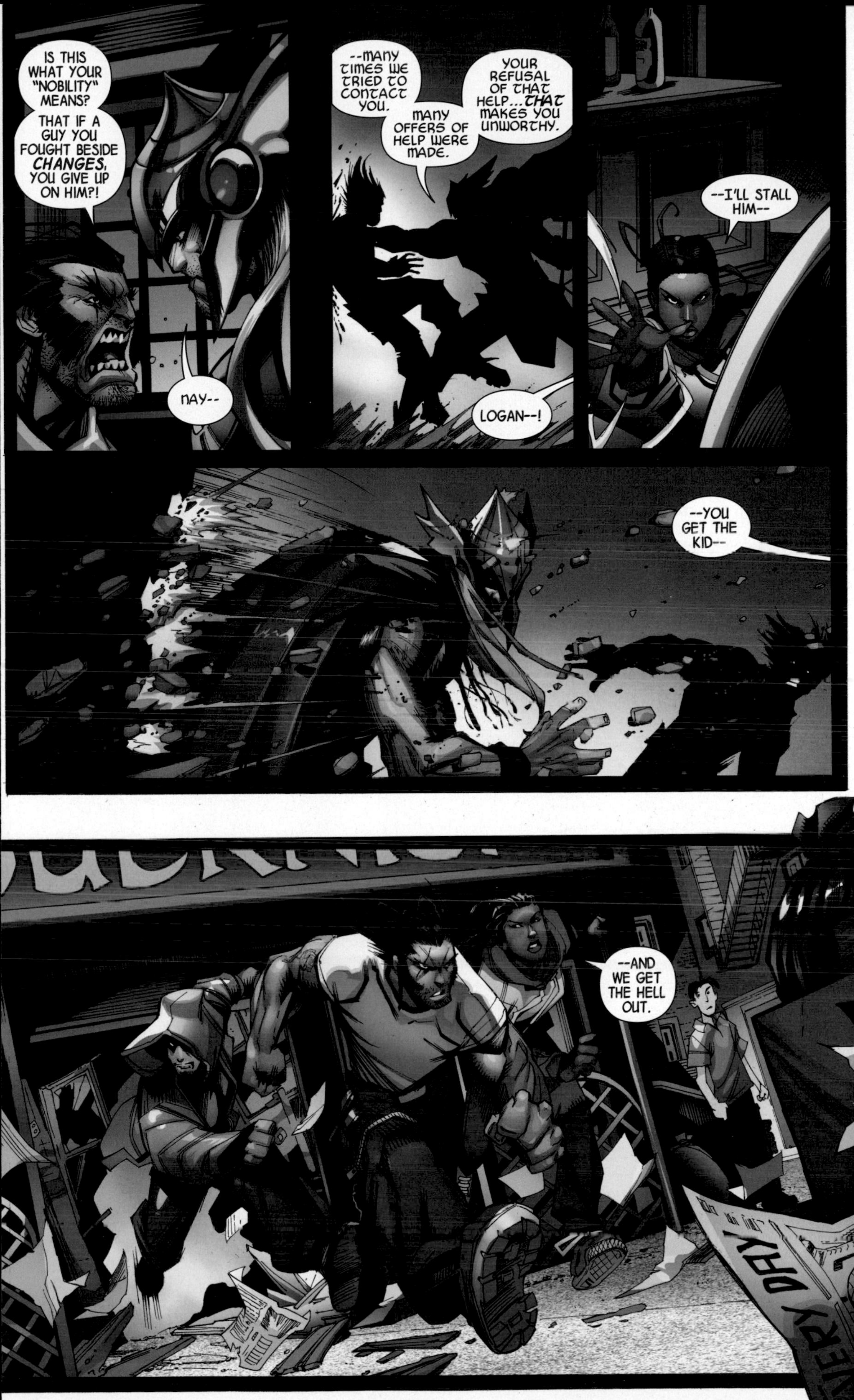

IS THIS WHAT YOUR "NOBILITY" MEANS?
THAT IF A GUY YOU FOUGHT BESIDE *CHANGES*, YOU GIVE UP ON HIM?!
NAY--
--MANY TIMES WE TRIED TO CONTACT YOU.
MANY OFFERS OF HELP WERE MADE.
YOUR REFUSAL OF THAT HELP...*THAT* MAKES YOU UNWORTHY.
LOGAN--!
--I'LL STALL HIM--
--YOU GET THE KID--
--AND WE GET THE HELL OUT.

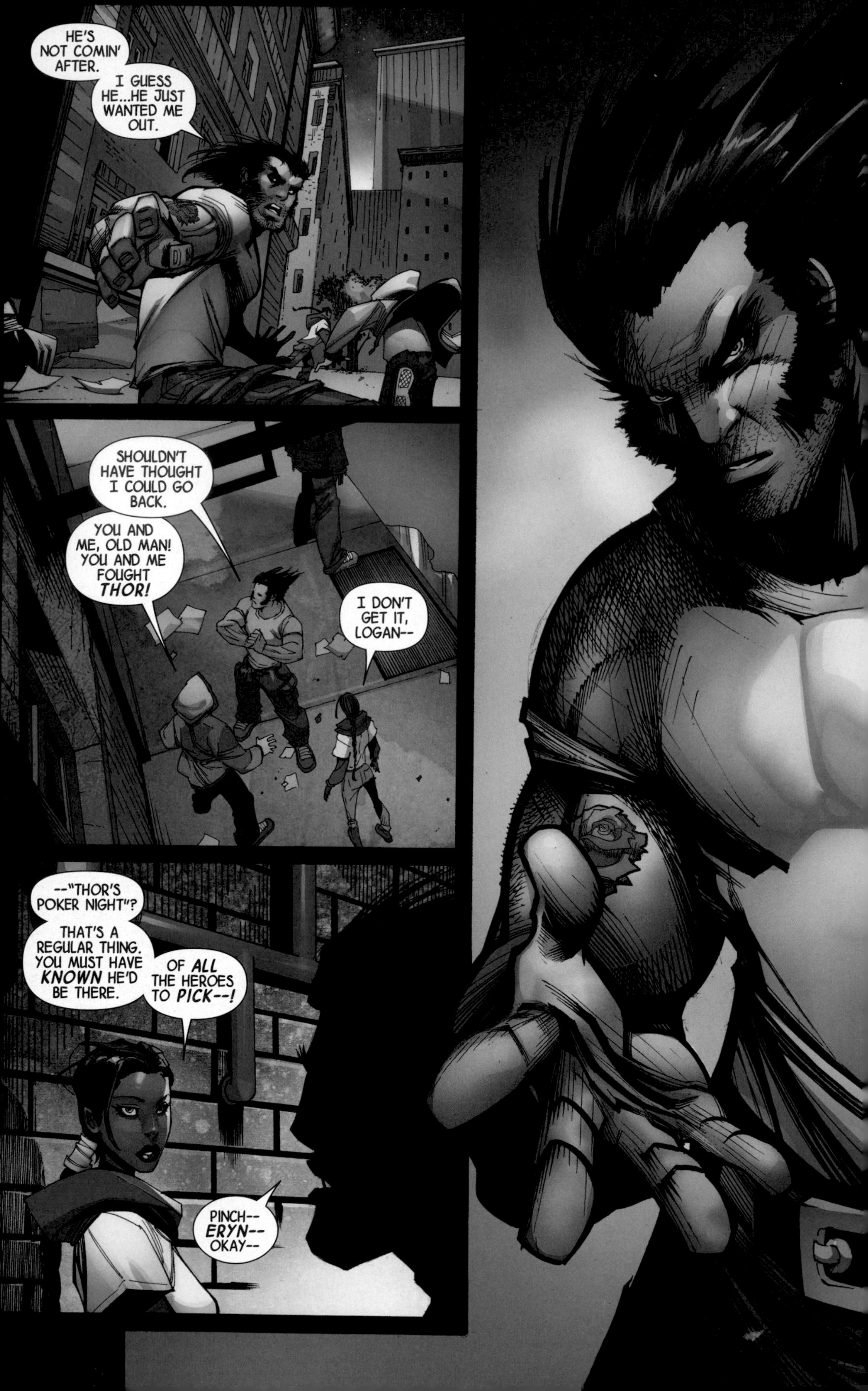
HE'S NOT COMIN' AFTER.
I GUESS HE...HE JUST WANTED ME OUT.
SHOULDN'T HAVE THOUGHT I COULD GO BACK.
YOU AND ME, OLD MAN! YOU AND ME FOUGHT THOR!
I DON'T GET IT, LOGAN--
--"THOR'S POKER NIGHT"?
THAT'S A REGULAR THING. YOU MUST HAVE KNOWN HE'D BE THERE.
OF ALL THE HEROES TO PICK--!
PINCH-- ERYN-- OKAY--

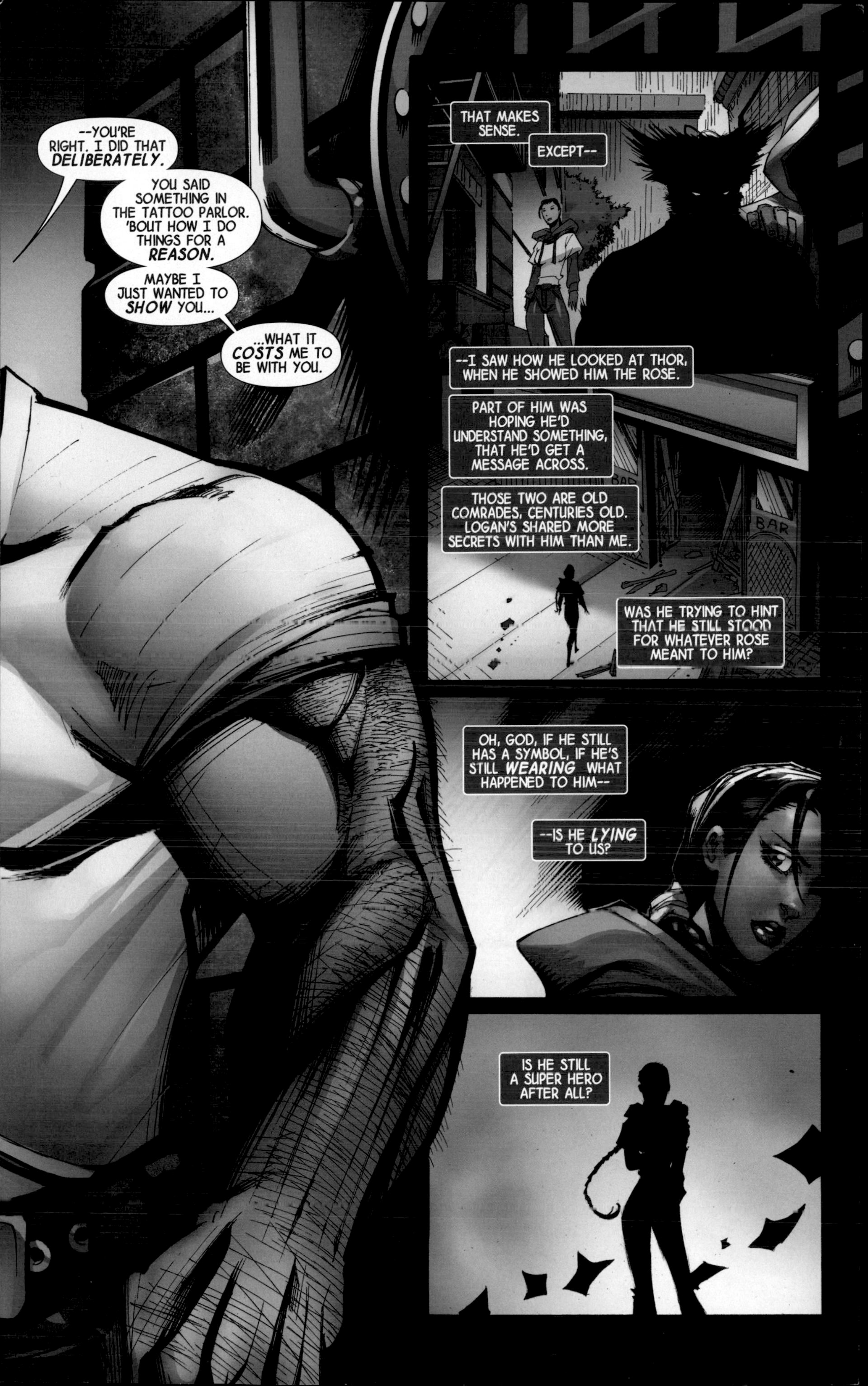

--YOU'RE RIGHT. I DID THAT DELIBERATELY.
YOU SAID SOMETHING IN THE TATTOO PARLOR. 'BOUT HOW I DO THINGS FOR A REASON.
MAYBE I JUST WANTED TO SHOW YOU...
...WHAT IT COSTS ME TO BE WITH YOU.
THAT MAKES SENSE.
EXCEPT--
--I SAW HOW HE LOOKED AT THOR, WHEN HE SHOWED HIM THE ROSE.
PART OF HIM WAS HOPING HE'D UNDERSTAND SOMETHING, THAT HE'D GET A MESSAGE ACROSS.
THOSE TWO ARE OLD COMRADES, CENTURIES OLD. LOGAN'S SHARED MORE SECRETS WITH HIM THAN ME.
BAR
BAR
WAS HE TRYING TO HINT THAT HE STILL STOOD FOR WHATEVER ROSE MEANT TO HIM?
OH, GOD, IF HE STILL HAS A SYMBOL, IF HE'S STILL WEARING WHAT HAPPENED TO HIM--
--IS HE LYING TO US?
IS HE STILL A SUPER HERO AFTER ALL?

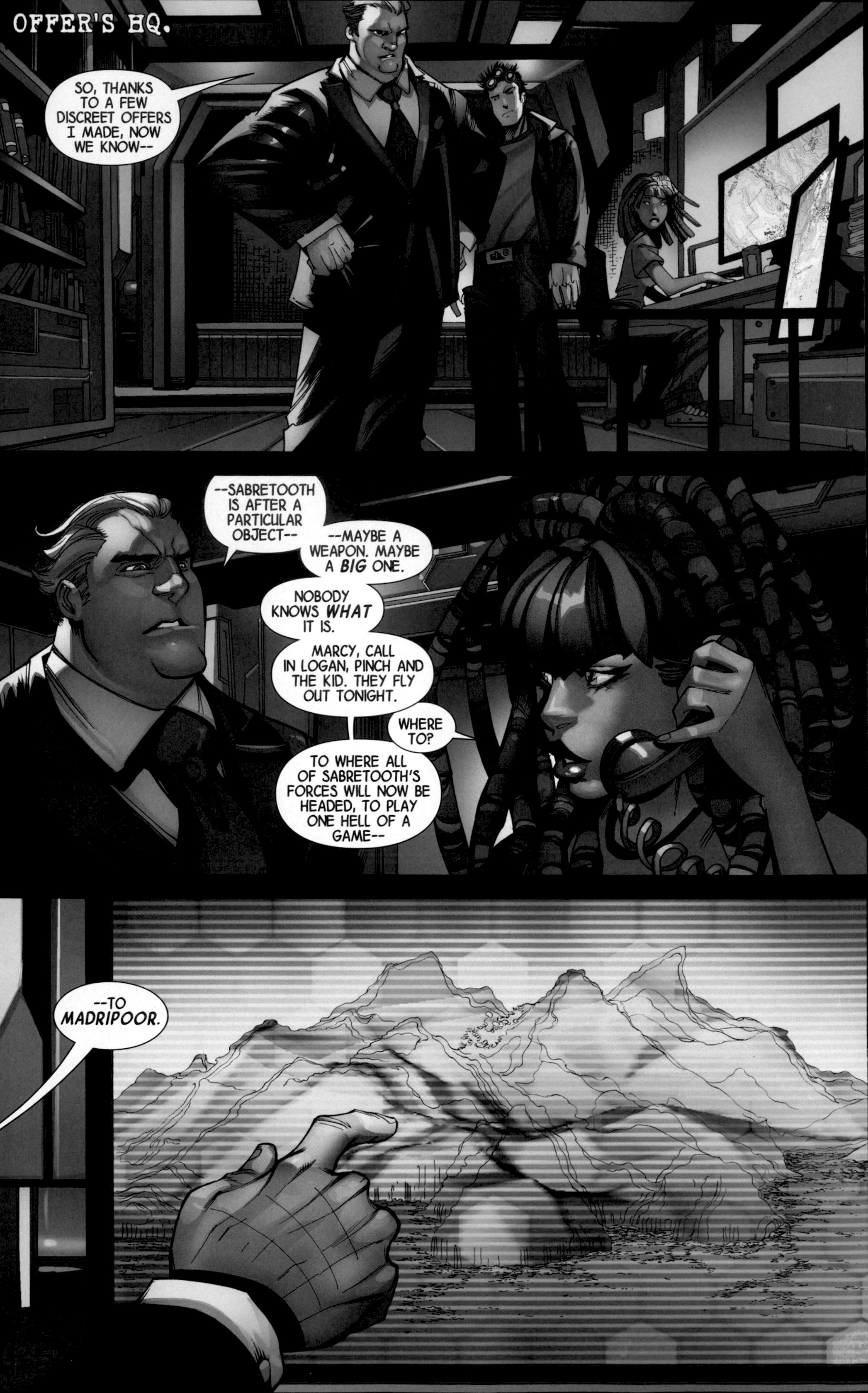
OFFER'S HQ.
SO, THANKS TO A FEW DISCREET OFFERS I MADE, NOW WE KNOW--
--SABRETOOTH IS AFTER A PARTICULAR OBJECT--
--MAYBE A WEAPON. MAYBE A BIG ONE.
NOBODY KNOWS WHAT IT IS.
MARCY, CALL IN LOGAN, PINCH AND THE KID. THEY FLY OUT TONIGHT.
WHERE TO?
TO WHERE ALL OF SABRETOOTH'S FORCES WILL NOW BE HEADED, TO PLAY ONE HELL OF A GAME--
--TO MADRIPOOR.

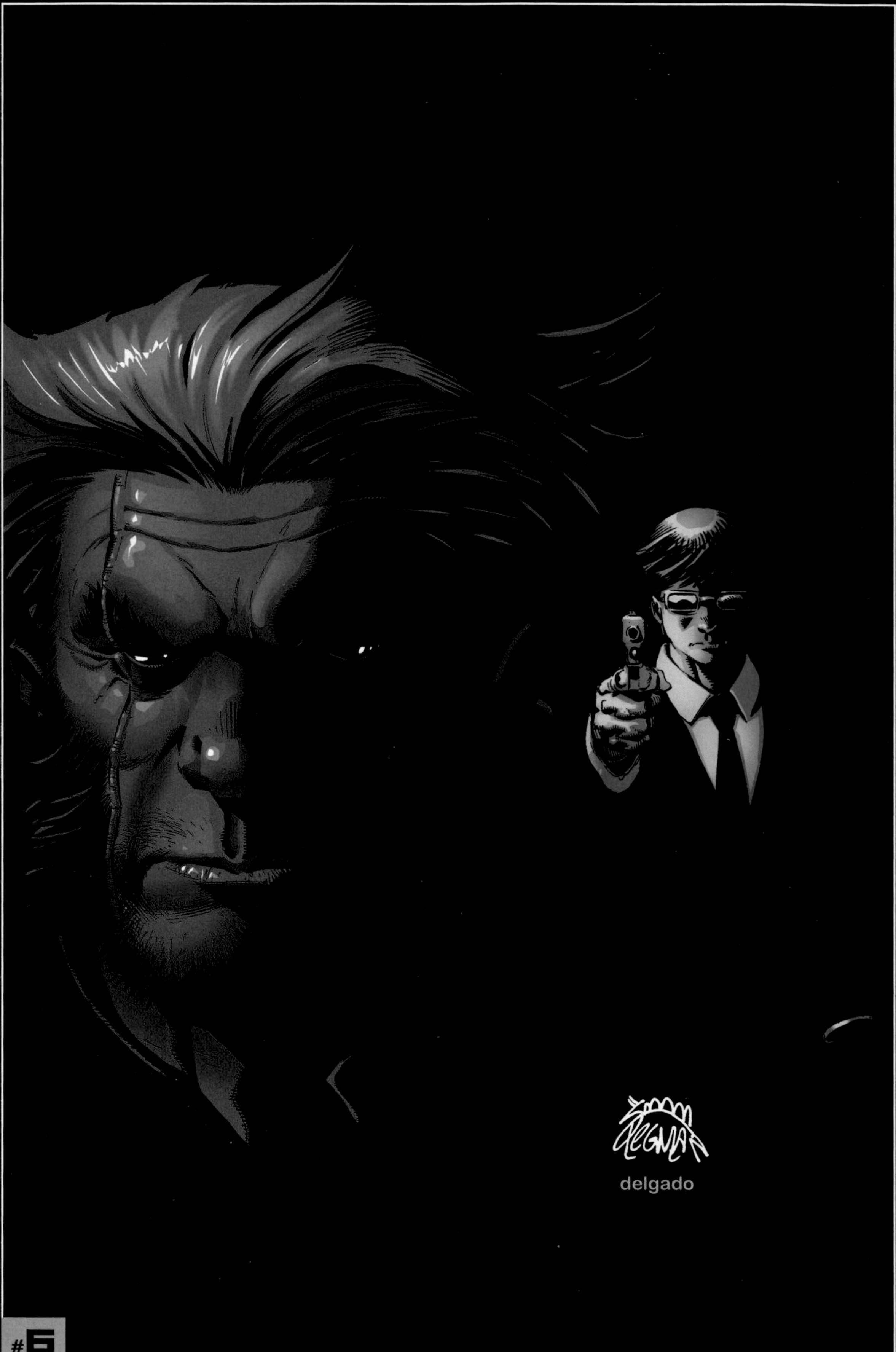
delgado

#6

THE MADRIPOOR JOB PART 1

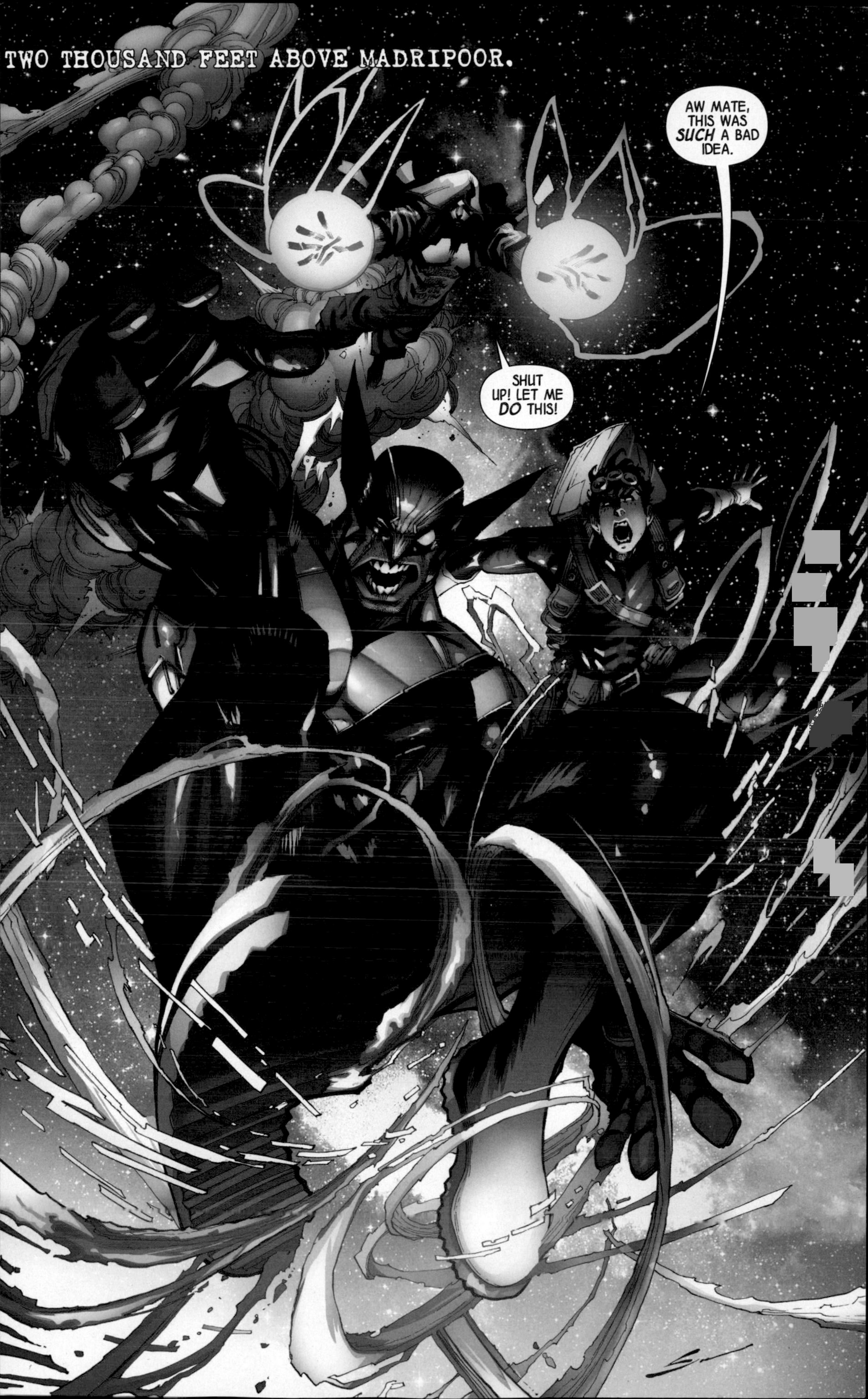
TWO THOUSAND FEET ABOVE MADRIPOOR.
AW MATE, THIS WAS SUCH A BAD IDEA.
SHUT UP! LET ME DO THIS!

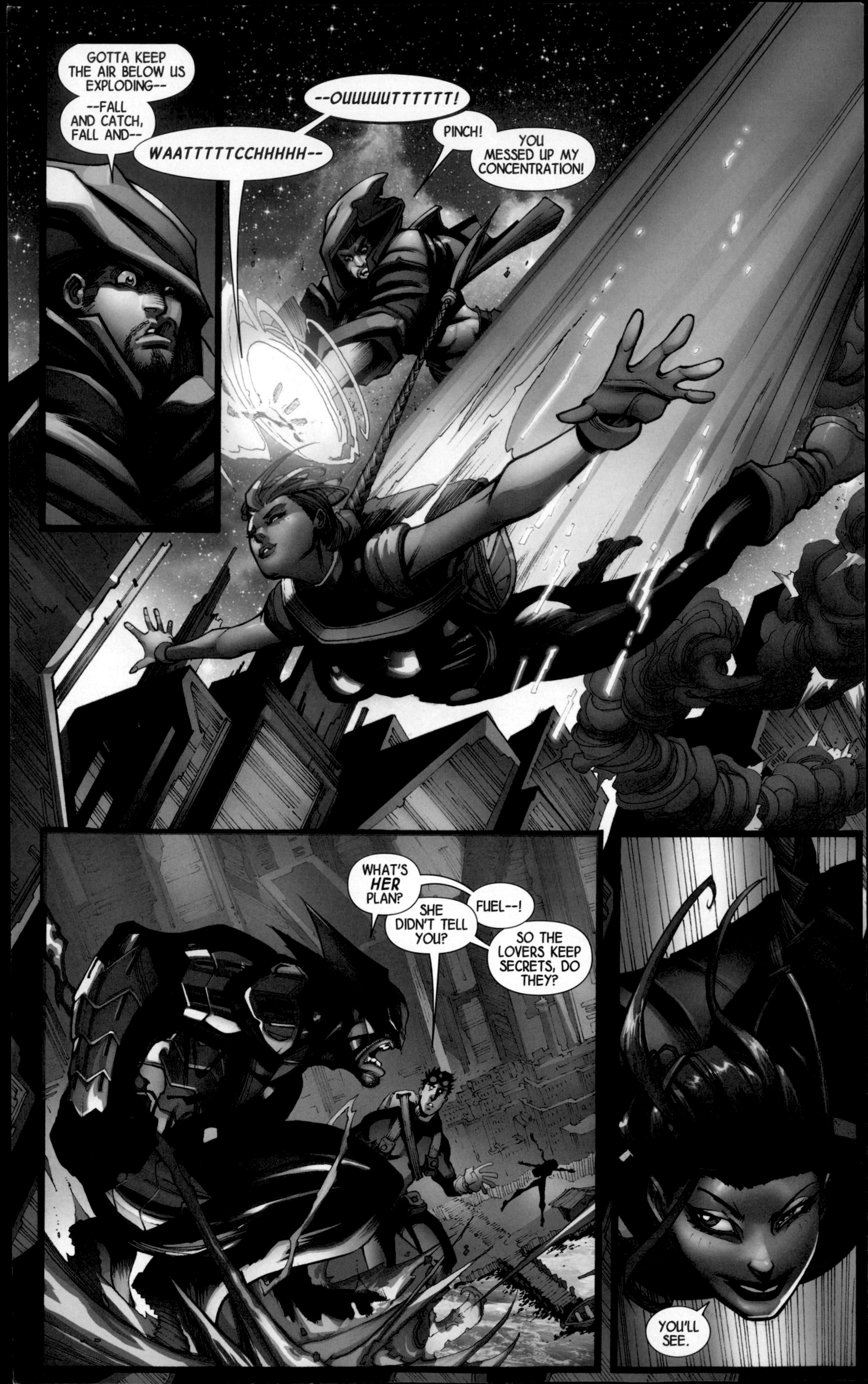
GOTTA KEEP THE AIR BELOW US EXPLODING--
--FALL AND CATCH, FALL AND--
--OUUUUUTTTTTT!
WAATTTTTCCHHHHH--
PINCH!
YOU MESSED UP MY CONCENTRATION!
WHAT'S HER PLAN?
FUEL--!
SHE DIDN'T TELL YOU?
SO THE LOVERS KEEP SECRETS, DO THEY?
YOU'LL SEE.

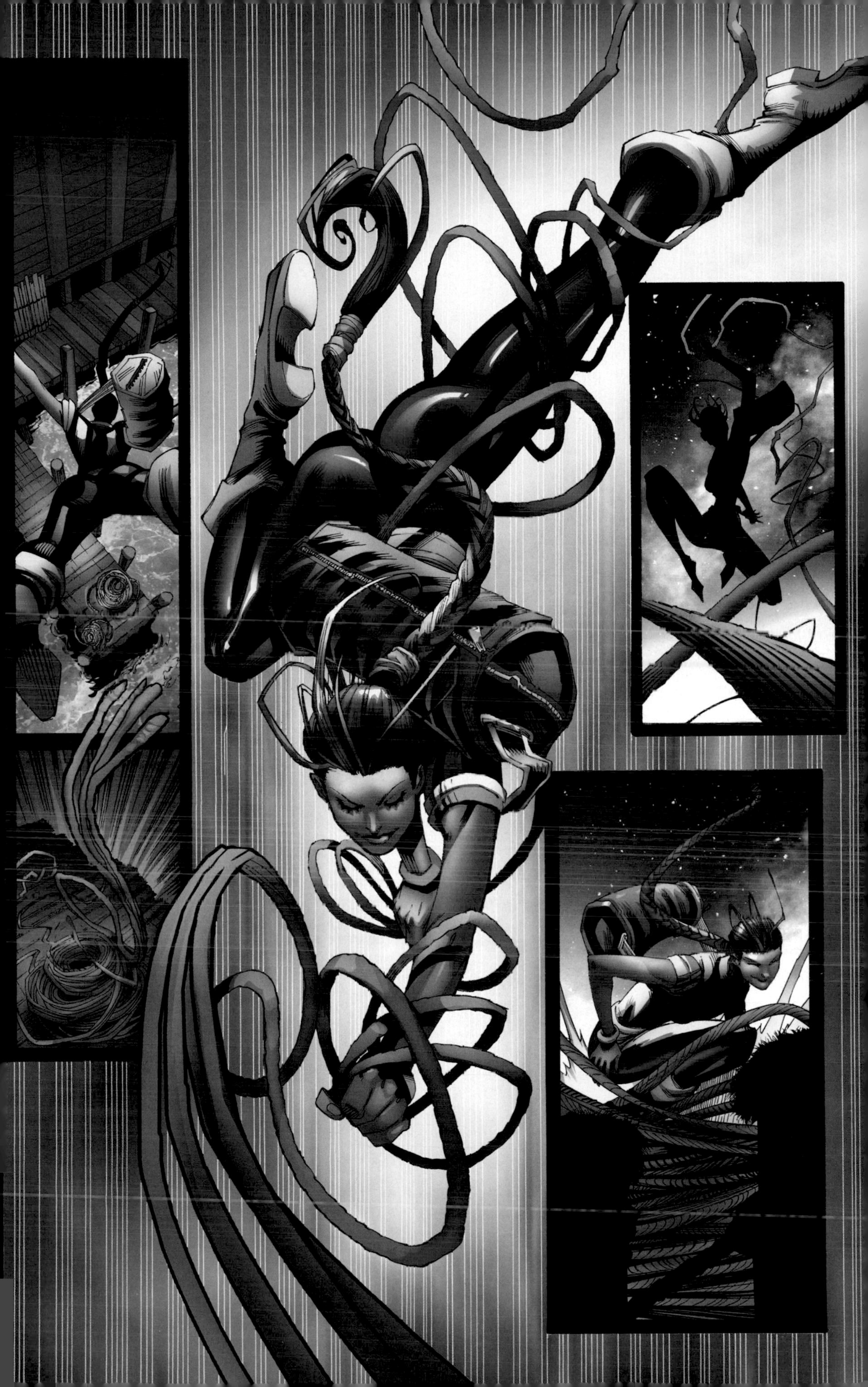

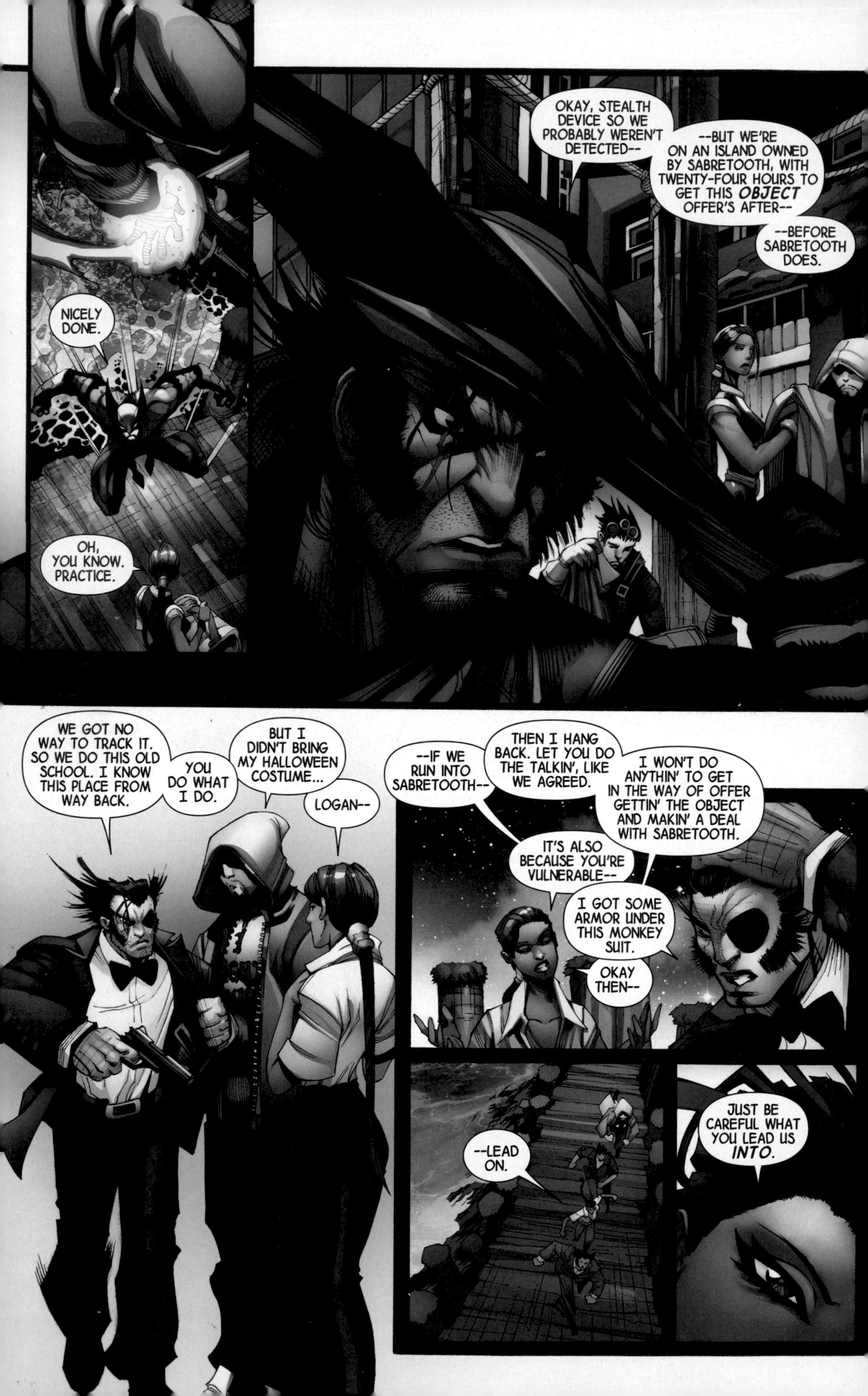
NICELY DONE.
OH, YOU KNOW. PRACTICE.
OKAY, STEALTH DEVICE SO WE PROBABLY WEREN'T DETECTED--
--BUT WE'RE ON AN ISLAND OWNED BY SABRETOOTH, WITH TWENTY-FOUR HOURS TO GET THIS OBJECT OFFER'S AFTER--
--BEFORE SABRETOOTH DOES.
WE GOT NO WAY TO TRACK IT. SO WE DO THIS OLD SCHOOL. I KNOW THIS PLACE FROM WAY BACK.
YOU DO WHAT I DO.
BUT I DIDN'T BRING MY HALLOWEEN COSTUME...
LOGAN--
--IF WE RUN INTO SABRETOOTH--
THEN I HANG BACK. LET YOU DO THE TALKIN', LIKE WE AGREED.
I WON'T DO ANYTHIN' TO GET IN THE WAY OF OFFER GETTIN' THE OBJECT AND MAKIN' A DEAL WITH SABRETOOTH.
IT'S ALSO BECAUSE YOU'RE VULNERABLE--
I GOT SOME ARMOR UNDER THIS MONKEY SUIT.
OKAY THEN--
--LEAD ON.
JUST BE CAREFUL WHAT YOU LEAD US INTO.

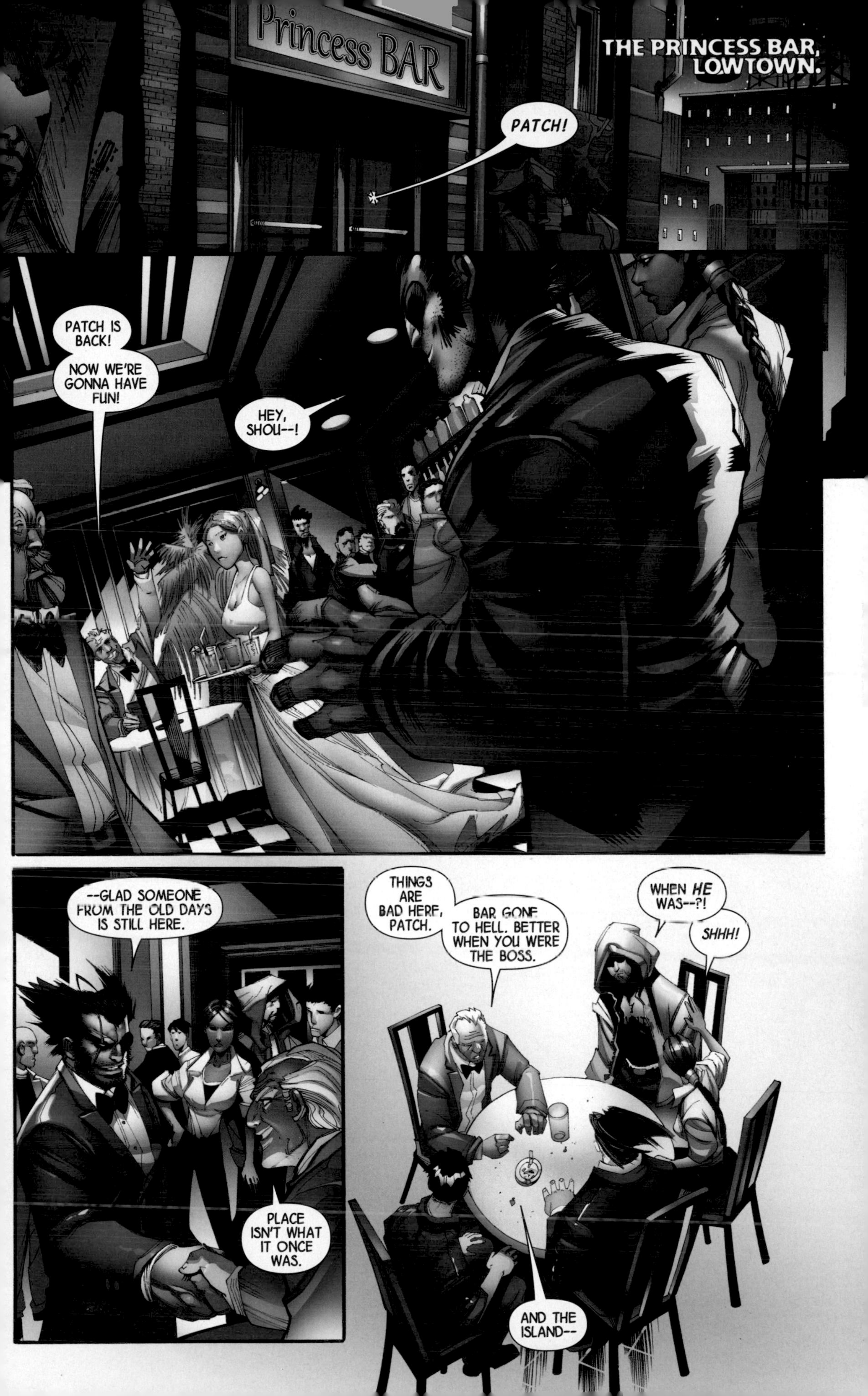
Princess BAR
THE PRINCESS BAR, LOWTOWN.
PATCH!
PATCH IS BACK!
NOW WE'RE GONNA HAVE FUN!
HEY, SHOU--!
--GLAD SOMEONE FROM THE OLD DAYS IS STILL HERE.
PLACE ISN'T WHAT IT ONCE WAS.
THINGS ARE BAD HERE, PATCH.
BAR GONE TO HELL. BETTER WHEN YOU WERE THE BOSS.
WHEN HE WAS--?!
SHHH!
AND THE ISLAND--

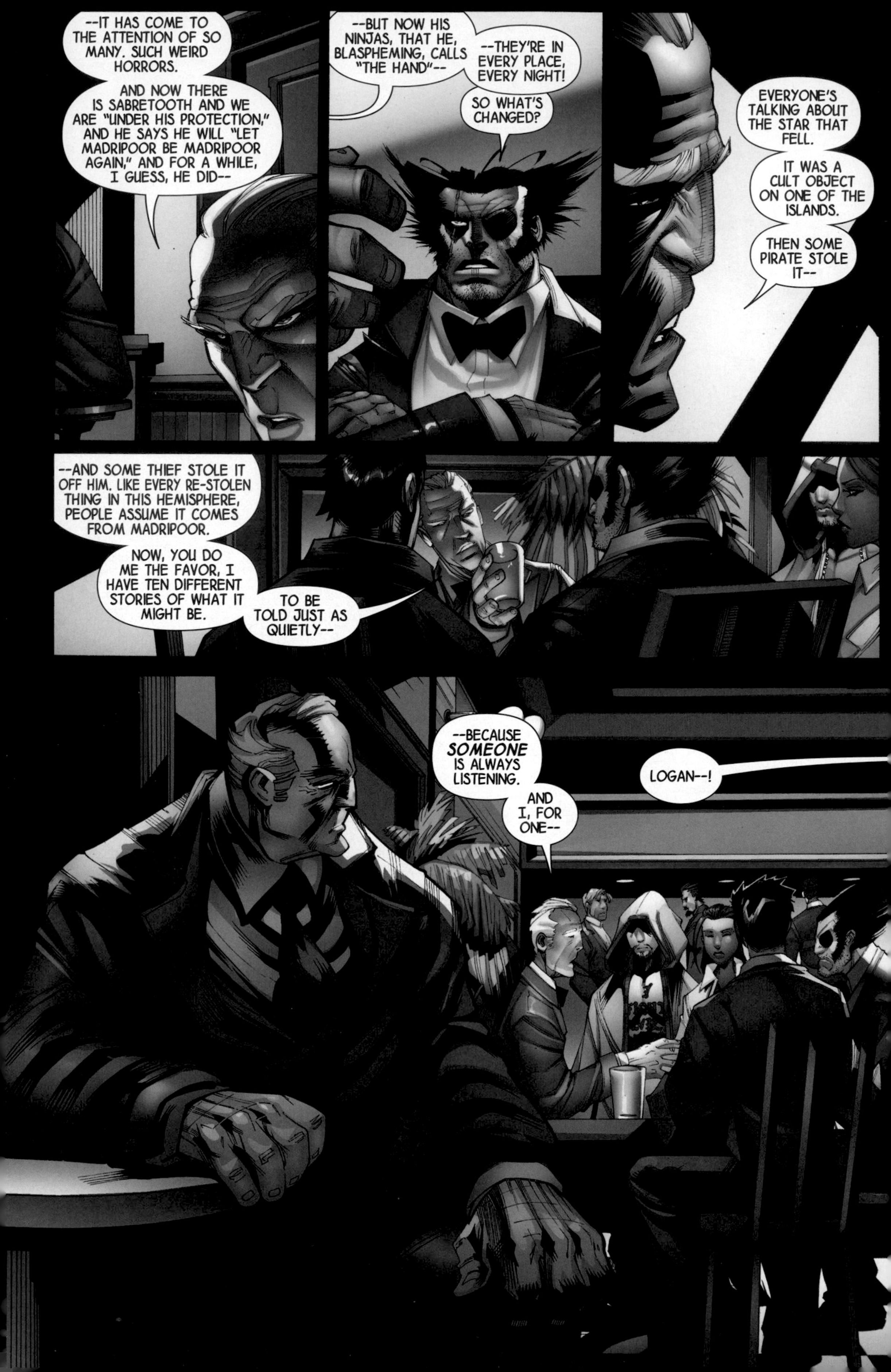
--IT HAS COME TO THE ATTENTION OF SO MANY. SUCH WEIRD HORRORS.
AND NOW THERE IS SABRETOOTH AND WE ARE "UNDER HIS PROTECTION," AND HE SAYS HE WILL "LET MADRIPOOR BE MADRIPOOR AGAIN," AND FOR A WHILE, I GUESS, HE DID--
--BUT NOW HIS NINJAS, THAT HE, BLASPHEMING, CALLS "THE HAND"--
--THEY'RE IN EVERY PLACE, EVERY NIGHT!
SO WHAT'S CHANGED?
EVERYONE'S TALKING ABOUT THE STAR THAT FELL.
IT WAS A CULT OBJECT ON ONE OF THE ISLANDS.
THEN SOME PIRATE STOLE IT--
--AND SOME THIEF STOLE IT OFF HIM. LIKE EVERY RE-STOLEN THING IN THIS HEMISPHERE, PEOPLE ASSUME IT COMES FROM MADRIPOOR.
NOW, YOU DO ME THE FAVOR, I HAVE TEN DIFFERENT STORIES OF WHAT IT MIGHT BE.
TO BE TOLD JUST AS QUIETLY--
--BECAUSE *SOMEONE* IS ALWAYS LISTENING.
AND I, FOR ONE--
LOGAN--!

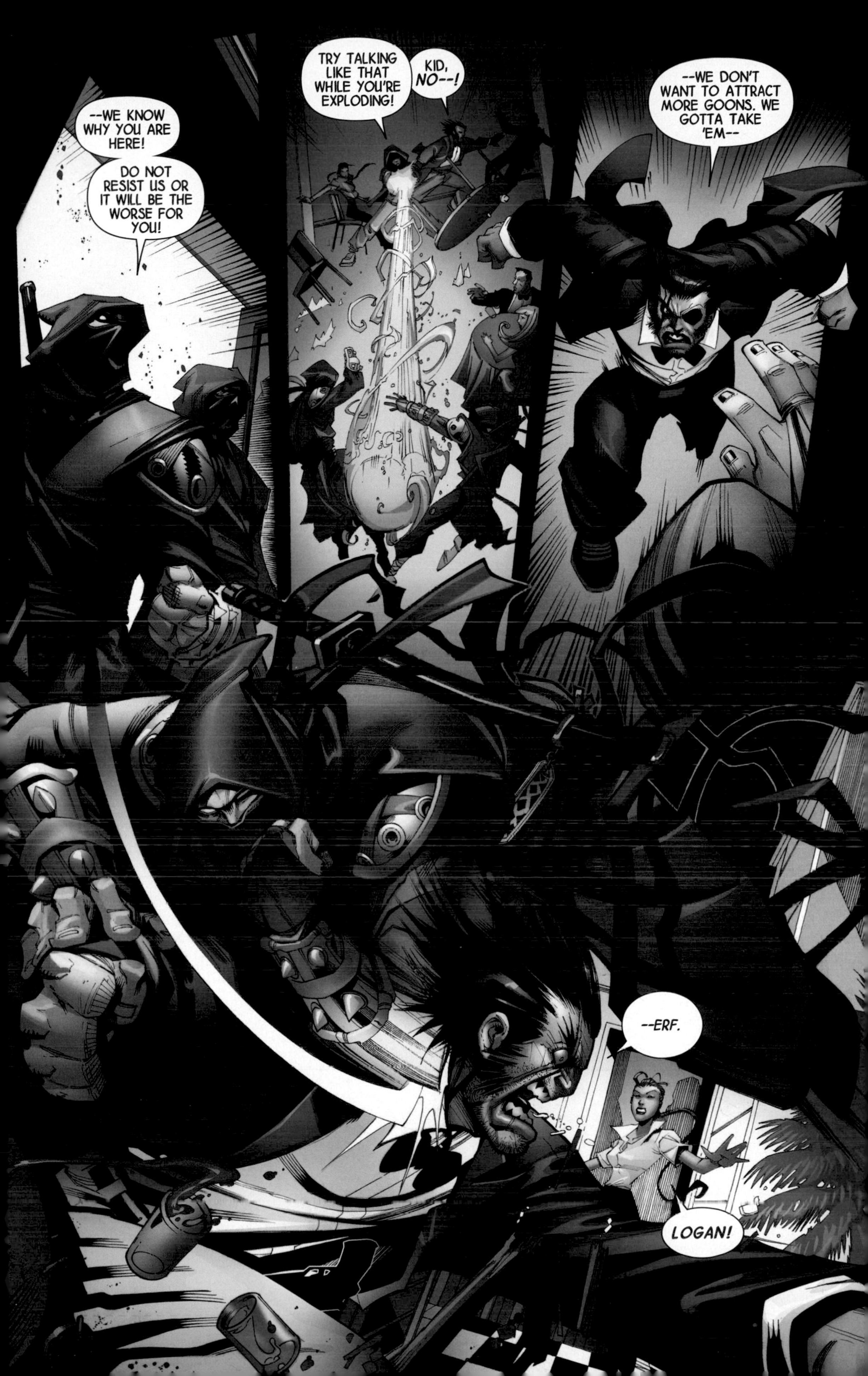
--WE KNOW WHY YOU ARE HERE!
DO NOT RESIST US OR IT WILL BE THE WORSE FOR YOU!
TRY TALKING LIKE THAT WHILE YOU'RE EXPLODING!
KID, NO--!
--WE DON'T WANT TO ATTRACT MORE GOONS. WE GOTTA TAKE 'EM--
--ERF.
LOGAN!

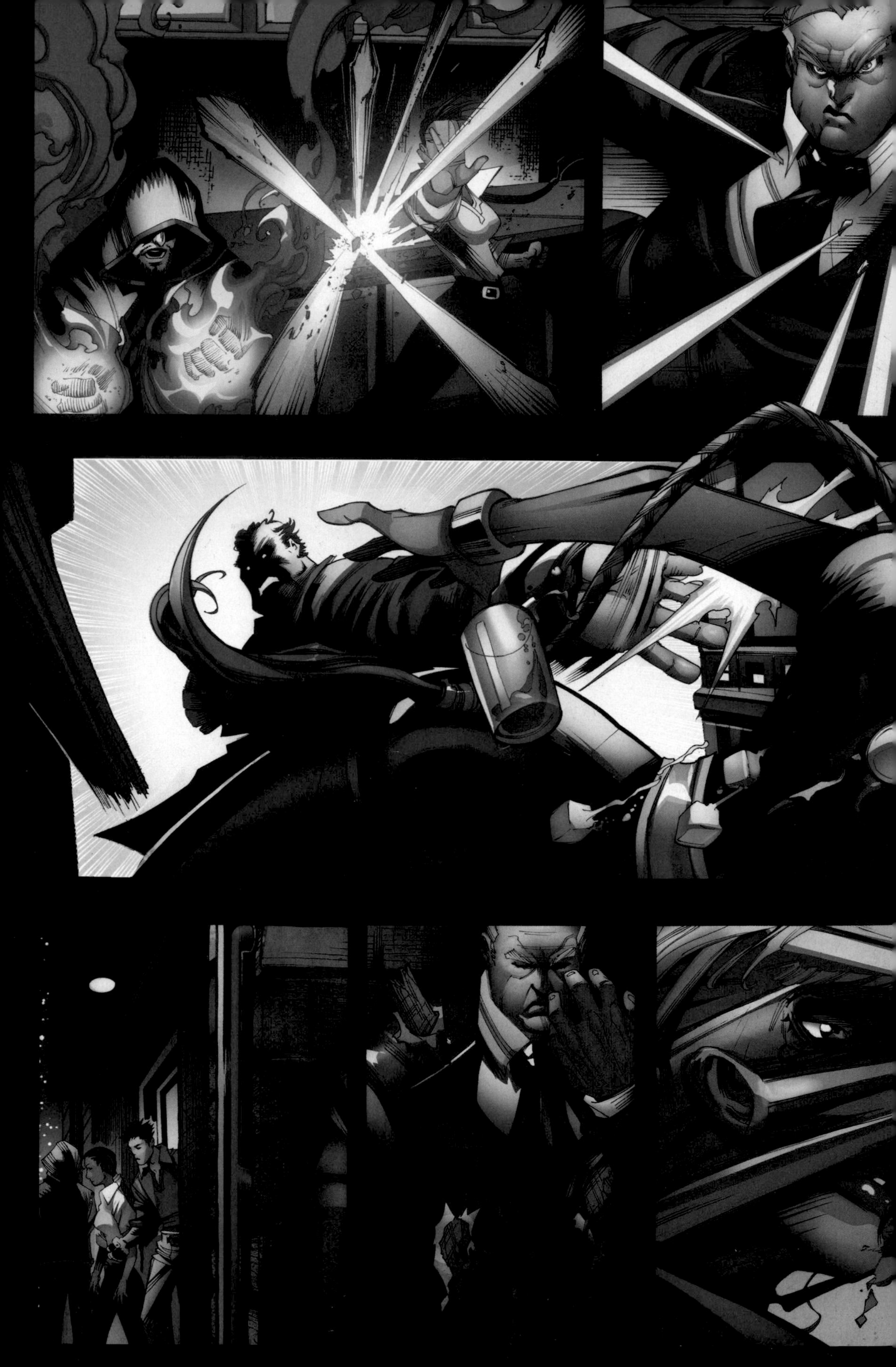

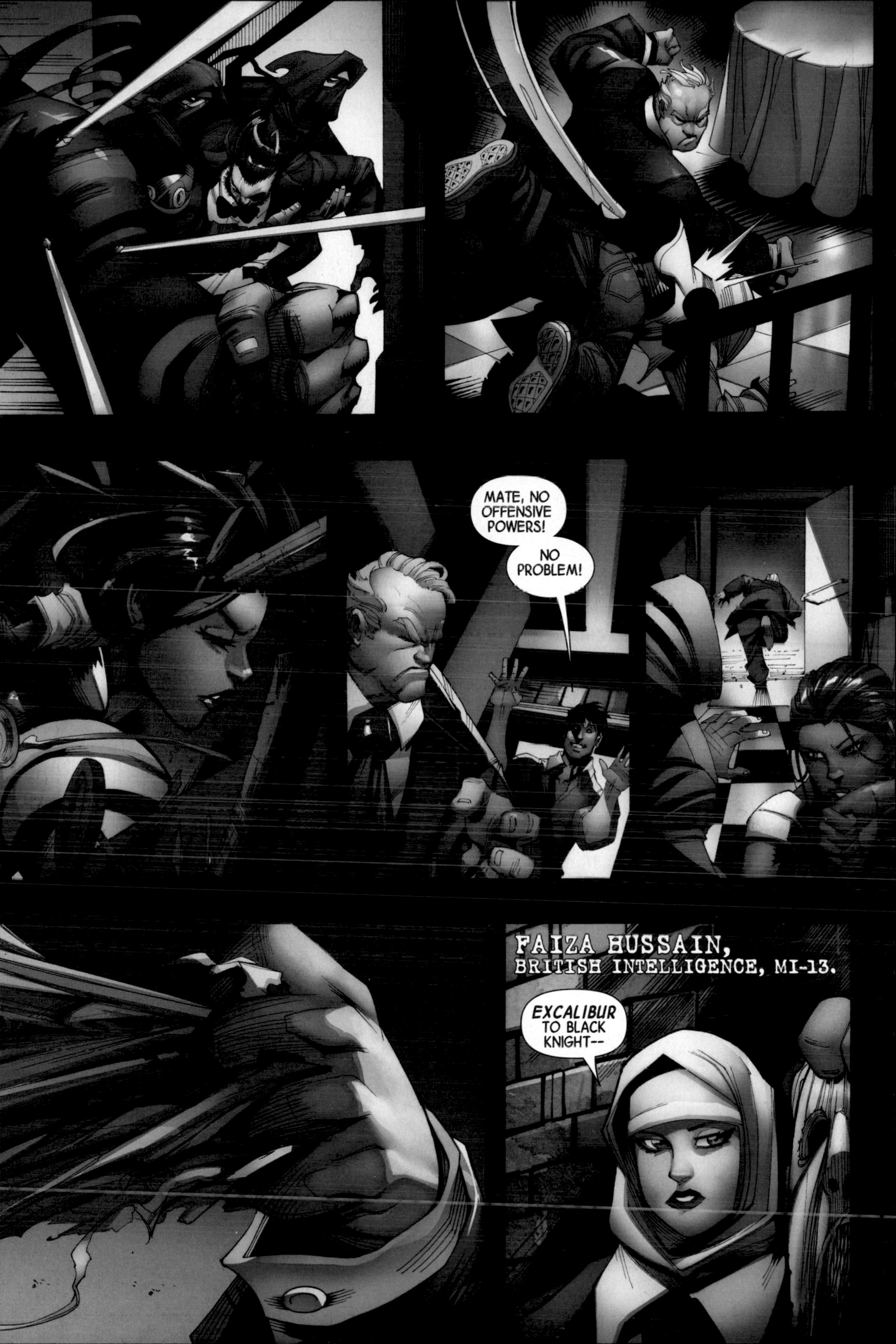
MATE, NO OFFENSIVE POWERS!
NO PROBLEM!
FAIZA HUSSAIN, BRITISH INTELLIGENCE, MI-13.
EXCALIBUR TO BLACK KNIGHT--

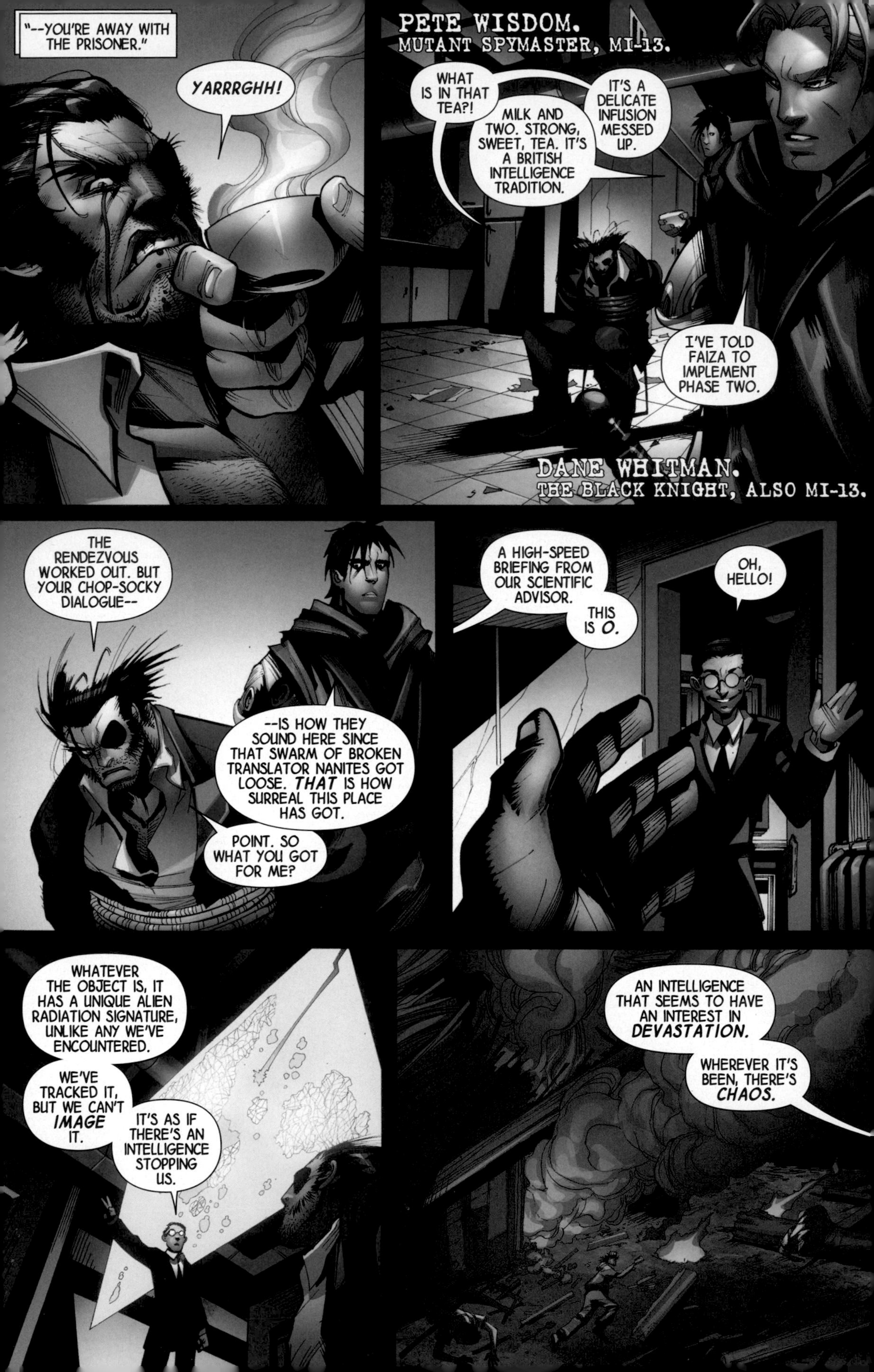
"--YOU'RE AWAY WITH THE PRISONER."
YARRRGHH!
PETE WISDOM. MUTANT SPYMASTER, MI-13.
WHAT IS IN THAT TEA?!
MILK AND TWO. STRONG, SWEET, TEA. IT'S A BRITISH INTELLIGENCE TRADITION.
IT'S A DELICATE INFUSION MESSED UP.
I'VE TOLD FAIZA TO IMPLEMENT PHASE TWO.
DANE WHITMAN. THE BLACK KNIGHT, ALSO MI-13.
THE RENDEZVOUS WORKED OUT. BUT YOUR CHOP-SOCKY DIALOGUE--
--IS HOW THEY SOUND HERE SINCE THAT SWARM OF BROKEN TRANSLATOR NANITES GOT LOOSE. THAT IS HOW SURREAL THIS PLACE HAS GOT.
POINT. SO WHAT YOU GOT FOR ME?
A HIGH-SPEED BRIEFING FROM OUR SCIENTIFIC ADVISOR.
THIS IS O.
OH, HELLO!
WHATEVER THE OBJECT IS, IT HAS A UNIQUE ALIEN RADIATION SIGNATURE, UNLIKE ANY WE'VE ENCOUNTERED.
WE'VE TRACKED IT, BUT WE CAN'T IMAGE IT.
IT'S AS IF THERE'S AN INTELLIGENCE STOPPING US.
AN INTELLIGENCE THAT SEEMS TO HAVE AN INTEREST IN DEVASTATION.
WHEREVER IT'S BEEN, THERE'S CHAOS.

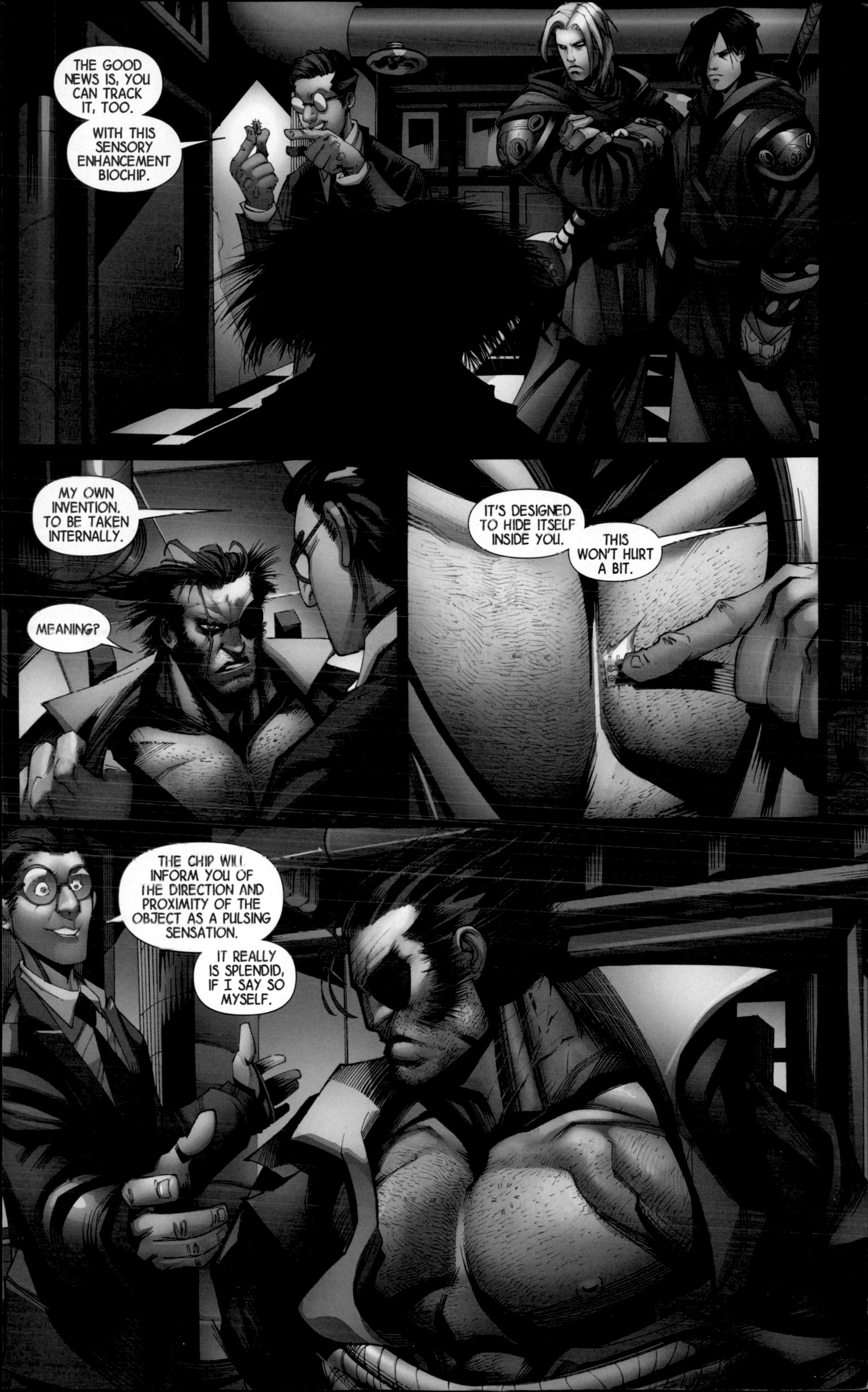
THE GOOD NEWS IS, YOU CAN TRACK IT, TOO.
WITH THIS SENSORY ENHANCEMENT BIOCHIP.
MY OWN INVENTION. TO BE TAKEN INTERNALLY.
MEANING?
IT'S DESIGNED TO HIDE ITSELF INSIDE YOU.
THIS WON'T HURT A BIT.
THE CHIP WILL INFORM YOU OF THE DIRECTION AND PROXIMITY OF THE OBJECT AS A PULSING SENSATION.
IT REALLY IS SPLENDID, IF I SAY SO MYSELF.

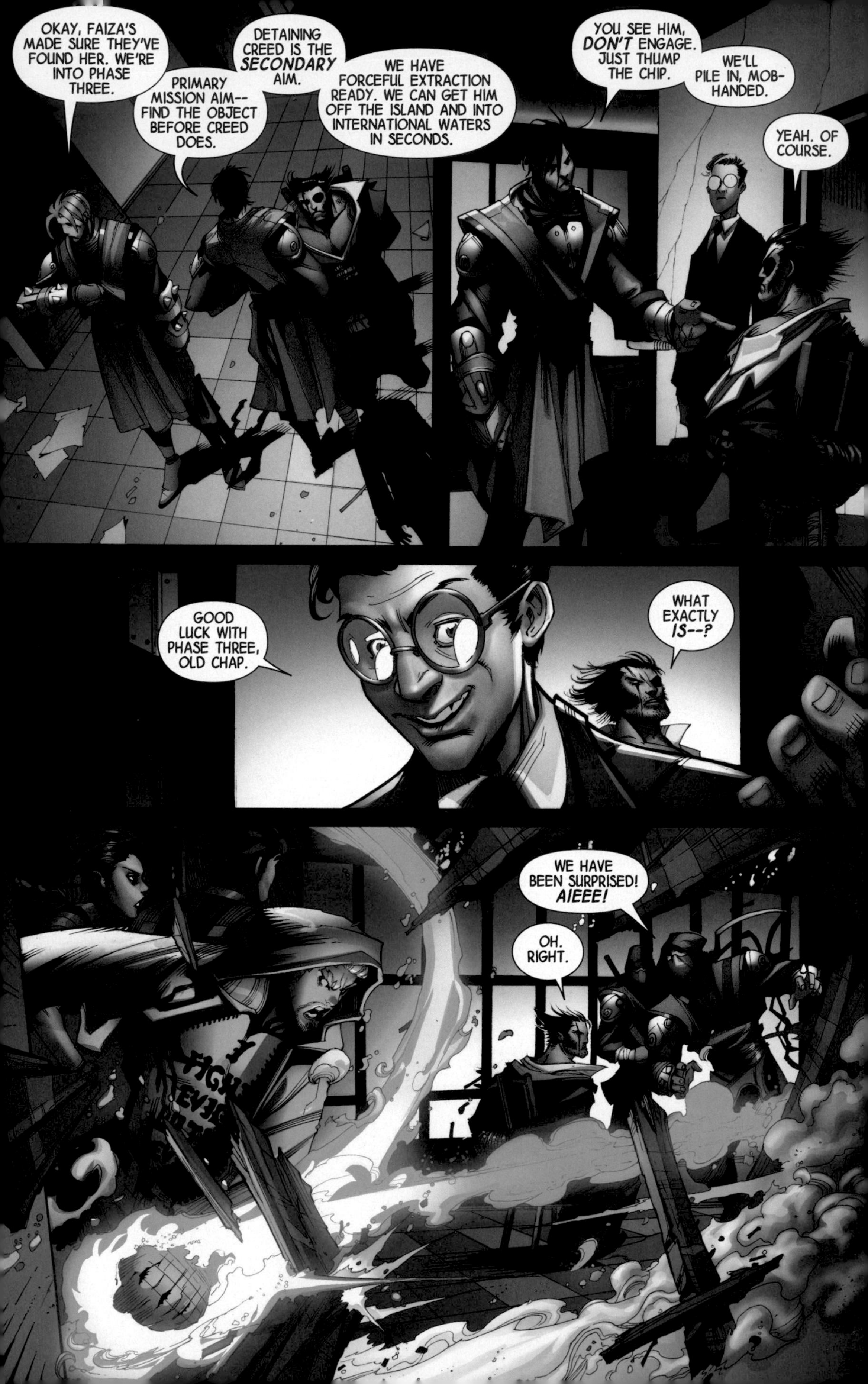
OKAY, FAIZA'S MADE SURE THEY'VE FOUND HER. WE'RE INTO PHASE THREE.
PRIMARY MISSION AIM-- FIND THE OBJECT BEFORE CREED DOES.
DETAINING CREED IS THE SECONDARY AIM.
WE HAVE FORCEFUL EXTRACTION READY. WE CAN GET HIM OFF THE ISLAND AND INTO INTERNATIONAL WATERS IN SECONDS.
YOU SEE HIM, DON'T ENGAGE. JUST THUMP THE CHIP.
WE'LL PILE IN, MOB-HANDED.
YEAH. OF COURSE.
GOOD LUCK WITH PHASE THREE, OLD CHAP.
WHAT EXACTLY IS--?
WE HAVE BEEN SURPRISED! AIEEE!
OH. RIGHT.

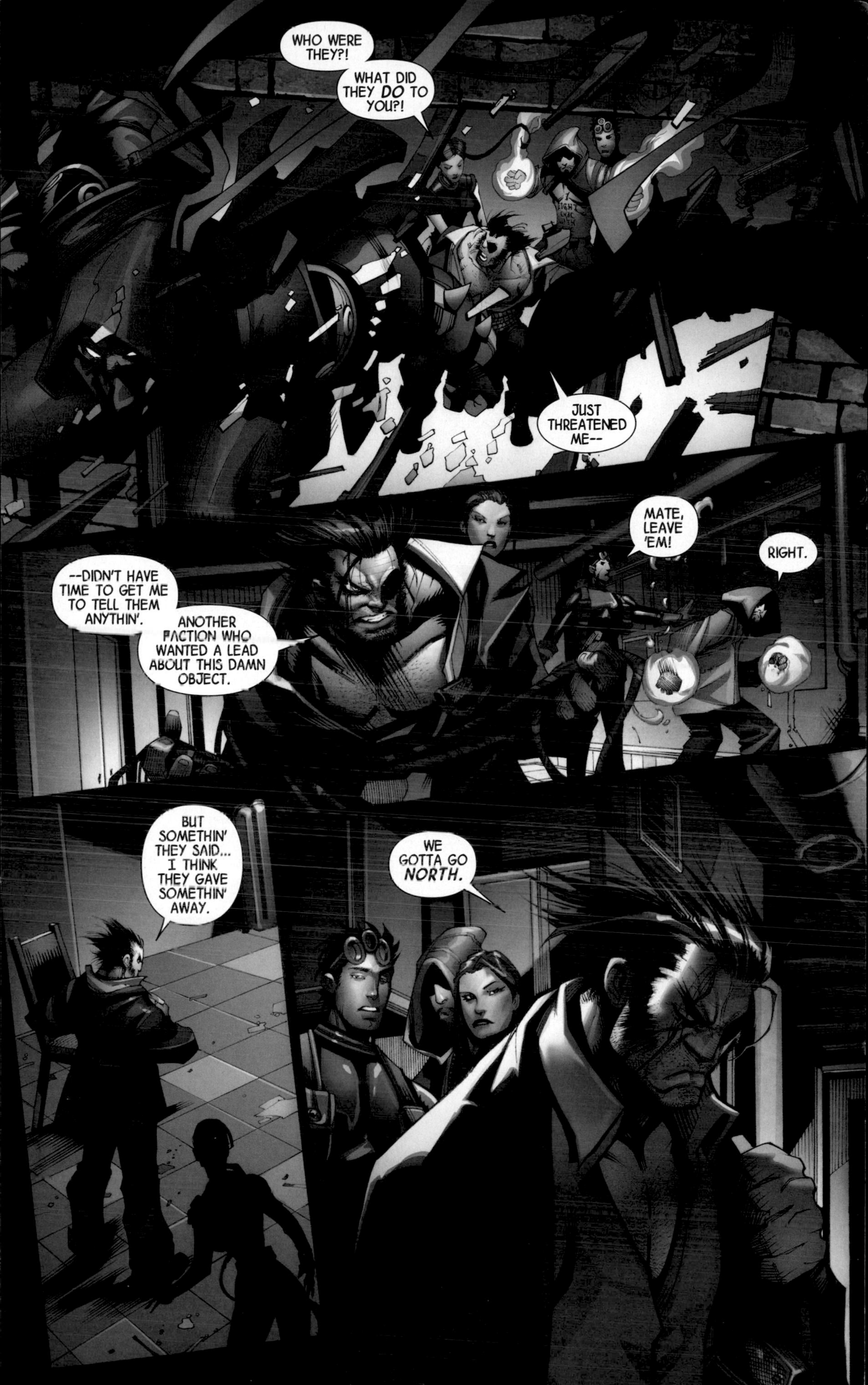
WHO WERE THEY?!
WHAT DID THEY DO TO YOU?!
JUST THREATENED ME--
--DIDN'T HAVE TIME TO GET ME TO TELL THEM ANYTHIN'.
ANOTHER FACTION WHO WANTED A LEAD ABOUT THIS DAMN OBJECT.
MATE, LEAVE 'EM!
RIGHT.
BUT SOMETHIN' THEY SAID... I THINK THEY GAVE SOMETHIN' AWAY.
WE GOTTA GO NORTH.

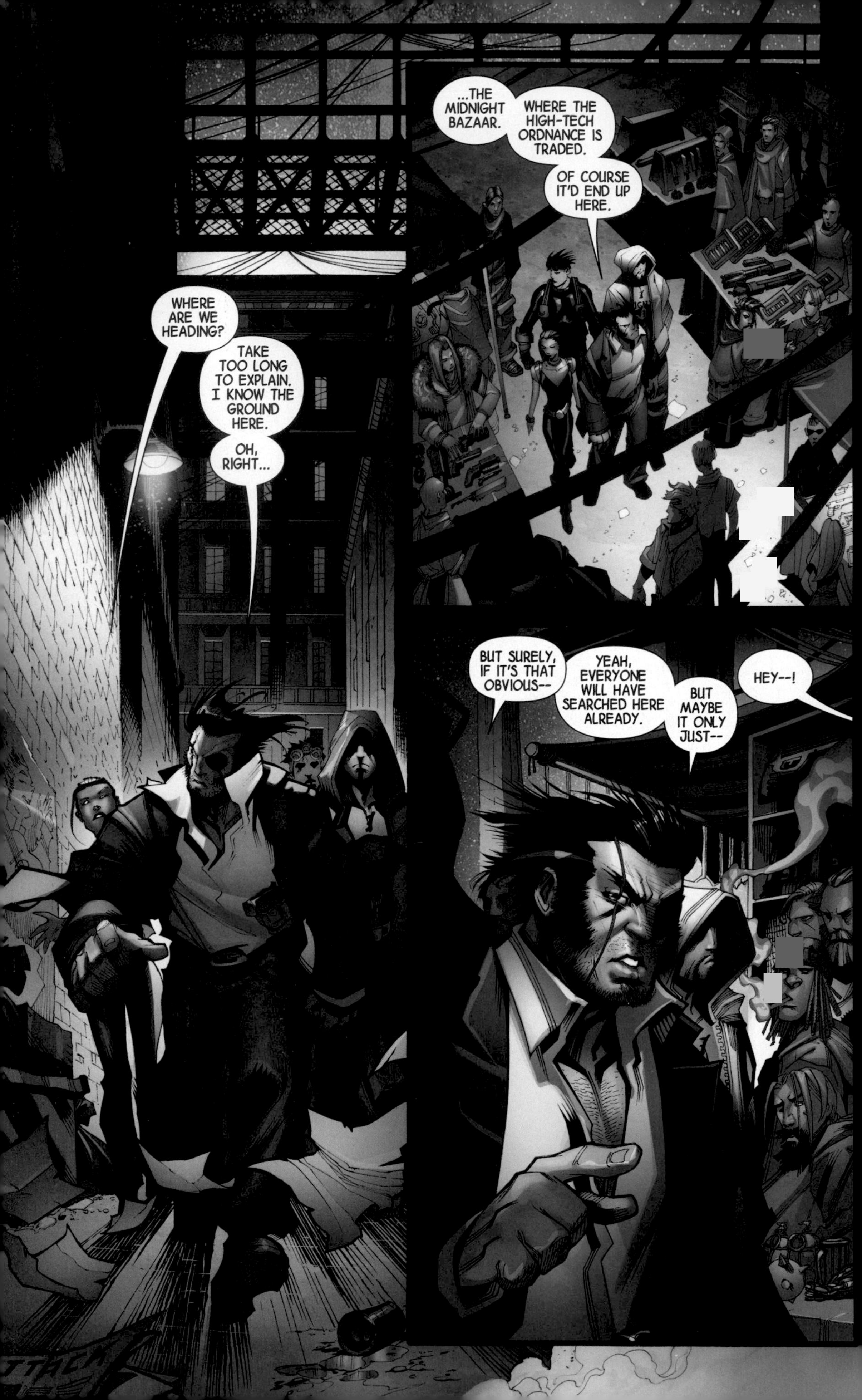
WHERE ARE WE HEADING?
TAKE TOO LONG TO EXPLAIN. I KNOW THE GROUND HERE.
OH, RIGHT...
...THE MIDNIGHT BAZAAR.
WHERE THE HIGH-TECH ORDNANCE IS TRADED.
OF COURSE IT'D END UP HERE.
BUT SURELY, IF IT'S THAT OBVIOUS--
YEAH, EVERYONE WILL HAVE SEARCHED HERE ALREADY.
BUT MAYBE IT ONLY JUST--
HEY--!

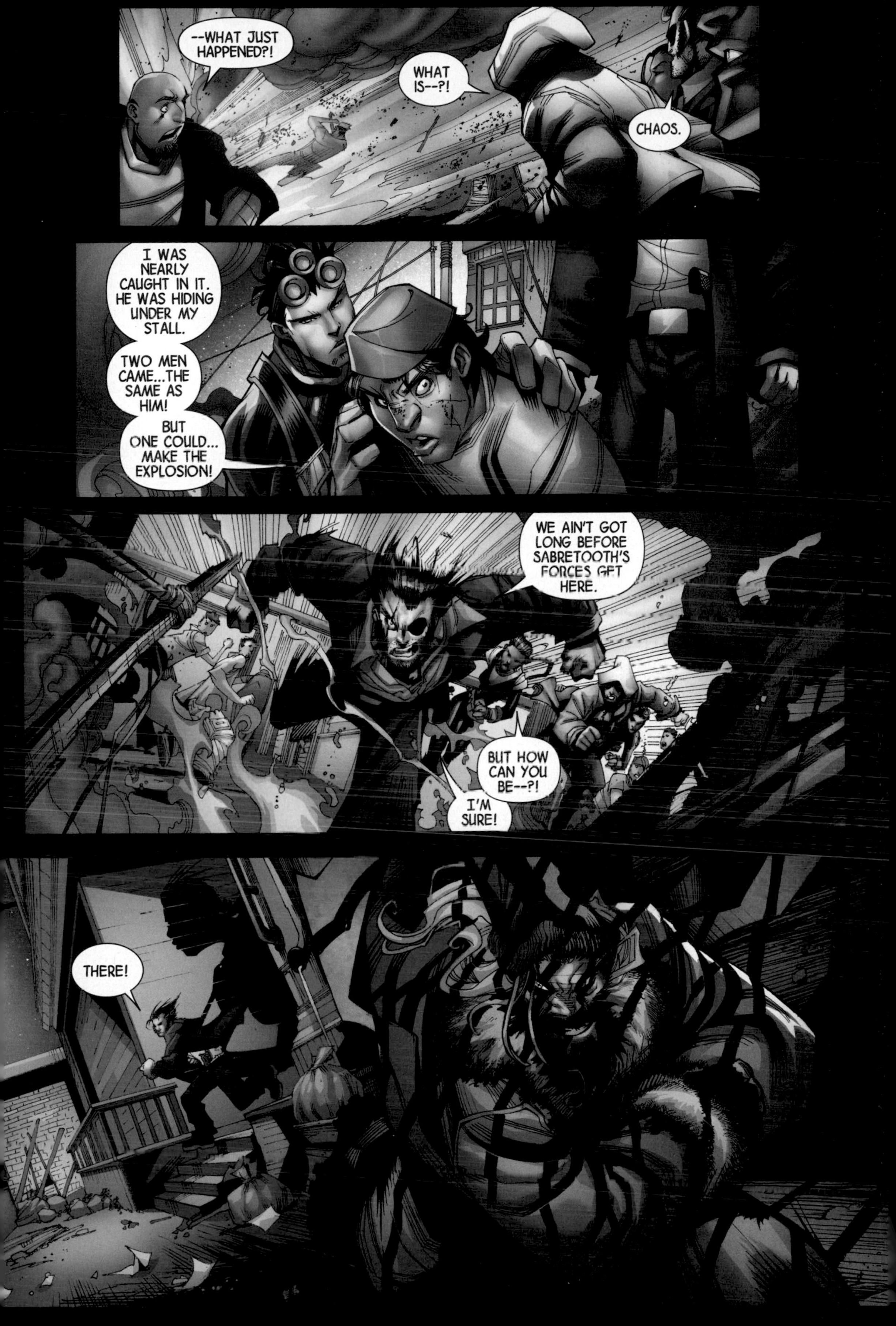
--WHAT JUST HAPPENED?!
WHAT IS--?!
CHAOS.
I WAS NEARLY CAUGHT IN IT. HE WAS HIDING UNDER MY STALL.
TWO MEN CAME...THE SAME AS HIM!
BUT ONE COULD... MAKE THE EXPLOSION!
WE AIN'T GOT LONG BEFORE SABRETOOTH'S FORCES GET HERE.
BUT HOW CAN YOU BE--?!
I'M SURE!
THERE!

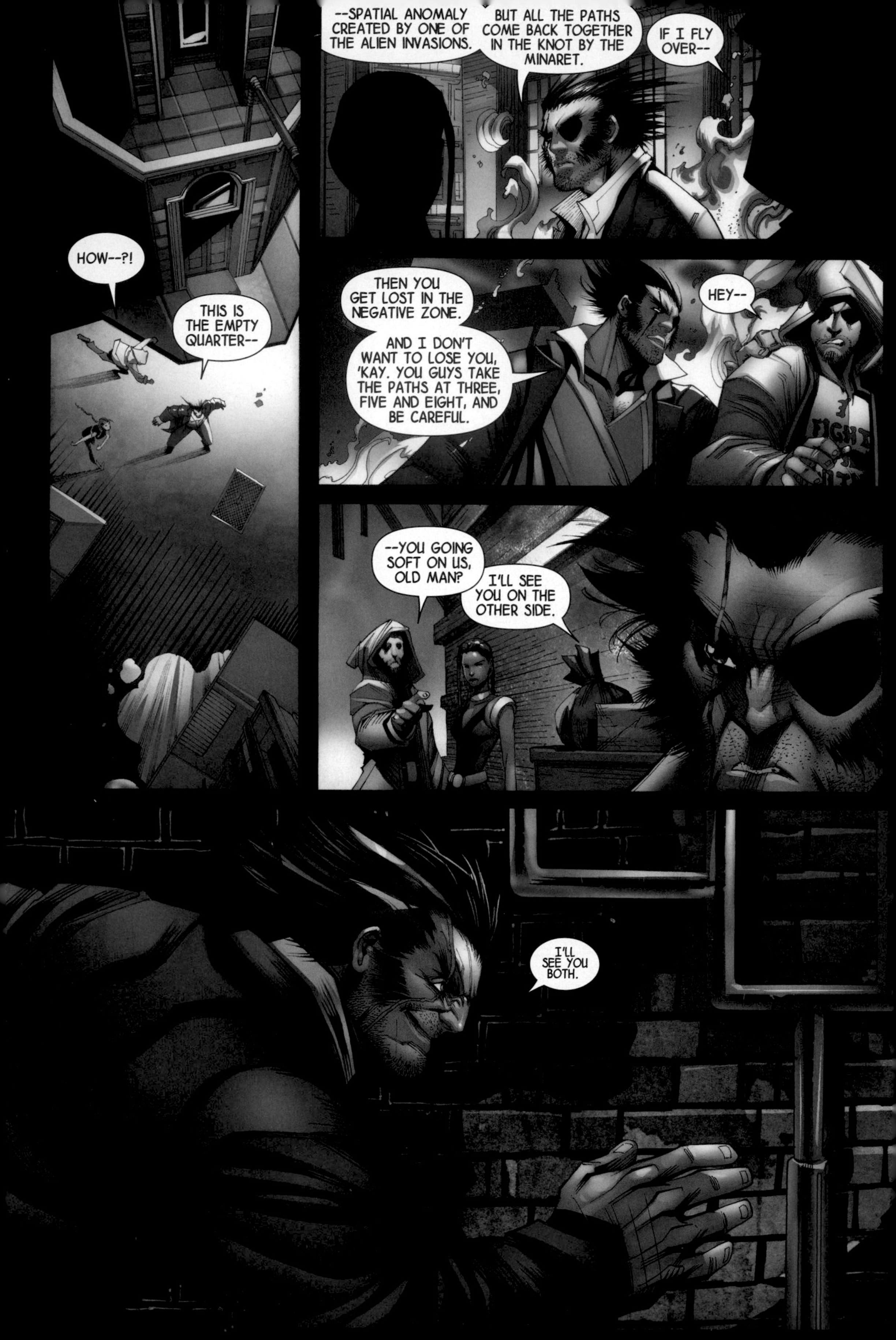

HOW--?!
THIS IS THE EMPTY QUARTER--
--SPATIAL ANOMALY CREATED BY ONE OF THE ALIEN INVASIONS.
BUT ALL THE PATHS COME BACK TOGETHER IN THE KNOT BY THE MINARET.
IF I FLY OVER--
THEN YOU GET LOST IN THE NEGATIVE ZONE.
AND I DON'T WANT TO LOSE YOU, 'KAY. YOU GUYS TAKE THE PATHS AT THREE, FIVE AND EIGHT, AND BE CAREFUL.
HEY--
--YOU GOING SOFT ON US, OLD MAN?
I'LL SEE YOU ON THE OTHER SIDE.
I'LL SEE YOU BOTH.

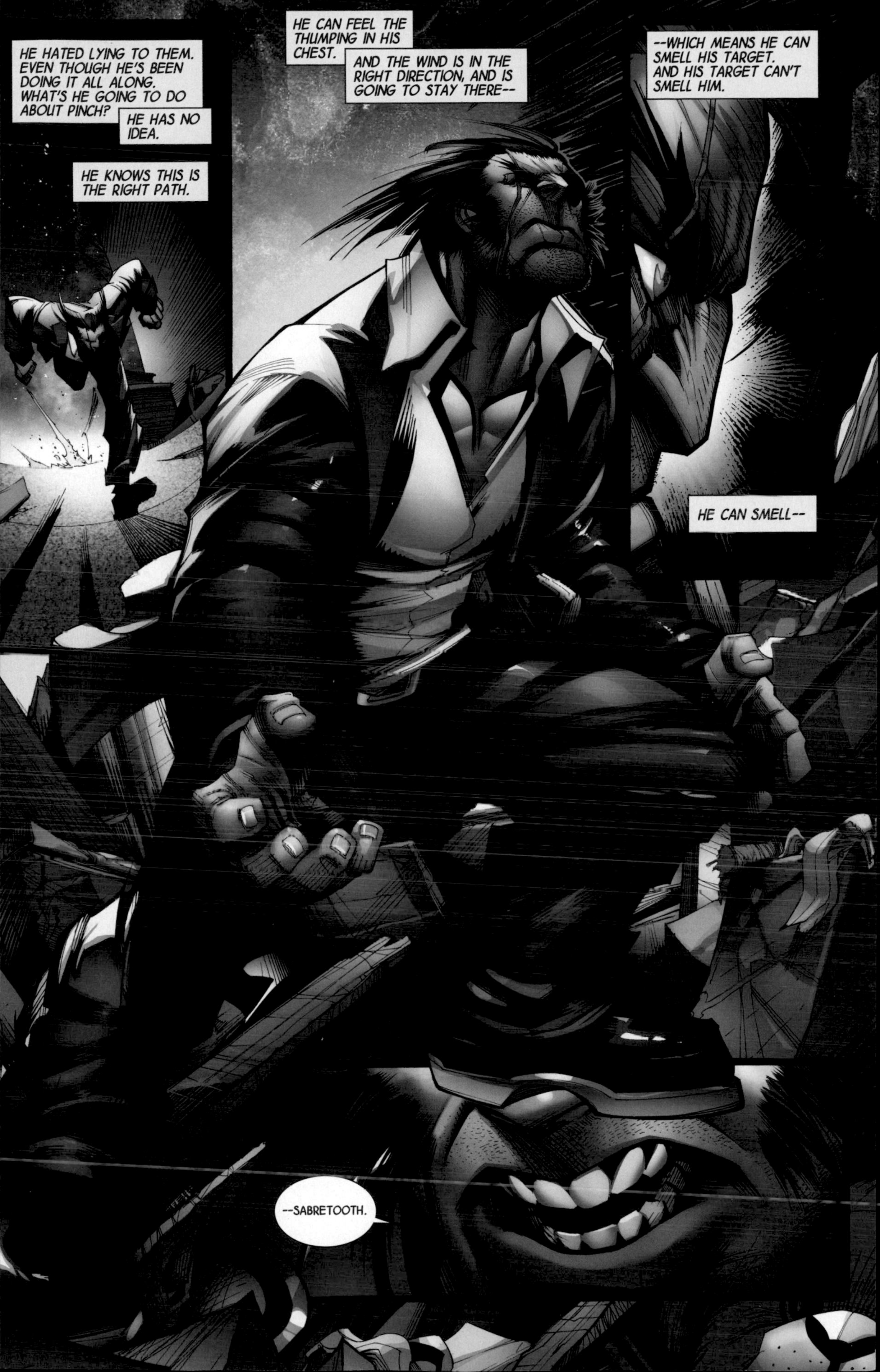
HE HATED LYING TO THEM. EVEN THOUGH HE'S BEEN DOING IT ALL ALONG. WHAT'S HE GOING TO DO ABOUT PINCH?
HE HAS NO IDEA.
HE KNOWS THIS IS THE RIGHT PATH.
HE CAN FEEL THE THUMPING IN HIS CHEST.
AND THE WIND IS IN THE RIGHT DIRECTION, AND IS GOING TO STAY THERE--
--WHICH MEANS HE CAN SMELL HIS TARGET. AND HIS TARGET CAN'T SMELL HIM.
HE CAN SMELL--
--SABRETOOTH.

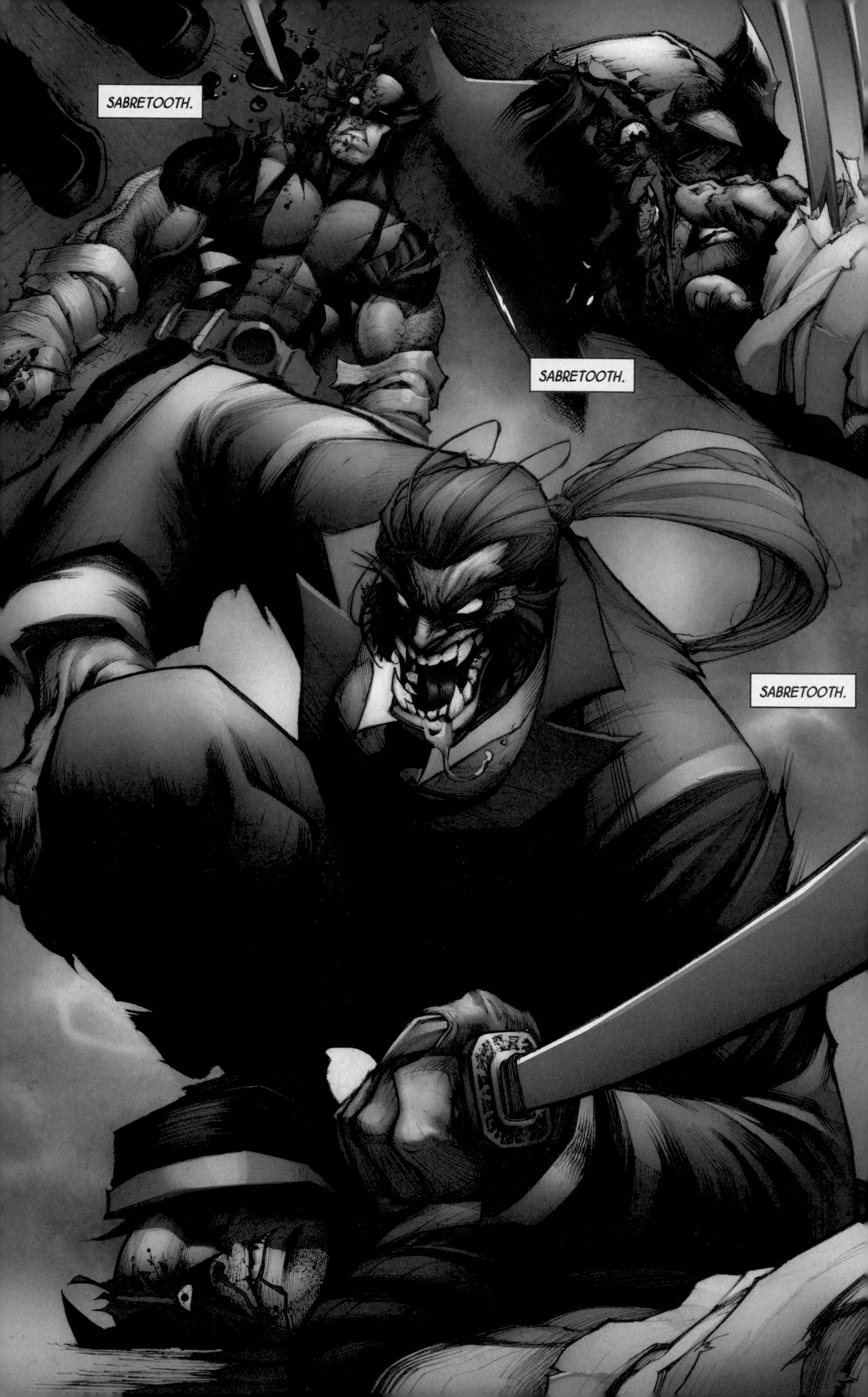
SABRETOOTH.
SABRETOOTH.
SABRETOOTH.

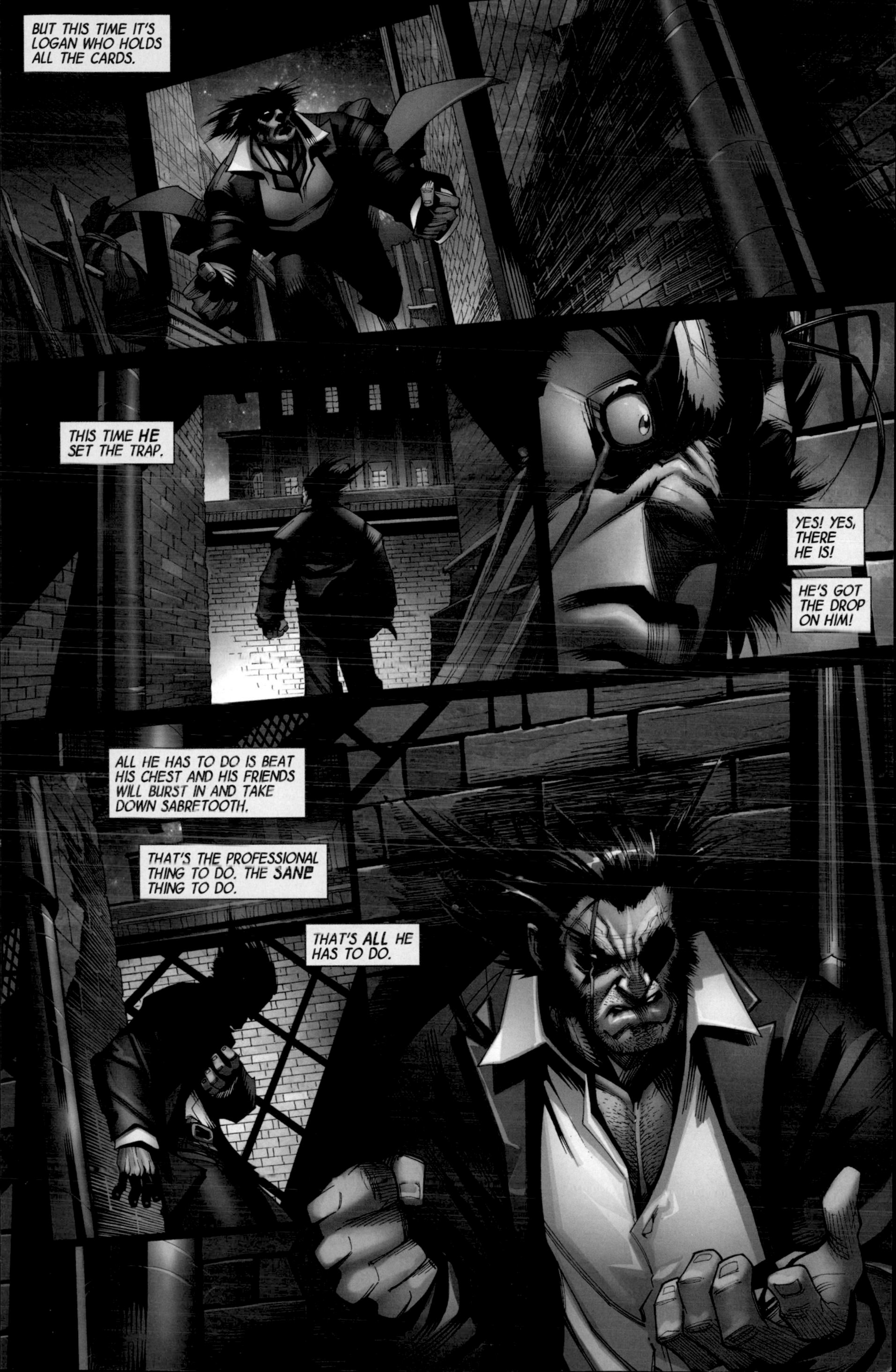
BUT THIS TIME IT'S LOGAN WHO HOLDS ALL THE CARDS.
THIS TIME HE SET THE TRAP.
YES! YES, THERE HE IS!
HE'S GOT THE DROP ON HIM!
ALL HE HAS TO DO IS BEAT HIS CHEST AND HIS FRIENDS WILL BURST IN AND TAKE DOWN SABRETOOTH.
THAT'S THE PROFESSIONAL THING TO DO. THE SANE THING TO DO.
THAT'S ALL HE HAS TO DO.

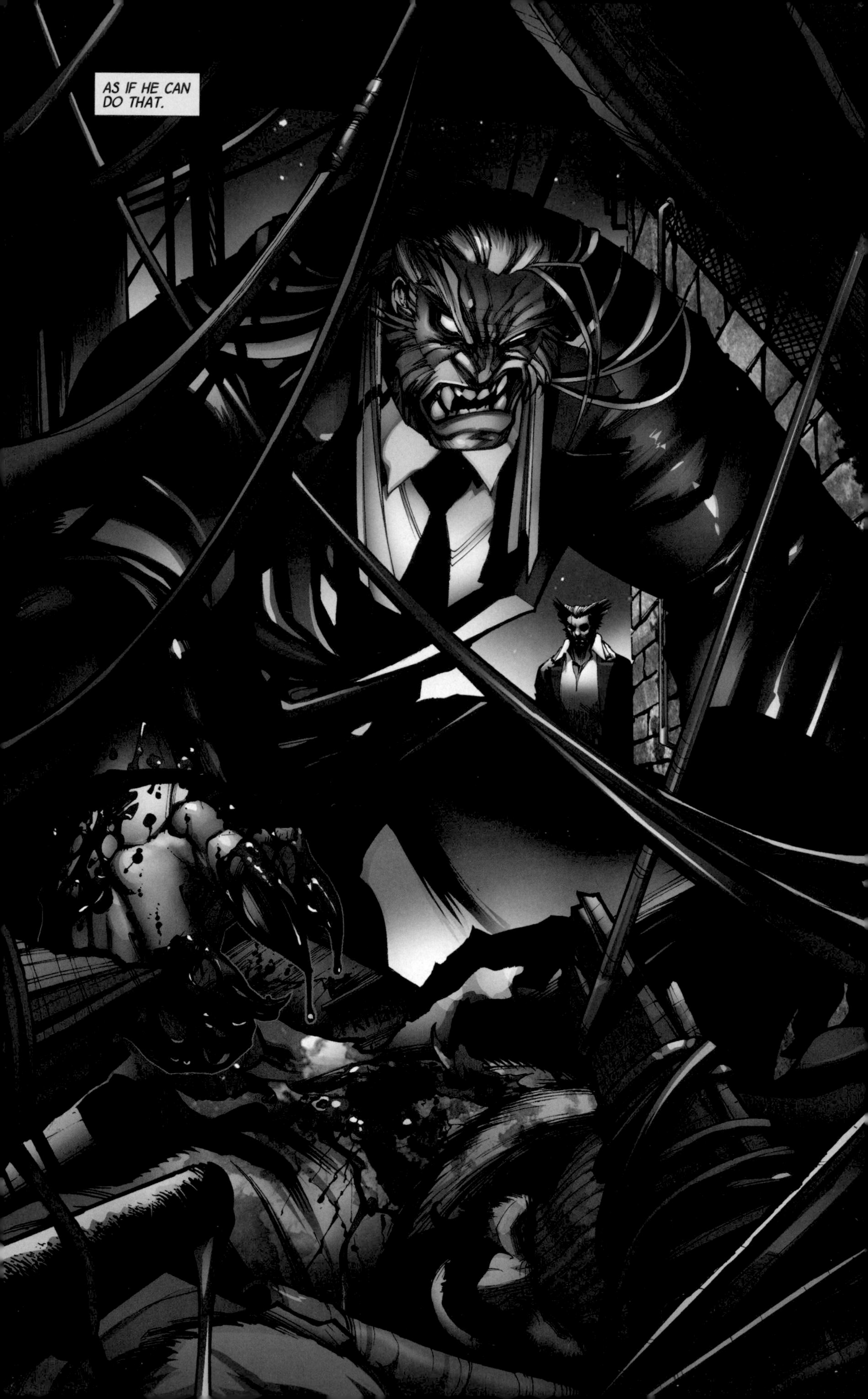
AS IF HE CAN
DO THAT.

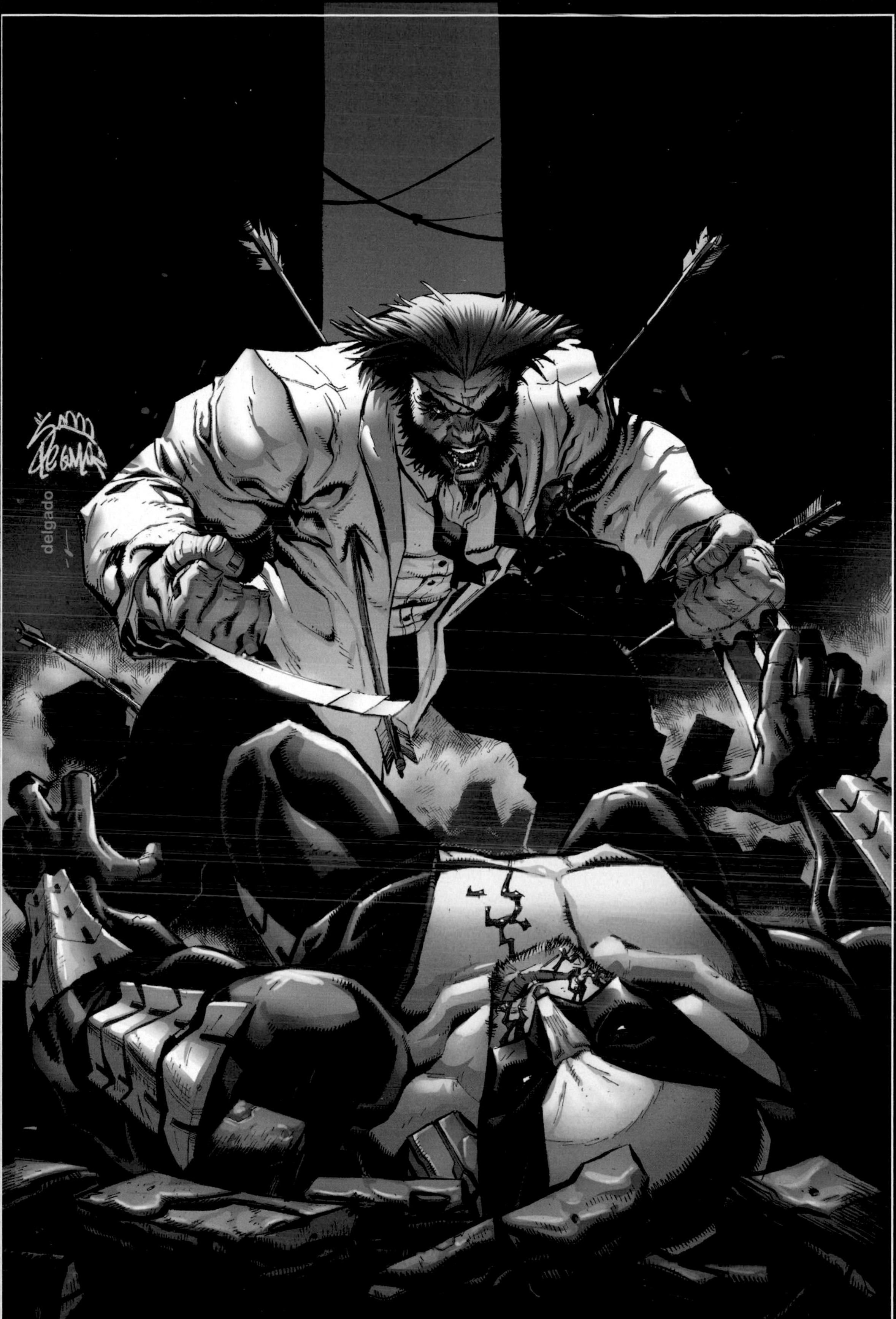
delgado

#7

THE MADRIPOOR JOB PART 2

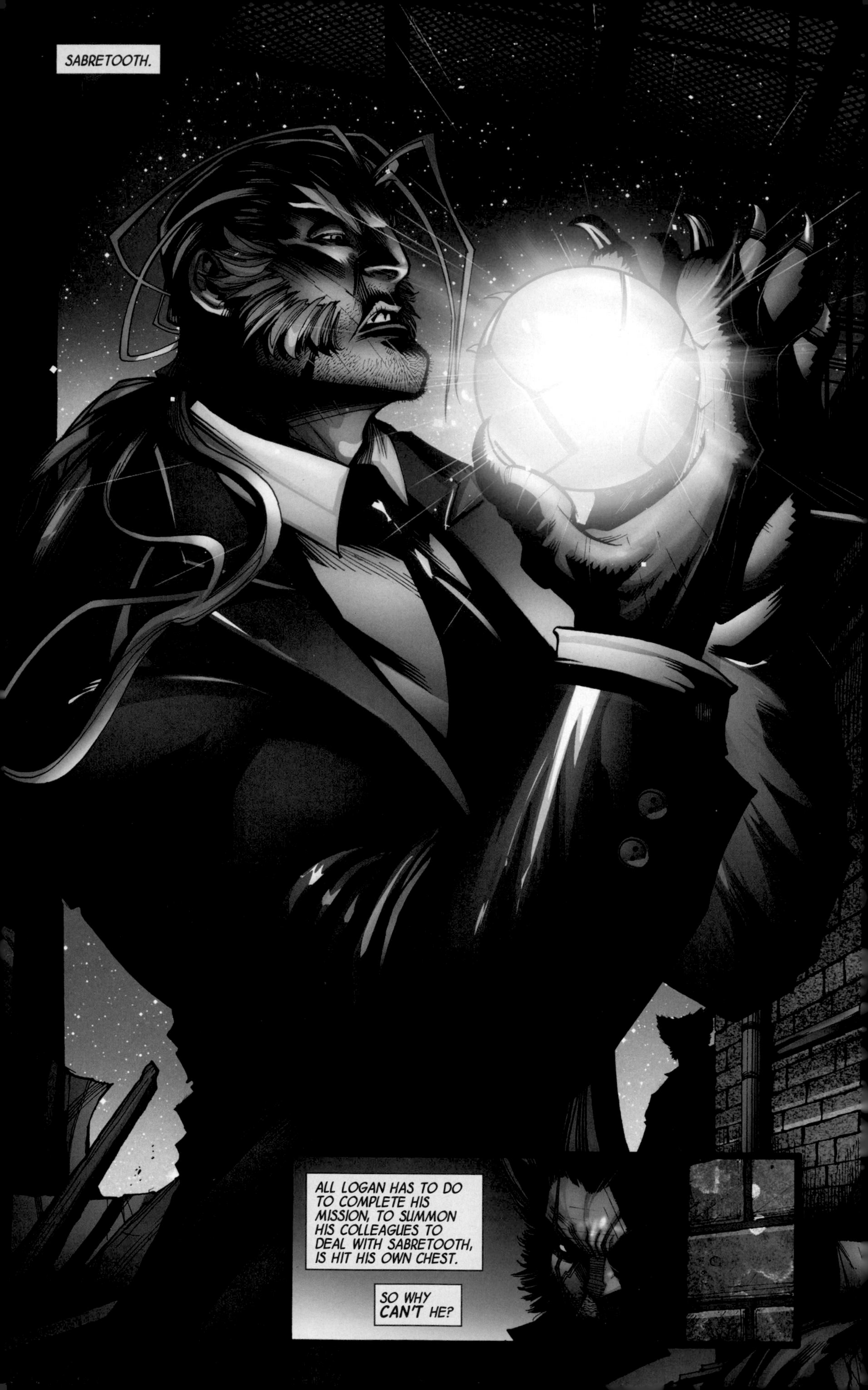
SABRETOOTH.
ALL LOGAN HAS TO DO TO COMPLETE HIS MISSION, TO SUMMON HIS COLLEAGUES TO DEAL WITH SABRETOOTH, IS HIT HIS OWN CHEST.
SO WHY CAN'T HE?

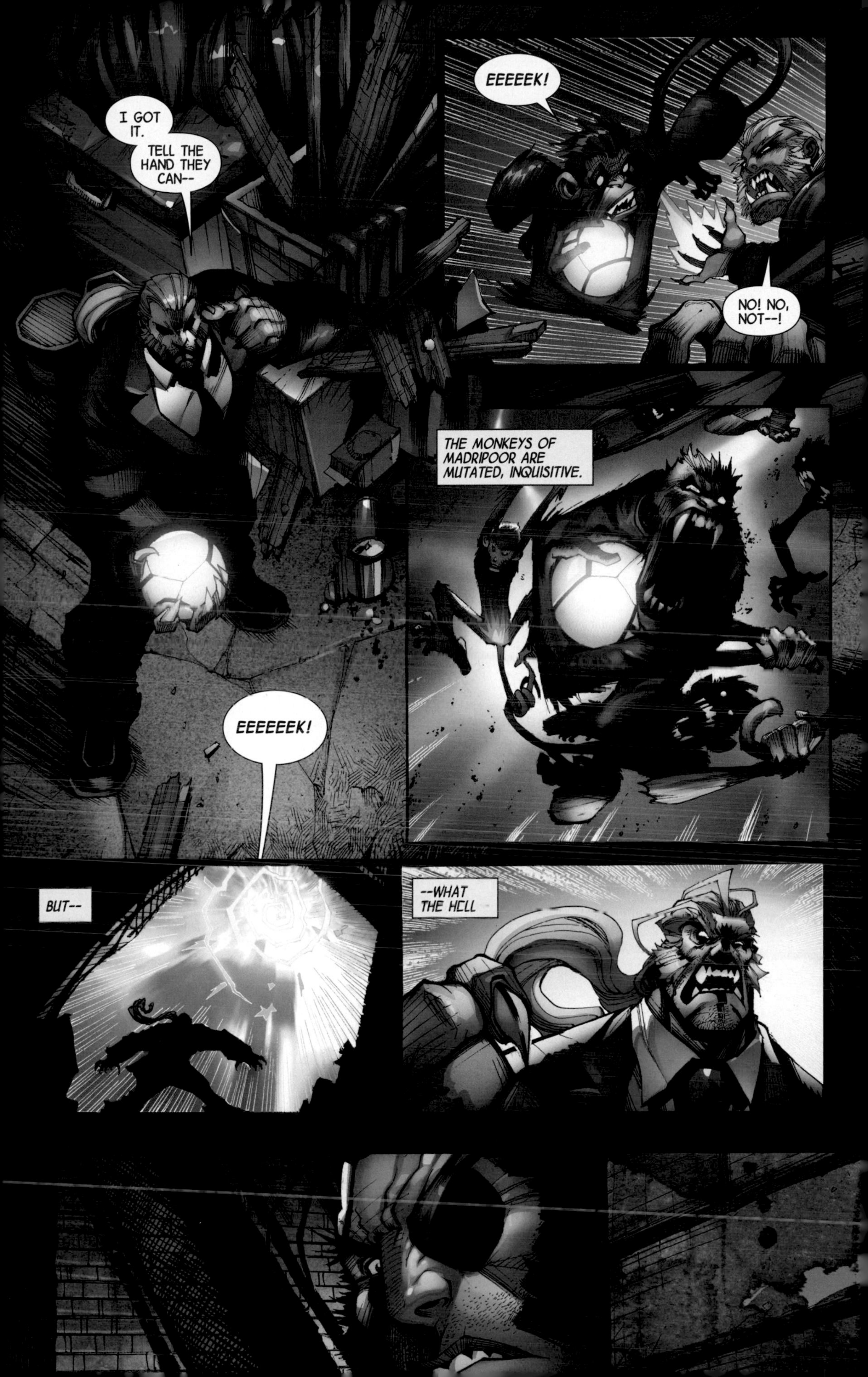
I GOT IT.
TELL THE HAND THEY CAN--
EEEEEK!
NO! NO, NOT--!
THE MONKEYS OF MADRIPOOR ARE MUTATED, INQUISITIVE.
EEEEEEK!
BUT--
--WHAT THE HELL

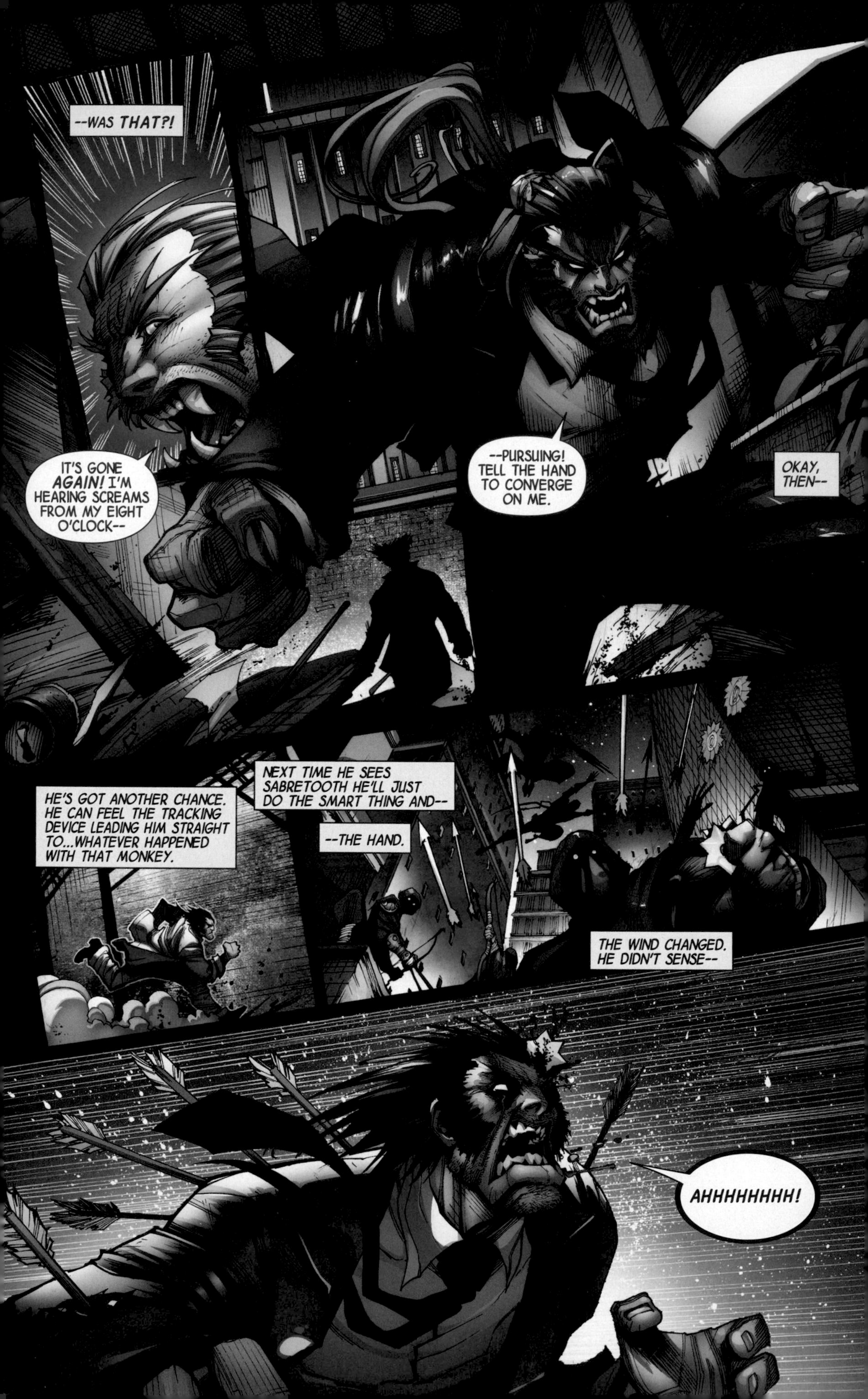
--WAS THAT?!
IT'S GONE AGAIN! I'M HEARING SCREAMS FROM MY EIGHT O'CLOCK--
--PURSUING! TELL THE HAND TO CONVERGE ON ME.
OKAY, THEN--
HE'S GOT ANOTHER CHANCE. HE CAN FEEL THE TRACKING DEVICE LEADING HIM STRAIGHT TO...WHATEVER HAPPENED WITH THAT MONKEY.
NEXT TIME HE SEES SABRETOOTH HE'LL JUST DO THE SMART THING AND--
--THE HAND.
THE WIND CHANGED. HE DIDN'T SENSE--
AHHHHHHHH!

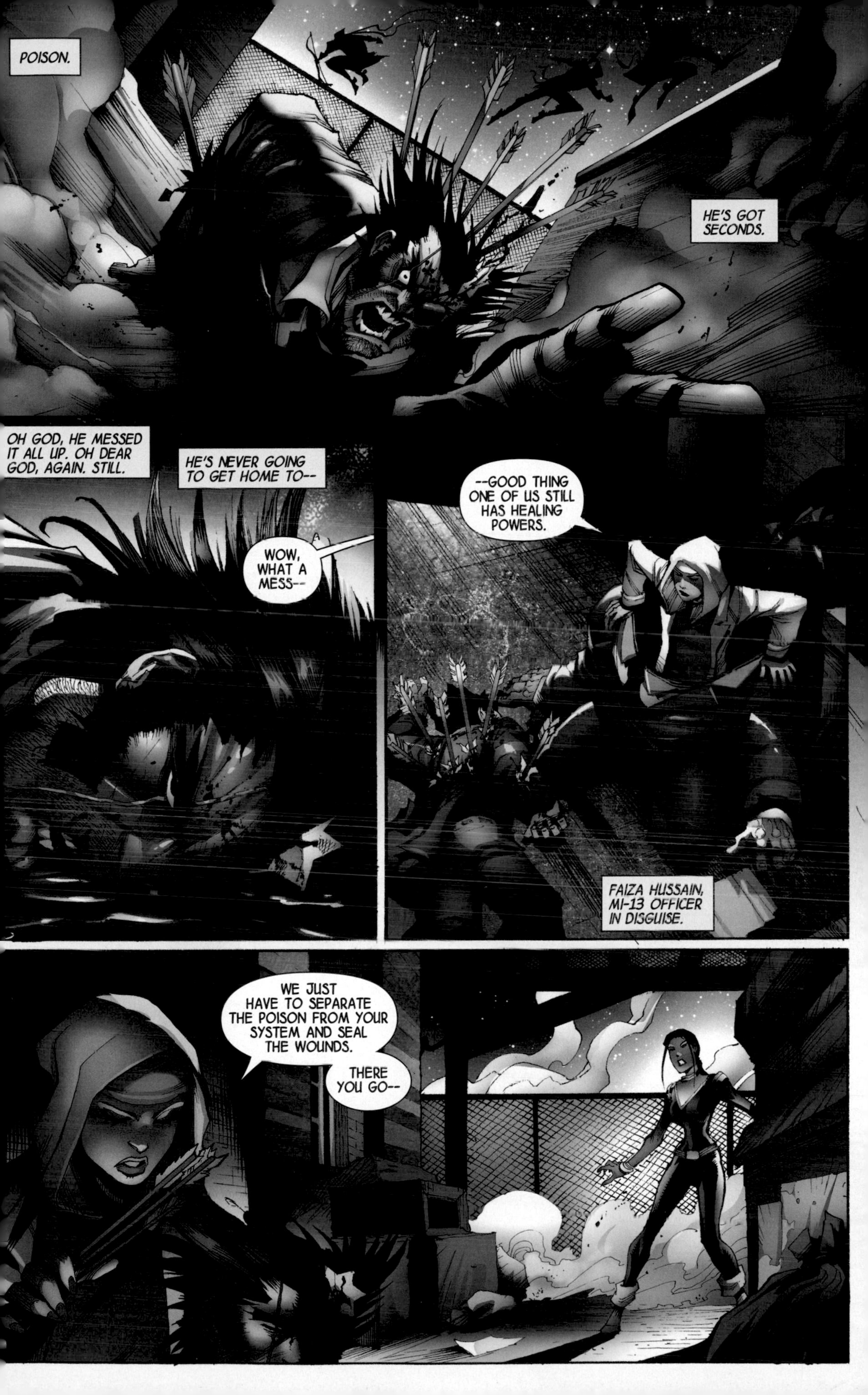
POISON.
HE'S GOT SECONDS.
OH GOD, HE MESSED IT ALL UP. OH DEAR GOD, AGAIN. STILL.
HE'S NEVER GOING TO GET HOME TO--
WOW, WHAT A MESS--
--GOOD THING ONE OF US STILL HAS HEALING POWERS.
FAIZA HUSSAIN, MI-13 OFFICER IN DISGUISE.
WE JUST HAVE TO SEPARATE THE POISON FROM YOUR SYSTEM AND SEAL THE WOUNDS.
THERE YOU GO--

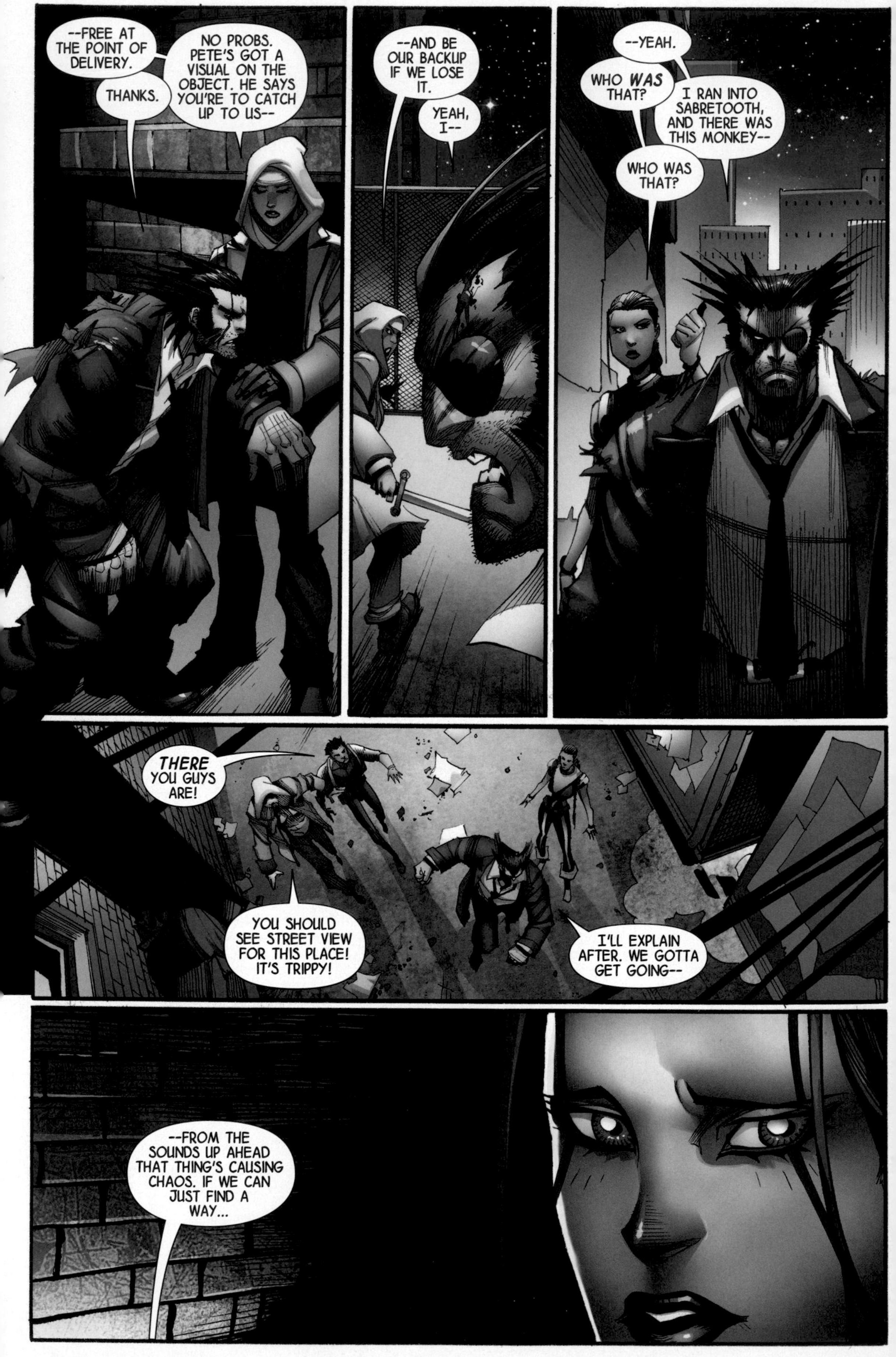
--FREE AT THE POINT OF DELIVERY.
NO PROBS. PETE'S GOT A VISUAL ON THE OBJECT. HE SAYS YOU'RE TO CATCH UP TO US--
THANKS.
--AND BE OUR BACKUP IF WE LOSE IT.
YEAH, I--
--YEAH.
WHO *WAS* THAT?
I RAN INTO SABRETOOTH, AND THERE WAS THIS MONKEY--
WHO WAS THAT?
THERE YOU GUYS ARE!
YOU SHOULD SEE STREET VIEW FOR THIS PLACE! IT'S TRIPPY!
I'LL EXPLAIN AFTER. WE GOTTA GET GOING--
--FROM THE SOUNDS UP AHEAD THAT THING'S CAUSING CHAOS. IF WE CAN JUST FIND A WAY...

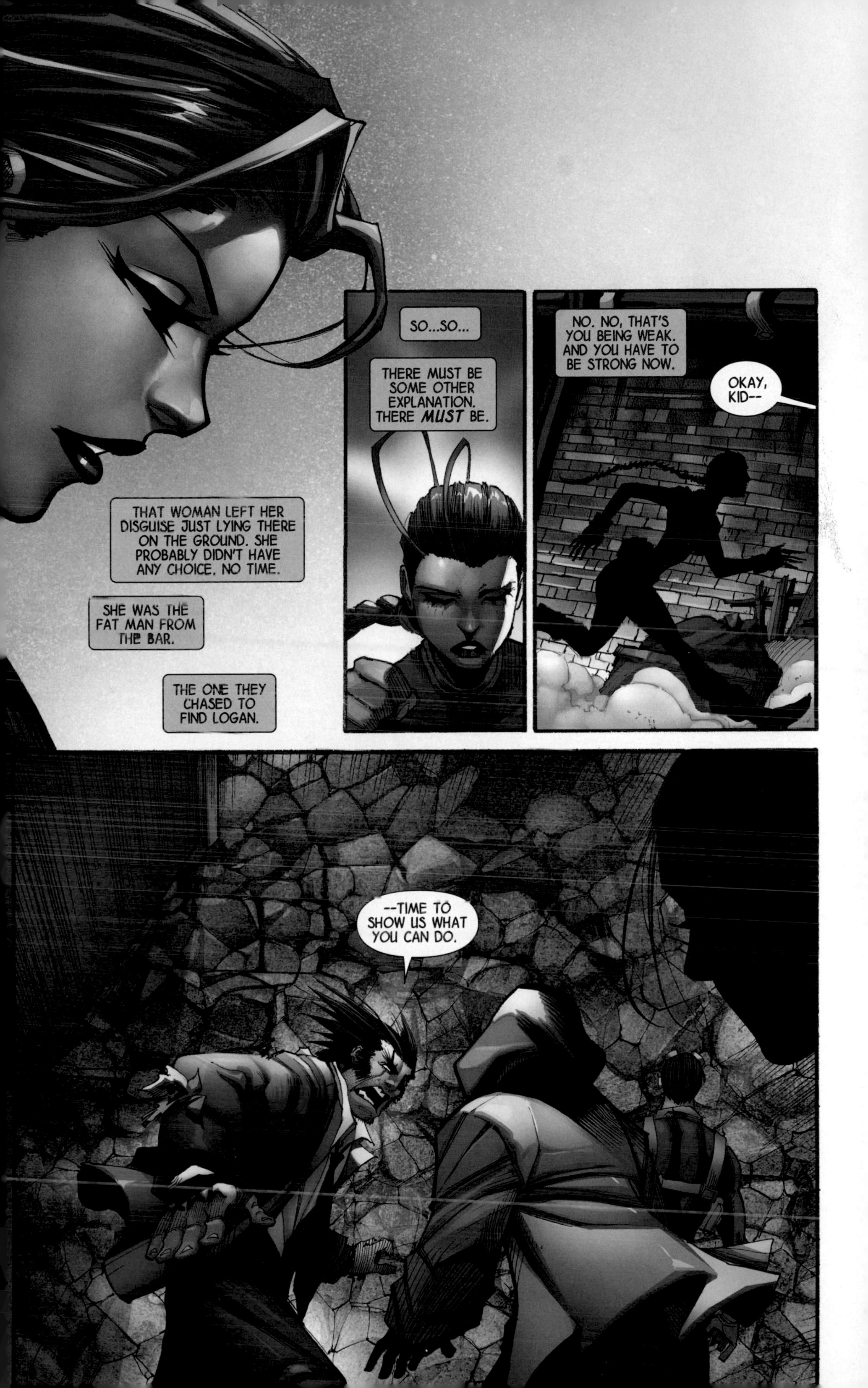
THAT WOMAN LEFT HER DISGUISE JUST LYING THERE ON THE GROUND. SHE PROBABLY DIDN'T HAVE ANY CHOICE. NO TIME.
SHE WAS THE FAT MAN FROM THE BAR.
THE ONE THEY CHASED TO FIND LOGAN.
SO...SO...
THERE MUST BE SOME OTHER EXPLANATION. THERE *MUST* BE.
NO. NO, THAT'S YOU BEING WEAK. AND YOU HAVE TO BE STRONG NOW.
OKAY, KID--
--TIME TO SHOW US WHAT YOU CAN DO.

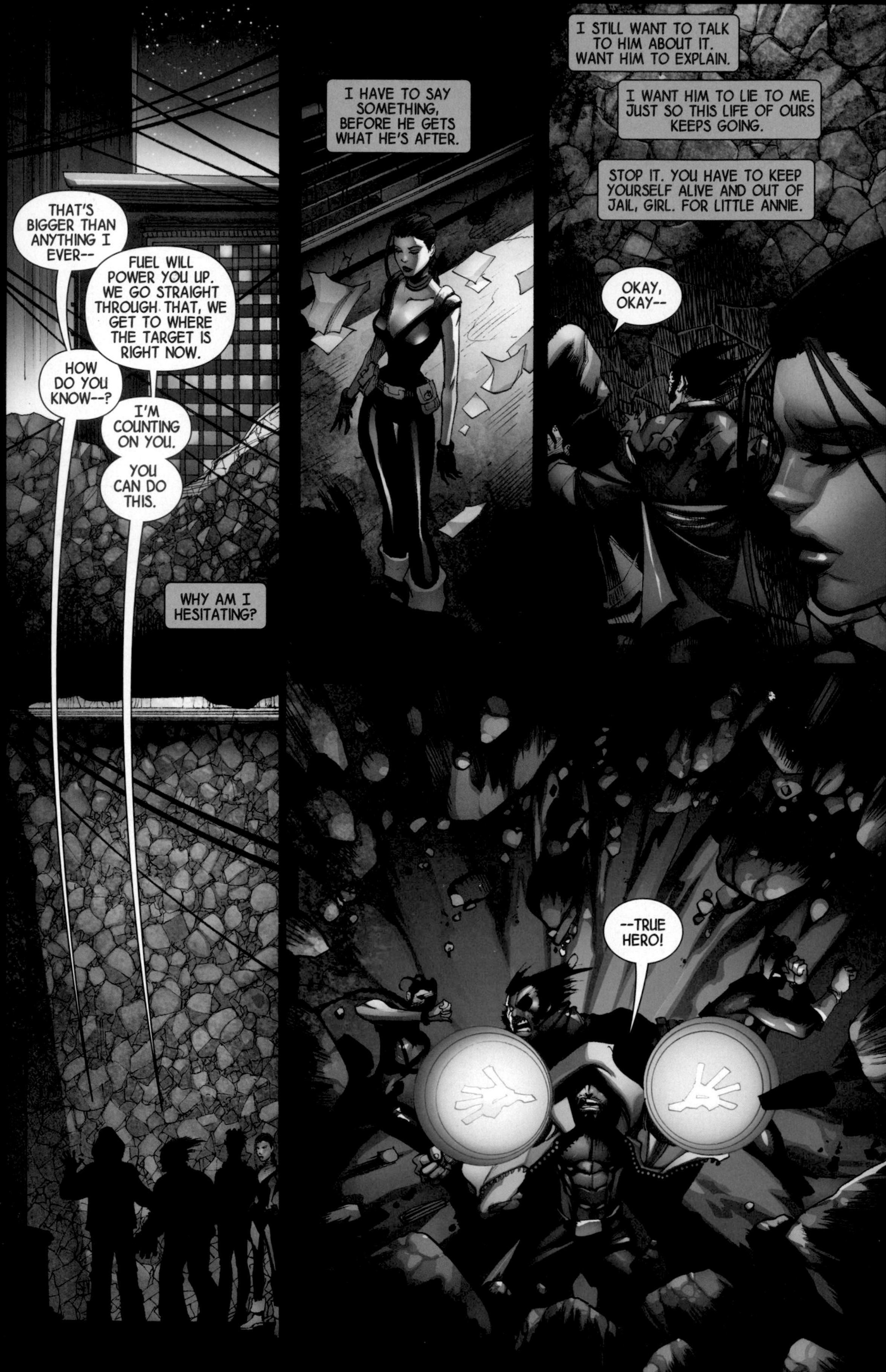
THAT'S BIGGER THAN ANYTHING I EVER--
FUEL WILL POWER YOU UP. WE GO STRAIGHT THROUGH THAT, WE GET TO WHERE THE TARGET IS RIGHT NOW.
HOW DO YOU KNOW--?
I'M COUNTING ON YOU.
YOU CAN DO THIS.
WHY AM I HESITATING?
I HAVE TO SAY SOMETHING, BEFORE HE GETS WHAT HE'S AFTER.
I STILL WANT TO TALK TO HIM ABOUT IT. WANT HIM TO EXPLAIN.
I WANT HIM TO LIE TO ME. JUST SO THIS LIFE OF OURS KEEPS GOING.
STOP IT. YOU HAVE TO KEEP YOURSELF ALIVE AND OUT OF JAIL, GIRL. FOR LITTLE ANNIE.
OKAY, OKAY--
--TRUE HERO!

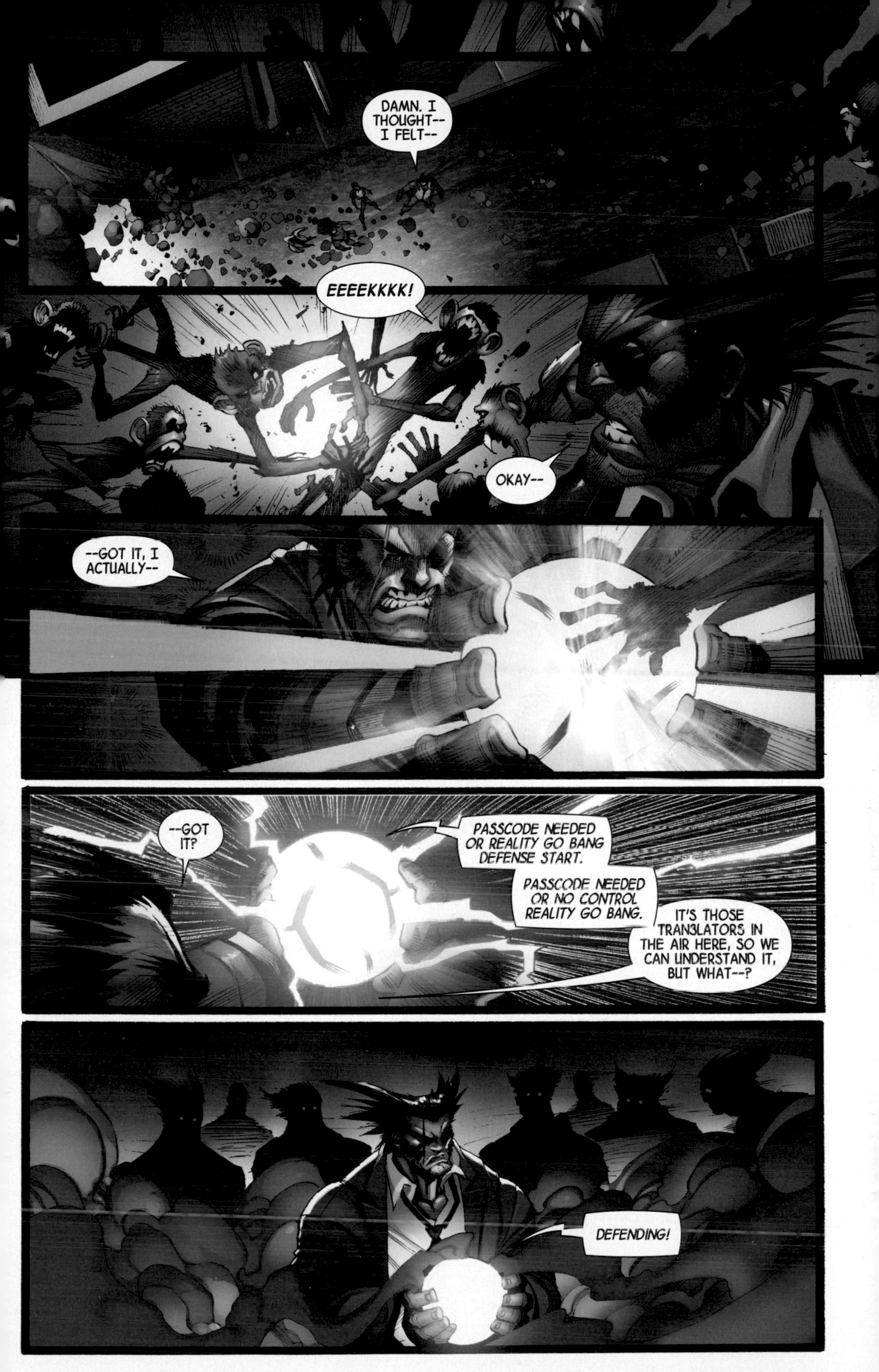
DAMN. I THOUGHT-- I FELT--
EEEEKKKK!
OKAY--
--GOT IT, I ACTUALLY--
--GOT IT?
PASSCODE NEEDED OR REALITY GO BANG DEFENSE START.
PASSCODE NEEDED OR NO CONTROL REALITY GO BANG.
IT'S THOSE TRANSLATORS IN THE AIR HERE, SO WE CAN UNDERSTAND IT, BUT WHAT--?
DEFENDING!

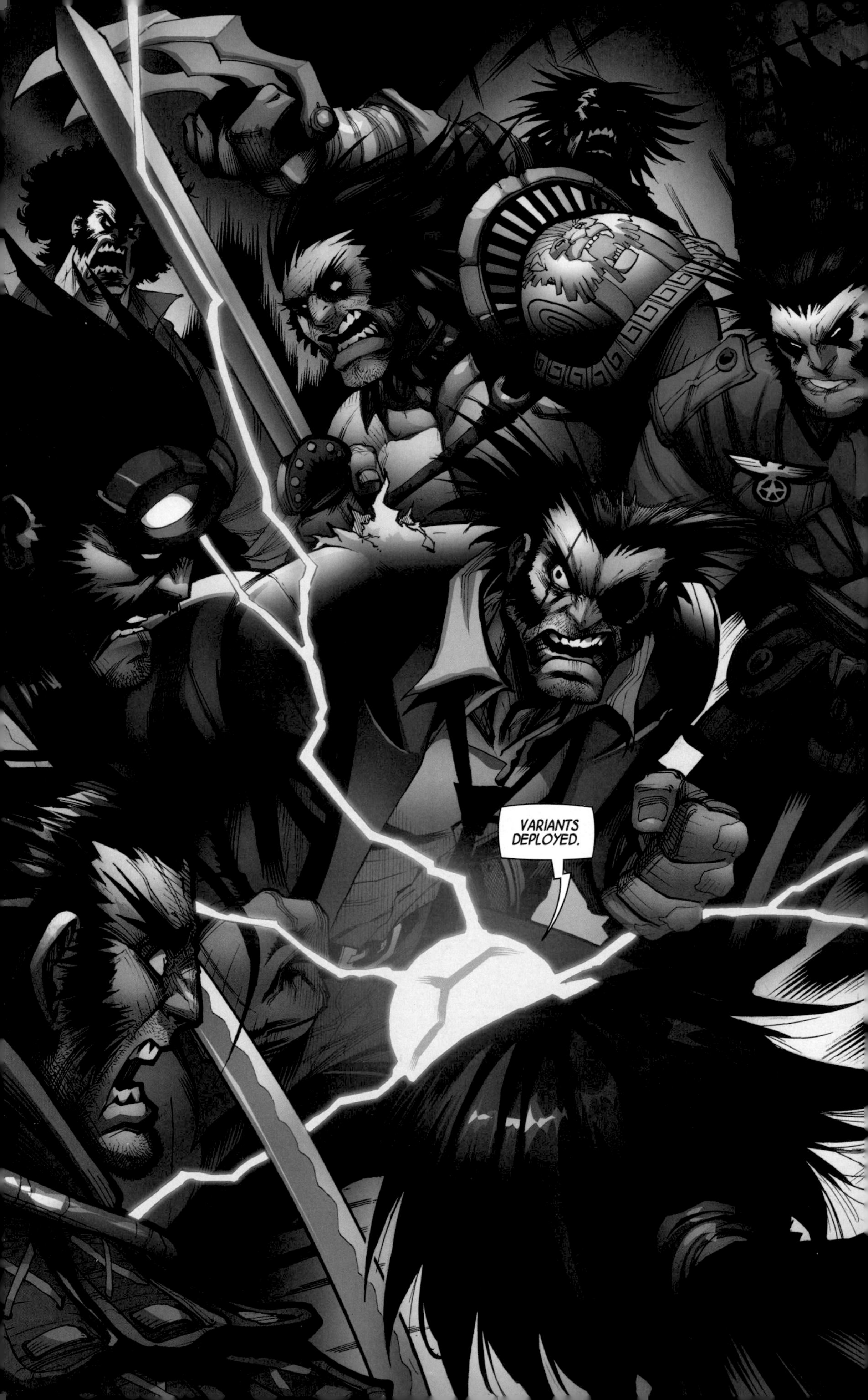
VARIANTS DEPLOYED.

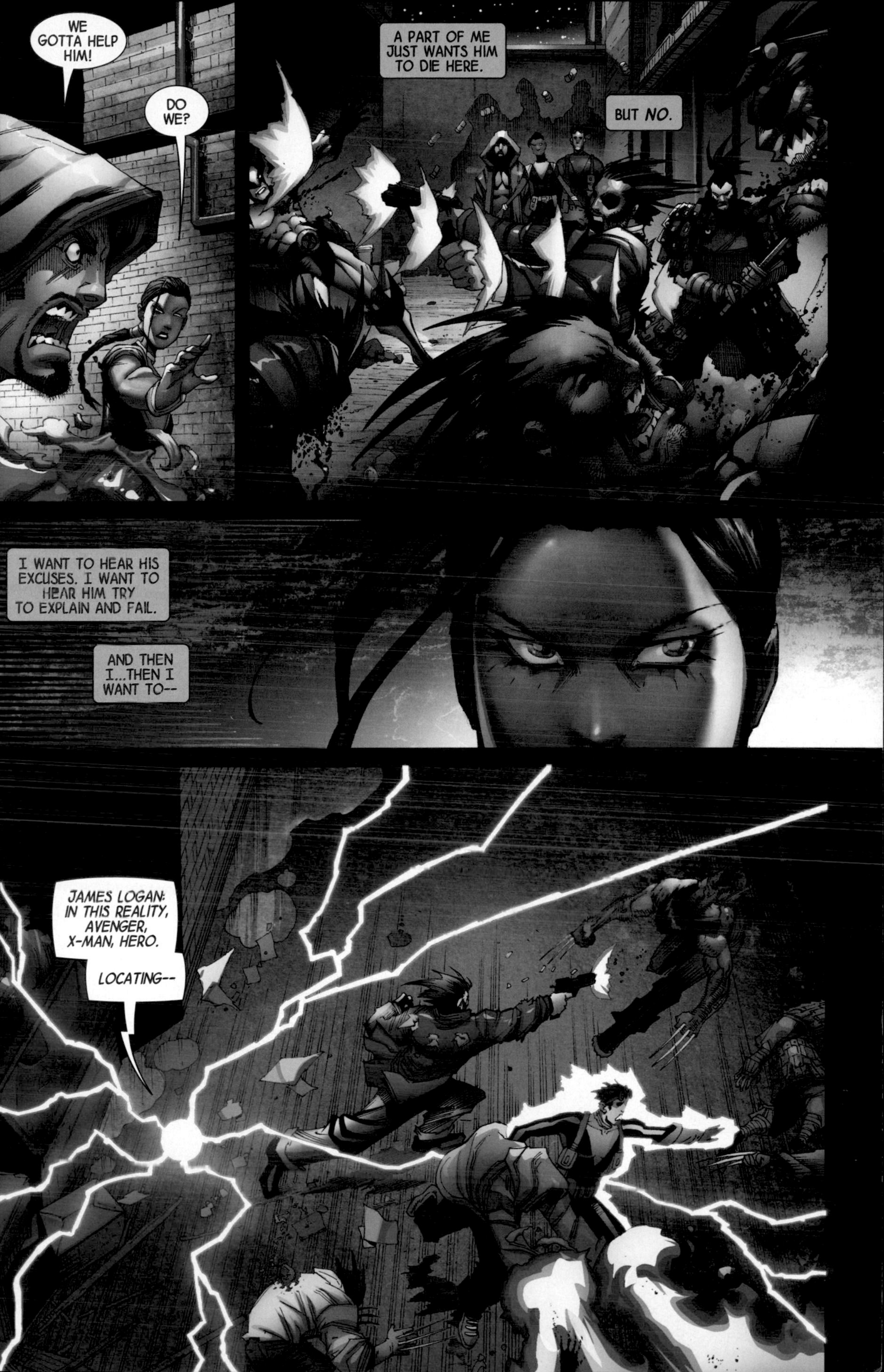
WE GOTTA HELP HIM!
DO WE?
A PART OF ME JUST WANTS HIM TO DIE HERE.
BUT NO.
I WANT TO HEAR HIS EXCUSES. I WANT TO HEAR HIM TRY TO EXPLAIN AND FAIL.
AND THEN I...THEN I WANT TO--
JAMES LOGAN: IN THIS REALITY, AVENGER, X-MAN, HERO.
LOCATING--

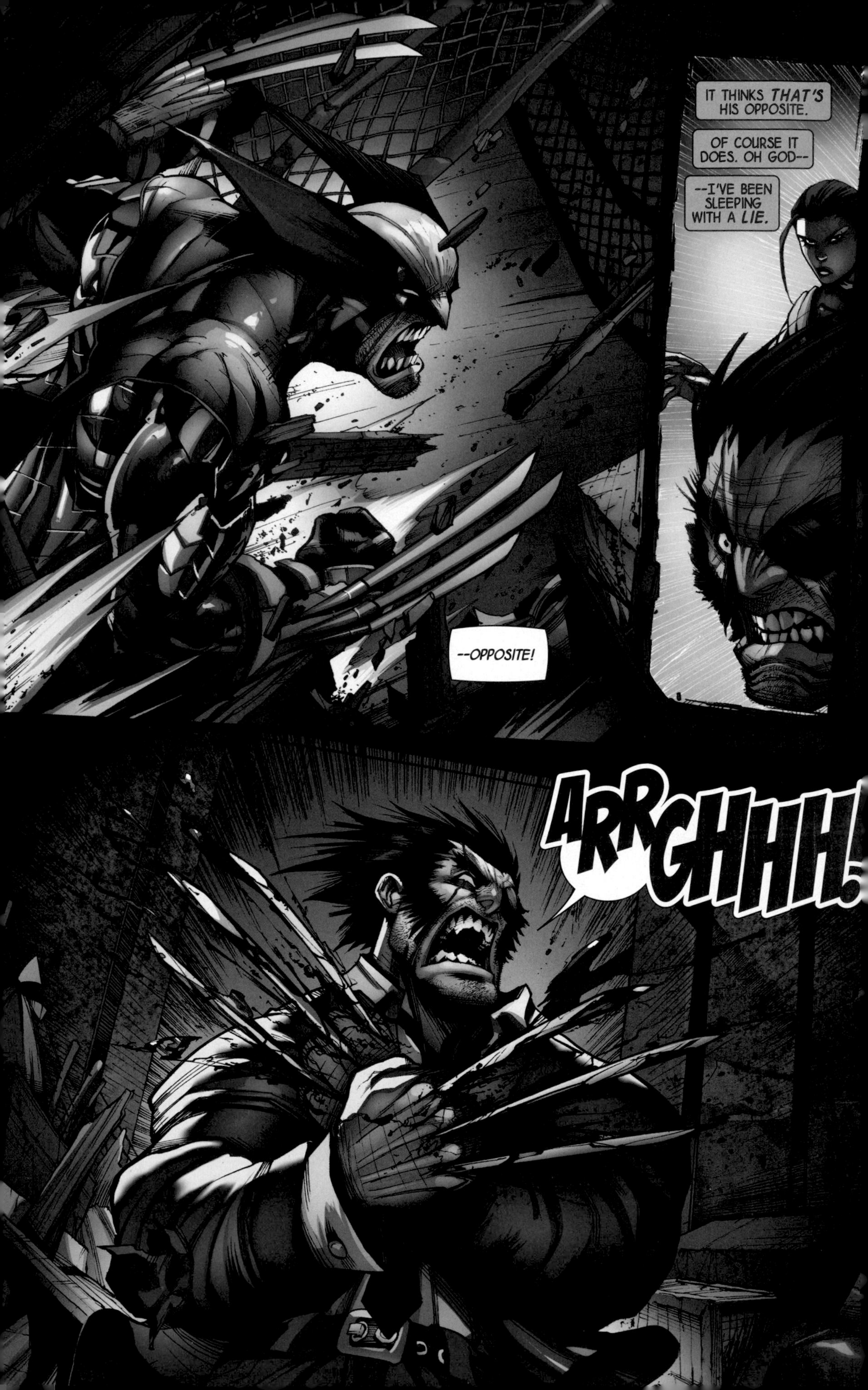
IT THINKS THAT'S HIS OPPOSITE.
OF COURSE IT DOES. OH GOD--
--I'VE BEEN SLEEPING WITH A LIE.
--OPPOSITE!
ARRGHHH!

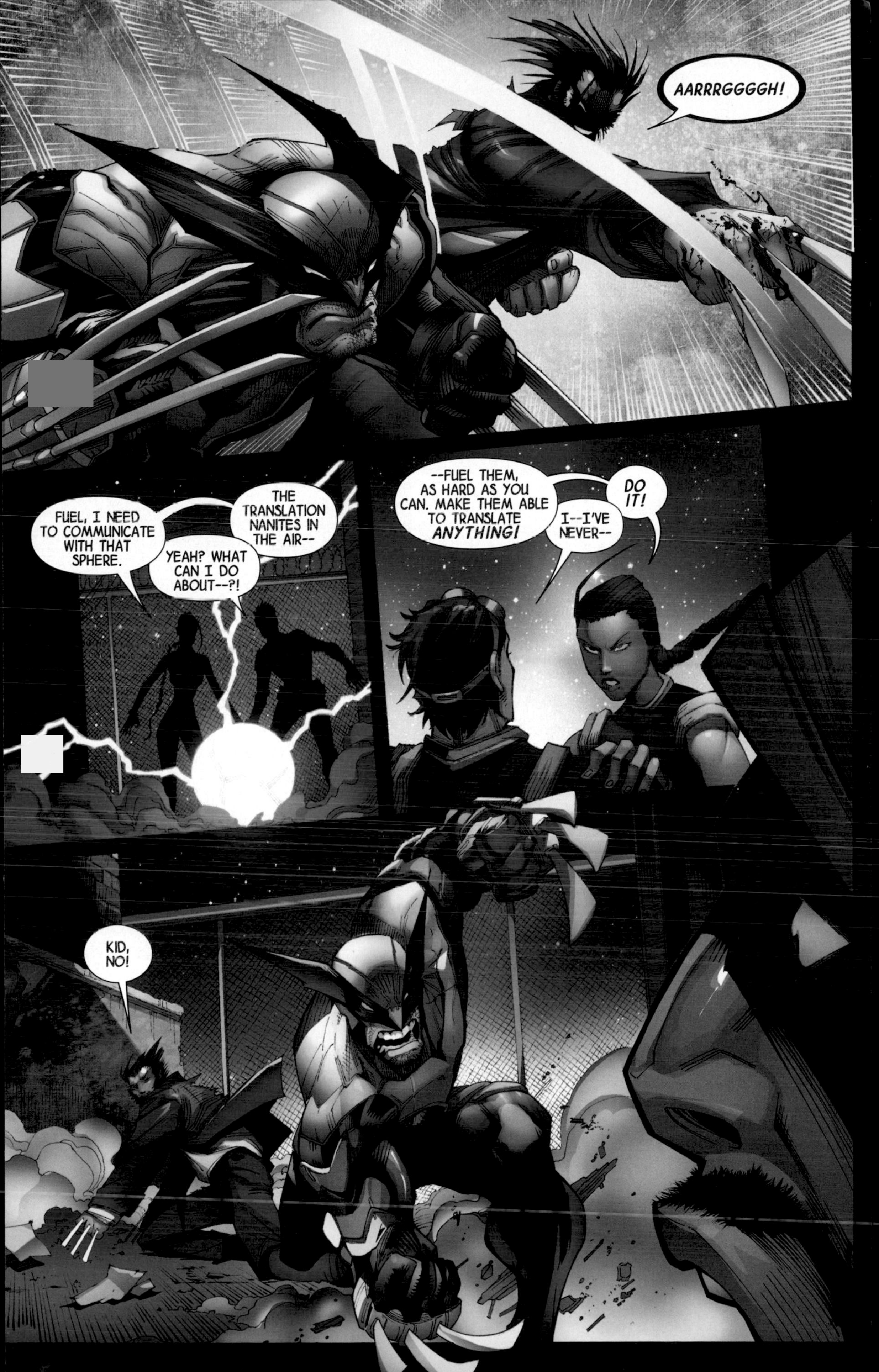
AARRRGGGGH!
FUEL, I NEED TO COMMUNICATE WITH THAT SPHERE.
THE TRANSLATION NANITES IN THE AIR--
YEAH? WHAT CAN I DO ABOUT--?!
--FUEL THEM, AS HARD AS YOU CAN. MAKE THEM ABLE TO TRANSLATE ANYTHING!
I--I'VE NEVER--
DO IT!
KID, NO!

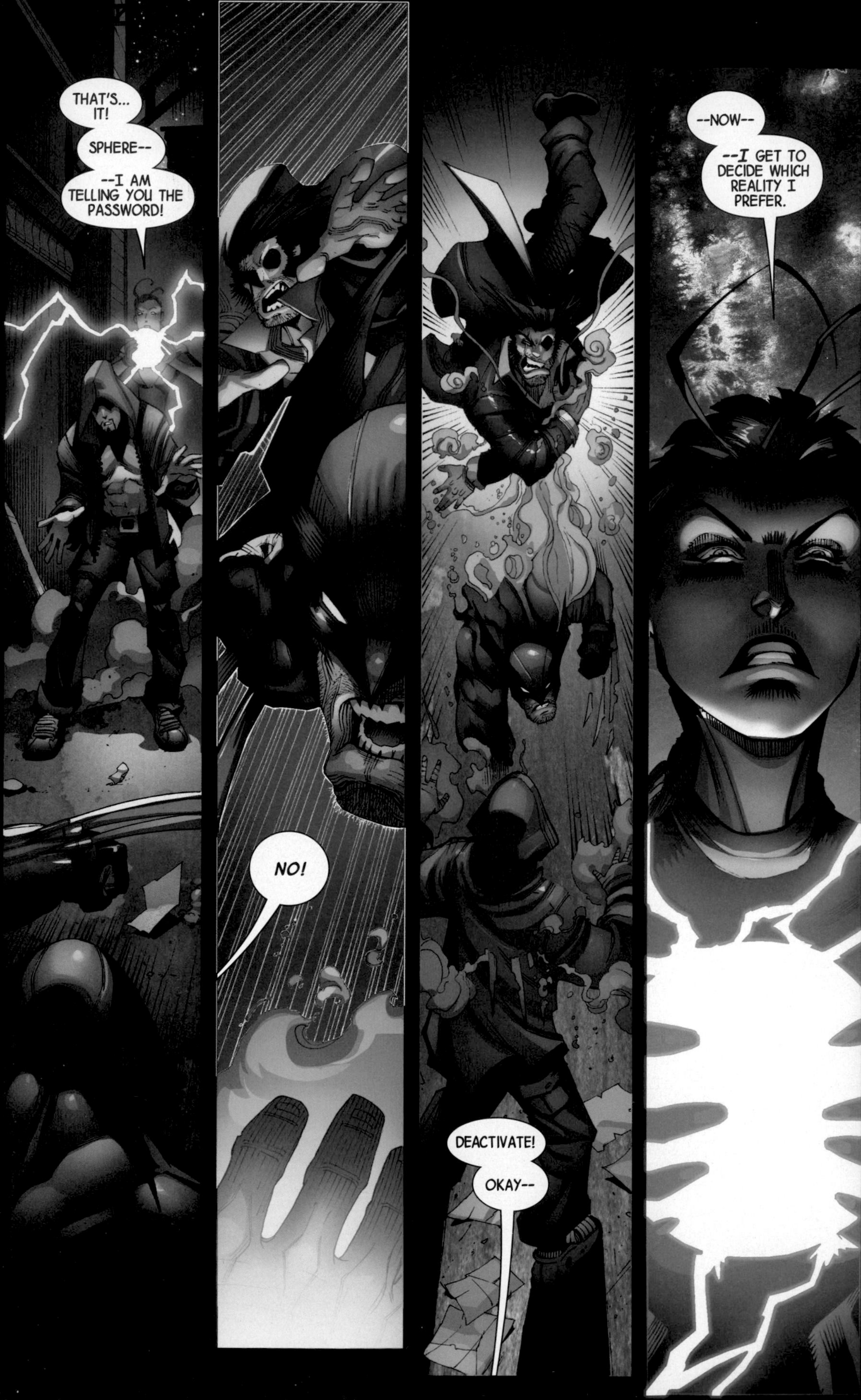
THAT'S... IT!
SPHERE--
--I AM TELLING YOU THE PASSWORD!
NO!
DEACTIVATE!
OKAY--
--NOW--
--I GET TO DECIDE WHICH REALITY I PREFER.

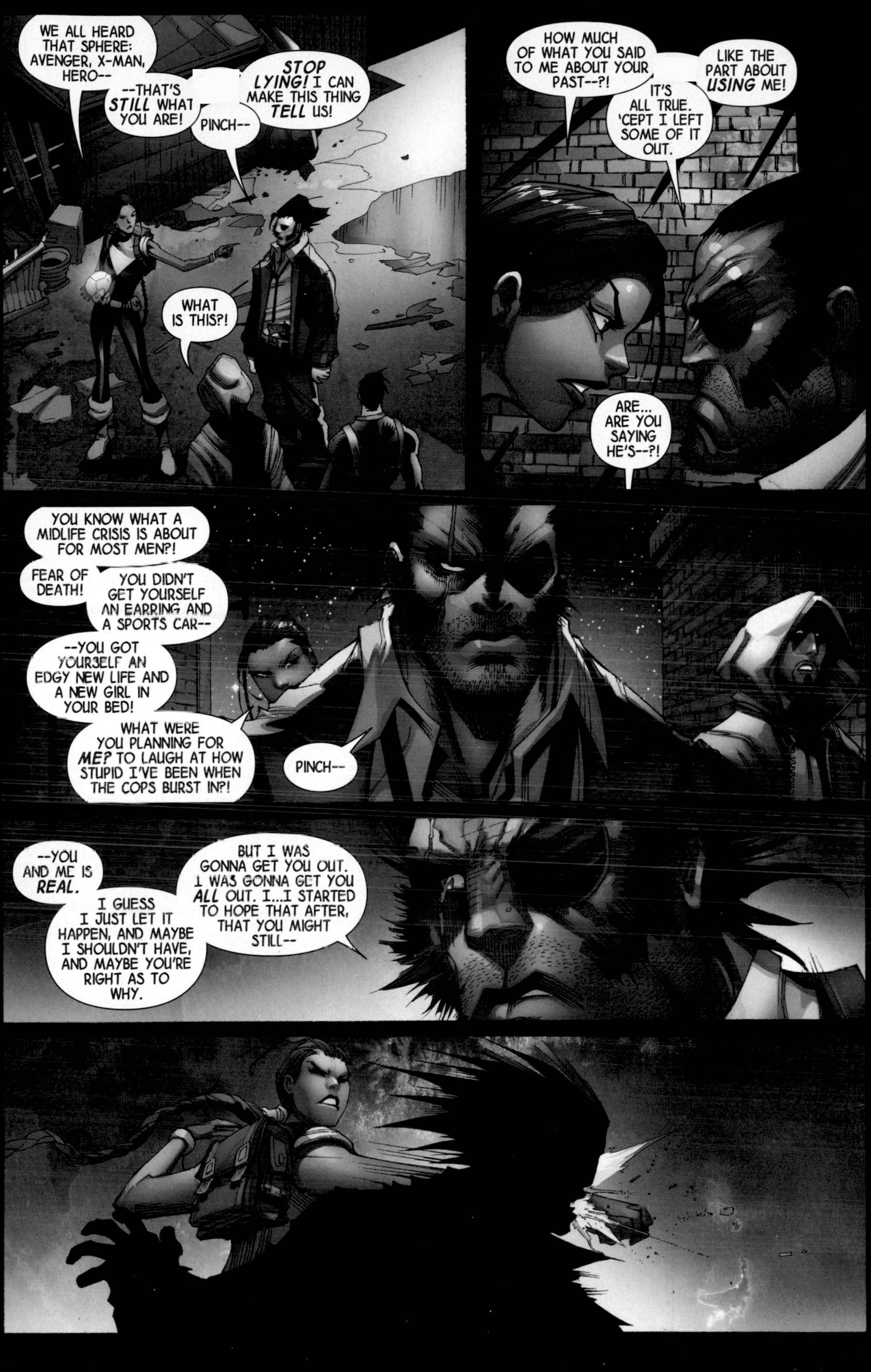
WE ALL HEARD THAT SPHERE: AVENGER, X-MAN, HERO--
--THAT'S STILL WHAT YOU ARE!
PINCH--
STOP LYING! I CAN MAKE THIS THING TELL US!
WHAT IS THIS?!
HOW MUCH OF WHAT YOU SAID TO ME ABOUT YOUR PAST--?!
IT'S ALL TRUE. 'CEPT I LEFT SOME OF IT OUT.
LIKE THE PART ABOUT USING ME!
ARE... ARE YOU SAYING HE'S--?!
YOU KNOW WHAT A MIDLIFE CRISIS IS ABOUT FOR MOST MEN?!
FEAR OF DEATH!
YOU DIDN'T GET YOURSELF AN EARRING AND A SPORTS CAR--
--YOU GOT YOURSELF AN EDGY NEW LIFE AND A NEW GIRL IN YOUR BED!
WHAT WERE YOU PLANNING FOR ME? TO LAUGH AT HOW STUPID I'VE BEEN WHEN THE COPS BURST IN?!
PINCH--
BUT I WAS GONNA GET YOU OUT. I WAS GONNA GET YOU ALL OUT. I...I STARTED TO HOPE THAT AFTER, THAT YOU MIGHT STILL--
--YOU AND ME IS REAL.
I GUESS I JUST LET IT HAPPEN, AND MAYBE I SHOULDN'T HAVE, AND MAYBE YOU'RE RIGHT AS TO WHY.

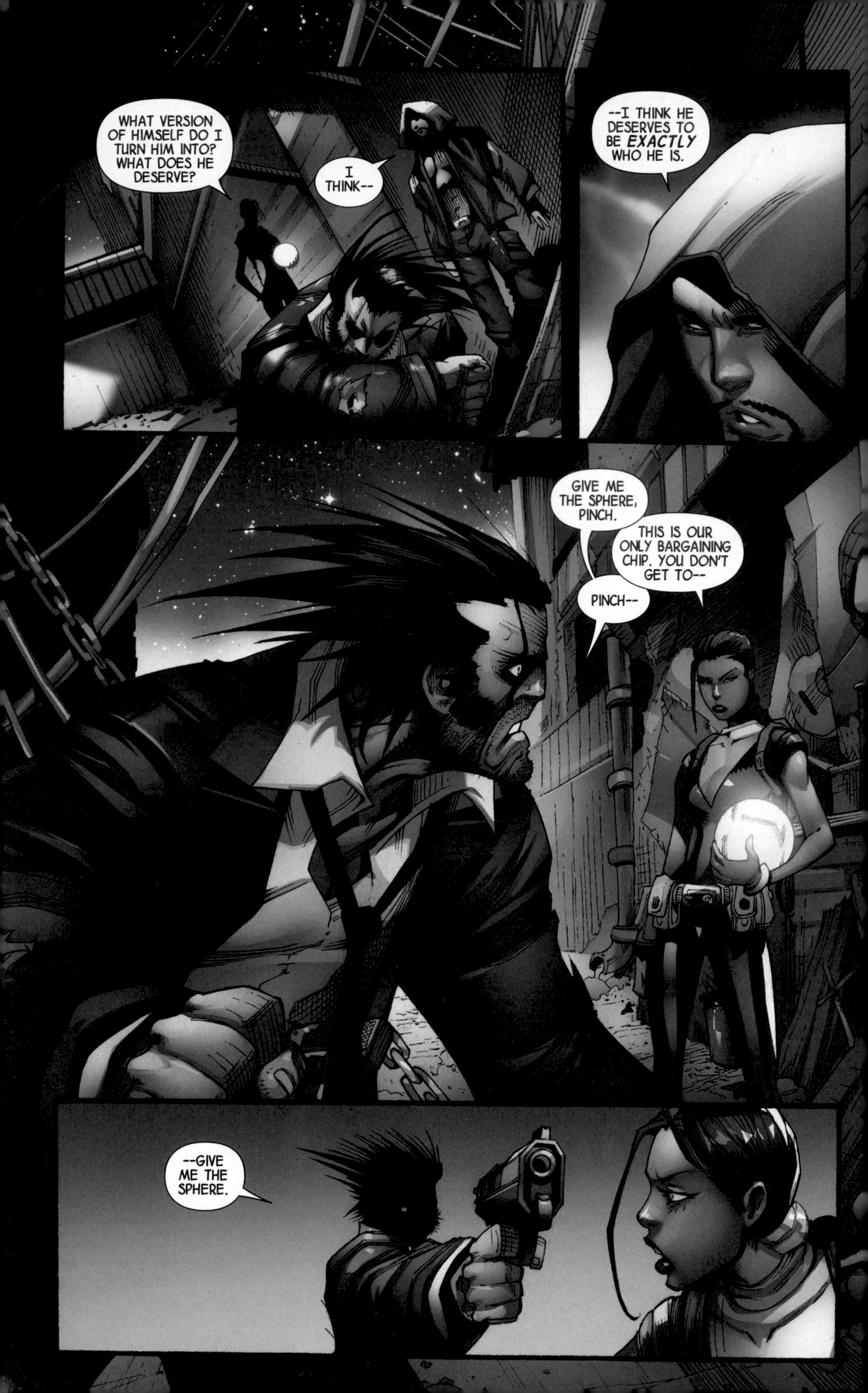
WHAT VERSION OF HIMSELF DO I TURN HIM INTO? WHAT DOES HE DESERVE?
I THINK--
--I THINK HE DESERVES TO BE *EXACTLY* WHO HE IS.
GIVE ME THE SPHERE, PINCH.
THIS IS OUR ONLY BARGAINING CHIP. YOU DON'T GET TO--
PINCH--
--GIVE ME THE SPHERE.

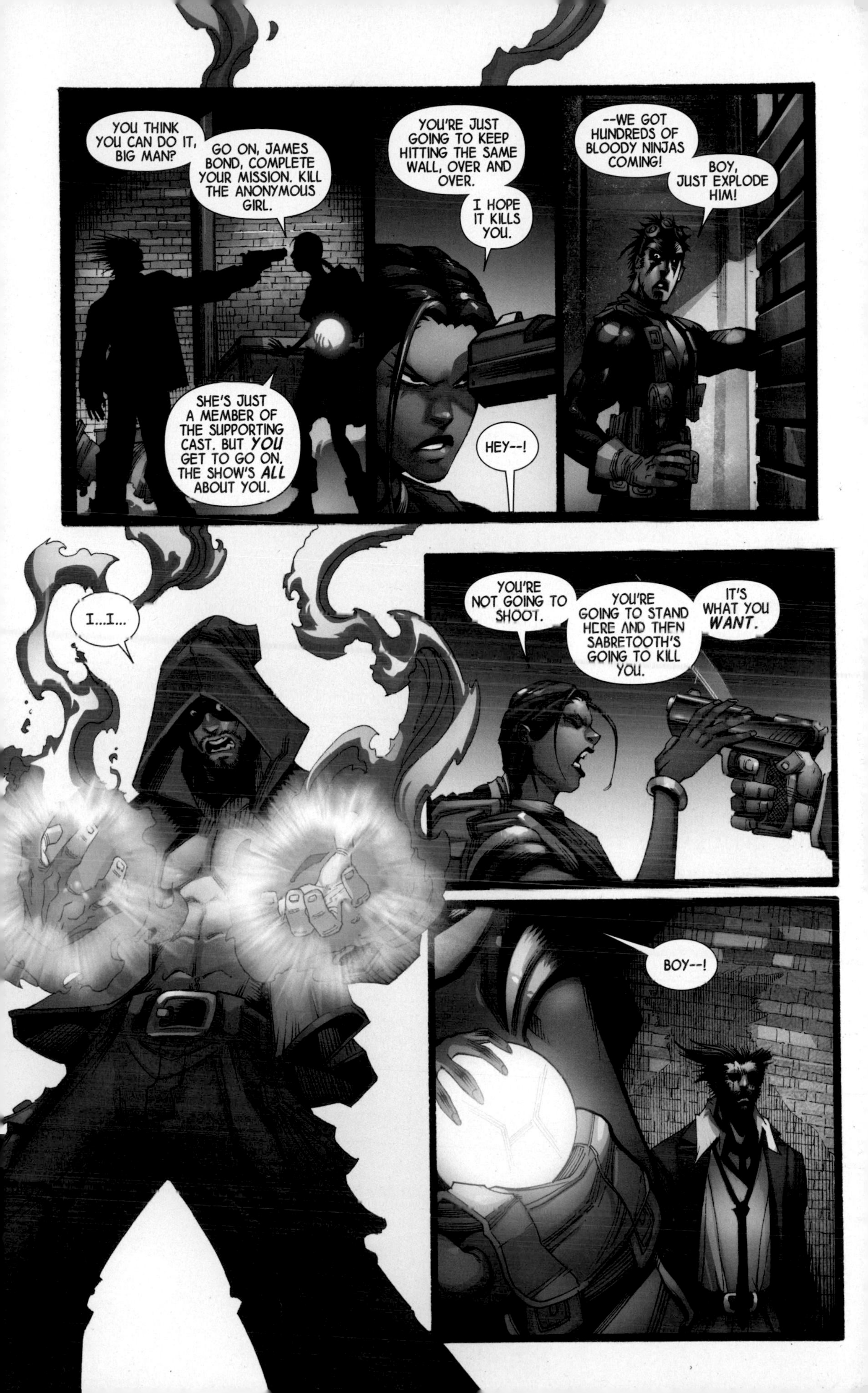
YOU THINK YOU CAN DO IT, BIG MAN?
GO ON, JAMES BOND, COMPLETE YOUR MISSION. KILL THE ANONYMOUS GIRL.
SHE'S JUST A MEMBER OF THE SUPPORTING CAST. BUT YOU GET TO GO ON. THE SHOW'S ALL ABOUT YOU.
YOU'RE JUST GOING TO KEEP HITTING THE SAME WALL, OVER AND OVER.
I HOPE IT KILLS YOU.
HEY--!
--WE GOT HUNDREDS OF BLOODY NINJAS COMING!
BOY, JUST EXPLODE HIM!
I...I...
YOU'RE NOT GOING TO SHOOT.
YOU'RE GOING TO STAND HERE AND THEN SABRETOOTH'S GOING TO KILL YOU.
IT'S WHAT YOU WANT.
BOY--!

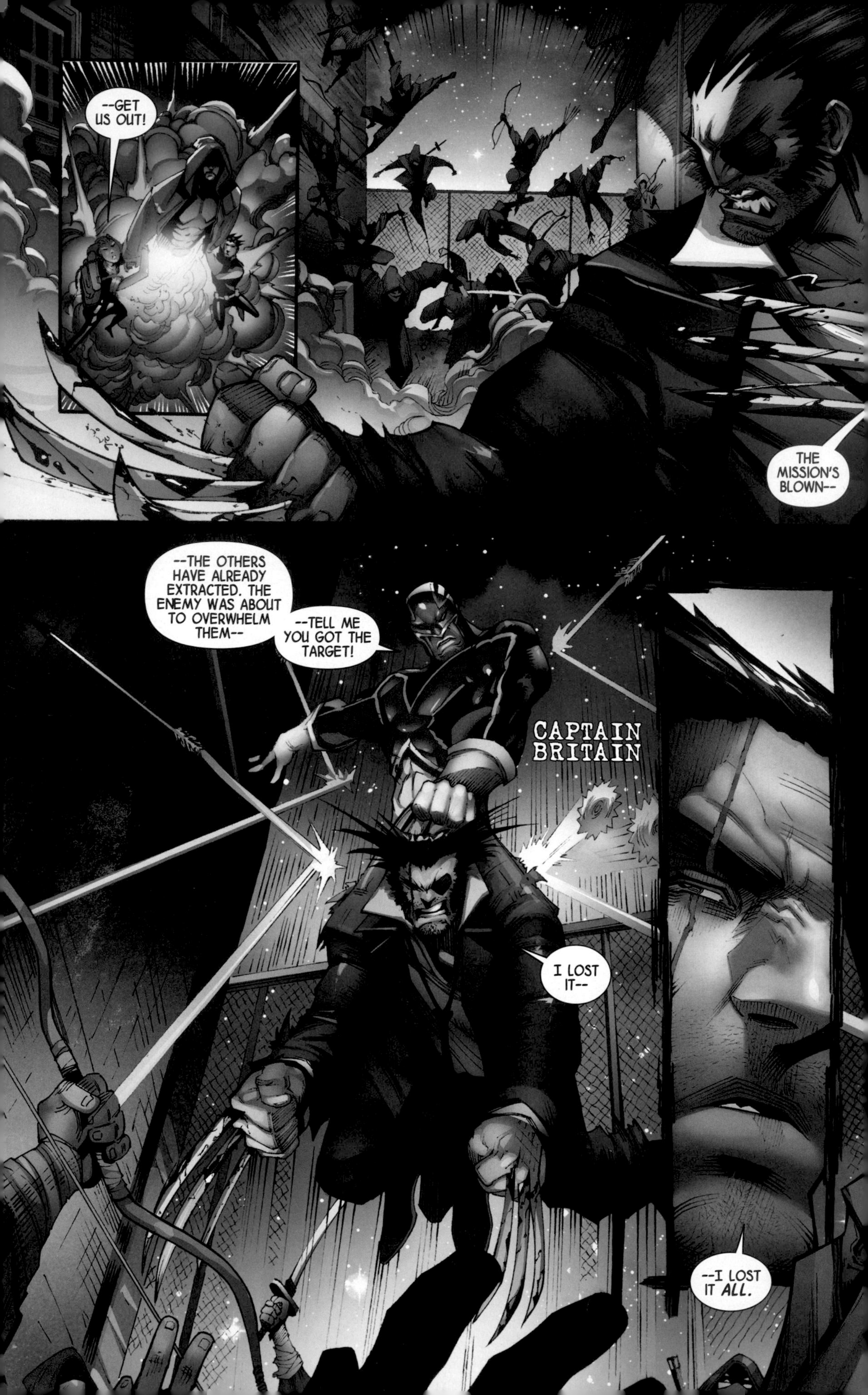
--GET US OUT!
THE MISSION'S BLOWN--
--THE OTHERS HAVE ALREADY EXTRACTED. THE ENEMY WAS ABOUT TO OVERWHELM THEM--
--TELL ME YOU GOT THE TARGET!
CAPTAIN BRITAIN
I LOST IT--
--I LOST IT ALL.

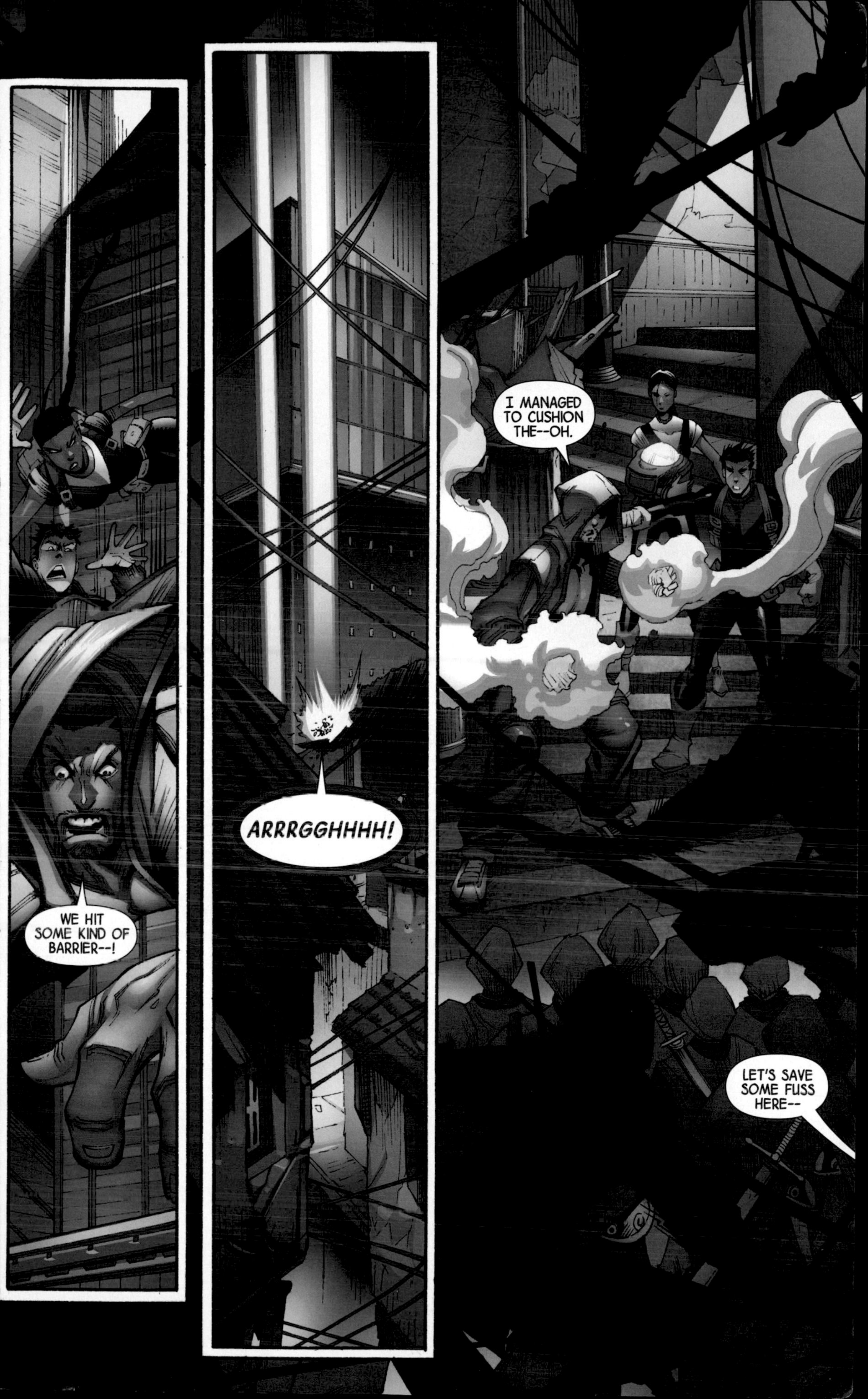
WE HIT SOME KIND OF BARRIER--!
ARRRGGHHHH!
I MANAGED TO CUSHION THE--OH.
LET'S SAVE SOME FUSS HERE--

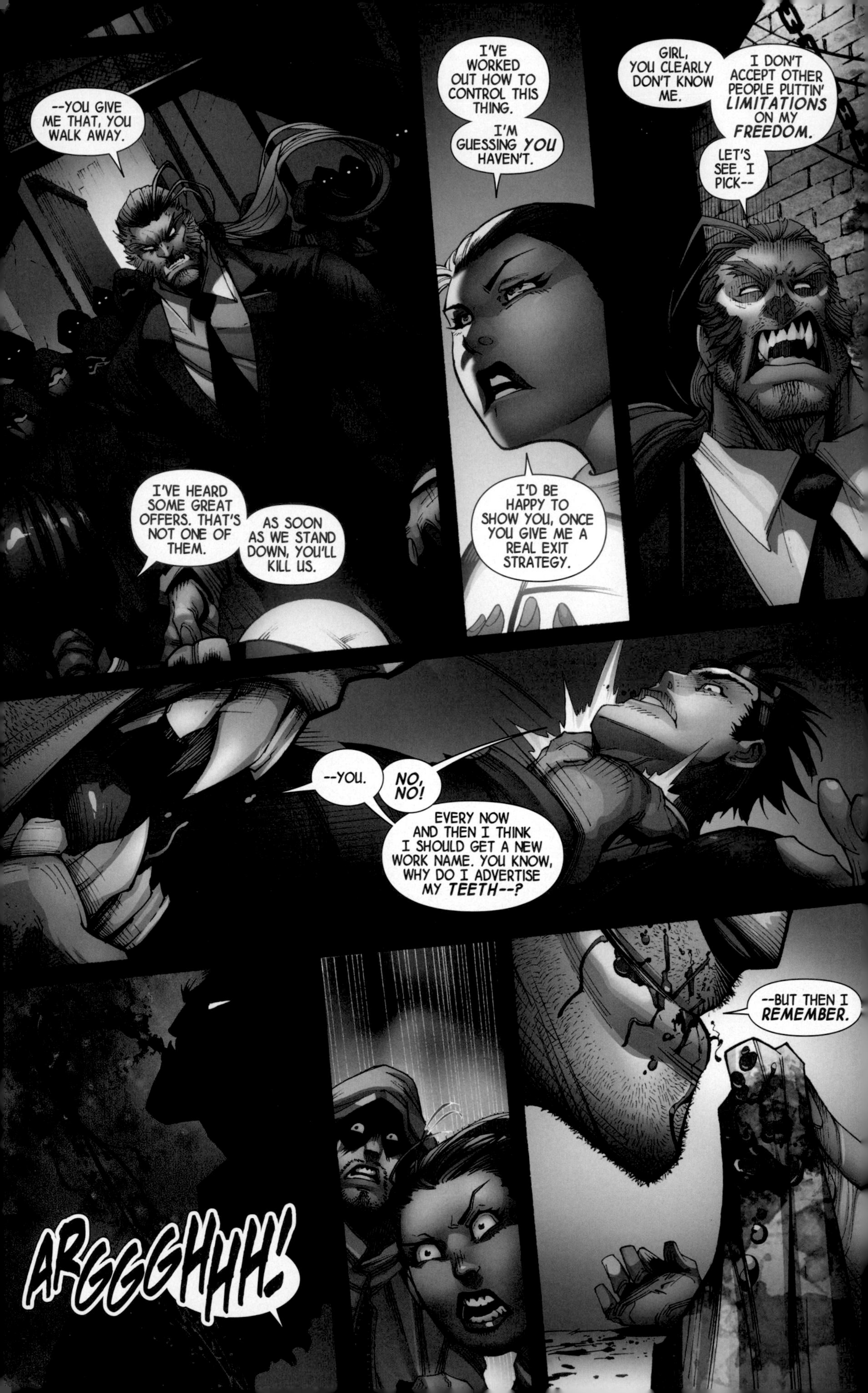
--YOU GIVE ME THAT, YOU WALK AWAY.
I'VE WORKED OUT HOW TO CONTROL THIS THING.
I'M GUESSING YOU HAVEN'T.
GIRL, YOU CLEARLY DON'T KNOW ME.
I DON'T ACCEPT OTHER PEOPLE PUTTIN' LIMITATIONS ON MY FREEDOM.
LET'S SEE. I PICK--
I'VE HEARD SOME GREAT OFFERS. THAT'S NOT ONE OF THEM.
AS SOON AS WE STAND DOWN, YOU'LL KILL US.
I'D BE HAPPY TO SHOW YOU, ONCE YOU GIVE ME A REAL EXIT STRATEGY.
--YOU.
NO, NO!
EVERY NOW AND THEN I THINK I SHOULD GET A NEW WORK NAME. YOU KNOW, WHY DO I ADVERTISE MY TEETH--?
--BUT THEN I REMEMBER.
ARGGGHHH!

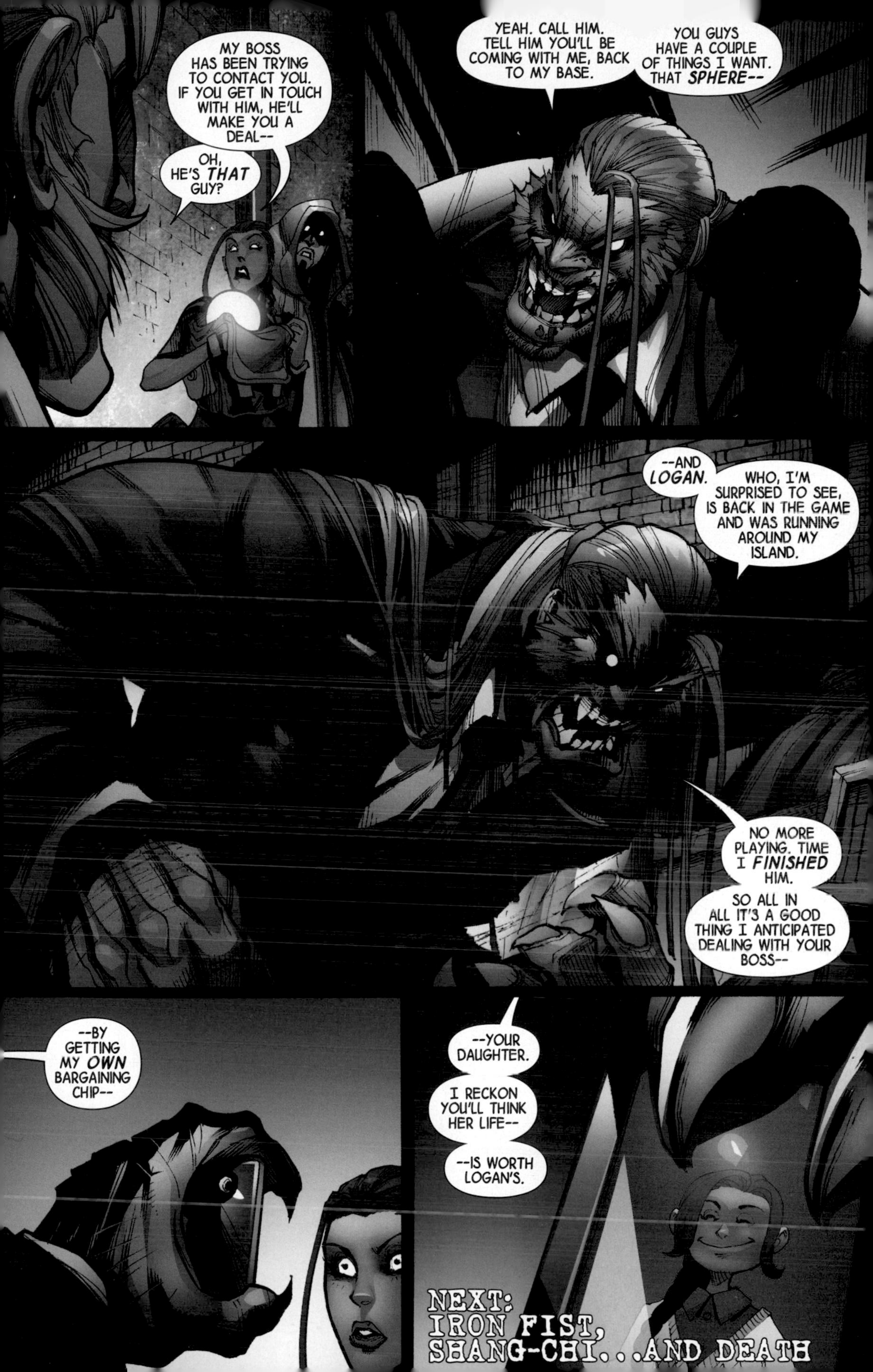
MY BOSS HAS BEEN TRYING TO CONTACT YOU. IF YOU GET IN TOUCH WITH HIM, HE'LL MAKE YOU A DEAL--
OH, HE'S THAT GUY?
YEAH. CALL HIM. TELL HIM YOU'LL BE COMING WITH ME, BACK TO MY BASE.
YOU GUYS HAVE A COUPLE OF THINGS I WANT. THAT SPHERE--
--AND LOGAN.
WHO, I'M SURPRISED TO SEE, IS BACK IN THE GAME AND WAS RUNNING AROUND MY ISLAND.
NO MORE PLAYING. TIME I FINISHED HIM.
SO ALL IN ALL IT'S A GOOD THING I ANTICIPATED DEALING WITH YOUR BOSS--
--BY GETTING MY OWN BARGAINING CHIP--
--YOUR DAUGHTER.
I RECKON YOU'LL THINK HER LIFE--
--IS WORTH LOGAN'S.
NEXT: IRON FIST, SHANG-CHI...AND DEATH

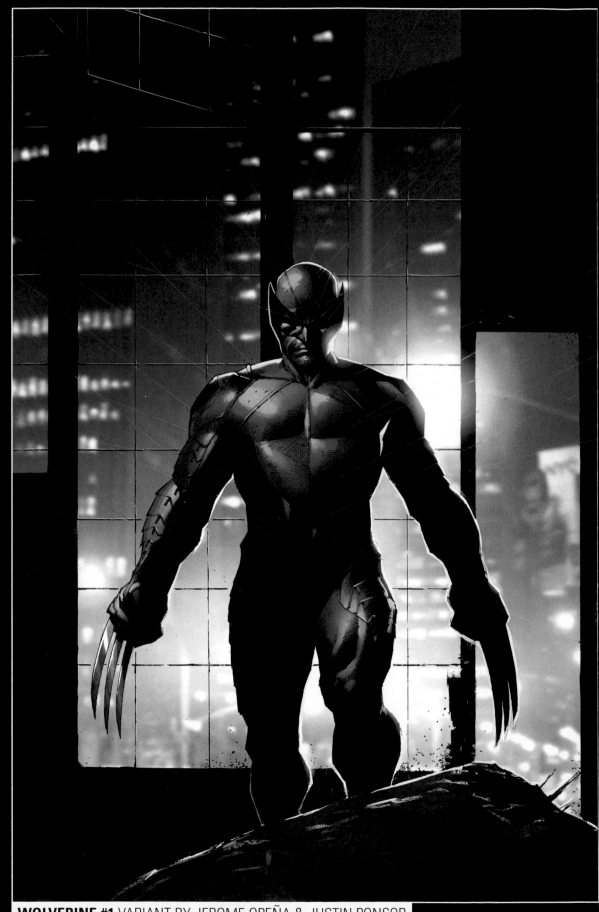

WOLVERINE #1 VARIANT BY JEROME OPEÑA & JUSTIN PONSOR

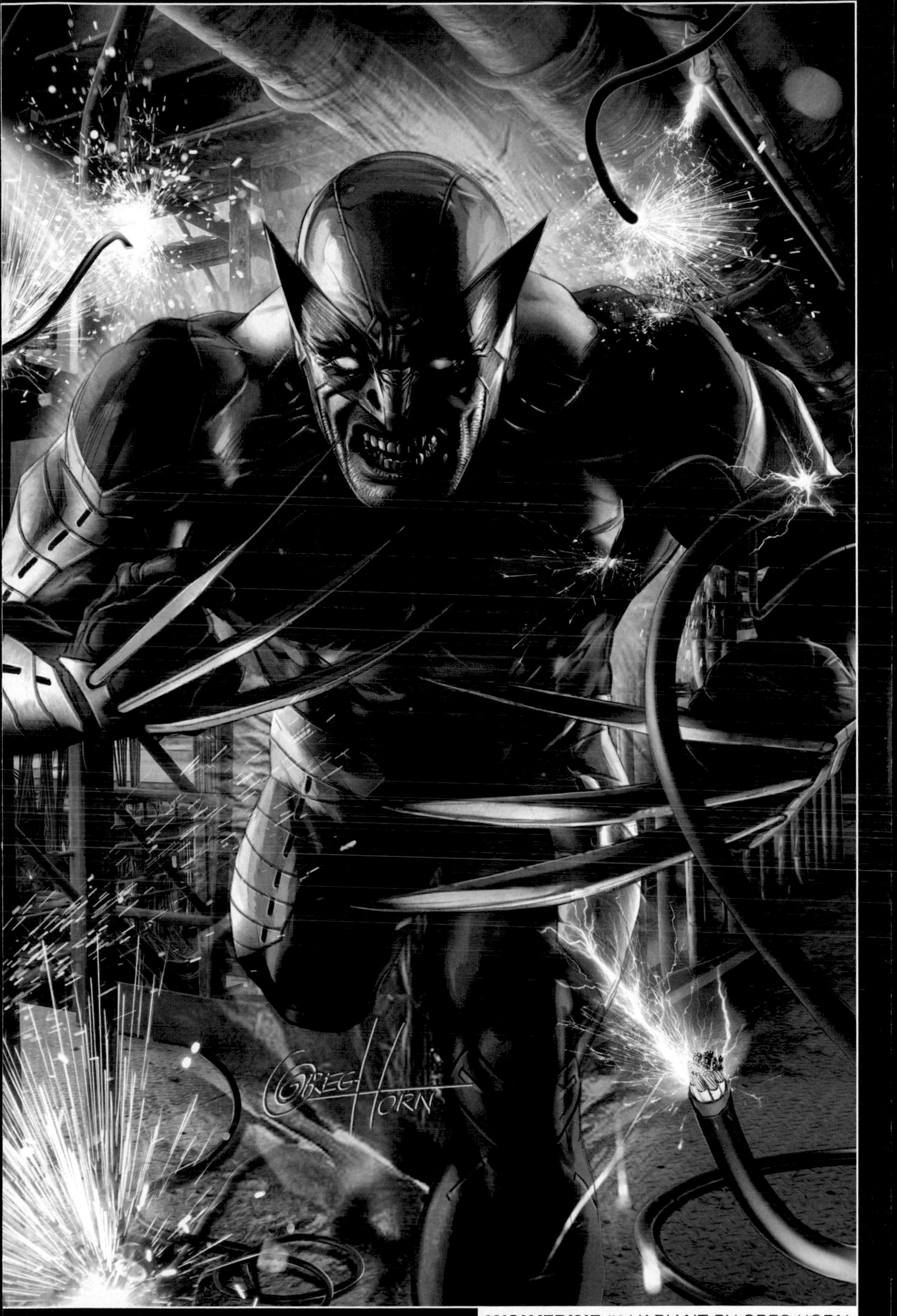
GREG HORN

WOLVERINE #1 VARIANT BY GREG HORN

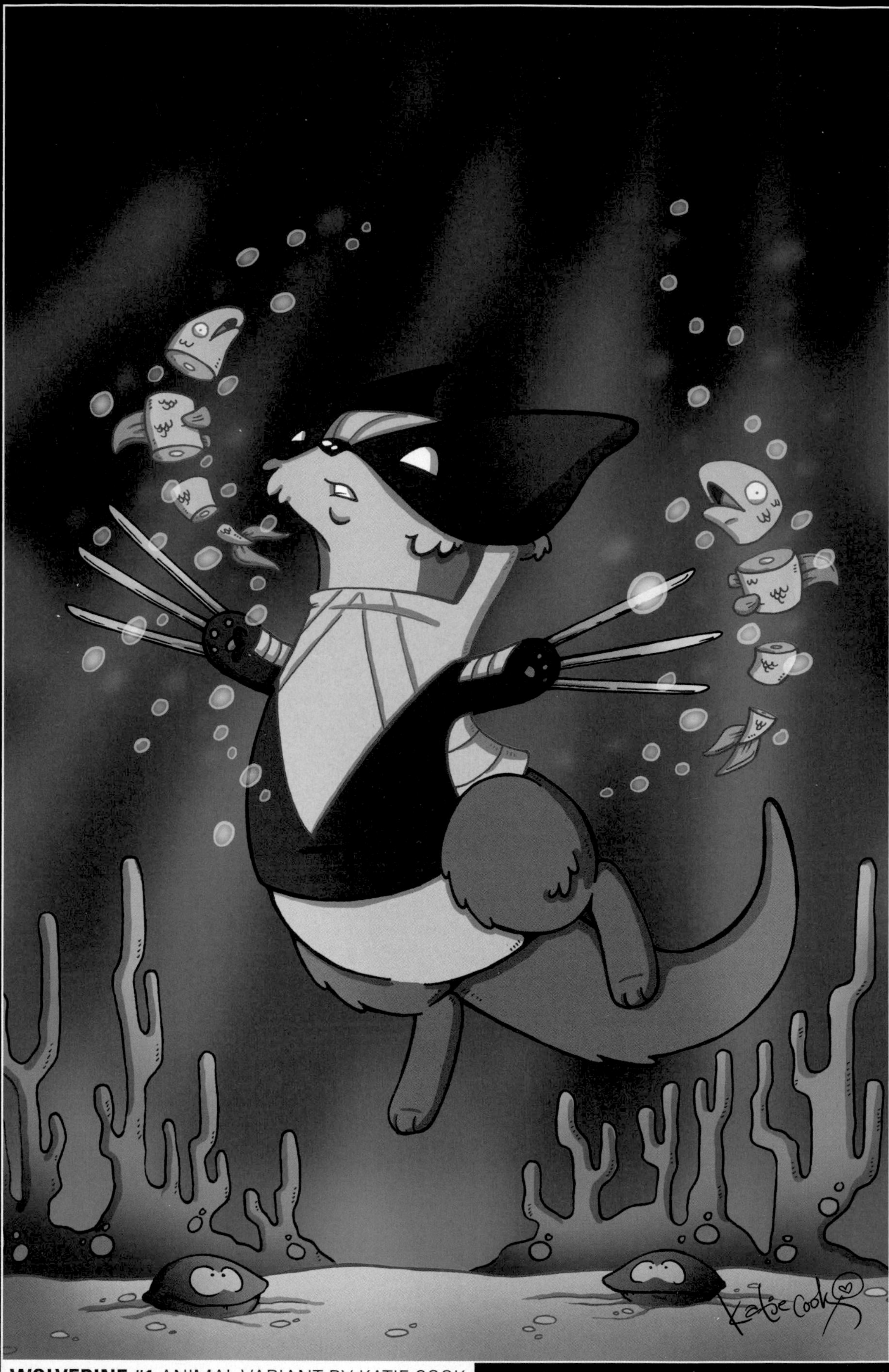
Katie Cook

WOLVERINE #1 ANIMAL VARIANT BY KATIE COOK

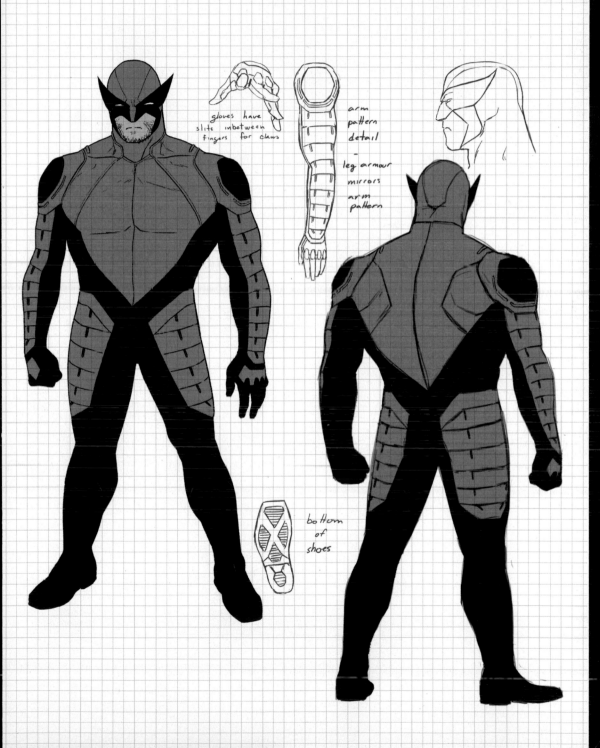

gloves have
slits inbetween
fingers for claws

arm
pattern
detail
-
leg armour
mirrors
arm
pattern

bottom
of
shoes

WOLVERINE #1 DESIGN VARIANT BY KRIS ANKA

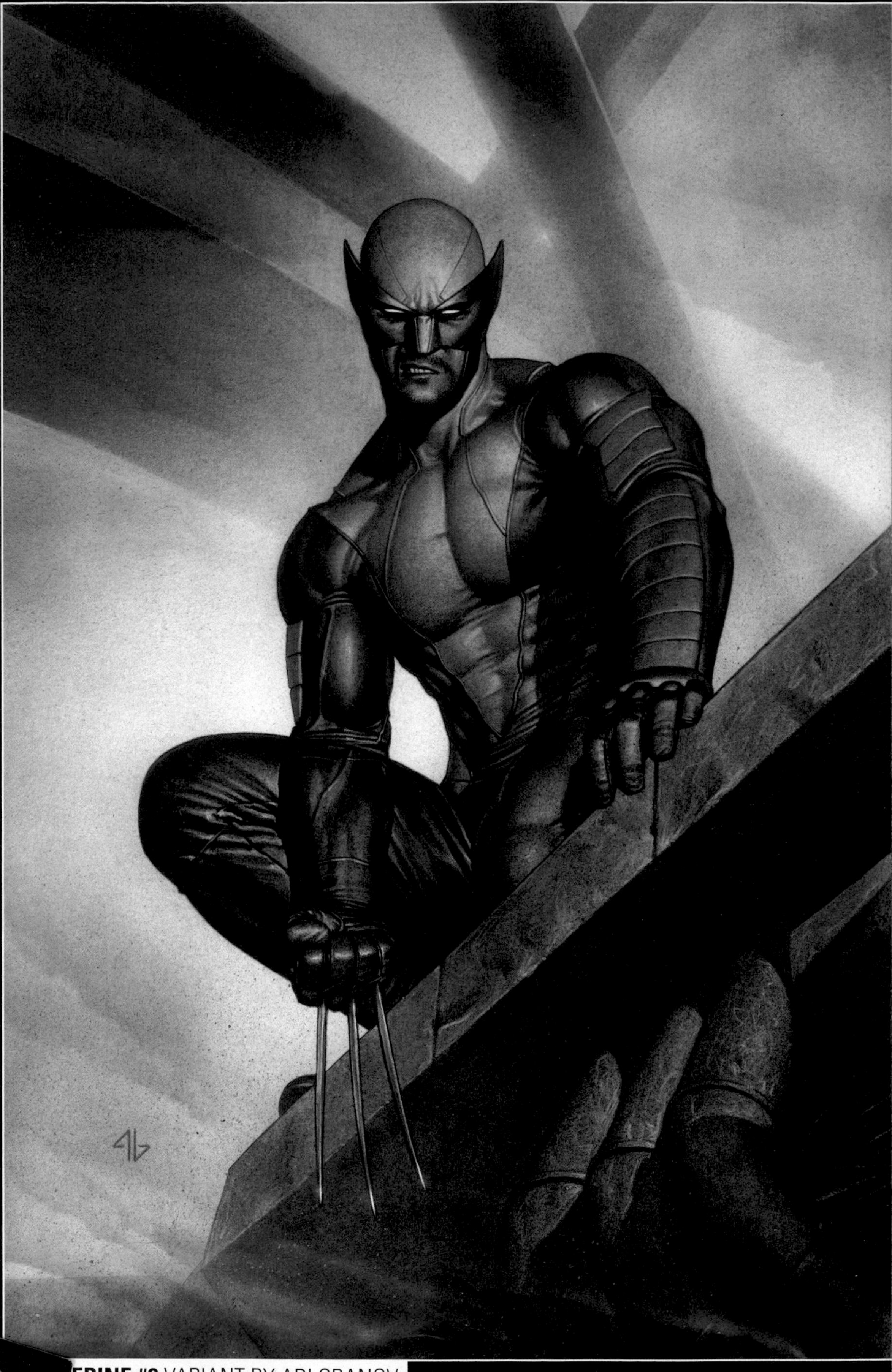

ERINE #2 VARIANT BY ADI GRANOV

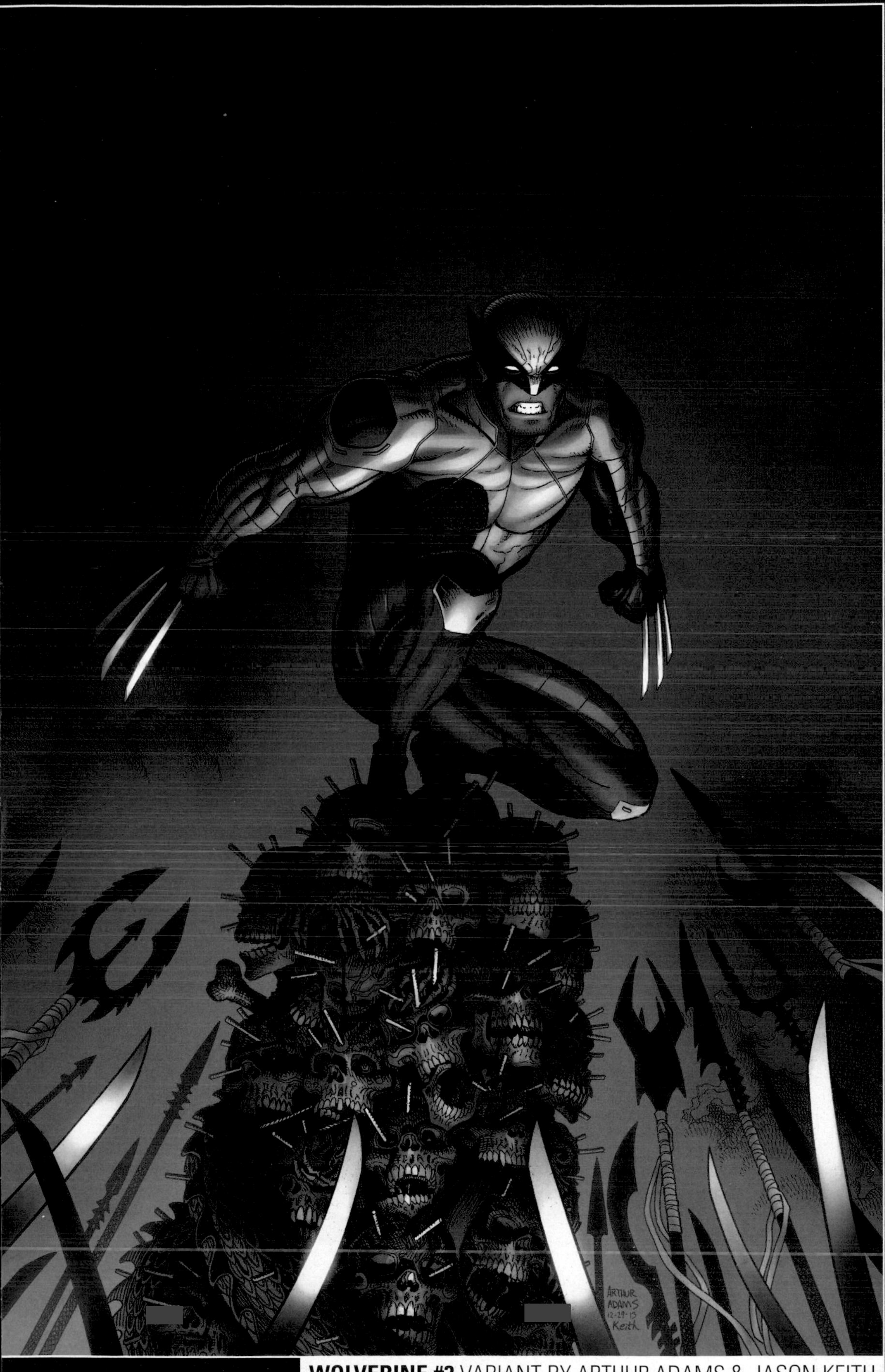
ARTHUR ADAMS
Keith

WOLVERINE #3 VARIANT BY ARTHUR ADAMS & JASON KEITH

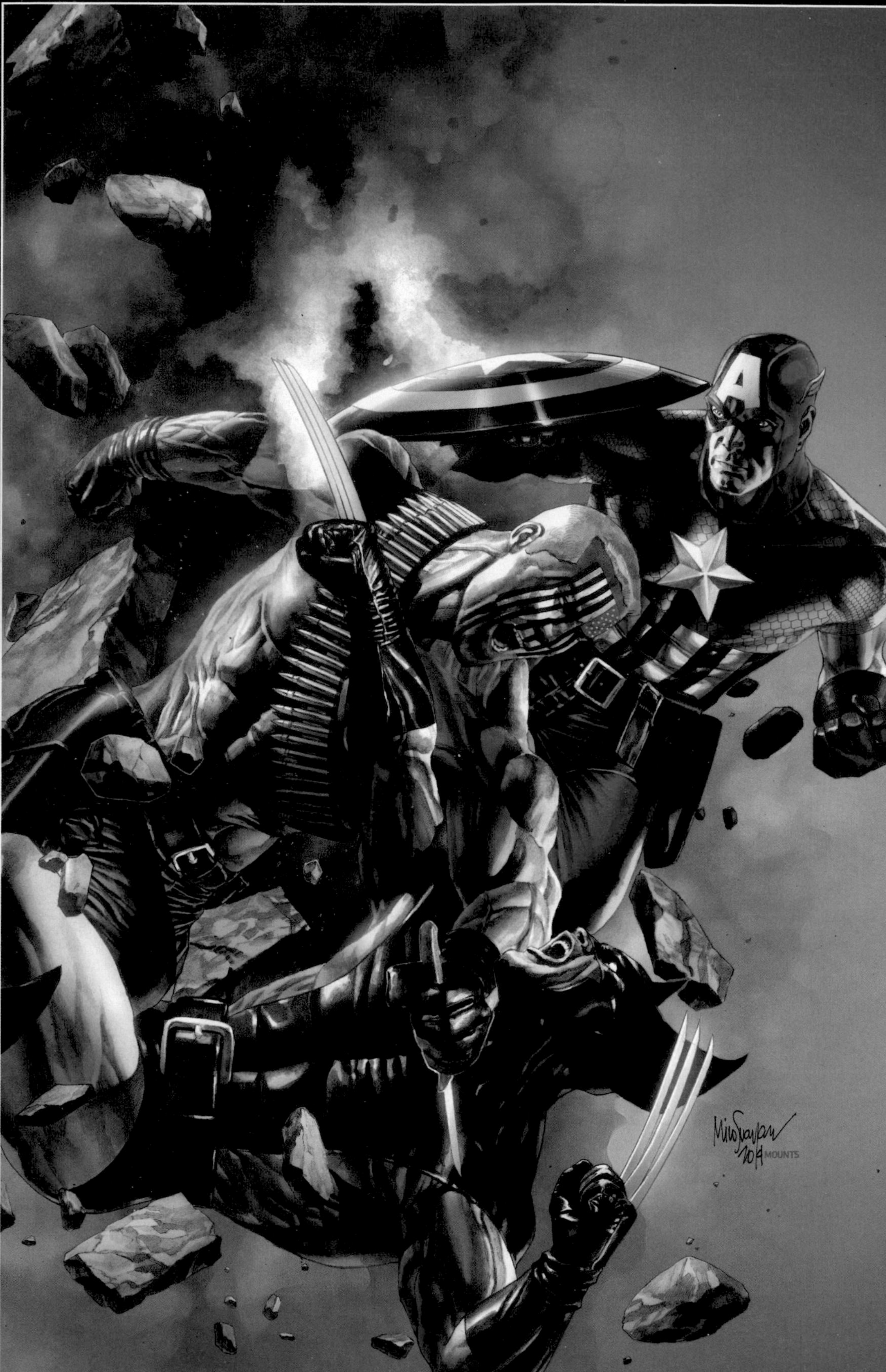

WOLVERINE #5 CAPTAIN AMERICA TEAM-UP VARIANT BY MICO SUAYAN & PAUL MOUNTS